CASE CLOSED

VOLUME 65

Gosho Aoyama

Case Briefing:

Subject:
Occupation:
Special Skills:
Equipment:

Jimmy Kudo, a.k.a. Conan Edogawa
High School Student/Detective
Analytical thinking and deductive reasoning, Soccer
Bow Tie Voice Transmitter, Super Sneakers,
Homing Glasses, Stretchy Suspenders

The subject is hot on the trail of a pair of suspicious men in black when he is attacked from behind and administered a strange substance which physically transforms him into a first grader. When the subject confides in the eccentric inventor Dr. Agasa, they decide to keep the subject's true identity a secret for the safety of everyone around him. Assuming the new identity of first-grader Conan Edogawa, the subject continues to assist the police force on their most baffling cases. The only problem is that most crime-solving professionals won't take a little kid's advice!

Table of Contents

CONFIDE

CASE CLOSED
Volume 65
Shonen Sunday Edition

Story and Art by GOSHO AOYAMA

MEITANTEI CONAN Vol. 65
by Gosho AOYAMA
© 1994 Gosho AOYAMA
All rights reserved.
Original Japanese edition published by SHOGAKUKAN.
English translation rights in the United States of America, Canada,
the United Kingdom and Ireland arranged with SHOGAKUKAN.

Translation
Tetsuichiro Miyaki

Touch-up & Lettering
Freeman Wong

Cover & Graphic Design
Andrea Rice

Editor
Shaenon K. Garrity

Printed in the U.S.A.

Published by VIZ Media, LLC
P.O. Box 77010
San Francisco, CA 94107

10 9 8 7 6 5 4 3 2 1
First printing, January 2018

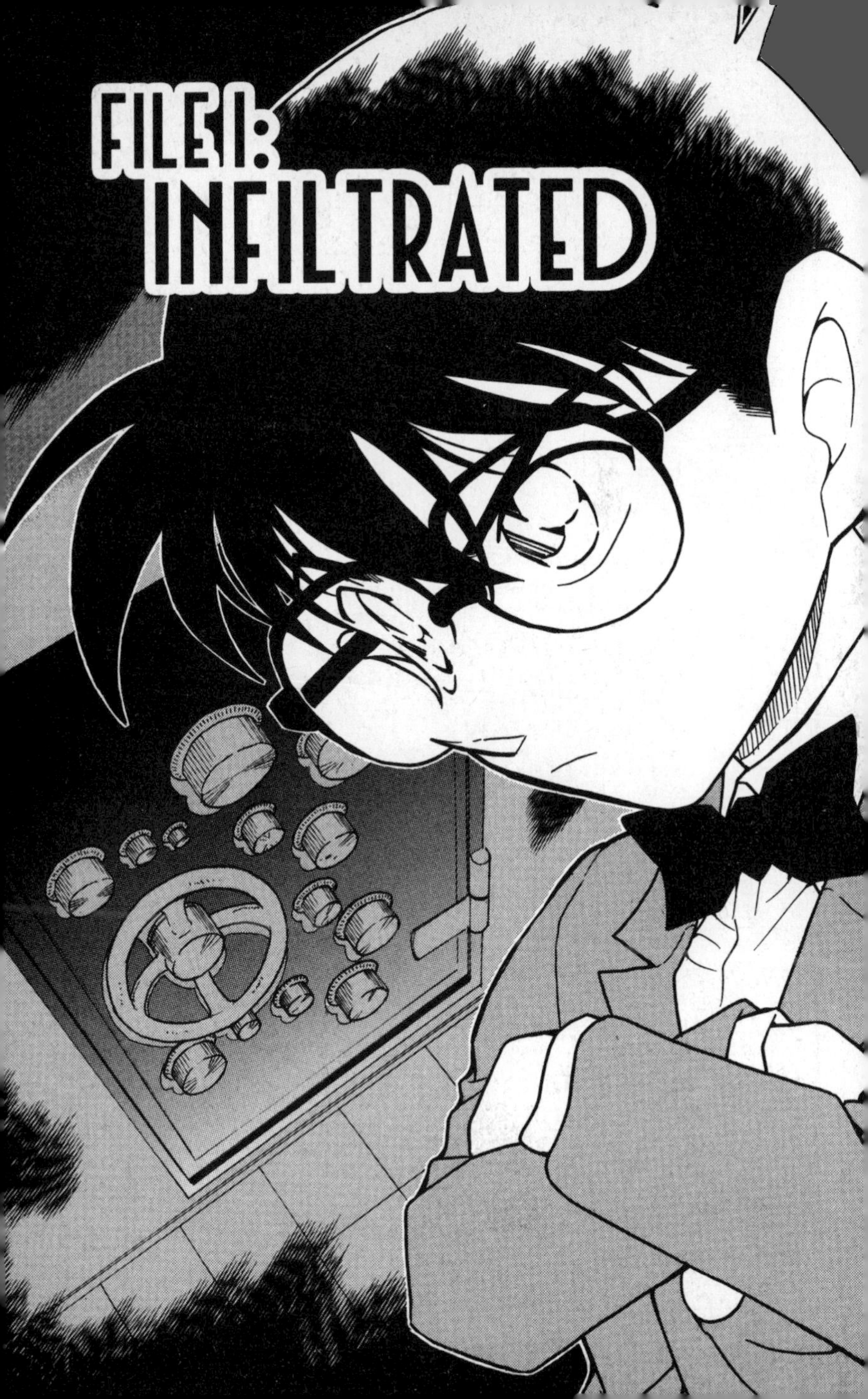
FILE 1:
INFILTRATED

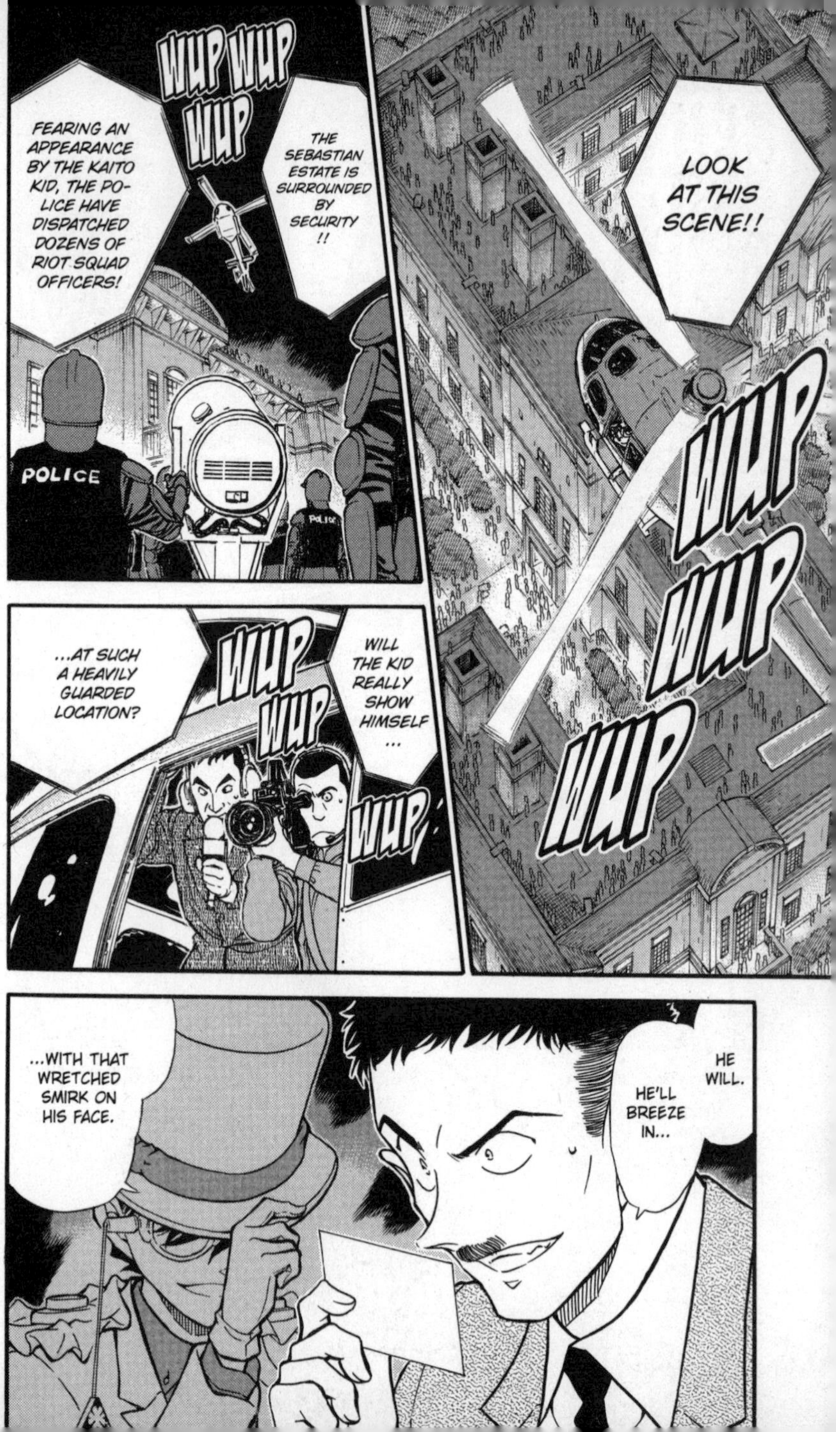
LOOK AT THIS SCENE!!
WUP WUP WUP
WUP WUP WUP
THE SEBASTIAN ESTATE IS SURROUNDED BY SECURITY!!
FEARING AN APPEARANCE BY THE KAITO KID, THE POLICE HAVE DISPATCHED DOZENS OF RIOT SQUAD OFFICERS!
POLICE
POLICE
WILL THE KID REALLY SHOW HIMSELF...
WUP WUP
...AT SUCH A HEAVILY GUARDED LOCATION?
WUP
HE WILL.
HE'LL BREEZE IN...
...WITH THAT WRETCHED SMIRK ON HIS FACE.

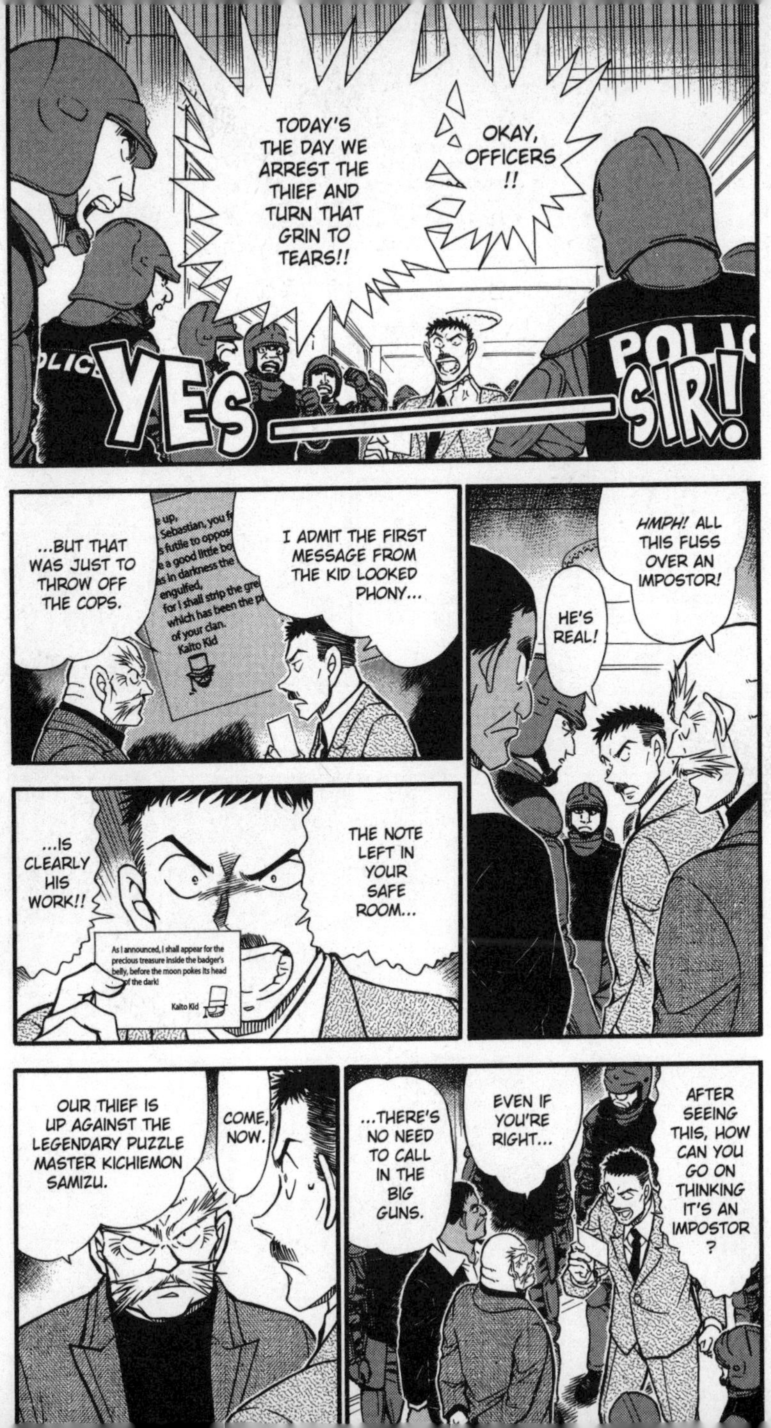
OKAY, OFFICERS!!
TODAY'S THE DAY WE ARREST THE THIEF AND TURN THAT GRIN TO TEARS!!
YES—SIR!
HMPH! ALL THIS FUSS OVER AN IMPOSTOR!
HE'S REAL!
I ADMIT THE FIRST MESSAGE FROM THE KID LOOKED PHONY...
...BUT THAT WAS JUST TO THROW OFF THE COPS.
Kaito Kid
THE NOTE LEFT IN YOUR SAFE ROOM...
...IS CLEARLY HIS WORK!!
As I announced, I shall appear for the precious treasure inside the badger's belly, before the moon pokes its head
of the dark!
Kaito Kid
AFTER SEEING THIS, HOW CAN YOU GO ON THINKING IT'S AN IMPOSTOR?
EVEN IF YOU'RE RIGHT...
...THERE'S NO NEED TO CALL IN THE BIG GUNS.
COME, NOW.
OUR THIEF IS UP AGAINST THE LEGENDARY PUZZLE MASTER KICHIEMON SAMIZU.

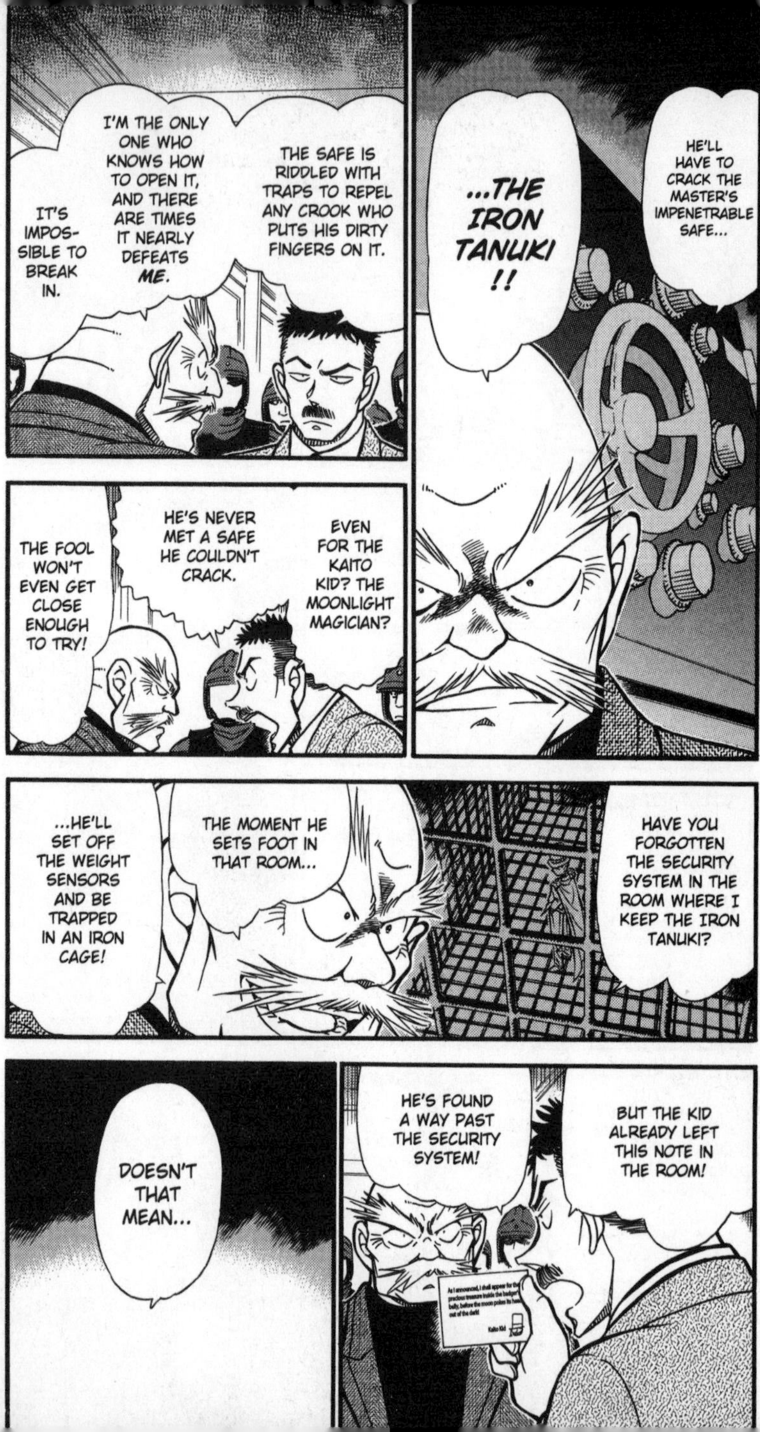
HE'LL HAVE TO CRACK THE MASTER'S IMPENETRABLE SAFE...
...THE IRON TANUKI!!
THE SAFE IS RIDDLED WITH TRAPS TO REPEL ANY CROOK WHO PUTS HIS DIRTY FINGERS ON IT.
I'M THE ONLY ONE WHO KNOWS HOW TO OPEN IT, AND THERE ARE TIMES IT NEARLY DEFEATS ***ME.***
IT'S IMPOSSIBLE TO BREAK IN.
EVEN FOR THE KAITO KID? THE MOONLIGHT MAGICIAN?
HE'S NEVER MET A SAFE HE COULDN'T CRACK.
THE FOOL WON'T EVEN GET CLOSE ENOUGH TO TRY!
HAVE YOU FORGOTTEN THE SECURITY SYSTEM IN THE ROOM WHERE I KEEP THE IRON TANUKI?
THE MOMENT HE SETS FOOT IN THAT ROOM...
...HE'LL SET OFF THE WEIGHT SENSORS AND BE TRAPPED IN AN IRON CAGE!
BUT THE KID ALREADY LEFT THIS NOTE IN THE ROOM!
HE'S FOUND A WAY PAST THE SECURITY SYSTEM!
Kaito Kid
DOESN'T THAT MEAN...

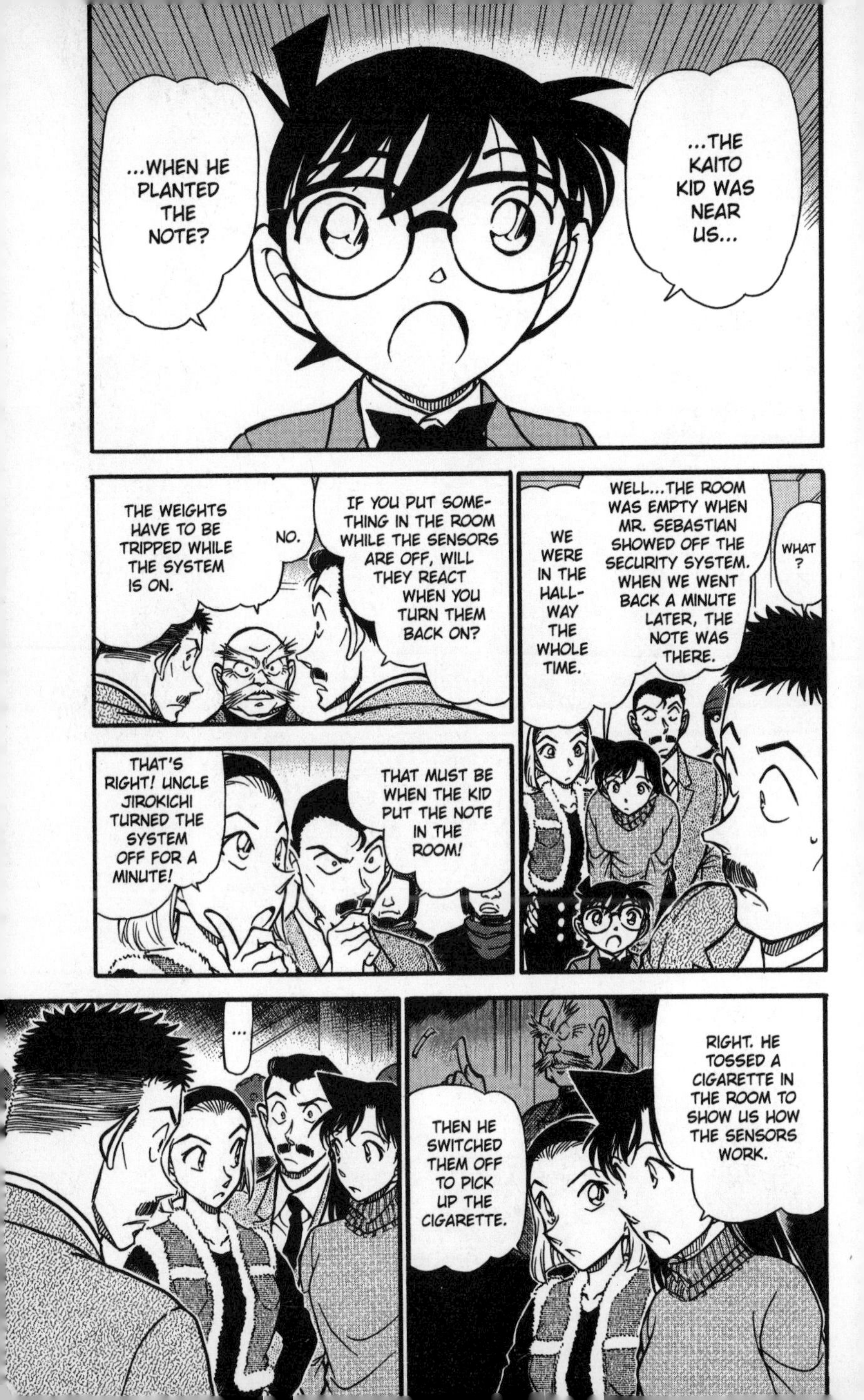
...THE KAITO KID WAS NEAR US...
...WHEN HE PLANTED THE NOTE?
WHAT?
WELL...THE ROOM WAS EMPTY WHEN MR. SEBASTIAN SHOWED OFF THE SECURITY SYSTEM. WHEN WE WENT BACK A MINUTE LATER, THE NOTE WAS THERE.
WE WERE IN THE HALLWAY THE WHOLE TIME.
IF YOU PUT SOMETHING IN THE ROOM WHILE THE SENSORS ARE OFF, WILL THEY REACT WHEN YOU TURN THEM BACK ON?
NO.
THE WEIGHTS HAVE TO BE TRIPPED WHILE THE SYSTEM IS ON.
THAT MUST BE WHEN THE KID PUT THE NOTE IN THE ROOM!
THAT'S RIGHT! UNCLE JIROKICHI TURNED THE SYSTEM OFF FOR A MINUTE!
RIGHT. HE TOSSED A CIGARETTE IN THE ROOM TO SHOW US HOW THE SENSORS WORK.
THEN HE SWITCHED THEM OFF TO PICK UP THE CIGARETTE.
...

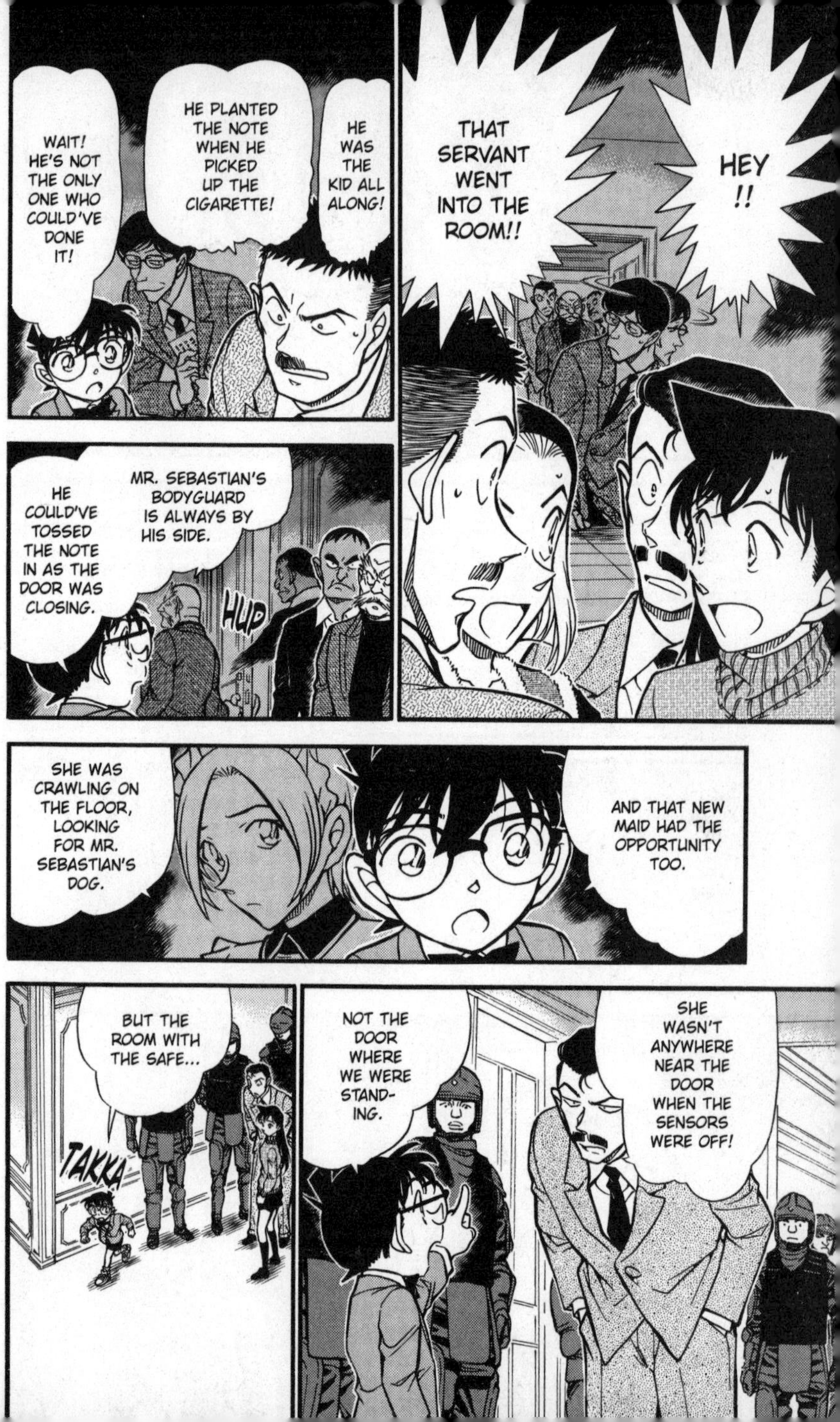
HEY!!
THAT SERVANT WENT INTO THE ROOM!!
HE WAS THE KID ALL ALONG!
HE PLANTED THE NOTE WHEN HE PICKED UP THE CIGARETTE!
WAIT! HE'S NOT THE ONLY ONE WHO COULD'VE DONE IT!
MR. SEBASTIAN'S BODYGUARD IS ALWAYS BY HIS SIDE.
HE COULD'VE TOSSED THE NOTE IN AS THE DOOR WAS CLOSING.
HUP
AND THAT NEW MAID HAD THE OPPORTUNITY TOO.
SHE WAS CRAWLING ON THE FLOOR, LOOKING FOR MR. SEBASTIAN'S DOG.
SHE WASN'T ANYWHERE NEAR THE DOOR WHEN THE SENSORS WERE OFF!
NOT THE DOOR WHERE WE WERE STAND-ING.
BUT THE ROOM WITH THE SAFE...
TAKKA

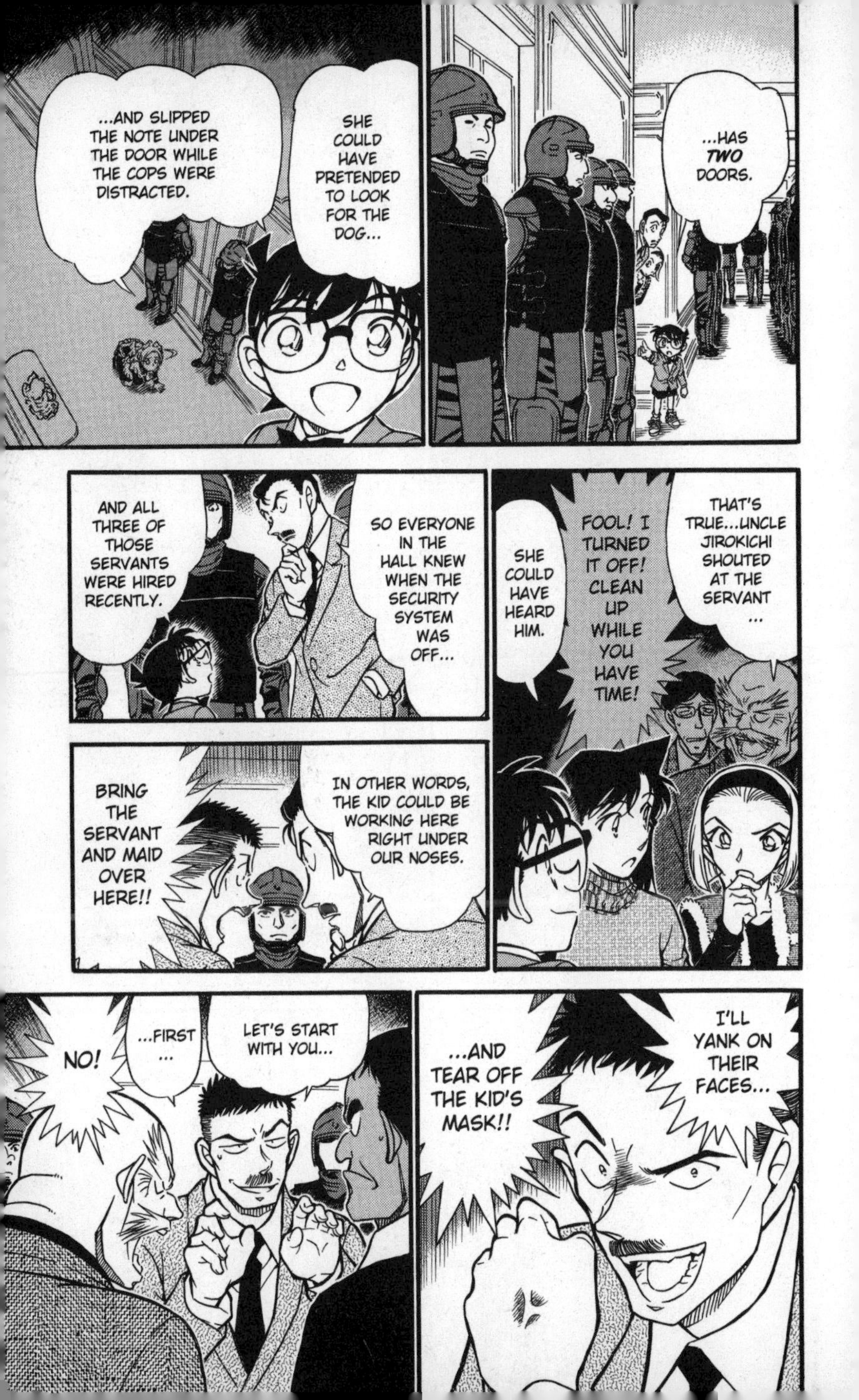
...HAS *TWO* DOORS.
SHE COULD HAVE PRETENDED TO LOOK FOR THE DOG...
...AND SLIPPED THE NOTE UNDER THE DOOR WHILE THE COPS WERE DISTRACTED.
THAT'S TRUE...UNCLE JIROKICHI SHOUTED AT THE SERVANT ...
FOOL! I TURNED IT OFF! CLEAN UP WHILE YOU HAVE TIME!
SHE COULD HAVE HEARD HIM.
SO EVERYONE IN THE HALL KNEW WHEN THE SECURITY SYSTEM WAS OFF...
AND ALL THREE OF THOSE SERVANTS WERE HIRED RECENTLY.
IN OTHER WORDS, THE KID COULD BE WORKING HERE RIGHT UNDER OUR NOSES.
BRING THE SERVANT AND MAID OVER HERE!!
I'LL YANK ON THEIR FACES...
...AND TEAR OFF THE KID'S MASK!!
LET'S START WITH YOU...
...FIRST ...
NO!

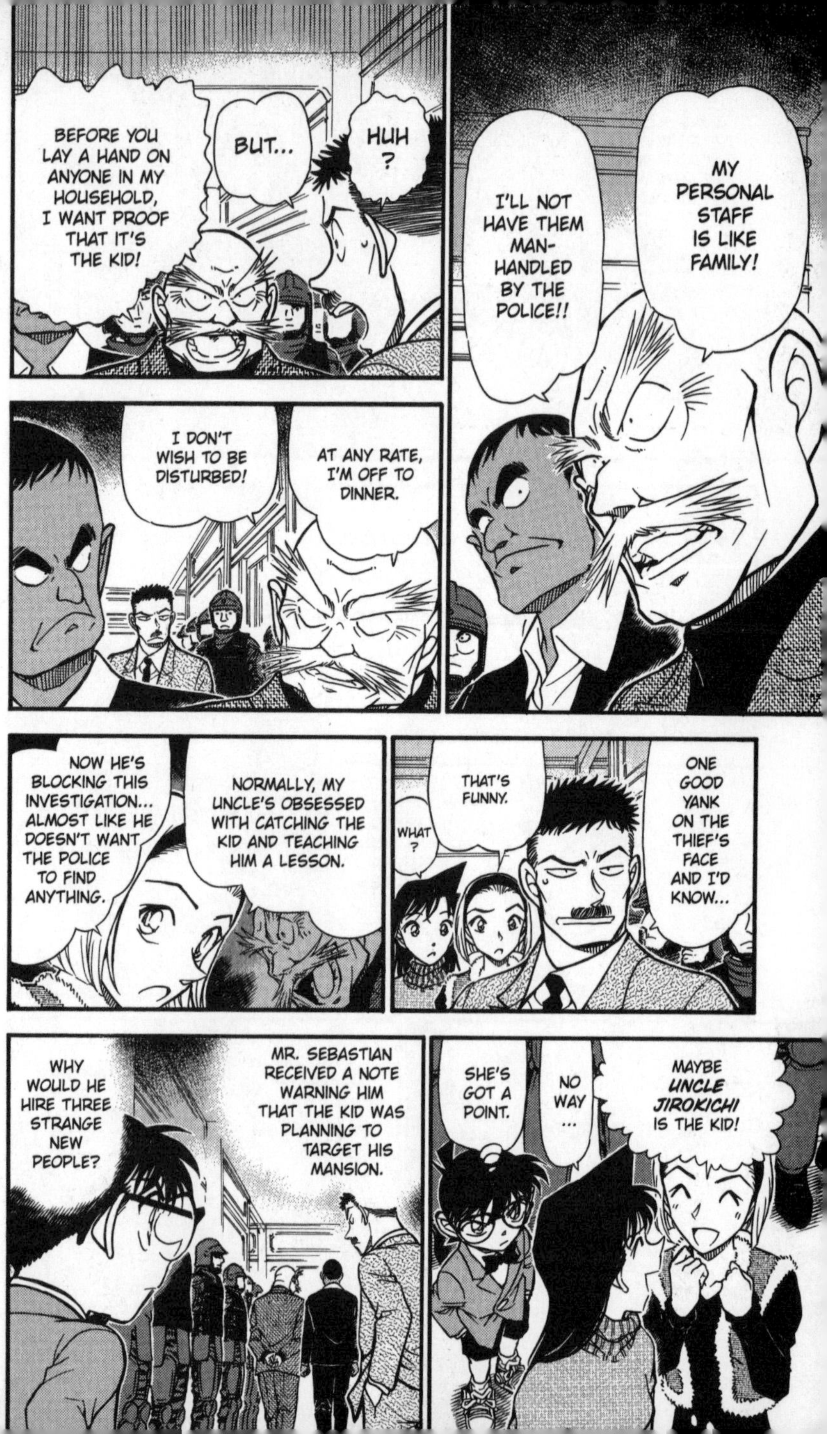
MY PERSONAL STAFF IS LIKE FAMILY!
I'LL NOT HAVE THEM MAN-HANDLED BY THE POLICE!!
HUH?
BUT...
BEFORE YOU LAY A HAND ON ANYONE IN MY HOUSEHOLD, I WANT PROOF THAT IT'S THE KID!
AT ANY RATE, I'M OFF TO DINNER.
I DON'T WISH TO BE DISTURBED!
ONE GOOD YANK ON THE THIEF'S FACE AND I'D KNOW...
THAT'S FUNNY.
WHAT?
NORMALLY, MY UNCLE'S OBSESSED WITH CATCHING THE KID AND TEACHING HIM A LESSON.
NOW HE'S BLOCKING THIS INVESTIGATION... ALMOST LIKE HE DOESN'T WANT THE POLICE TO FIND ANYTHING.
MAYBE *UNCLE JIROKICHI* IS THE KID!
NO WAY...
SHE'S GOT A POINT.
MR. SEBASTIAN RECEIVED A NOTE WARNING HIM THAT THE KID WAS PLANNING TO TARGET HIS MANSION.
WHY WOULD HE HIRE THREE STRANGE NEW PEOPLE?

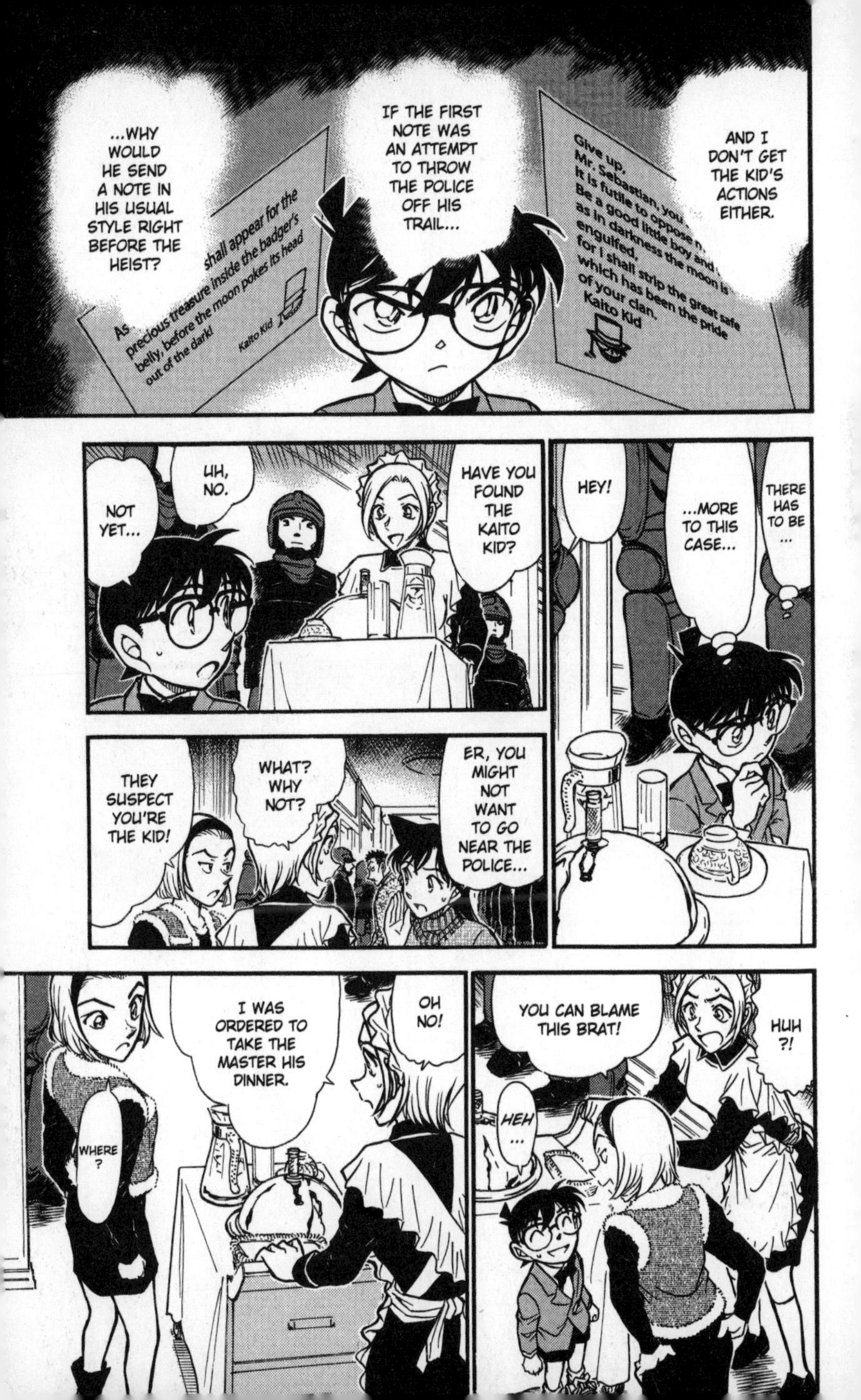
AND I DON'T GET THE KID'S ACTIONS EITHER.
Give up,
Mr. Sebastian, you
It is futile to oppose m
Be a good little boy and
as in darkness the moon is
engulfed,
for I shall strip the great safe
which has been the pride
of your clan.
Kaito Kid
IF THE FIRST NOTE WAS AN ATTEMPT TO THROW THE POLICE OFF HIS TRAIL...
...WHY WOULD HE SEND A NOTE IN HIS USUAL STYLE RIGHT BEFORE THE HEIST?
As
shall appear for the
precious treasure inside the badger's
belly, before the moon pokes its head
out of the dark!
Kaito Kid
THERE HAS TO BE ...
...MORE TO THIS CASE...
HEY!
HAVE YOU FOUND THE KAITO KID?
UH, NO.
NOT YET...
ER, YOU MIGHT NOT WANT TO GO NEAR THE POLICE...
WHAT? WHY NOT?
THEY SUSPECT YOU'RE THE KID!
HUH ?!
YOU CAN BLAME THIS BRAT!
HEH ...
OH NO!
I WAS ORDERED TO TAKE THE MASTER HIS DINNER.
WHERE ?

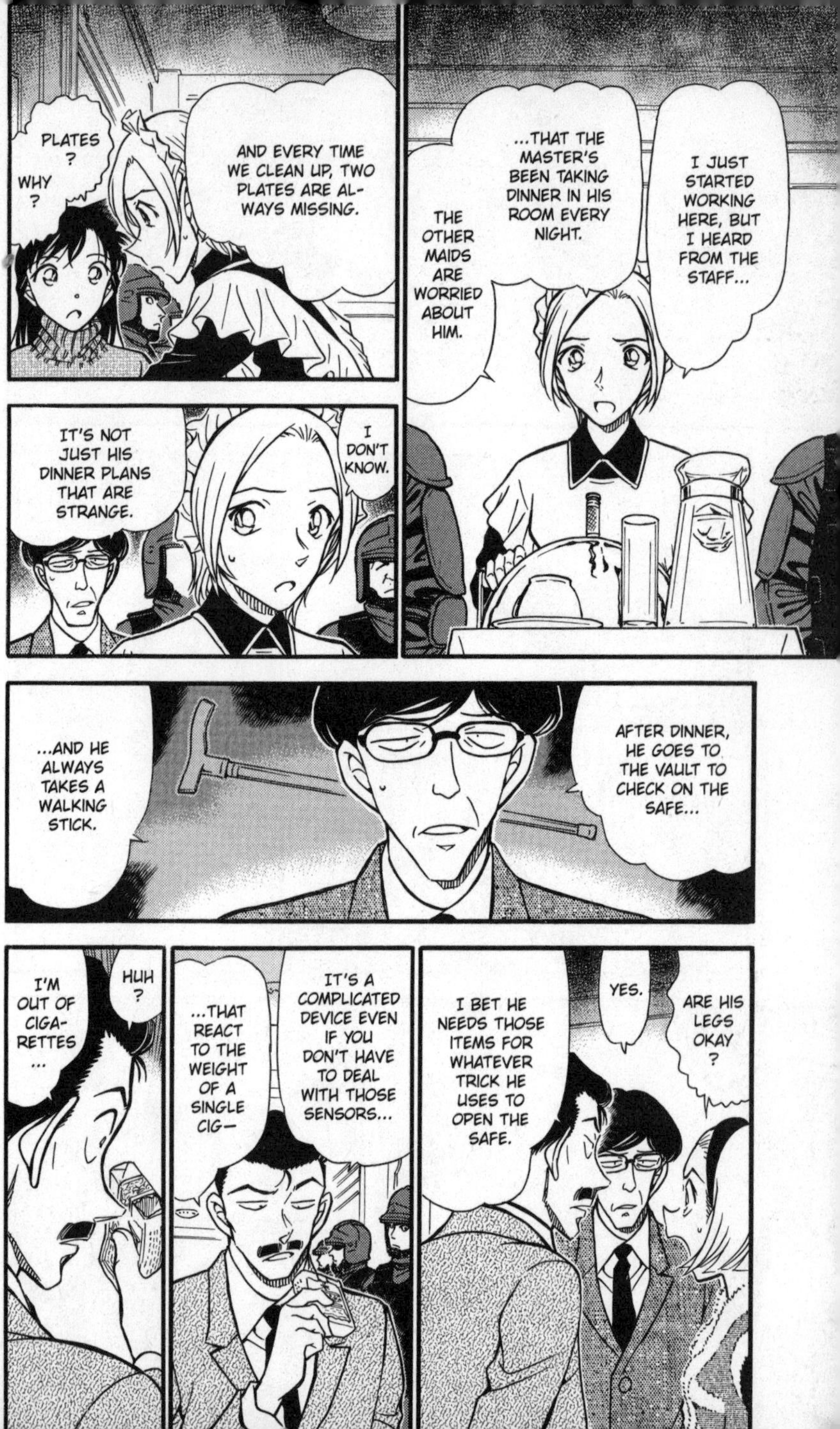
I JUST STARTED WORKING HERE, BUT I HEARD FROM THE STAFF...
...THAT THE MASTER'S BEEN TAKING DINNER IN HIS ROOM EVERY NIGHT.
THE OTHER MAIDS ARE WORRIED ABOUT HIM.
AND EVERY TIME WE CLEAN UP, TWO PLATES ARE AL-WAYS MISSING.
PLATES?
WHY?
I DON'T KNOW.
IT'S NOT JUST HIS DINNER PLANS THAT ARE STRANGE.
AFTER DINNER, HE GOES TO THE VAULT TO CHECK ON THE SAFE...
...AND HE ALWAYS TAKES A WALKING STICK.
ARE HIS LEGS OKAY?
YES.
I BET HE NEEDS THOSE ITEMS FOR WHATEVER TRICK HE USES TO OPEN THE SAFE.
IT'S A COMPLICATED DEVICE EVEN IF YOU DON'T HAVE TO DEAL WITH THOSE SENSORS...
...THAT REACT TO THE WEIGHT OF A SINGLE CIG—
HUH?
I'M OUT OF CIGA-RETTES...

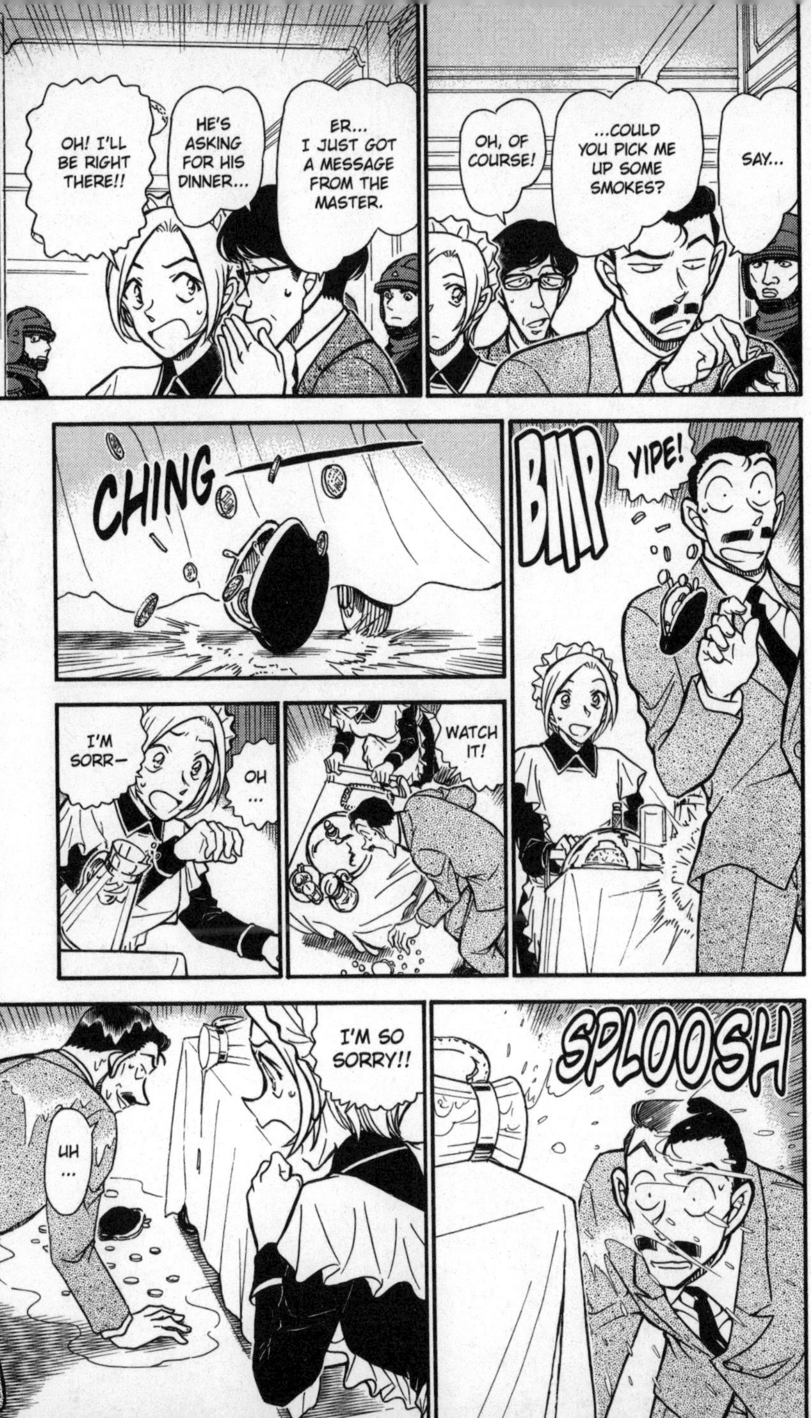
SAY...
...COULD YOU PICK ME UP SOME SMOKES?
OH, OF COURSE!
ER... I JUST GOT A MESSAGE FROM THE MASTER.
HE'S ASKING FOR HIS DINNER...
OH! I'LL BE RIGHT THERE!!
BMP
YIPE!
CHING
WATCH IT!
I'M SORR—
OH ...
SPLOOSH
I'M SO SORRY!!
UH ...

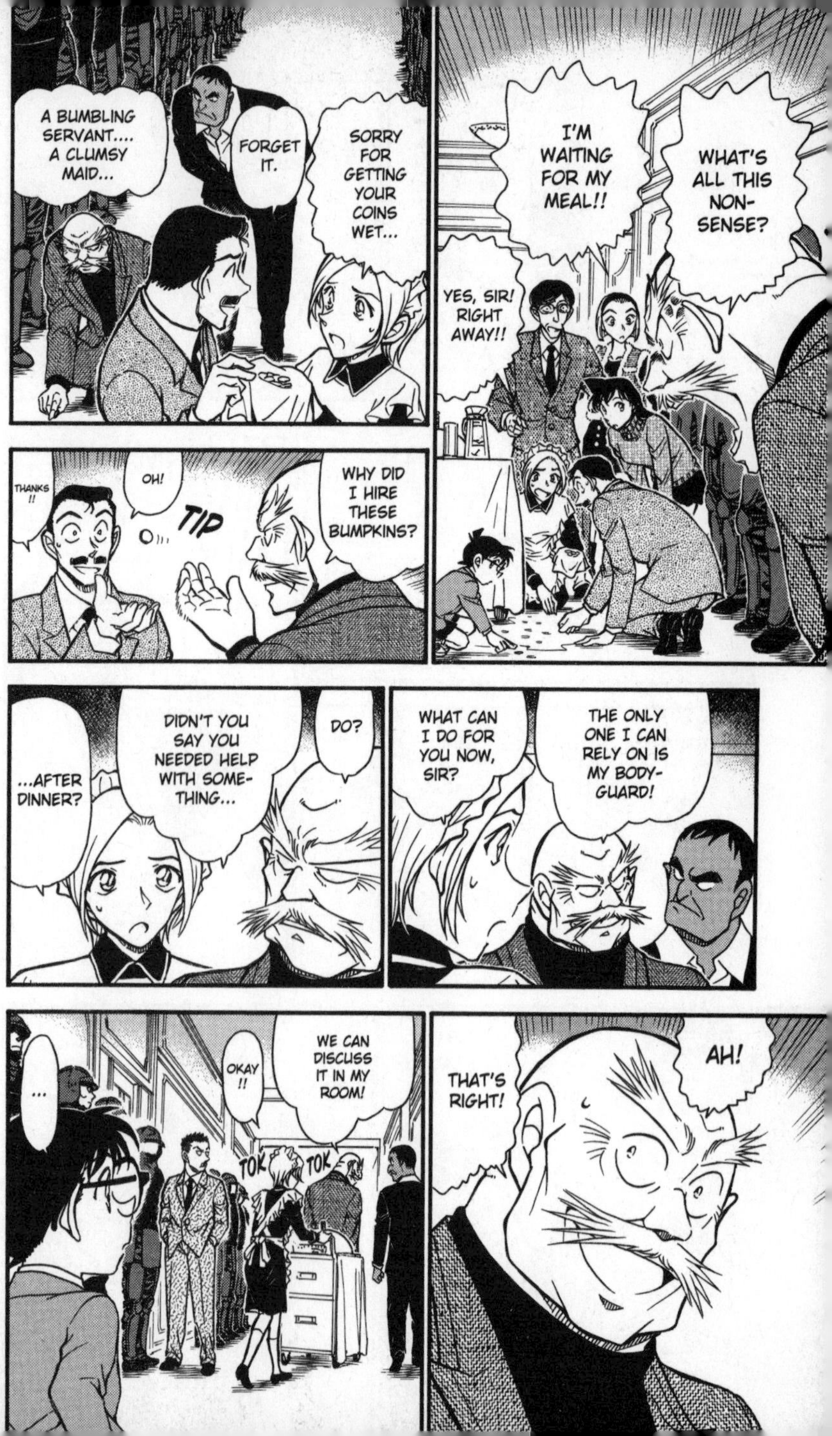
WHAT'S ALL THIS NON-SENSE?
I'M WAITING FOR MY MEAL!!
YES, SIR! RIGHT AWAY!!
SORRY FOR GETTING YOUR COINS WET...
FORGET IT.
A BUMBLING SERVANT.... A CLUMSY MAID...
WHY DID I HIRE THESE BUMPKINS?
TIP
OH!
THANKS!!
THE ONLY ONE I CAN RELY ON IS MY BODY-GUARD!
WHAT CAN I DO FOR YOU NOW, SIR?
DO?
DIDN'T YOU SAY YOU NEEDED HELP WITH SOME-THING...
...AFTER DINNER?
AH!
THAT'S RIGHT!
WE CAN DISCUSS IT IN MY ROOM!
OKAY!!
TOK
TOK
...

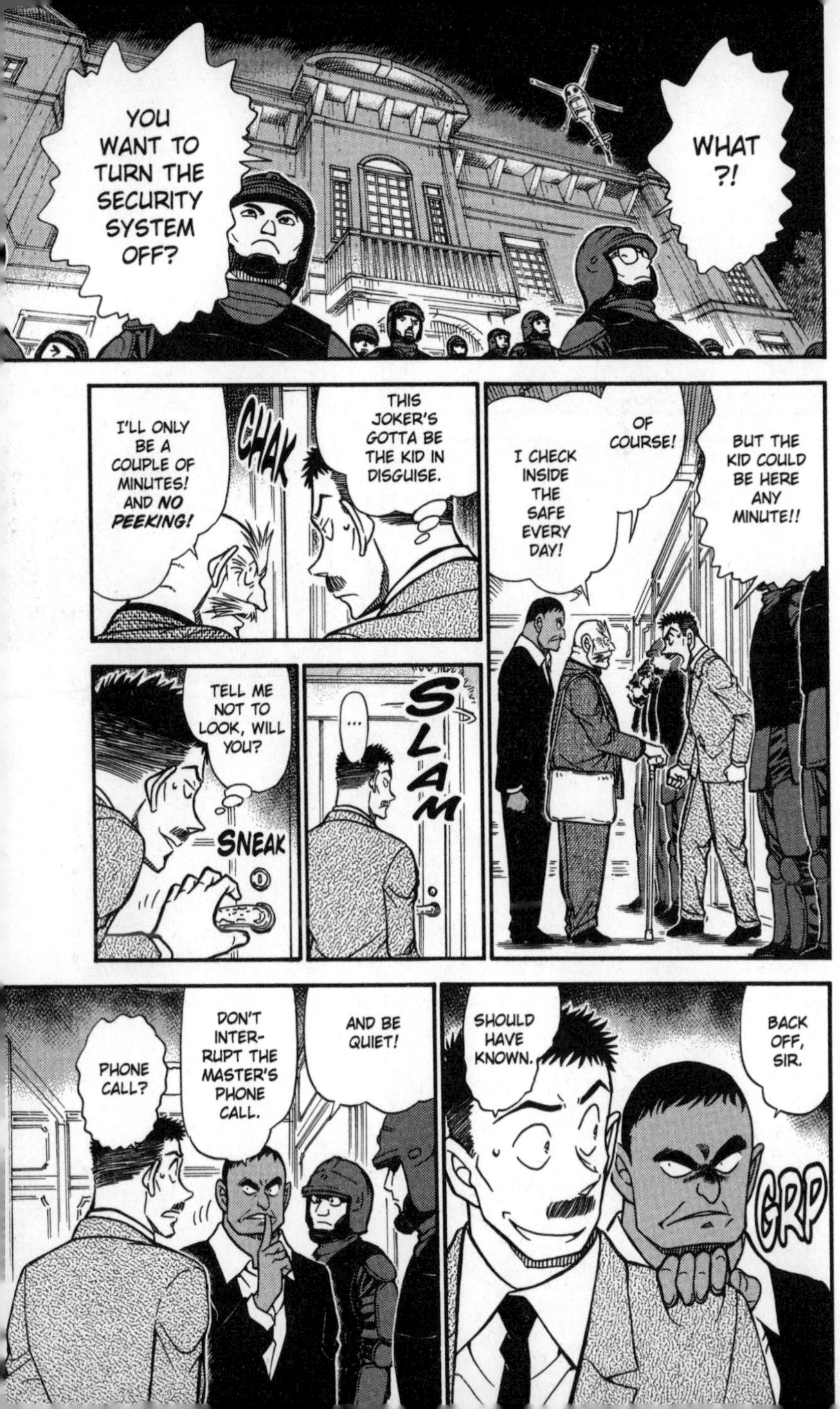
WHAT?!
YOU WANT TO TURN THE SECURITY SYSTEM OFF?
BUT THE KID COULD BE HERE ANY MINUTE!!
OF COURSE!
I CHECK INSIDE THE SAFE EVERY DAY!
THIS JOKER'S GOTTA BE THE KID IN DISGUISE.
CHAK
I'LL ONLY BE A COUPLE OF MINUTES! AND *NO PEEKING!*
SLAM
...
TELL ME NOT TO LOOK, WILL YOU?
SNEAK
BACK OFF, SIR.
SHOULD HAVE KNOWN.
GRP
AND BE QUIET!
DON'T INTER-RUPT THE MASTER'S PHONE CALL.
PHONE CALL?

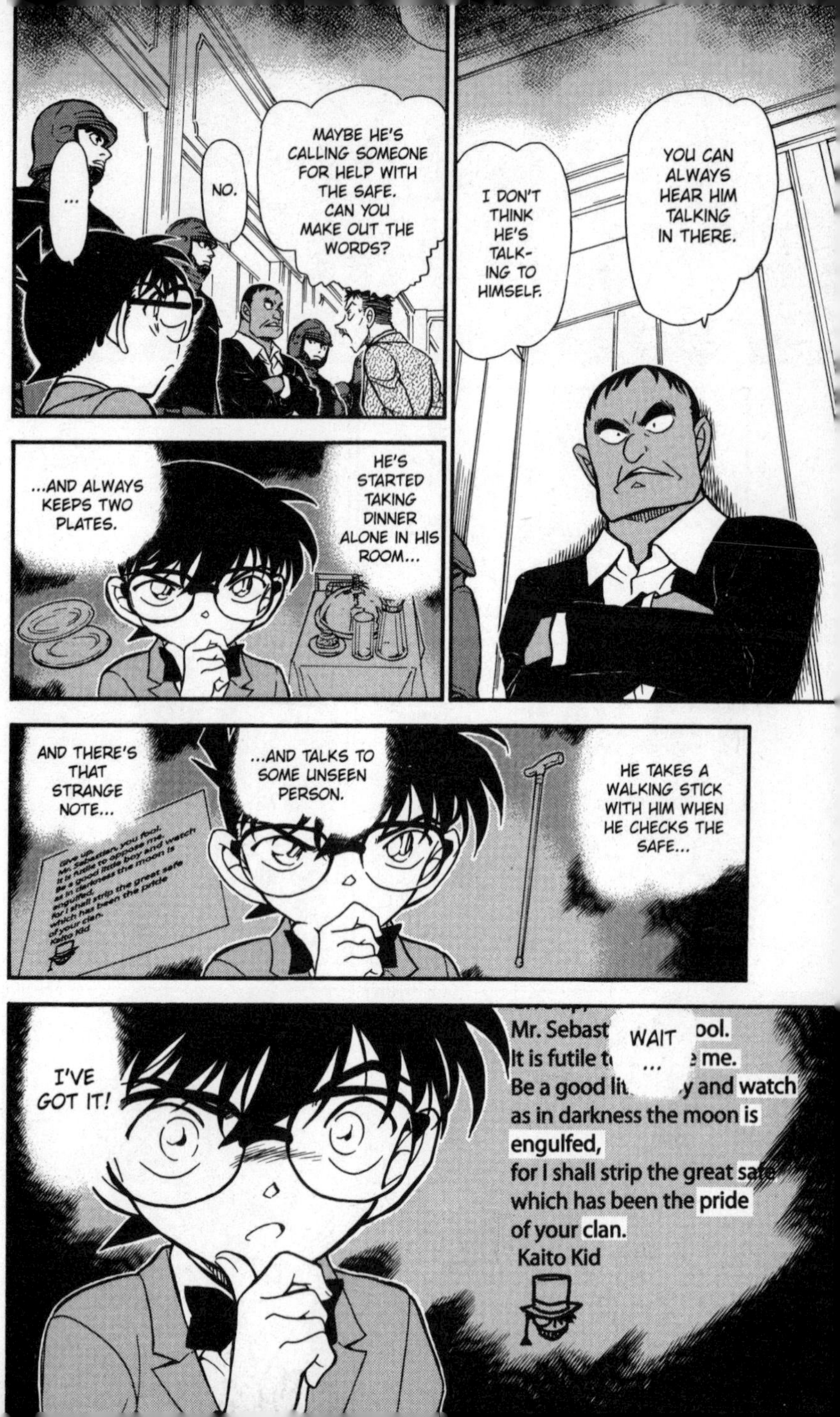
YOU CAN ALWAYS HEAR HIM TALKING IN THERE.
I DON'T THINK HE'S TALK-ING TO HIMSELF.
MAYBE HE'S CALLING SOMEONE FOR HELP WITH THE SAFE. CAN YOU MAKE OUT THE WORDS?
NO.
...
HE'S STARTED TAKING DINNER ALONE IN HIS ROOM...
...AND ALWAYS KEEPS TWO PLATES.
HE TAKES A WALKING STICK WITH HIM WHEN HE CHECKS THE SAFE...
...AND TALKS TO SOME UNSEEN PERSON.
AND THERE'S THAT STRANGE NOTE...
Mr. Sebast ool.
It is futile t e me.
Be a good lit y and watch
as in darkness the moon is
engulfed,
for I shall strip the great safe
which has been the pride
of your clan.
Kaito Kid
WAIT ...
I'VE GOT IT!

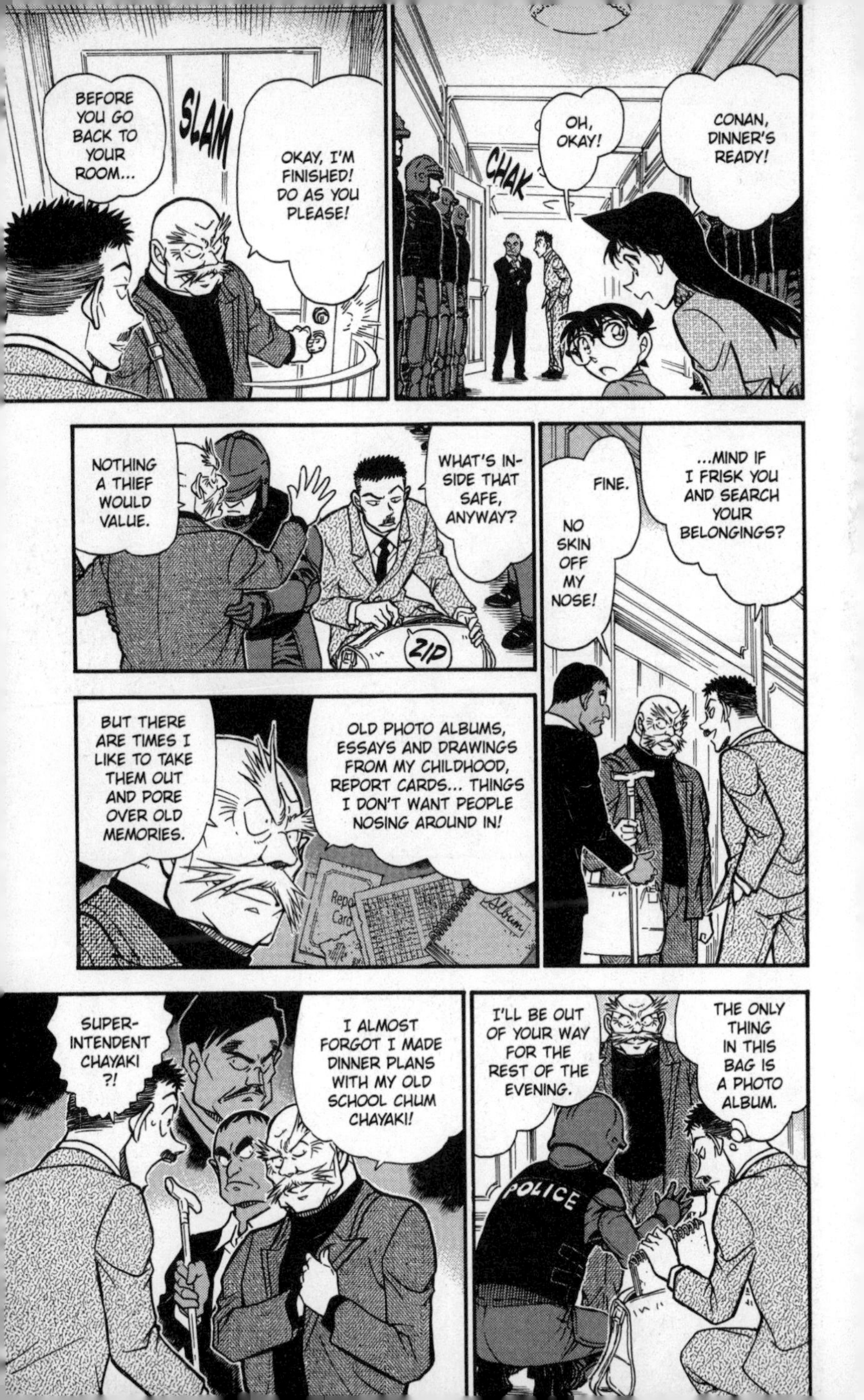
CONAN, DINNER'S READY!
OH, OKAY!
CHAK
OKAY, I'M FINISHED! DO AS YOU PLEASE!
SLAM
BEFORE YOU GO BACK TO YOUR ROOM...
...MIND IF I FRISK YOU AND SEARCH YOUR BELONGINGS?
FINE.
NO SKIN OFF MY NOSE!
WHAT'S IN-SIDE THAT SAFE, ANYWAY?
NOTHING A THIEF WOULD VALUE.
ZIP
OLD PHOTO ALBUMS, ESSAYS AND DRAWINGS FROM MY CHILDHOOD, REPORT CARDS... THINGS I DON'T WANT PEOPLE NOSING AROUND IN!
BUT THERE ARE TIMES I LIKE TO TAKE THEM OUT AND PORE OVER OLD MEMORIES.
Album
THE ONLY THING IN THIS BAG IS A PHOTO ALBUM.
I'LL BE OUT OF YOUR WAY FOR THE REST OF THE EVENING.
POLICE
I ALMOST FORGOT I MADE DINNER PLANS WITH MY OLD SCHOOL CHUM CHAYAKI!
SUPER-INTENDENT CHAYAKI ?!

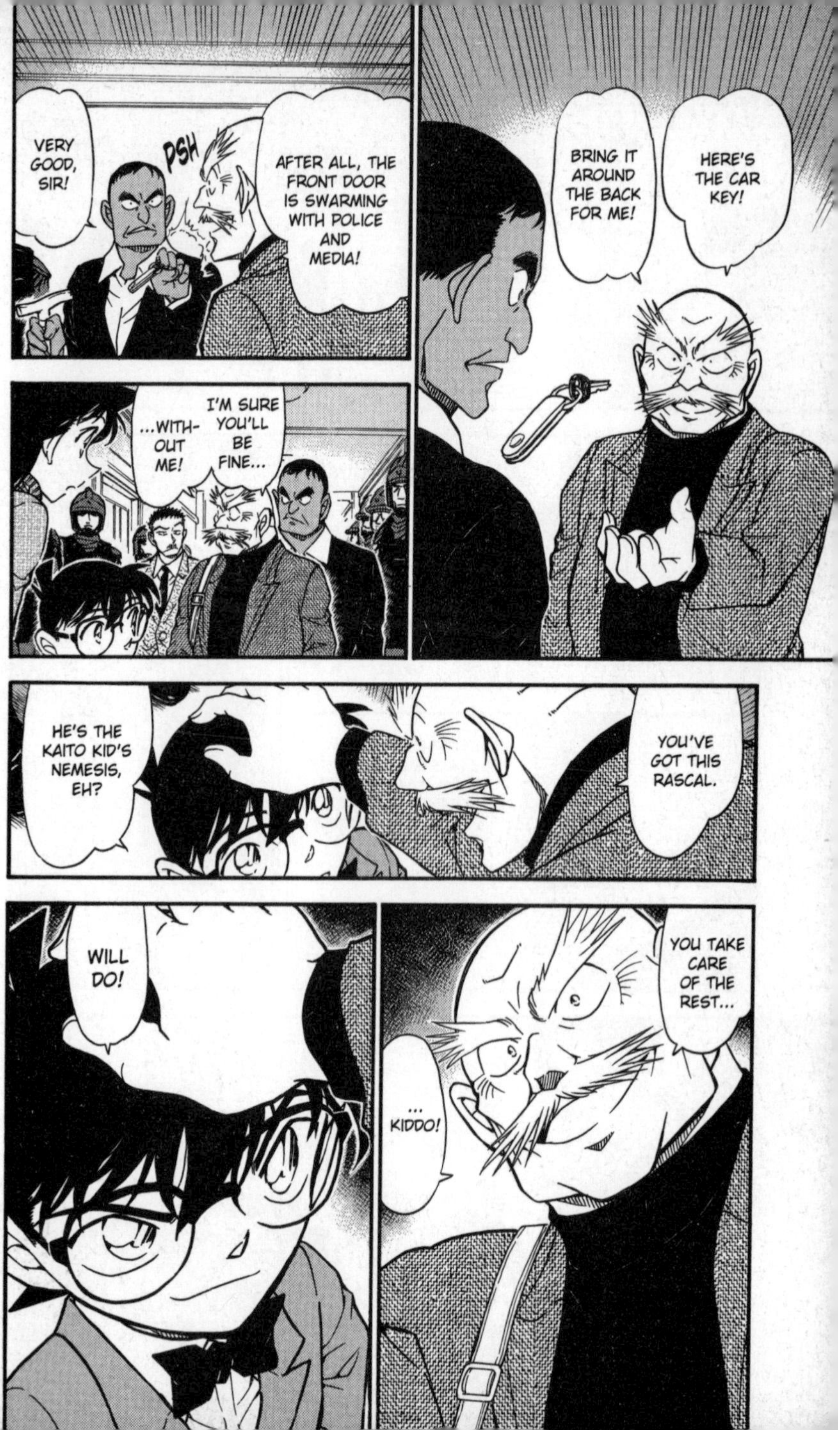
HERE'S THE CAR KEY!
BRING IT AROUND THE BACK FOR ME!
AFTER ALL, THE FRONT DOOR IS SWARMING WITH POLICE AND MEDIA!
PSH
VERY GOOD, SIR!
I'M SURE YOU'LL BE FINE...
...WITH-OUT ME!
YOU'VE GOT THIS RASCAL.
HE'S THE KAITO KID'S NEMESIS, EH?
YOU TAKE CARE OF THE REST...
...KIDDO!
WILL DO!

FILE 2: UNLOCKED

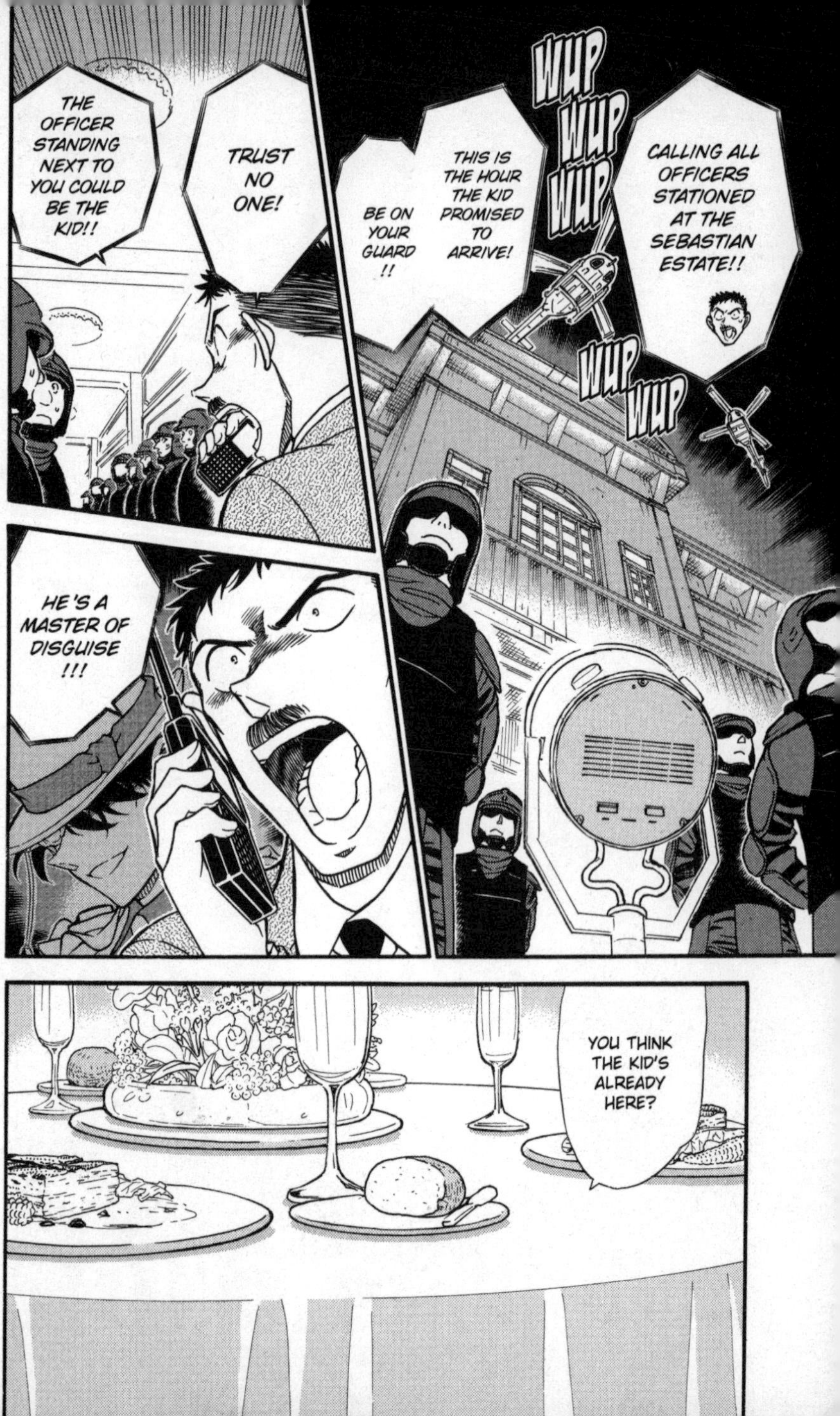
CALLING ALL OFFICERS STATIONED AT THE SEBASTIAN ESTATE!!
WUP WUP WUP
WUP WUP
THIS IS THE HOUR THE KID PROMISED TO ARRIVE!
BE ON YOUR GUARD!!
TRUST NO ONE!
THE OFFICER STANDING NEXT TO YOU COULD BE THE KID!!
HE'S A MASTER OF DISGUISE!!!
YOU THINK THE KID'S ALREADY HERE?

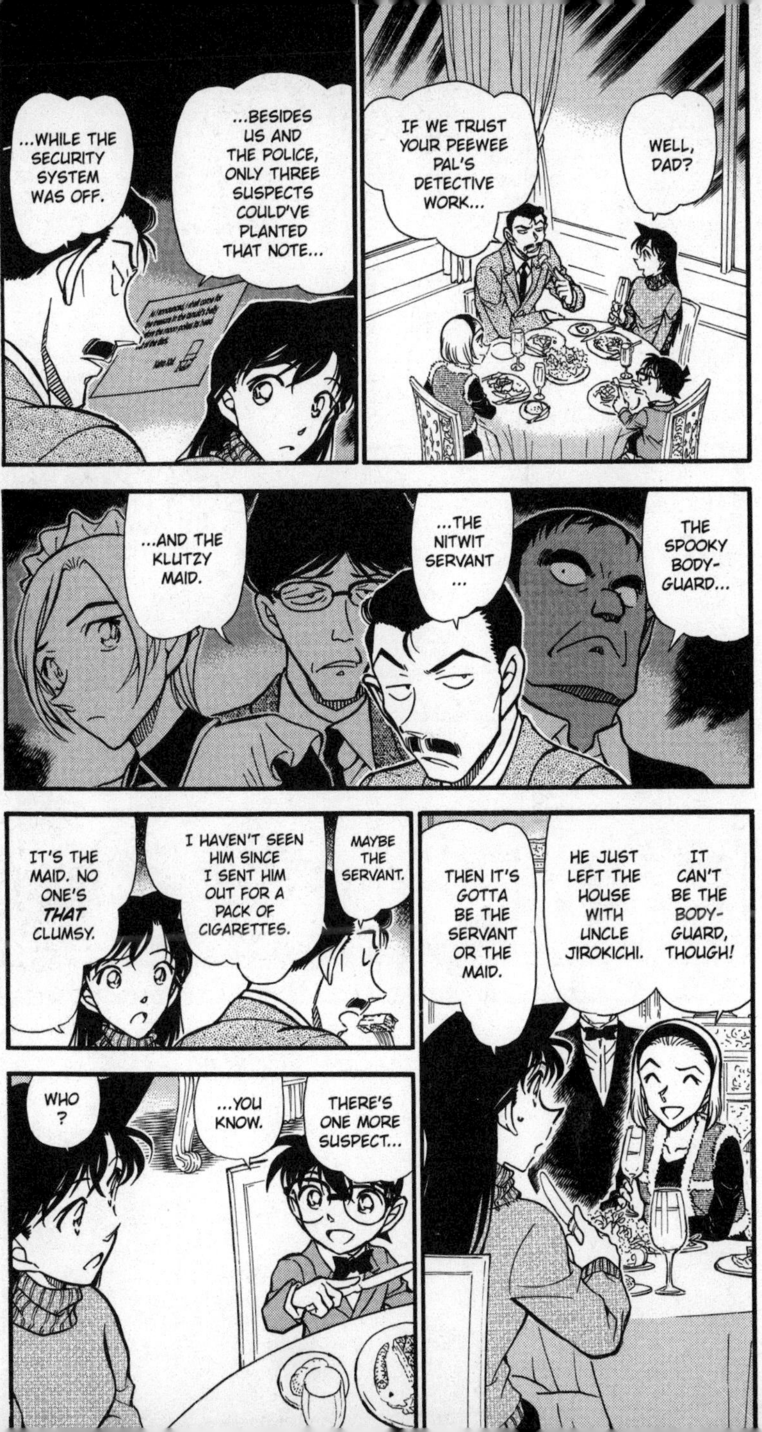
WELL, DAD?
IF WE TRUST YOUR PEEWEE PAL'S DETECTIVE WORK...
...BESIDES US AND THE POLICE, ONLY THREE SUSPECTS COULD'VE PLANTED THAT NOTE...
...WHILE THE SECURITY SYSTEM WAS OFF.
THE SPOOKY BODY-GUARD...
...THE NITWIT SERVANT ...
...AND THE KLUTZY MAID.
IT CAN'T BE THE BODY-GUARD, THOUGH!
HE JUST LEFT THE HOUSE WITH UNCLE JIROKICHI.
THEN IT'S GOTTA BE THE SERVANT OR THE MAID.
MAYBE THE SERVANT.
I HAVEN'T SEEN HIM SINCE I SENT HIM OUT FOR A PACK OF CIGARETTES.
IT'S THE MAID. NO ONE'S *THAT* CLUMSY.
THERE'S ONE MORE SUSPECT...
...YOU KNOW.
WHO ?

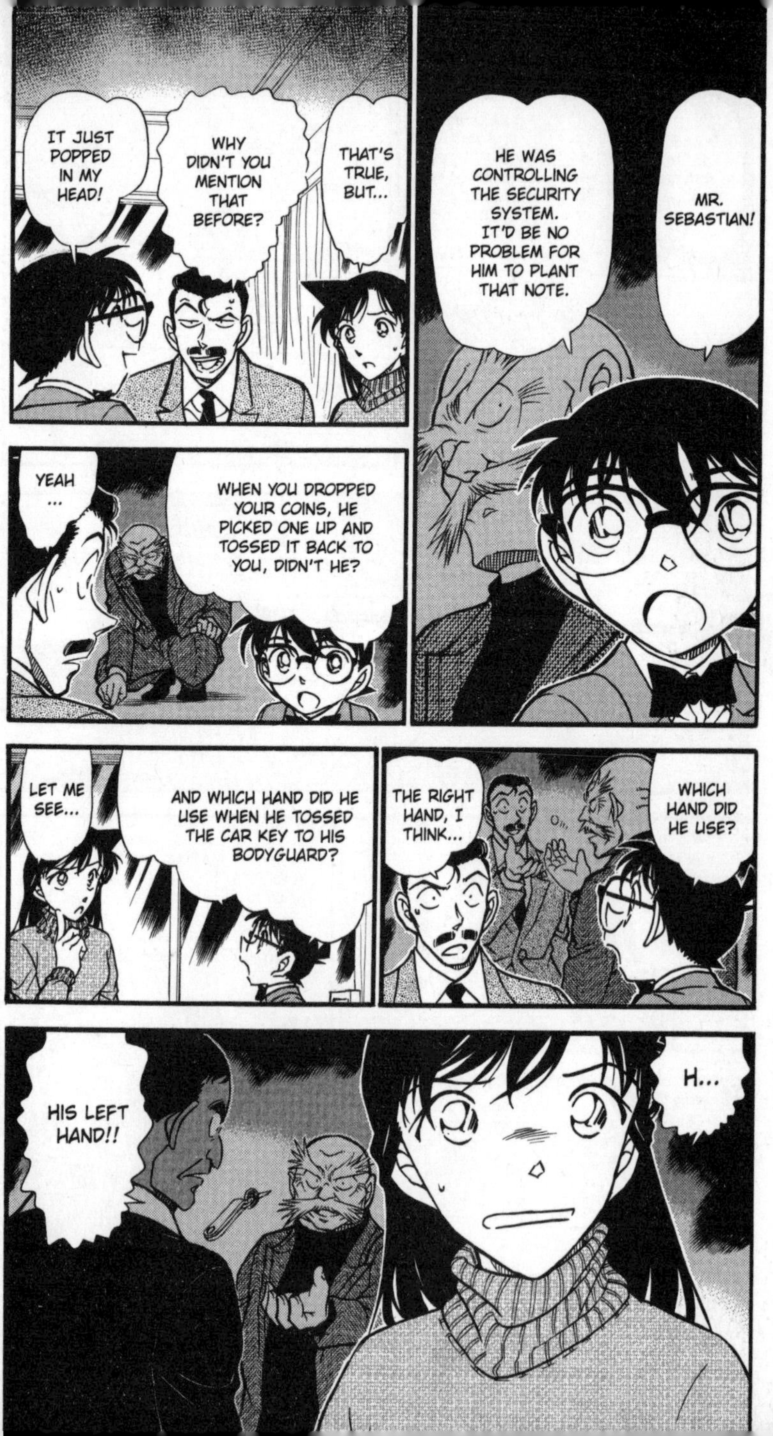
MR. SEBASTIAN!
HE WAS CONTROLLING THE SECURITY SYSTEM. IT'D BE NO PROBLEM FOR HIM TO PLANT THAT NOTE.
THAT'S TRUE, BUT...
WHY DIDN'T YOU MENTION THAT BEFORE?
IT JUST POPPED IN MY HEAD!
WHEN YOU DROPPED YOUR COINS, HE PICKED ONE UP AND TOSSED IT BACK TO YOU, DIDN'T HE?
YEAH ...
WHICH HAND DID HE USE?
THE RIGHT HAND, I THINK...
AND WHICH HAND DID HE USE WHEN HE TOSSED THE CAR KEY TO HIS BODYGUARD?
LET ME SEE...
H...
HIS LEFT HAND!!

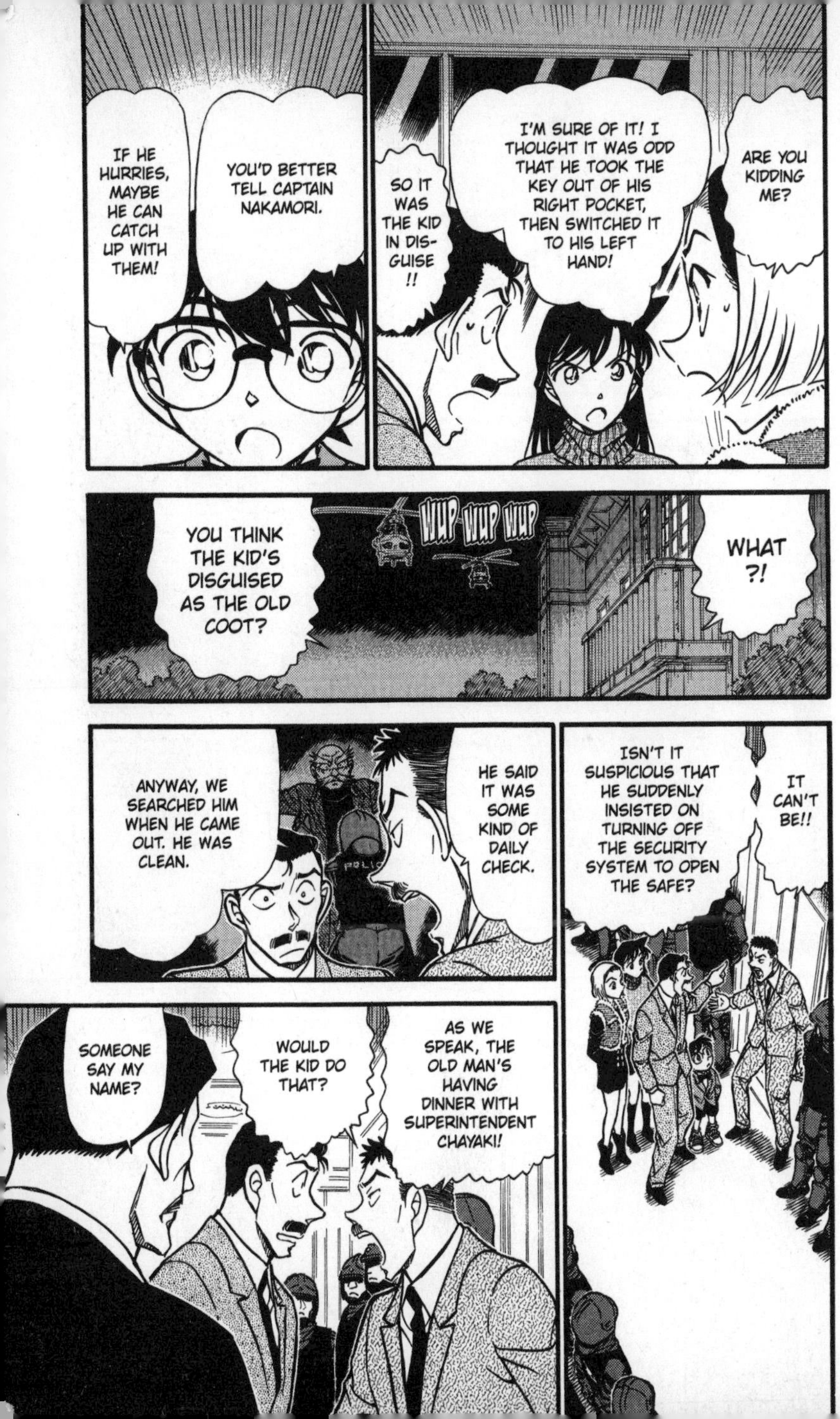
ARE YOU KIDDING ME?
I'M SURE OF IT! I THOUGHT IT WAS ODD THAT HE TOOK THE KEY OUT OF HIS RIGHT POCKET, THEN SWITCHED IT TO HIS LEFT HAND!
SO IT WAS THE KID IN DIS-GUISE!!
YOU'D BETTER TELL CAPTAIN NAKAMORI.
IF HE HURRIES, MAYBE HE CAN CATCH UP WITH THEM!
WHAT?!
WUP WUP WUP
YOU THINK THE KID'S DISGUISED AS THE OLD COOT?
IT CAN'T BE!!
ISN'T IT SUSPICIOUS THAT HE SUDDENLY INSISTED ON TURNING OFF THE SECURITY SYSTEM TO OPEN THE SAFE?
HE SAID IT WAS SOME KIND OF DAILY CHECK.
ANYWAY, WE SEARCHED HIM WHEN HE CAME OUT. HE WAS CLEAN.
AS WE SPEAK, THE OLD MAN'S HAVING DINNER WITH SUPERINTENDENT CHAYAKI!
WOULD THE KID DO THAT?
SOMEONE SAY MY NAME?

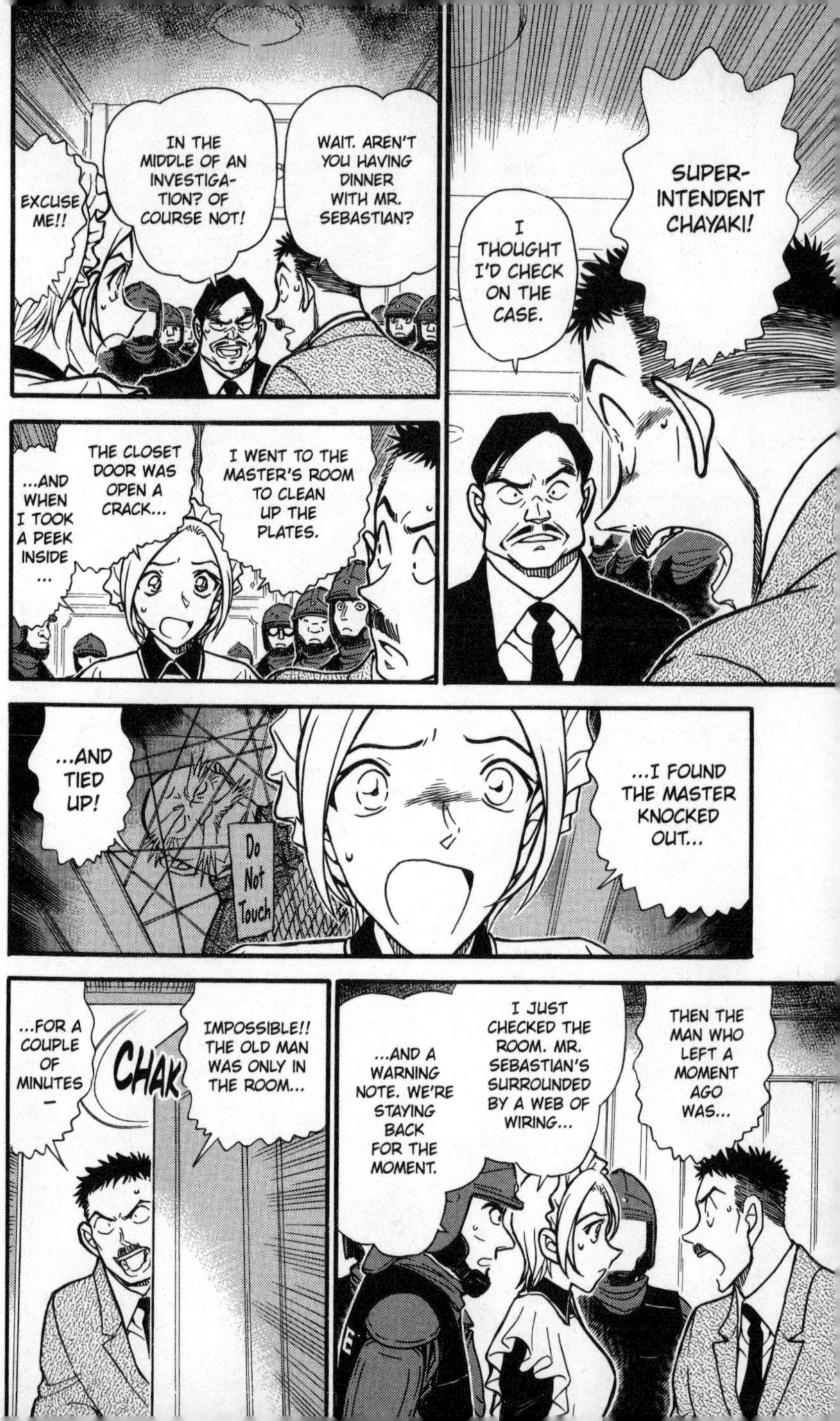
SUPER-INTENDENT CHAYAKI!
I THOUGHT I'D CHECK ON THE CASE.
WAIT. AREN'T YOU HAVING DINNER WITH MR. SEBASTIAN?
IN THE MIDDLE OF AN INVESTIGA-TION? OF COURSE NOT!
EXCUSE ME!!
I WENT TO THE MASTER'S ROOM TO CLEAN UP THE PLATES.
THE CLOSET DOOR WAS OPEN A CRACK...
...AND WHEN I TOOK A PEEK INSIDE ...
...I FOUND THE MASTER KNOCKED OUT...
Do Not Touch
...AND TIED UP!
THEN THE MAN WHO LEFT A MOMENT AGO WAS...
I JUST CHECKED THE ROOM. MR. SEBASTIAN'S SURROUNDED BY A WEB OF WIRING...
...AND A WARNING NOTE. WE'RE STAYING BACK FOR THE MOMENT.
IMPOSSIBLE!! THE OLD MAN WAS ONLY IN THE ROOM...
CHAK
...FOR A COUPLE OF MINUTES—

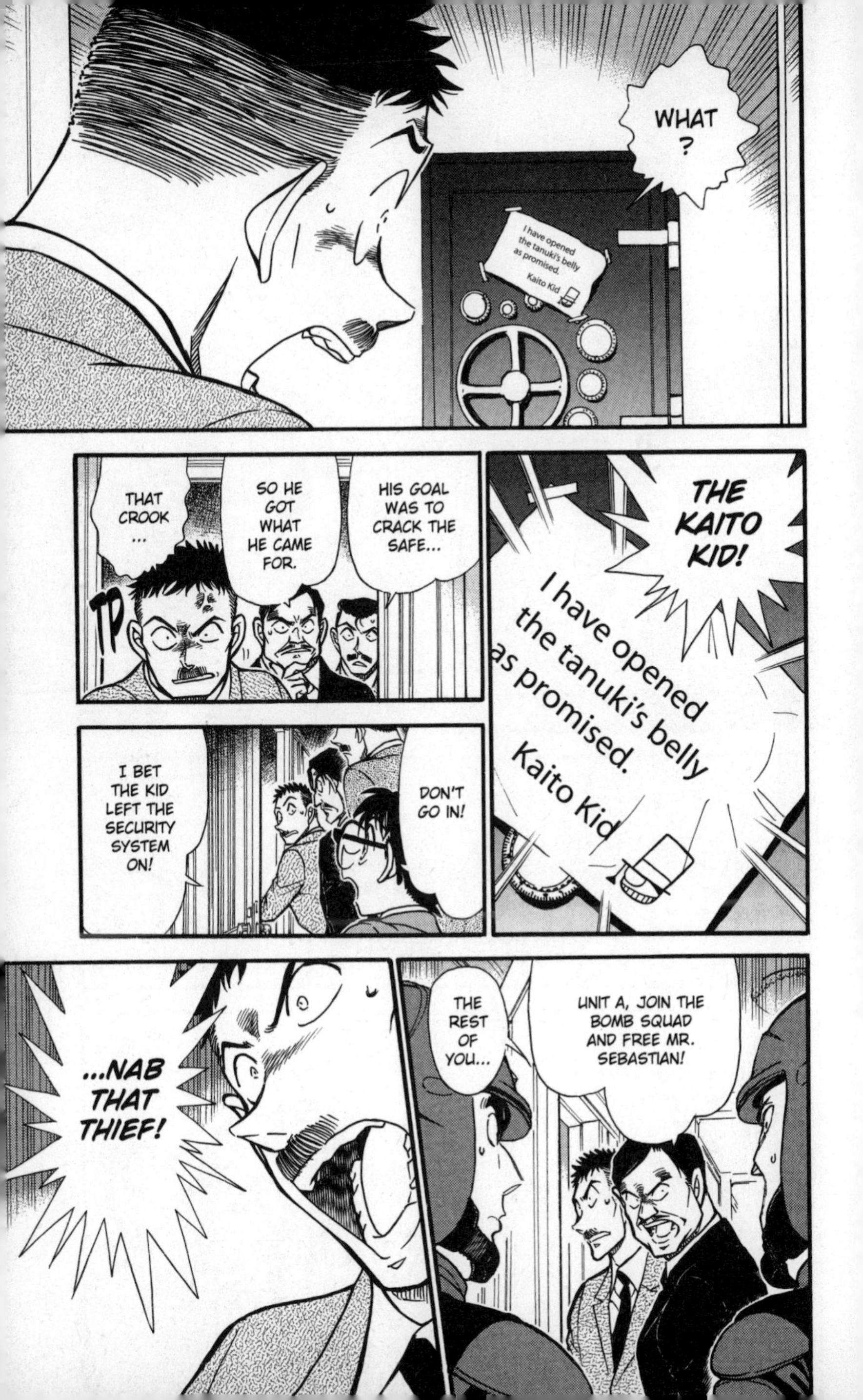
WHAT?
I have opened the tanuki's belly as promised.
Kaito Kid
THE KAITO KID!
I have opened the tanuki's belly as promised.
Kaito Kid
HIS GOAL WAS TO CRACK THE SAFE...
SO HE GOT WHAT HE CAME FOR.
THAT CROOK...
TP
DON'T GO IN!
I BET THE KID LEFT THE SECURITY SYSTEM ON!
UNIT A, JOIN THE BOMB SQUAD AND FREE MR. SEBASTIAN!
THE REST OF YOU...
...NAB THAT THIEF!

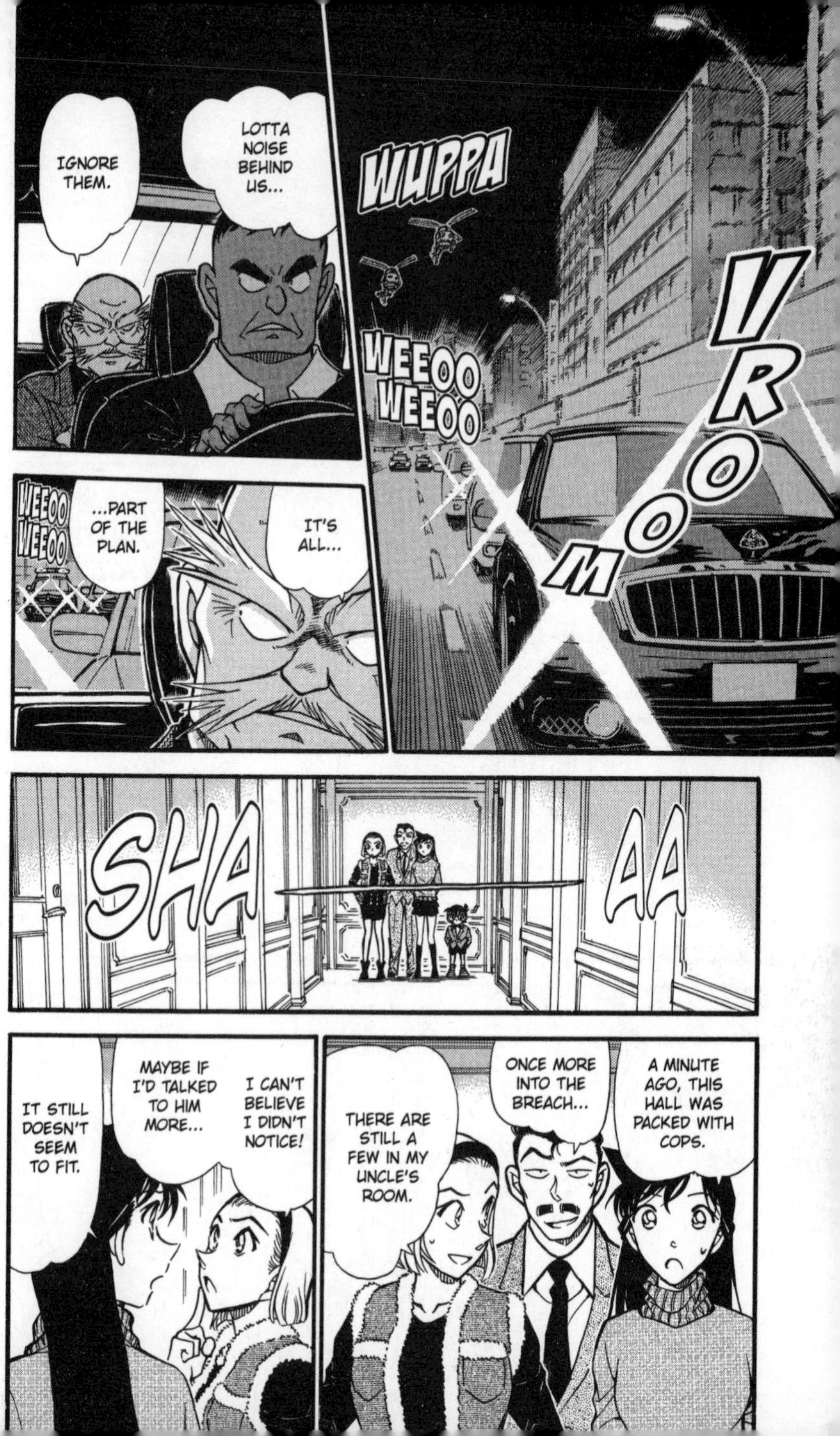
WUPPA
WEEOO WEEOO
VROOM
LOTTA NOISE BEHIND US...
IGNORE THEM.
IT'S ALL...
...PART OF THE PLAN.
WEEOO WEEOO
SHA AA
A MINUTE AGO, THIS HALL WAS PACKED WITH COPS.
ONCE MORE INTO THE BREACH...
THERE ARE STILL A FEW IN MY UNCLE'S ROOM.
I CAN'T BELIEVE I DIDN'T NOTICE!
MAYBE IF I'D TALKED TO HIM MORE...
IT STILL DOESN'T SEEM TO FIT.

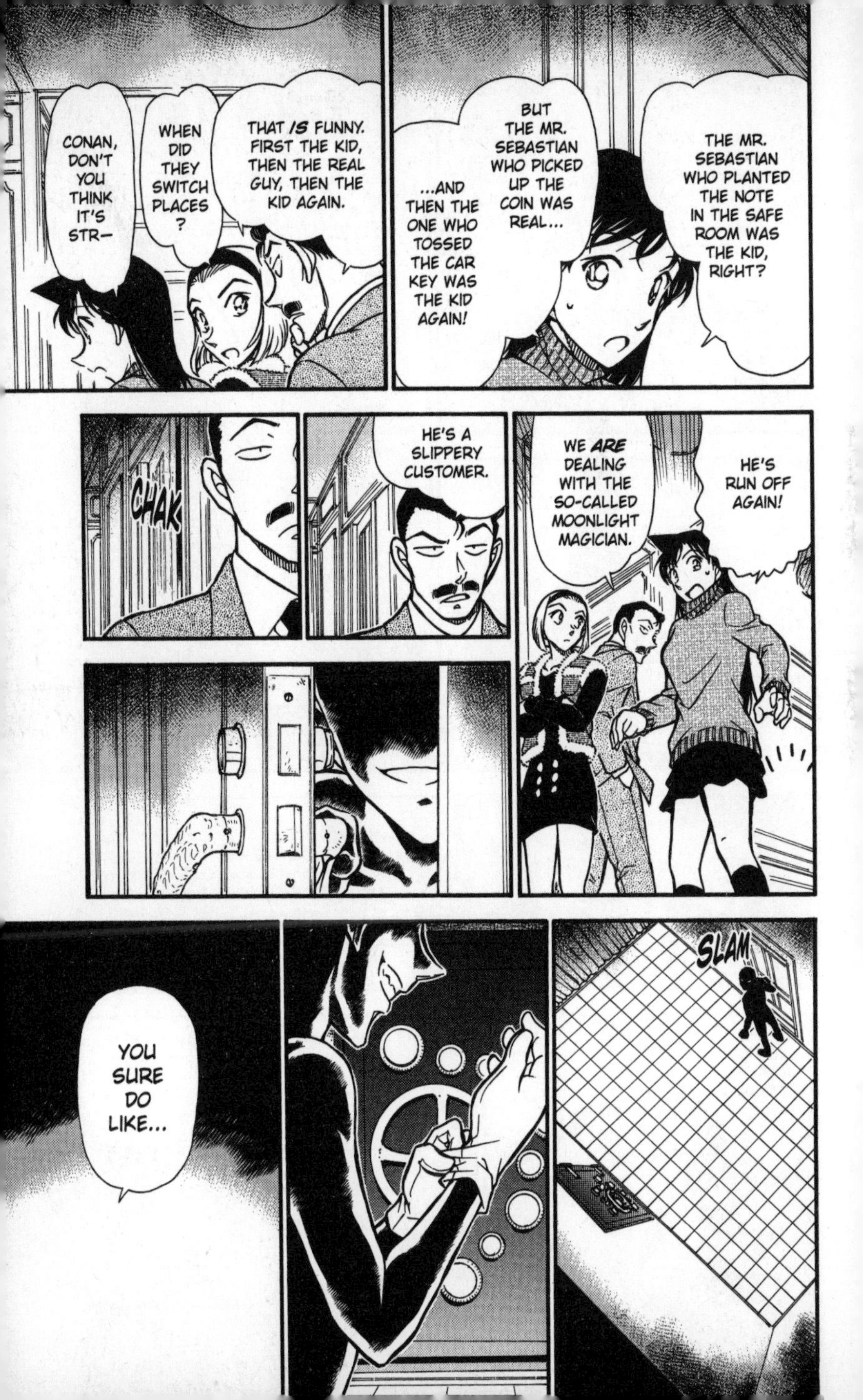
THE MR. SEBASTIAN WHO PLANTED THE NOTE IN THE SAFE ROOM WAS THE KID, RIGHT?
BUT THE MR. SEBASTIAN WHO PICKED UP THE COIN WAS REAL...
...AND THEN THE ONE WHO TOSSED THE CAR KEY WAS THE KID AGAIN!
THAT IS FUNNY. FIRST THE KID, THEN THE REAL GUY, THEN THE KID AGAIN.
WHEN DID THEY SWITCH PLACES?
CONAN, DON'T YOU THINK IT'S STR—
HE'S RUN OFF AGAIN!
WE ARE DEALING WITH THE SO-CALLED MOONLIGHT MAGICIAN.
HE'S A SLIPPERY CUSTOMER.
CHAK
SLAM
YOU SURE DO LIKE...

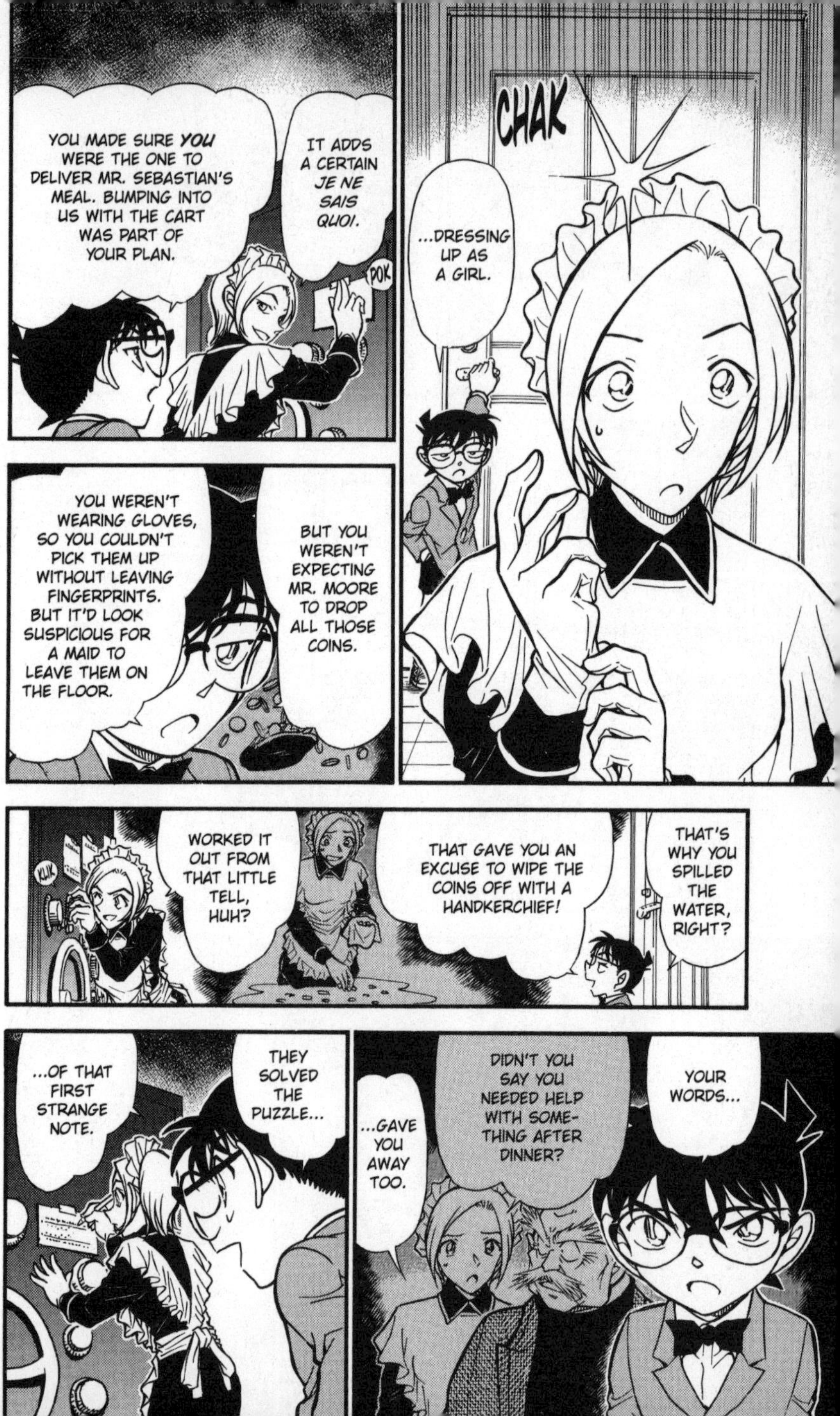
CHAK
...DRESSING UP AS A GIRL.
IT ADDS A CERTAIN *JE NE SAIS QUOI.*
YOU MADE SURE *YOU* WERE THE ONE TO DELIVER MR. SEBASTIAN'S MEAL. BUMPING INTO US WITH THE CART WAS PART OF YOUR PLAN.
POK
BUT YOU WEREN'T EXPECTING MR. MOORE TO DROP ALL THOSE COINS.
YOU WEREN'T WEARING GLOVES, SO YOU COULDN'T PICK THEM UP WITHOUT LEAVING FINGERPRINTS. BUT IT'D LOOK SUSPICIOUS FOR A MAID TO LEAVE THEM ON THE FLOOR.
THAT'S WHY YOU SPILLED THE WATER, RIGHT?
THAT GAVE YOU AN EXCUSE TO WIPE THE COINS OFF WITH A HANDKERCHIEF!
WORKED IT OUT FROM THAT LITTLE TELL, HUH?
KLIK
YOUR WORDS...
DIDN'T YOU SAY YOU NEEDED HELP WITH SOME-THING AFTER DINNER?
...GAVE YOU AWAY TOO.
THEY SOLVED THE PUZZLE...
...OF THAT FIRST STRANGE NOTE.

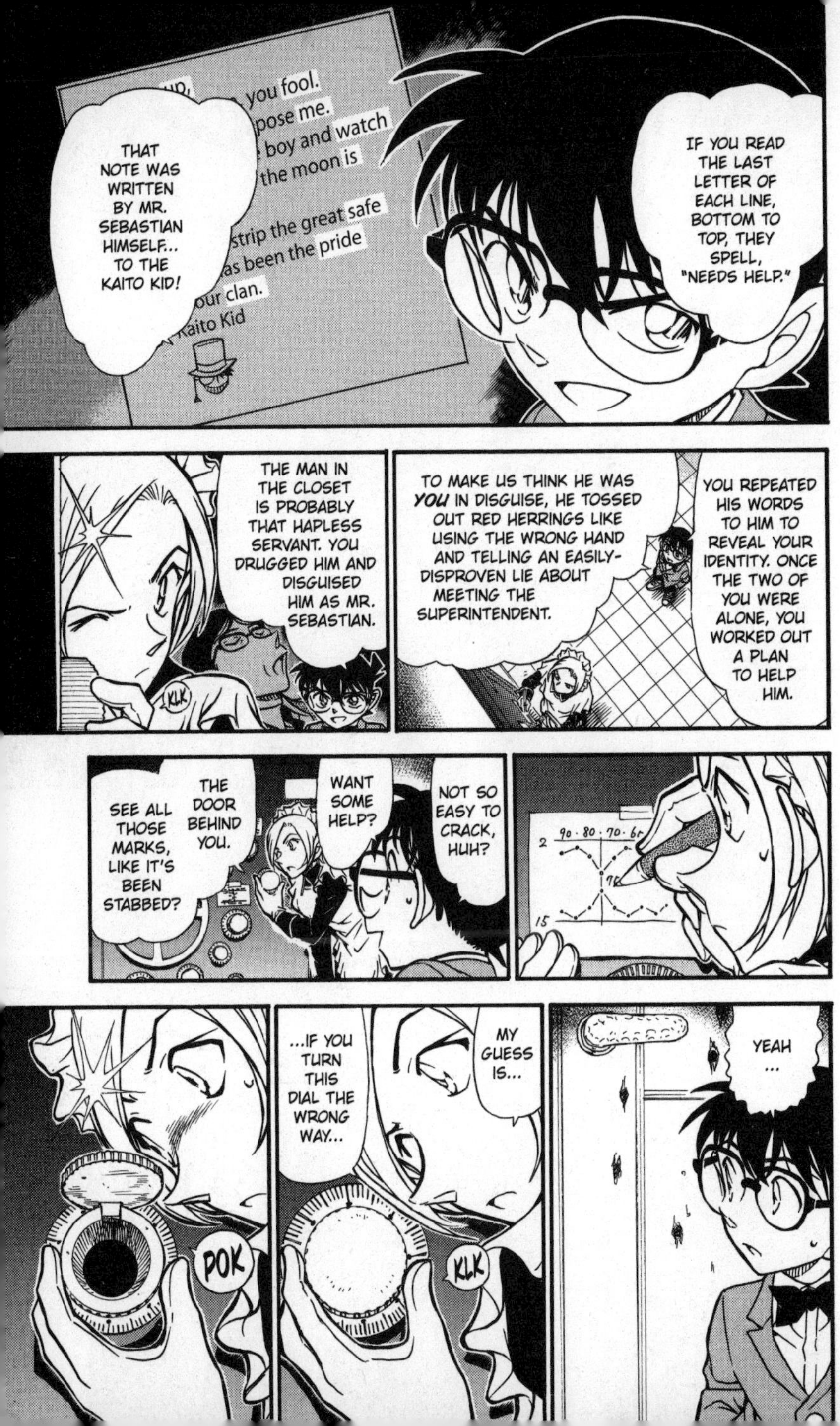
IF YOU READ THE LAST LETTER OF EACH LINE, BOTTOM TO TOP, THEY SPELL, "NEEDS HELP."
you fool.
pose me.
boy and watch
the moon is
strip the great safe
as been the pride
our clan.
Kaito Kid
THAT NOTE WAS WRITTEN BY MR. SEBASTIAN HIMSELF... TO THE KAITO KID!
YOU REPEATED HIS WORDS TO HIM TO REVEAL YOUR IDENTITY. ONCE THE TWO OF YOU WERE ALONE, YOU WORKED OUT A PLAN TO HELP HIM.
TO MAKE US THINK HE WAS *YOU* IN DISGUISE, HE TOSSED OUT RED HERRINGS LIKE USING THE WRONG HAND AND TELLING AN EASILY-DISPROVEN LIE ABOUT MEETING THE SUPERINTENDENT.
THE MAN IN THE CLOSET IS PROBABLY THAT HAPLESS SERVANT. YOU DRUGGED HIM AND DISGUISED HIM AS MR. SEBASTIAN.
KLK
NOT SO EASY TO CRACK, HUH?
WANT SOME HELP?
THE DOOR BEHIND YOU.
SEE ALL THOSE MARKS, LIKE IT'S BEEN STABBED?
YEAH ...
MY GUESS IS...
...IF YOU TURN THIS DIAL THE WRONG WAY...
KLK
POK

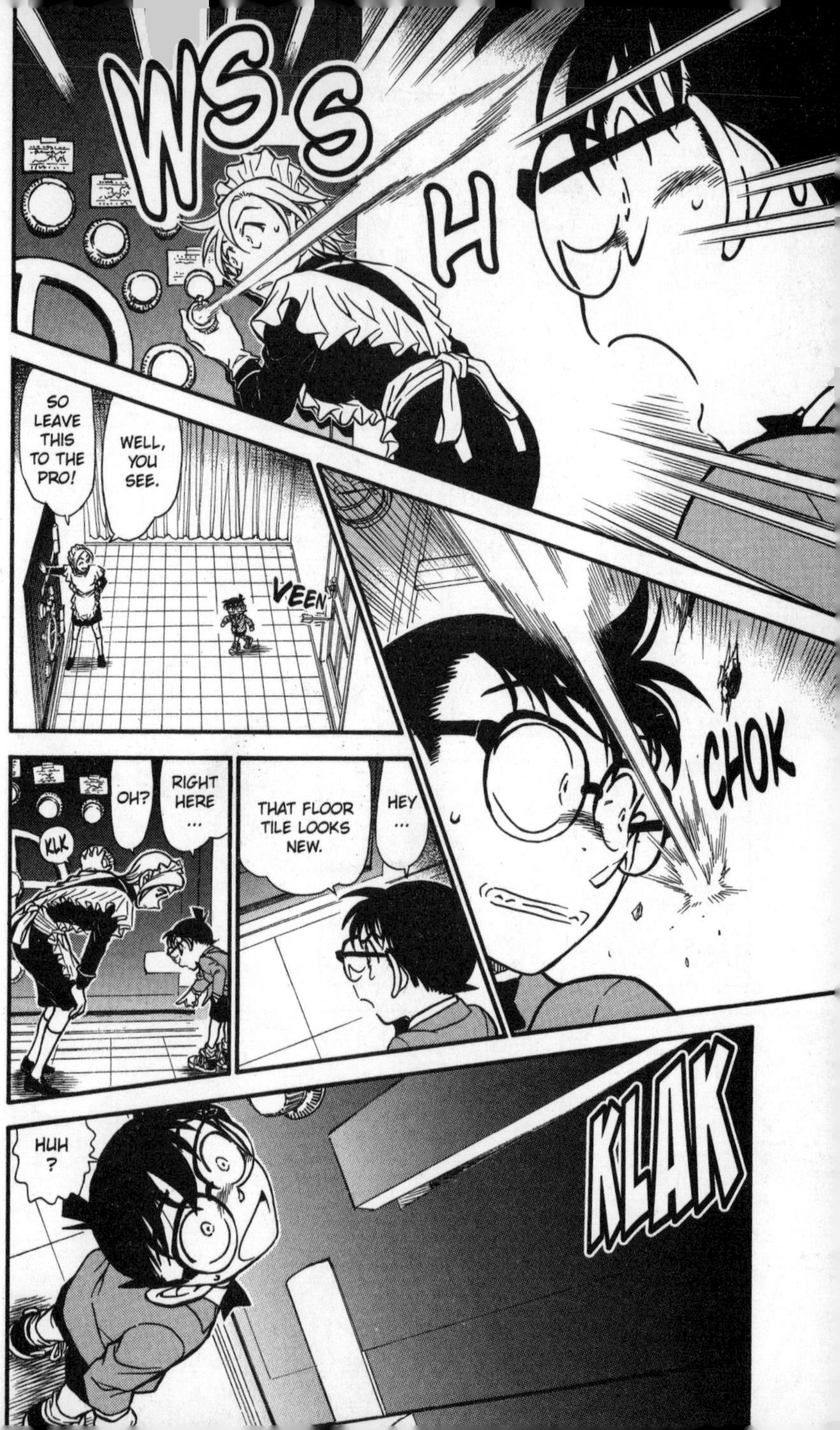
WSSH
CHOK
WELL, YOU SEE.
SO LEAVE THIS TO THE PRO!
VEEN
HEY ...
THAT FLOOR TILE LOOKS NEW.
RIGHT HERE ...
OH?
KLK
KLAK
HUH ?

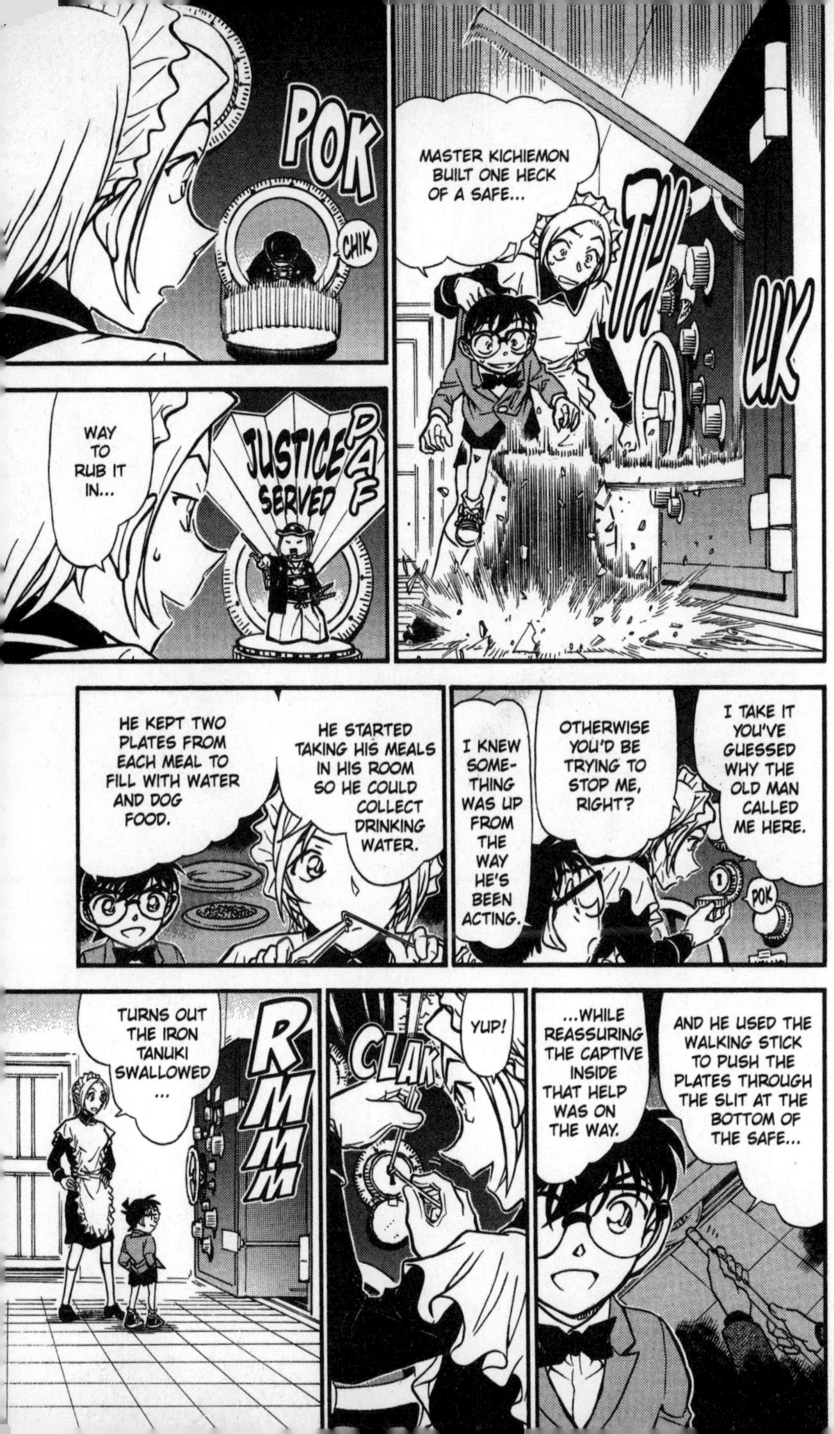
MASTER KICHIEMON BUILT ONE HECK OF A SAFE...
POK
CHIK
WAY TO RUB IT IN...
JUSTICE SERVED
PAF
I TAKE IT YOU'VE GUESSED WHY THE OLD MAN CALLED ME HERE.
OTHERWISE YOU'D BE TRYING TO STOP ME, RIGHT?
I KNEW SOMETHING WAS UP FROM THE WAY HE'S BEEN ACTING.
POK
HE STARTED TAKING HIS MEALS IN HIS ROOM SO HE COULD COLLECT DRINKING WATER.
HE KEPT TWO PLATES FROM EACH MEAL TO FILL WITH WATER AND DOG FOOD.
AND HE USED THE WALKING STICK TO PUSH THE PLATES THROUGH THE SLIT AT THE BOTTOM OF THE SAFE...
...WHILE REASSURING THE CAPTIVE INSIDE THAT HELP WAS ON THE WAY.
YUP!
CLAK
RMMM
TURNS OUT THE IRON TANUKI SWALLOWED ...

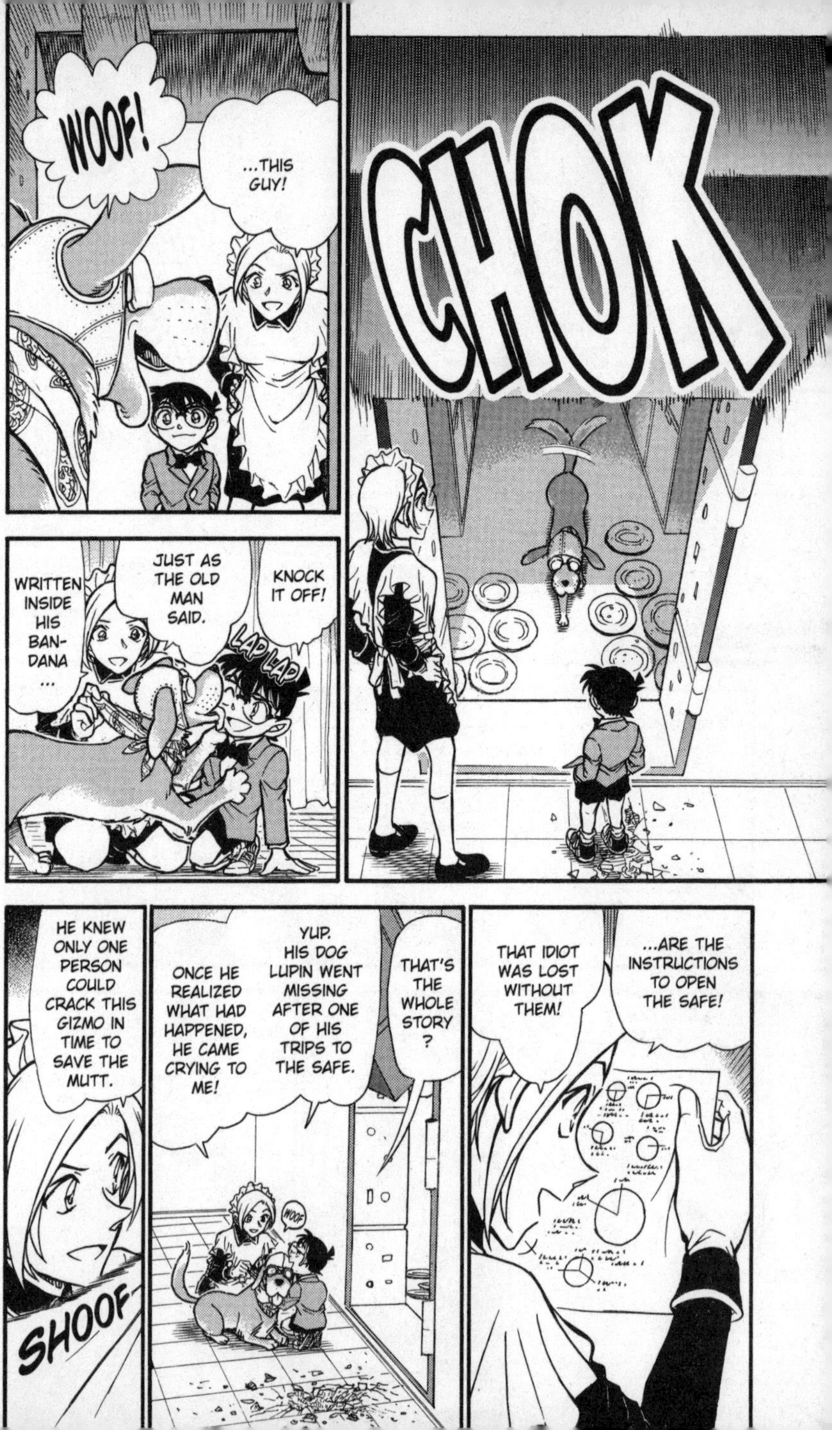
CHOK
...THIS GUY!
WOOF!
KNOCK IT OFF!
JUST AS THE OLD MAN SAID.
WRITTEN INSIDE HIS BAN-DANA ...
LAP LAP
...ARE THE INSTRUCTIONS TO OPEN THE SAFE!
THAT IDIOT WAS LOST WITHOUT THEM!
THAT'S THE WHOLE STORY ?
YUP. HIS DOG LUPIN WENT MISSING AFTER ONE OF HIS TRIPS TO THE SAFE.
ONCE HE REALIZED WHAT HAD HAPPENED, HE CAME CRYING TO ME!
WOOF
HE KNEW ONLY ONE PERSON COULD CRACK THIS GIZMO IN TIME TO SAVE THE MUTT.
SHOOF

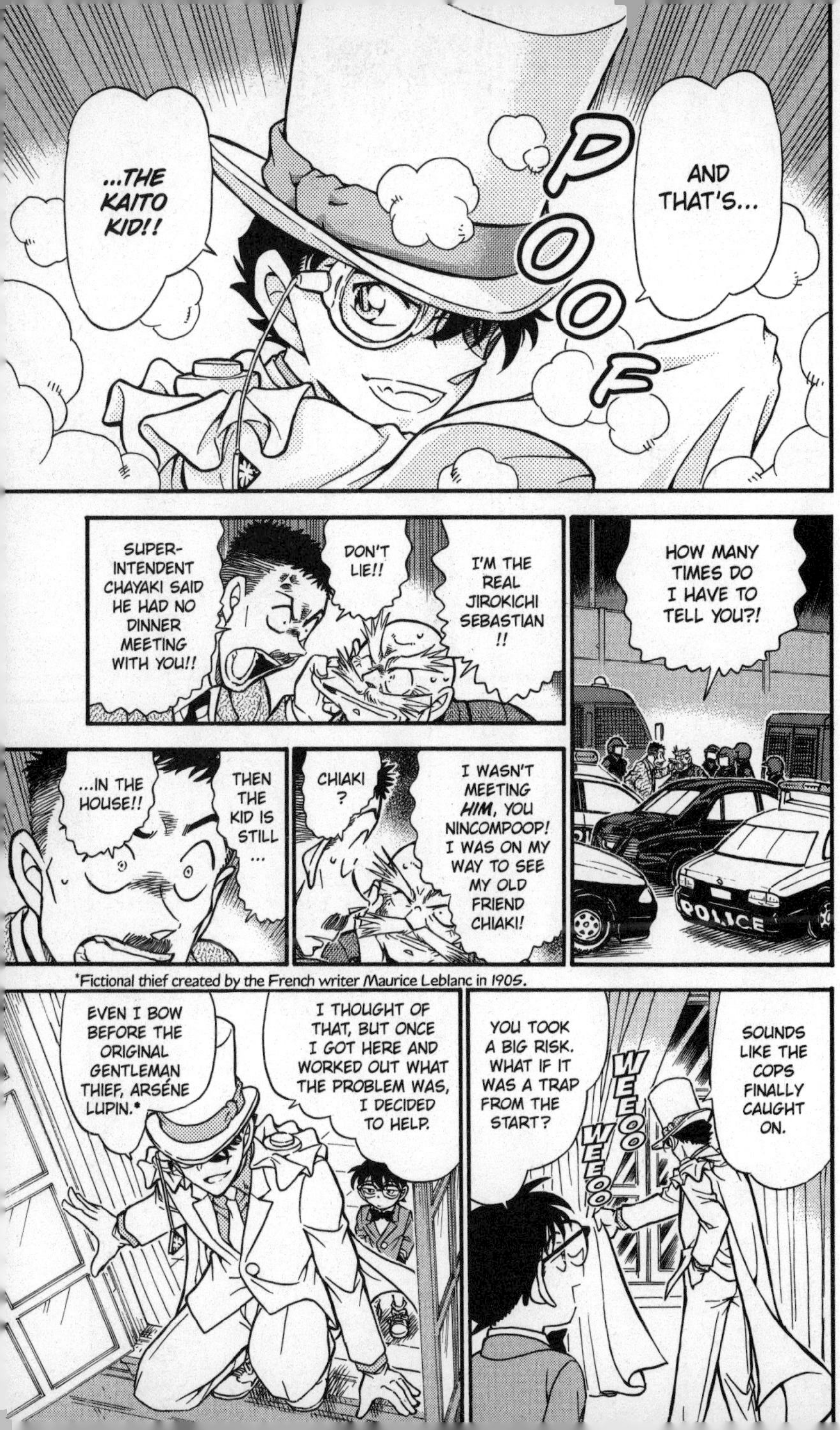
AND THAT'S...
POOOF
...THE KAITO KID!!
HOW MANY TIMES DO I HAVE TO TELL YOU?!
I'M THE REAL JIROKICHI SEBASTIAN !!
DON'T LIE!!
SUPER-INTENDENT CHAYAKI SAID HE HAD NO DINNER MEETING WITH YOU!!
I WASN'T MEETING *HIM*, YOU NINCOMPOOP! I WAS ON MY WAY TO SEE MY OLD FRIEND CHIAKI!
CHIAKI ?
THEN THE KID IS STILL ...
...IN THE HOUSE!!
POLICE
SOUNDS LIKE THE COPS FINALLY CAUGHT ON.
WEEOO
WEEOO
YOU TOOK A BIG RISK. WHAT IF IT WAS A TRAP FROM THE START?
I THOUGHT OF THAT, BUT ONCE I GOT HERE AND WORKED OUT WHAT THE PROBLEM WAS, I DECIDED TO HELP.
EVEN I BOW BEFORE THE ORIGINAL GENTLEMAN THIEF, ARSÉNE LUPIN.*

*Fictional thief created by the French writer Maurice Leblanc in 1905.

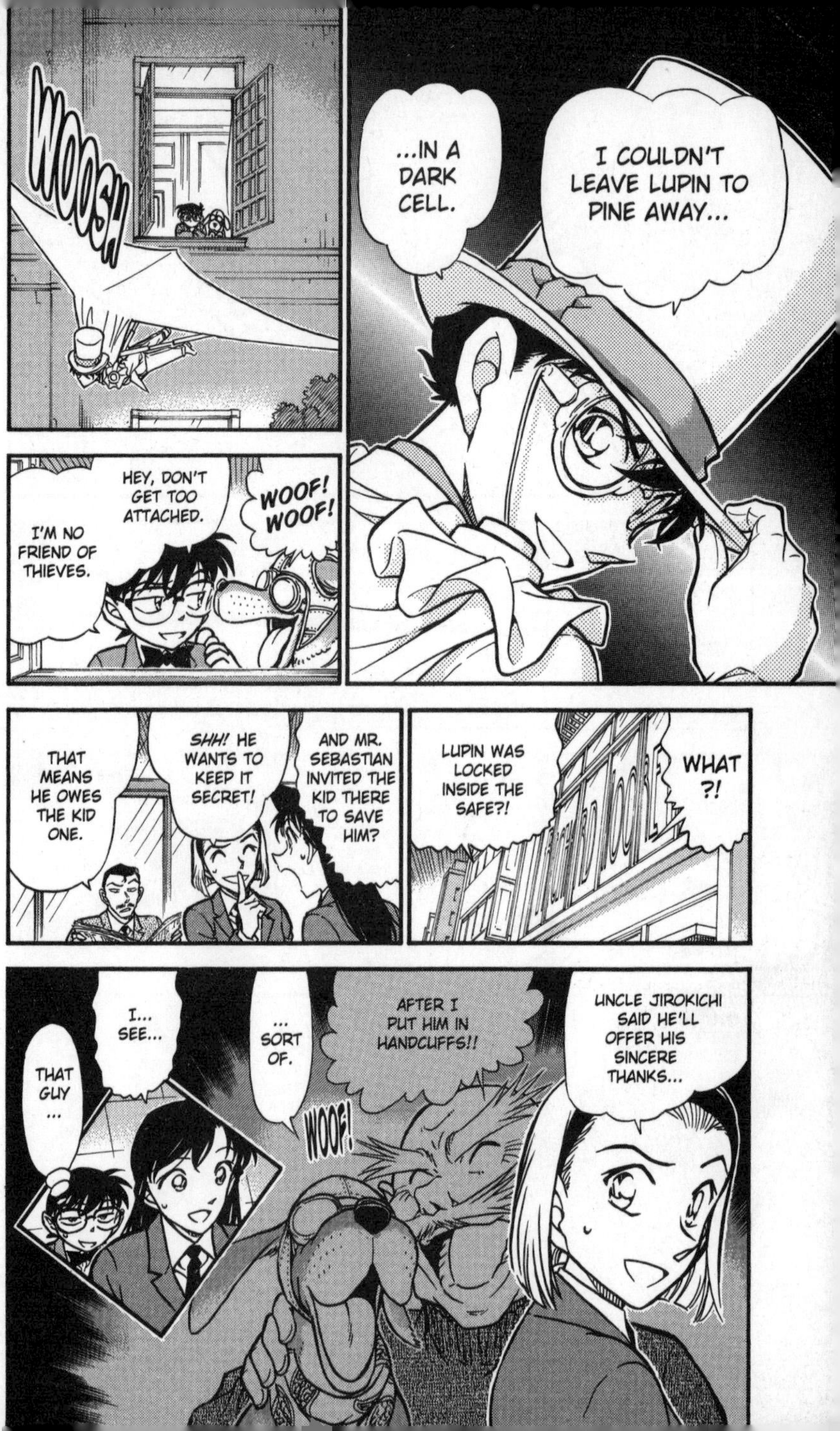
I COULDN'T LEAVE LUPIN TO PINE AWAY...
...IN A DARK CELL.
WOOSH
WOOF! WOOF!
HEY, DON'T GET TOO ATTACHED.
I'M NO FRIEND OF THIEVES.
WHAT ?!
LUPIN WAS LOCKED INSIDE THE SAFE?!
AND MR. SEBASTIAN INVITED THE KID THERE TO SAVE HIM?
SHH! HE WANTS TO KEEP IT SECRET!
THAT MEANS HE OWES THE KID ONE.
UNCLE JIROKICHI SAID HE'LL OFFER HIS SINCERE THANKS...
AFTER I PUT HIM IN HANDCUFFS!!
WOOF!
... SORT OF.
I... SEE...
THAT GUY ...

A TWIST OF FATE

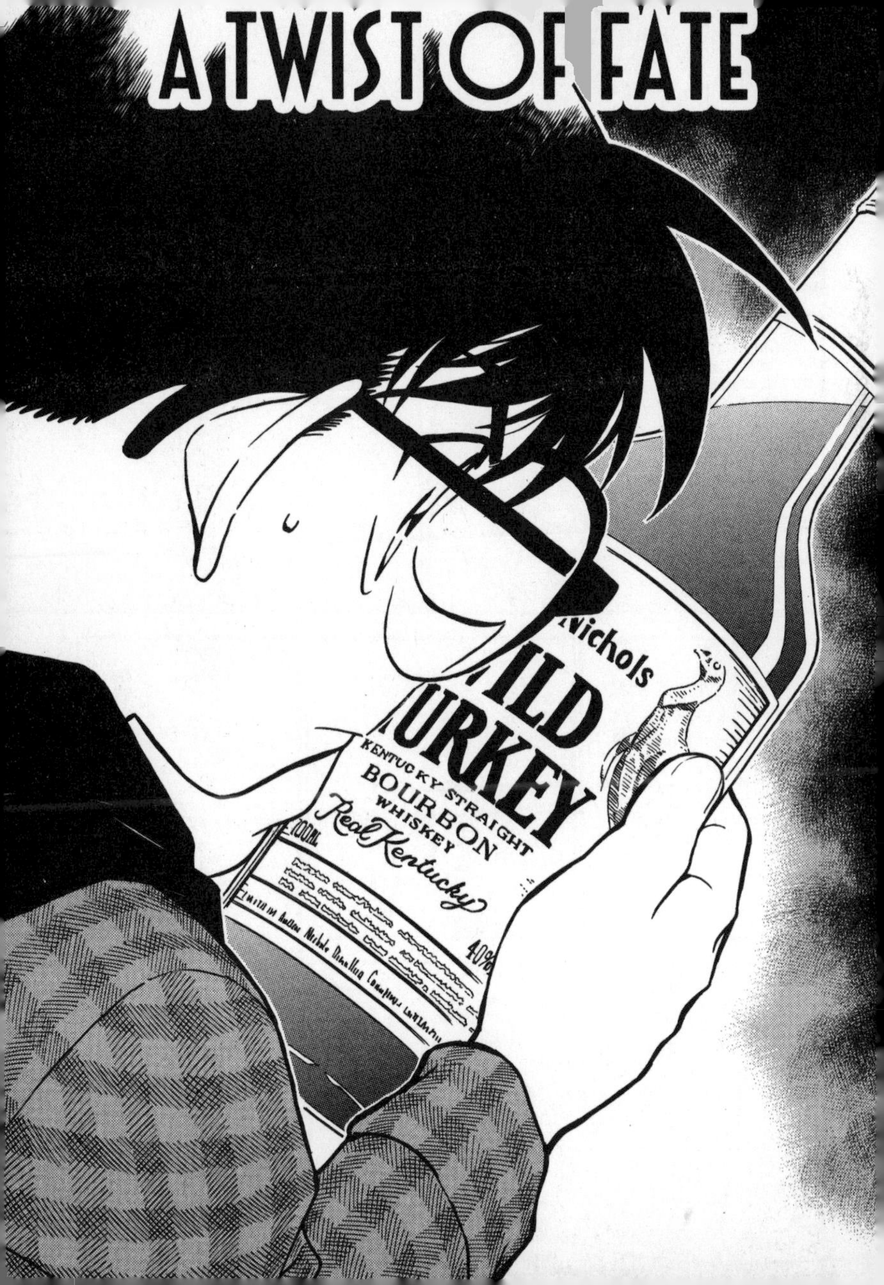
Nichols
KENTUCKY STRAIGHT
BOURBON
WHISKEY
Real Kentucky
700ml
40%

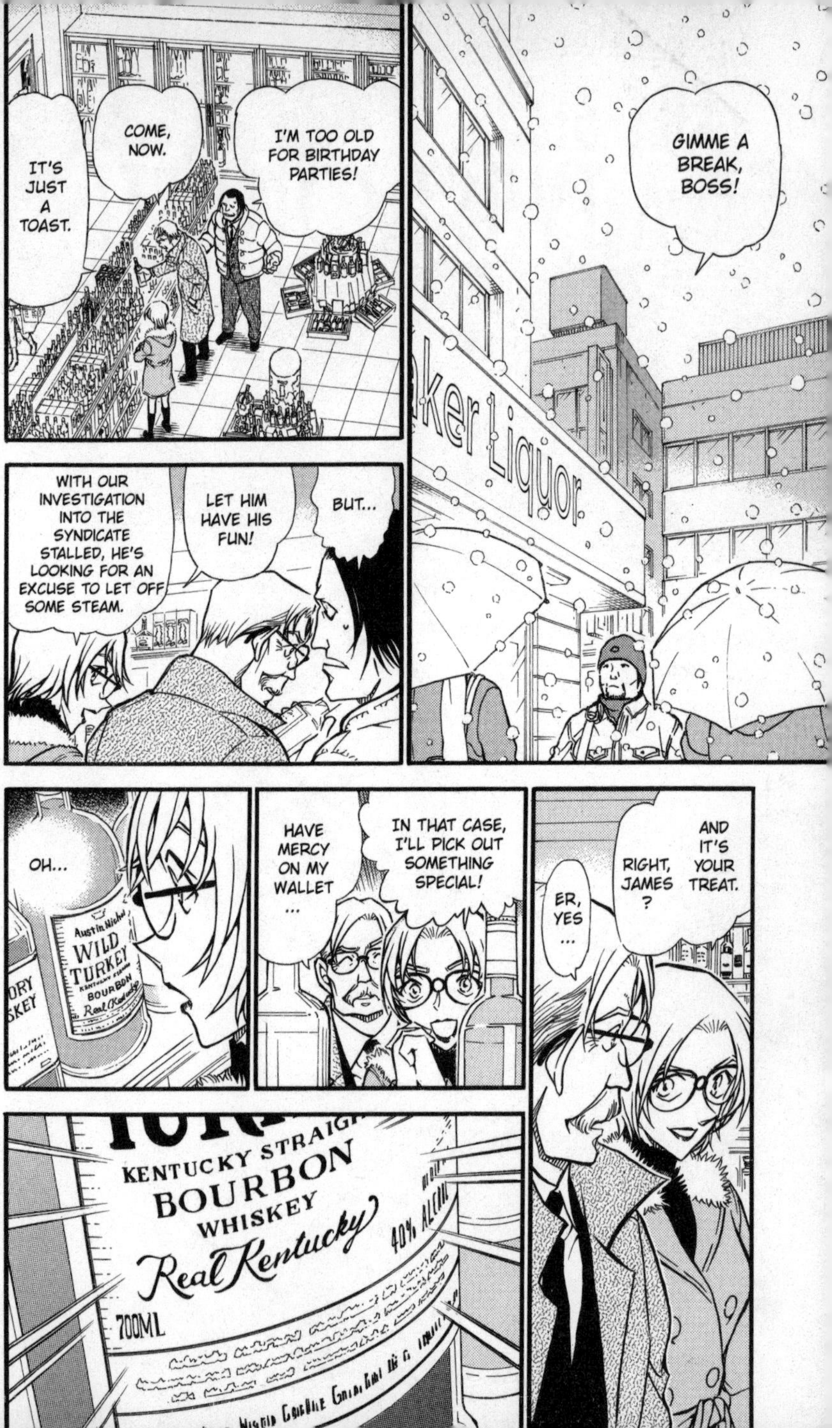
GIMME A BREAK, BOSS!
ker Liquor
I'M TOO OLD FOR BIRTHDAY PARTIES!
COME, NOW.
IT'S JUST A TOAST.
BUT...
LET HIM HAVE HIS FUN!
WITH OUR INVESTIGATION INTO THE SYNDICATE STALLED, HE'S LOOKING FOR AN EXCUSE TO LET OFF SOME STEAM.
AND IT'S YOUR TREAT.
RIGHT, JAMES?
ER, YES ...
IN THAT CASE, I'LL PICK OUT SOMETHING SPECIAL!
HAVE MERCY ON MY WALLET ...
OH...
Austin Nichols
WILD TURKEY
BOURBON
Real Kentucky
KENTUCKY STRAIG
BOURBON
WHISKEY
Real Kentucky
40% ALC
700ML

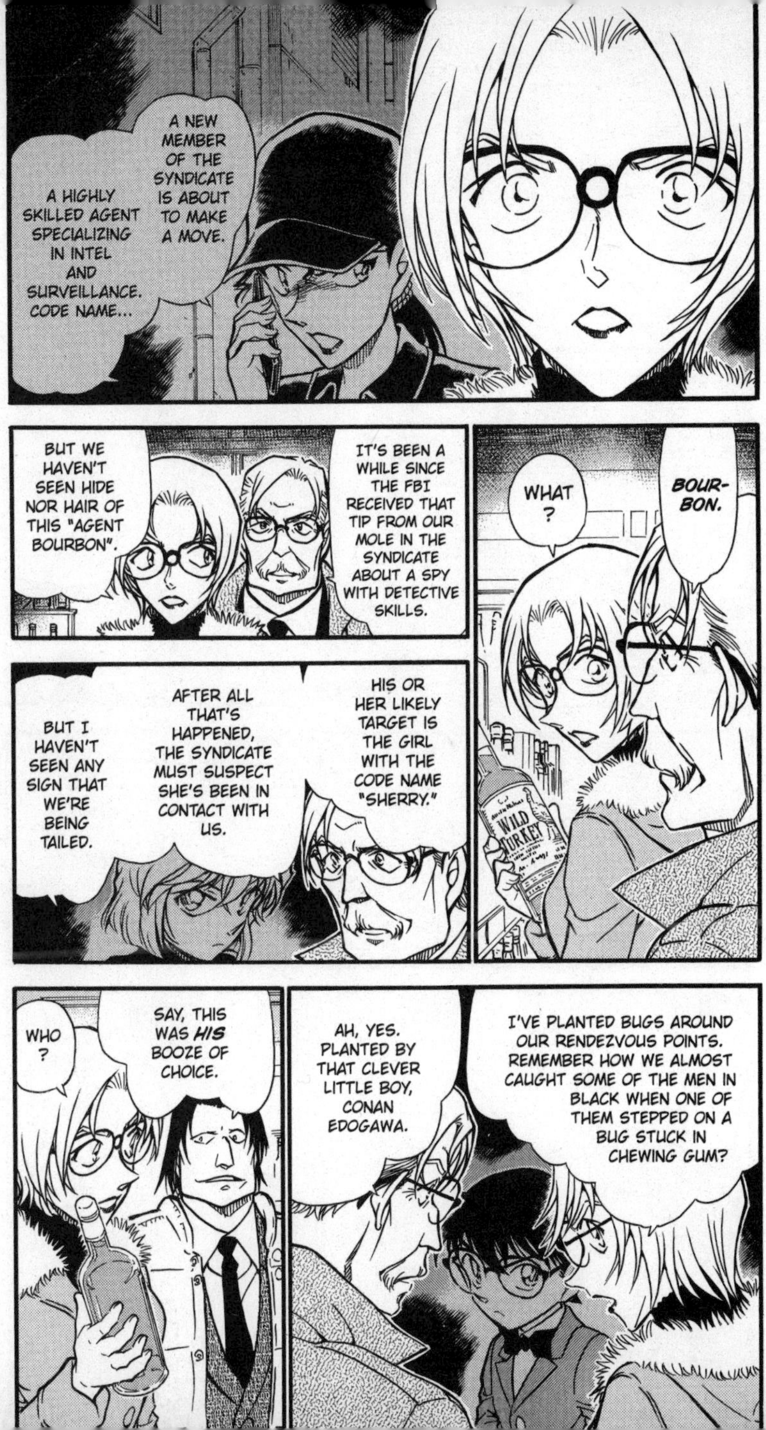
A NEW MEMBER OF THE SYNDICATE IS ABOUT TO MAKE A MOVE.
A HIGHLY SKILLED AGENT SPECIALIZING IN INTEL AND SURVEILLANCE. CODE NAME...
BOURBON.
WHAT?
WILD TURKEY
IT'S BEEN A WHILE SINCE THE FBI RECEIVED THAT TIP FROM OUR MOLE IN THE SYNDICATE ABOUT A SPY WITH DETECTIVE SKILLS.
BUT WE HAVEN'T SEEN HIDE NOR HAIR OF THIS "AGENT BOURBON".
HIS OR HER LIKELY TARGET IS THE GIRL WITH THE CODE NAME "SHERRY."
AFTER ALL THAT'S HAPPENED, THE SYNDICATE MUST SUSPECT SHE'S BEEN IN CONTACT WITH US.
BUT I HAVEN'T SEEN ANY SIGN THAT WE'RE BEING TAILED.
I'VE PLANTED BUGS AROUND OUR RENDEZVOUS POINTS. REMEMBER HOW WE ALMOST CAUGHT SOME OF THE MEN IN BLACK WHEN ONE OF THEM STEPPED ON A BUG STUCK IN CHEWING GUM?
AH, YES. PLANTED BY THAT CLEVER LITTLE BOY, CONAN EDOGAWA.
SAY, THIS WAS *HIS* BOOZE OF CHOICE.
WHO?

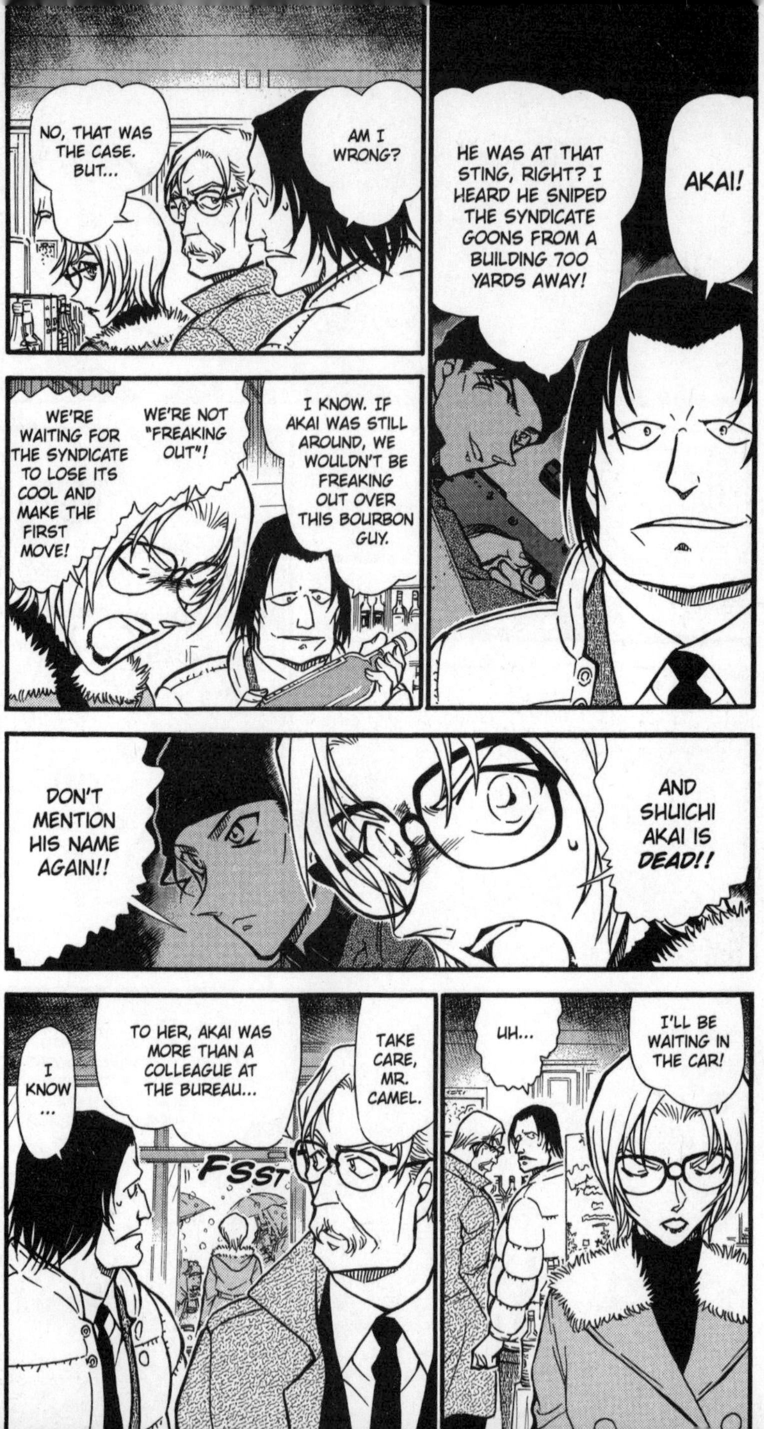
AKAI!
HE WAS AT THAT STING, RIGHT? I HEARD HE SNIPED THE SYNDICATE GOONS FROM A BUILDING 700 YARDS AWAY!
AM I WRONG?
NO, THAT WAS THE CASE. BUT...
I KNOW. IF AKAI WAS STILL AROUND, WE WOULDN'T BE FREAKING OUT OVER THIS BOURBON GUY.
WE'RE NOT "FREAKING OUT"!
WE'RE WAITING FOR THE SYNDICATE TO LOSE ITS COOL AND MAKE THE FIRST MOVE!
AND SHUICHI AKAI IS DEAD!!
DON'T MENTION HIS NAME AGAIN!!
I'LL BE WAITING IN THE CAR!
UH...
TAKE CARE, MR. CAMEL.
TO HER, AKAI WAS MORE THAN A COLLEAGUE AT THE BUREAU...
FSST
I KNOW...

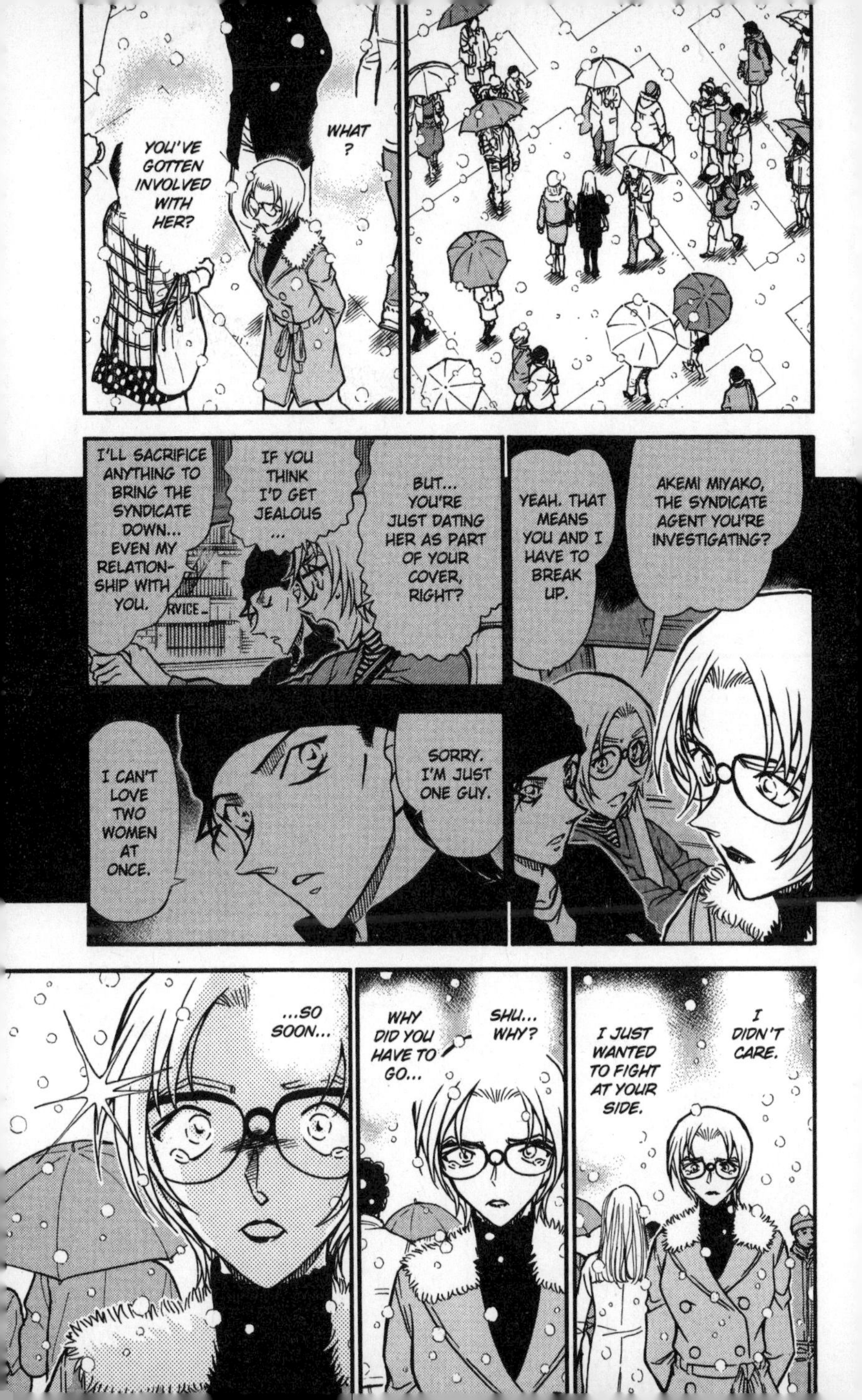
WHAT?
YOU'VE GOTTEN INVOLVED WITH HER?
AKEMI MIYAKO, THE SYNDICATE AGENT YOU'RE INVESTIGATING?
YEAH. THAT MEANS YOU AND I HAVE TO BREAK UP.
BUT... YOU'RE JUST DATING HER AS PART OF YOUR COVER, RIGHT?
IF YOU THINK I'D GET JEALOUS...
I'LL SACRIFICE ANYTHING TO BRING THE SYNDICATE DOWN... EVEN MY RELATIONSHIP WITH YOU.
SORRY. I'M JUST ONE GUY.
I CAN'T LOVE TWO WOMEN AT ONCE.
I DIDN'T CARE.
I JUST WANTED TO FIGHT AT YOUR SIDE.
SHU... WHY?
WHY DID YOU HAVE TO GO...
...SO SOON...

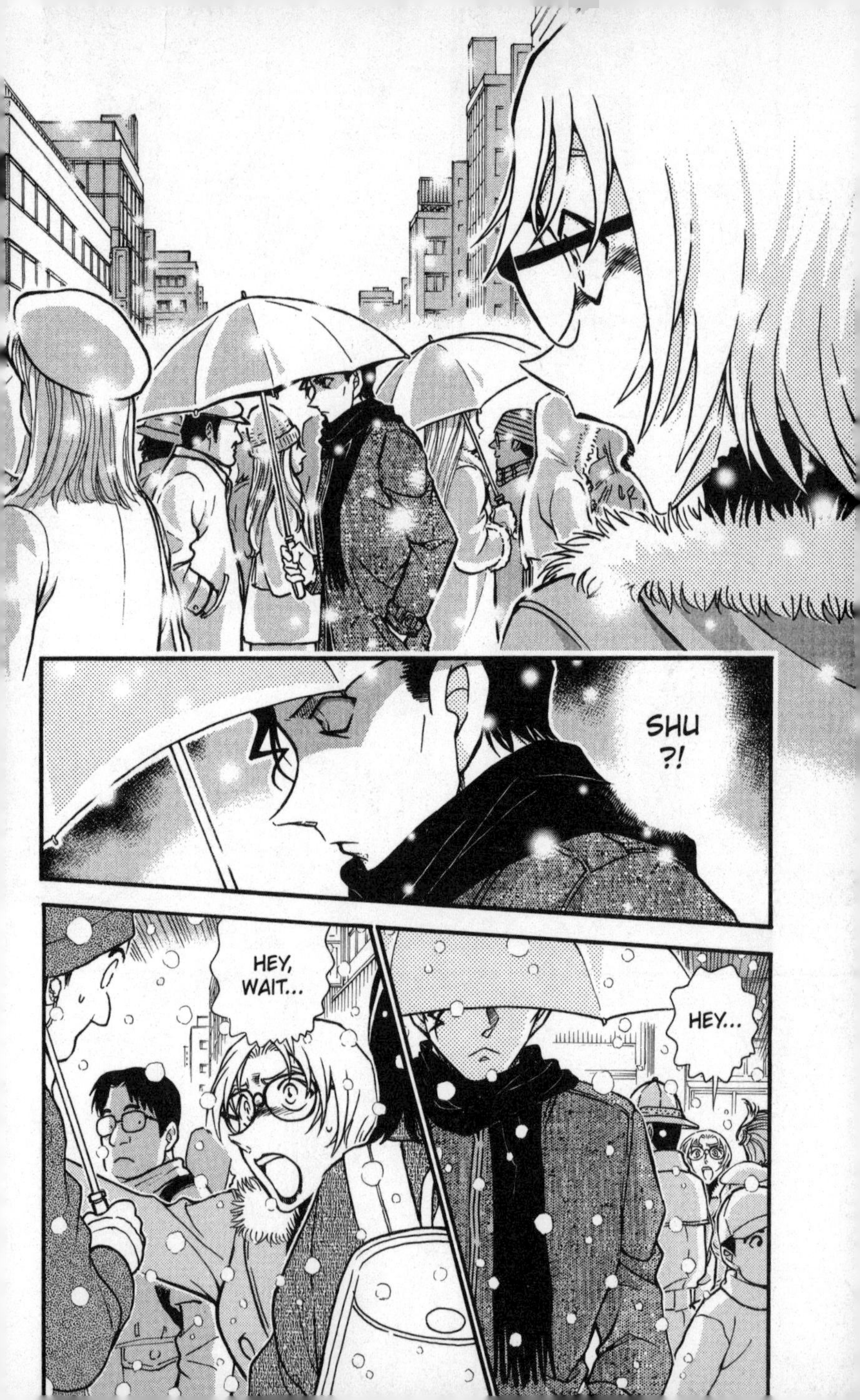
SHU
?!
HEY...
HEY,
WAIT...

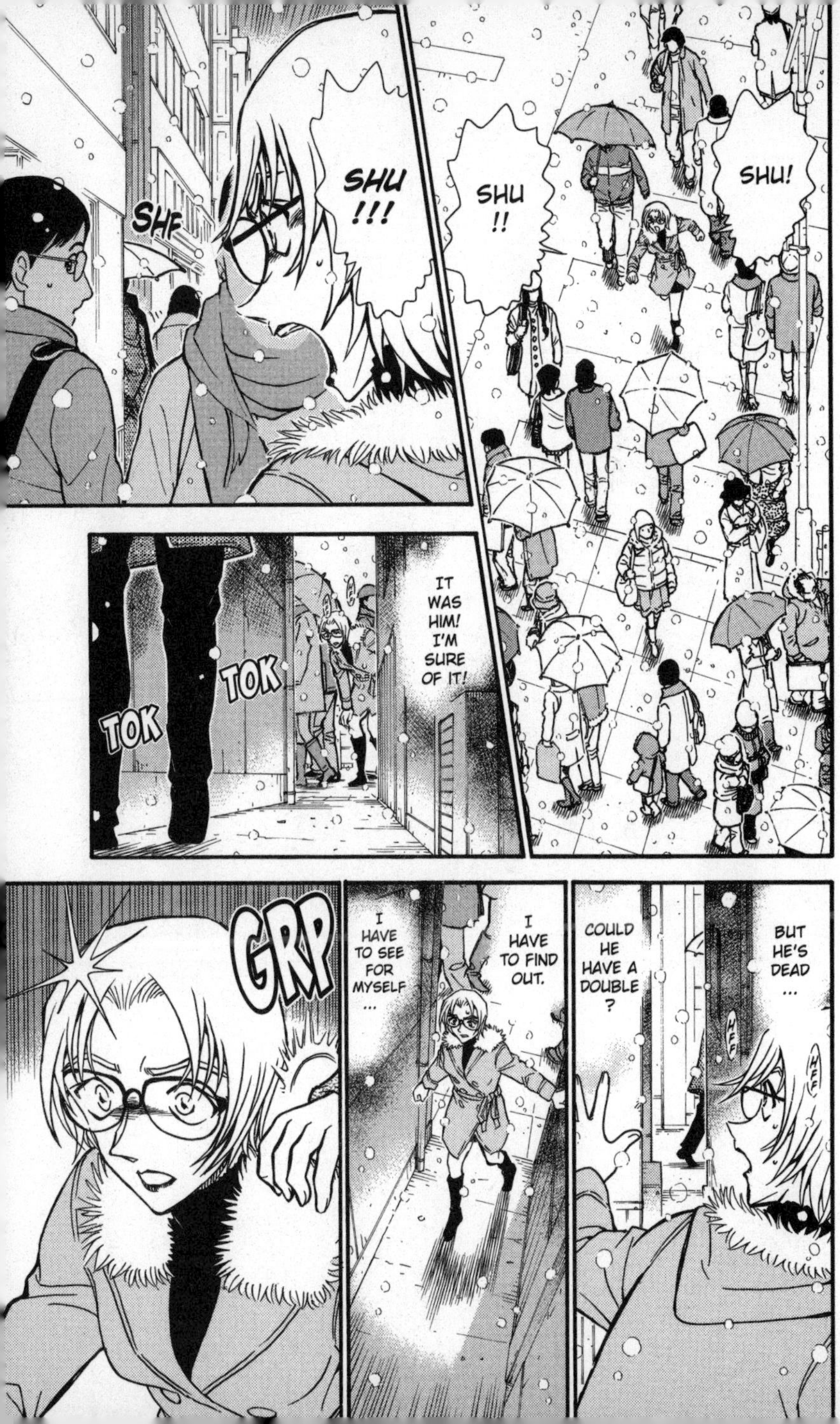
SHU!
SHU !!
SHU !!!
SHF
IT WAS HIM! I'M SURE OF IT!
TOK
TOK
BUT HE'S DEAD ...
HFF
HFF
COULD HE HAVE A DOUBLE ?
I HAVE TO FIND OUT.
I HAVE TO SEE FOR MYSELF ...
GRP

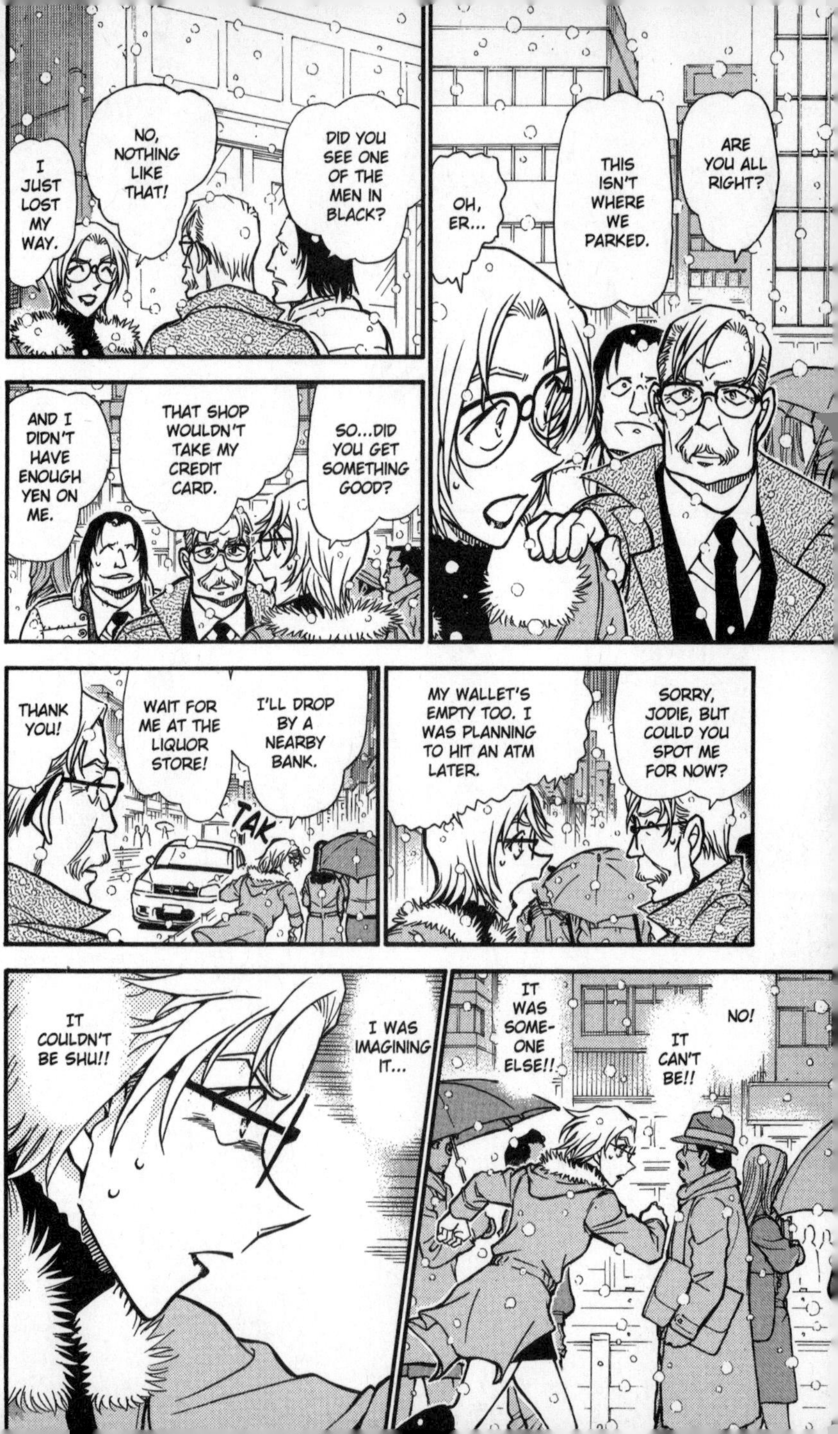
ARE YOU ALL RIGHT?
THIS ISN'T WHERE WE PARKED.
OH, ER...
DID YOU SEE ONE OF THE MEN IN BLACK?
NO, NOTHING LIKE THAT!
I JUST LOST MY WAY.
SO...DID YOU GET SOMETHING GOOD?
THAT SHOP WOULDN'T TAKE MY CREDIT CARD.
AND I DIDN'T HAVE ENOUGH YEN ON ME.
SORRY, JODIE, BUT COULD YOU SPOT ME FOR NOW?
MY WALLET'S EMPTY TOO. I WAS PLANNING TO HIT AN ATM LATER.
I'LL DROP BY A NEARBY BANK.
WAIT FOR ME AT THE LIQUOR STORE!
TAK
THANK YOU!
NO!
IT CAN'T BE!!
IT WAS SOME-ONE ELSE!!
I WAS IMAGINING IT...
IT COULDN'T BE SHU!!

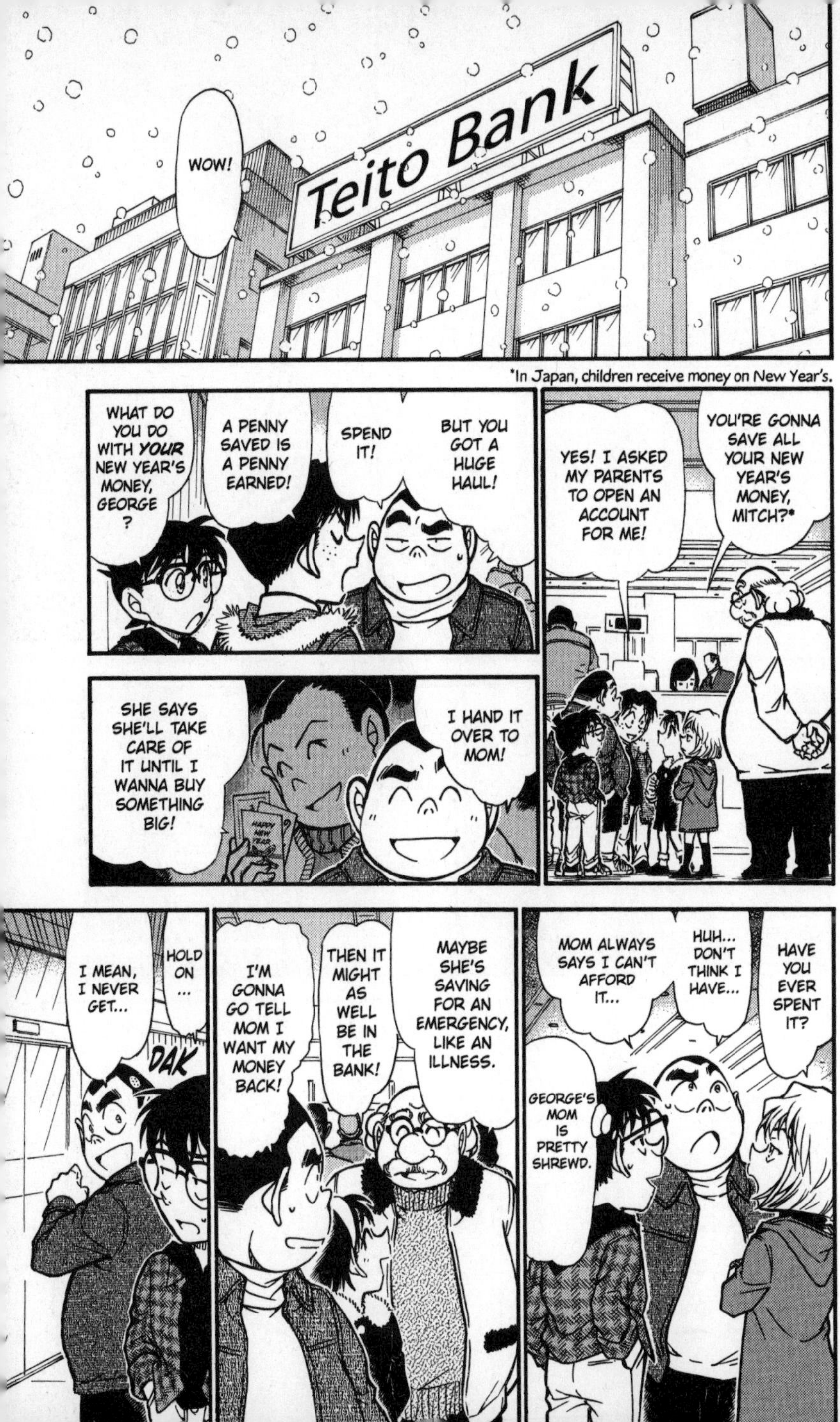
Teito Bank
WOW!
YOU'RE GONNA SAVE ALL YOUR NEW YEAR'S MONEY, MITCH?*
YES! I ASKED MY PARENTS TO OPEN AN ACCOUNT FOR ME!
BUT YOU GOT A HUGE HAUL!
SPEND IT!
A PENNY SAVED IS A PENNY EARNED!
WHAT DO YOU DO WITH *YOUR* NEW YEAR'S MONEY, GEORGE?
I HAND IT OVER TO MOM!
SHE SAYS SHE'LL TAKE CARE OF IT UNTIL I WANNA BUY SOMETHING BIG!
HAVE YOU EVER SPENT IT?
HUH... DON'T THINK I HAVE...
MOM ALWAYS SAYS I CAN'T AFFORD IT...
GEORGE'S MOM IS PRETTY SHREWD.
MAYBE SHE'S SAVING FOR AN EMERGENCY, LIKE AN ILLNESS.
THEN IT MIGHT AS WELL BE IN THE BANK!
I'M GONNA GO TELL MOM I WANT MY MONEY BACK!
HOLD ON...
DAK
I MEAN, I NEVER GET...

*In Japan, children receive money on New Year's.

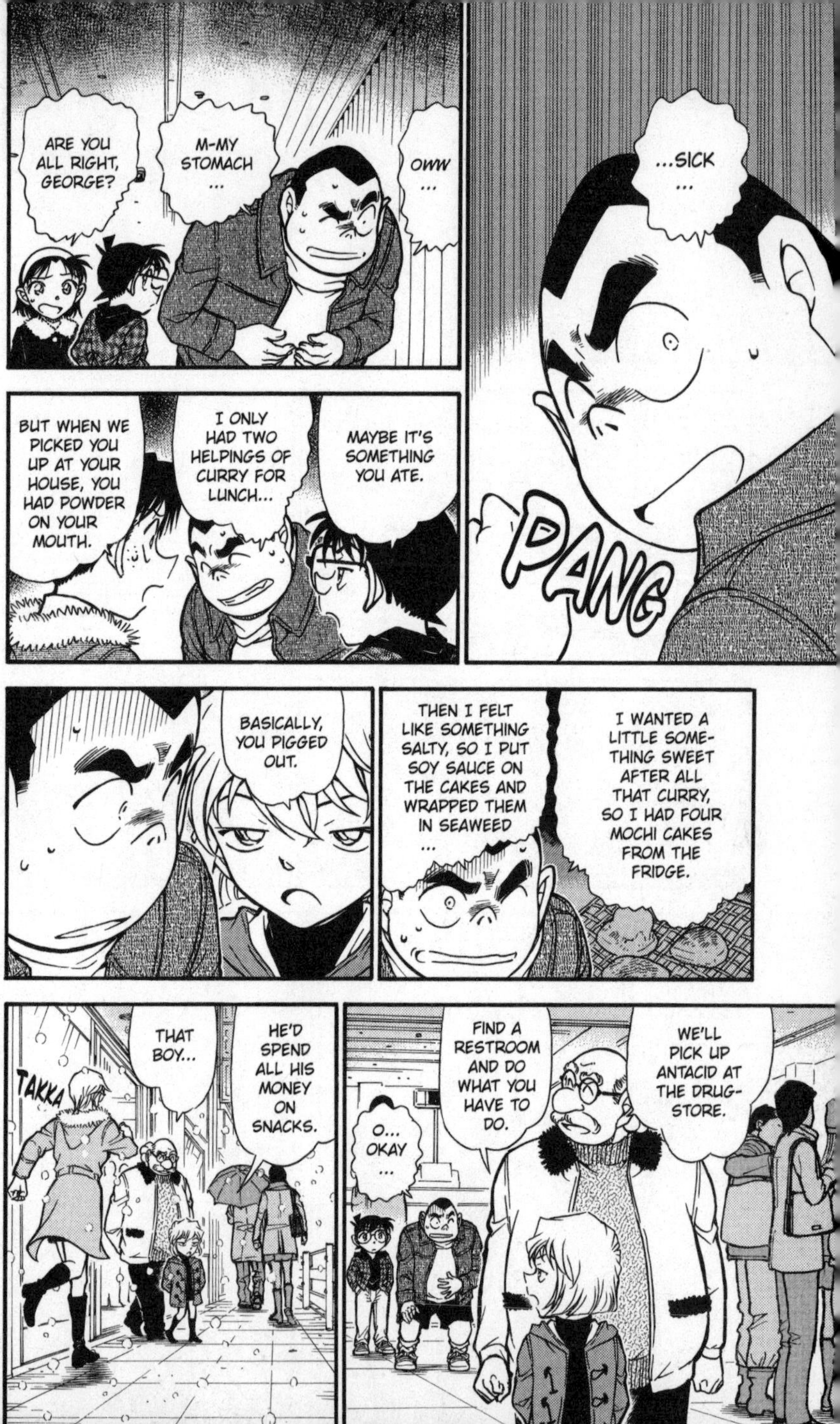
...SICK ...
PANG
OWW ...
M-MY STOMACH ...
ARE YOU ALL RIGHT, GEORGE?
MAYBE IT'S SOMETHING YOU ATE.
I ONLY HAD TWO HELPINGS OF CURRY FOR LUNCH...
BUT WHEN WE PICKED YOU UP AT YOUR HOUSE, YOU HAD POWDER ON YOUR MOUTH.
I WANTED A LITTLE SOME-THING SWEET AFTER ALL THAT CURRY, SO I HAD FOUR MOCHI CAKES FROM THE FRIDGE.
THEN I FELT LIKE SOMETHING SALTY, SO I PUT SOY SAUCE ON THE CAKES AND WRAPPED THEM IN SEAWEED ...
BASICALLY, YOU PIGGED OUT.
WE'LL PICK UP ANTACID AT THE DRUG-STORE.
FIND A RESTROOM AND DO WHAT YOU HAVE TO DO.
O... OKAY ...
HE'D SPEND ALL HIS MONEY ON SNACKS.
THAT BOY...
TAKKA

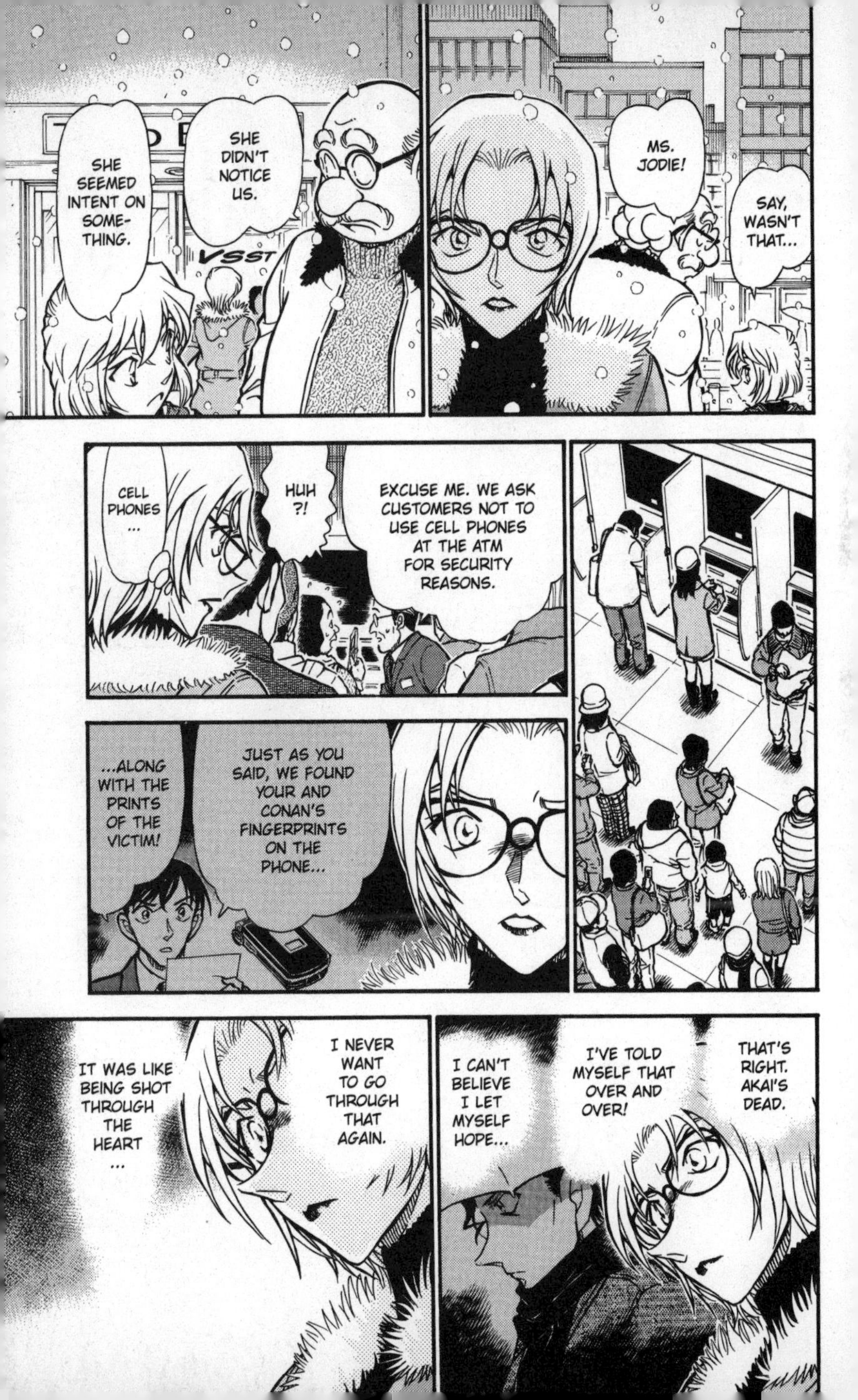
SAY, WASN'T THAT...
MS. JODIE!
SHE DIDN'T NOTICE US.
VSST
SHE SEEMED INTENT ON SOME-THING.
EXCUSE ME. WE ASK CUSTOMERS NOT TO USE CELL PHONES AT THE ATM FOR SECURITY REASONS.
HUH?!
CELL PHONES...
JUST AS YOU SAID, WE FOUND YOUR AND CONAN'S FINGERPRINTS ON THE PHONE...
...ALONG WITH THE PRINTS OF THE VICTIM!
THAT'S RIGHT. AKAI'S DEAD.
I'VE TOLD MYSELF THAT OVER AND OVER!
I CAN'T BELIEVE I LET MYSELF HOPE...
I NEVER WANT TO GO THROUGH THAT AGAIN.
IT WAS LIKE BEING SHOT THROUGH THE HEART...

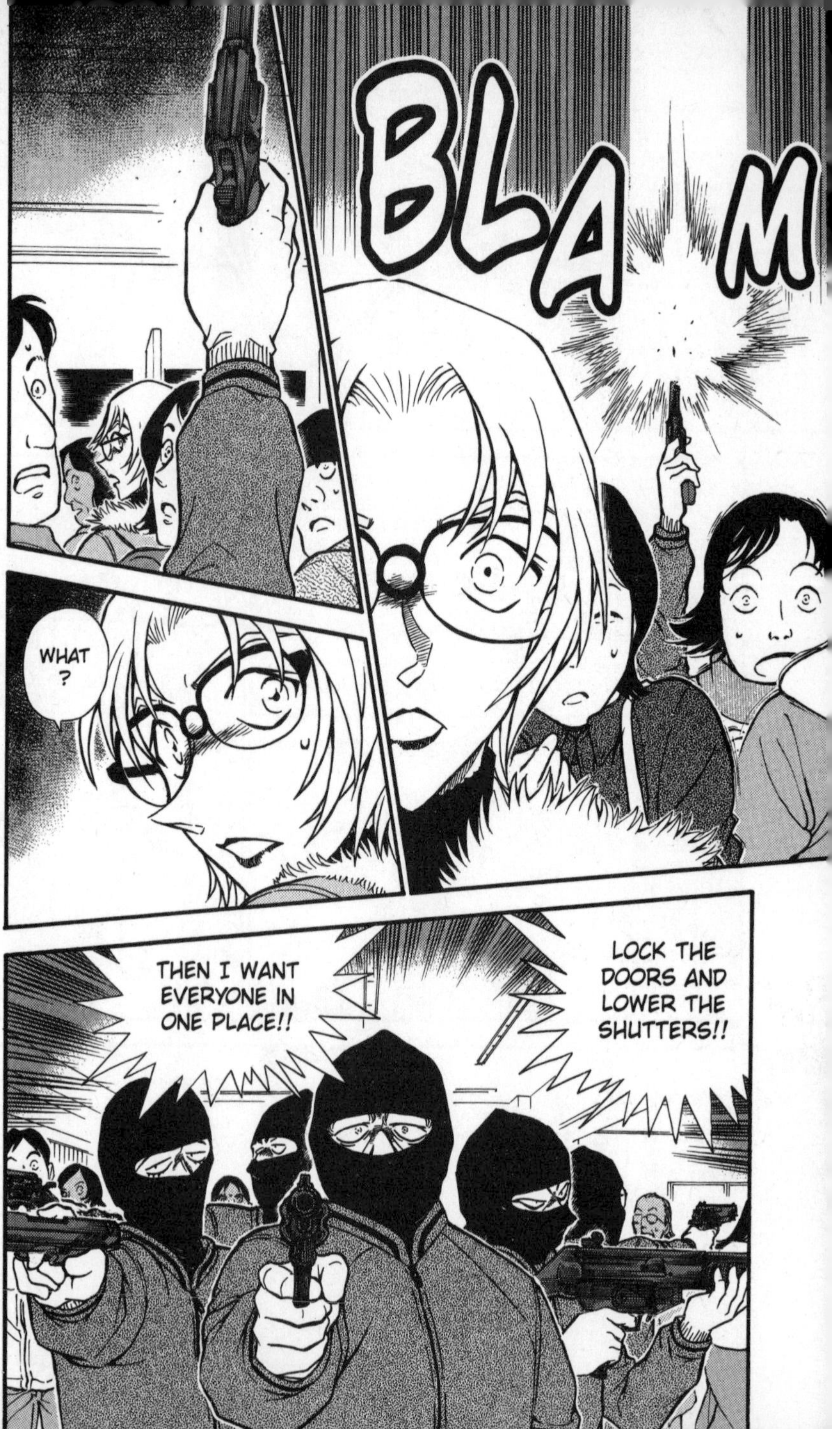
BLAM
WHAT?
LOCK THE DOORS AND LOWER THE SHUTTERS!!
THEN I WANT EVERYONE IN ONE PLACE!!

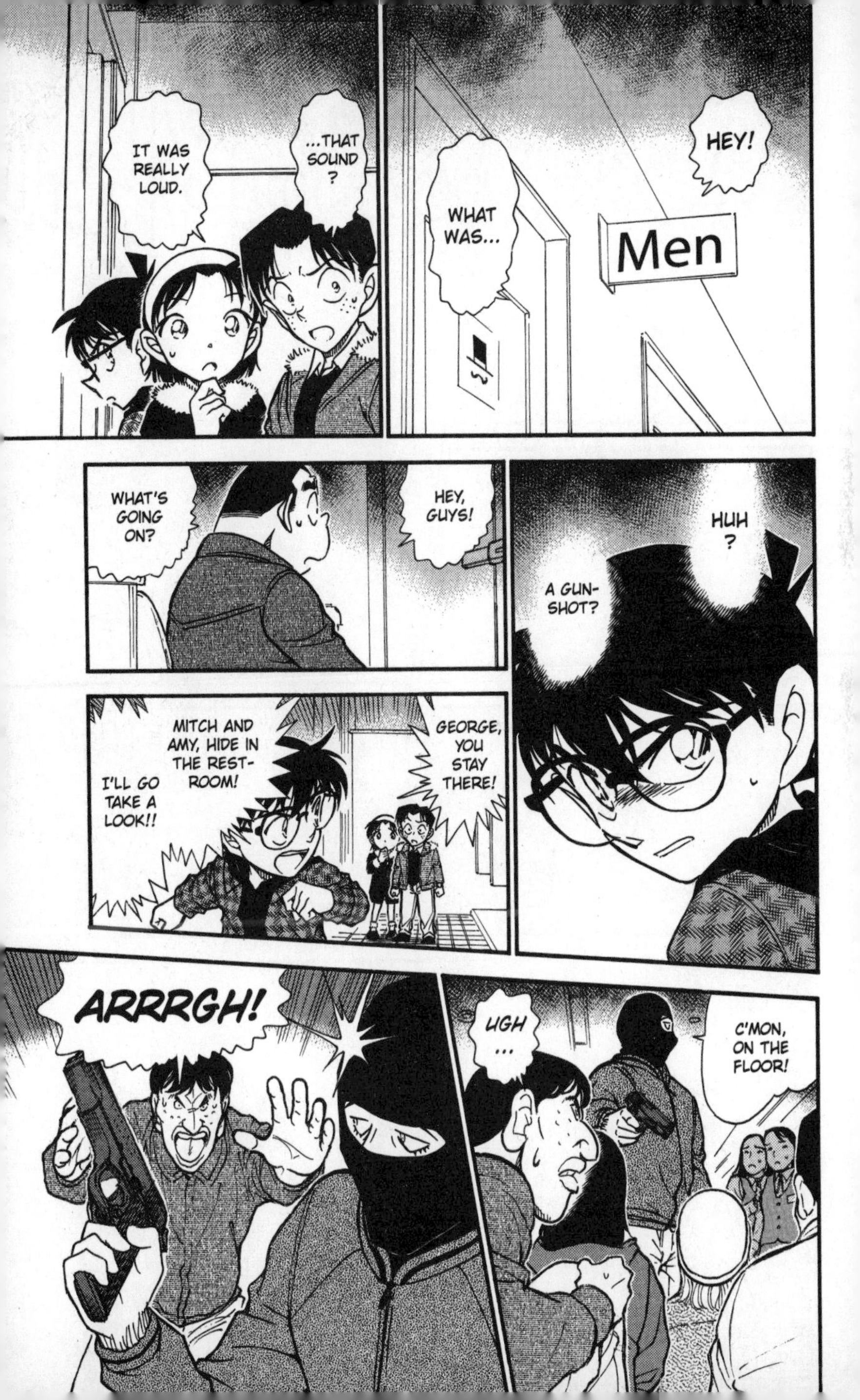
HEY!
WHAT WAS...
Men
...THAT SOUND?
IT WAS REALLY LOUD.
HUH?
A GUN-SHOT?
HEY, GUYS!
WHAT'S GOING ON?
GEORGE, YOU STAY THERE!
MITCH AND AMY, HIDE IN THE REST-ROOM!
I'LL GO TAKE A LOOK!!
C'MON, ON THE FLOOR!
UGH...
ARRRGH!

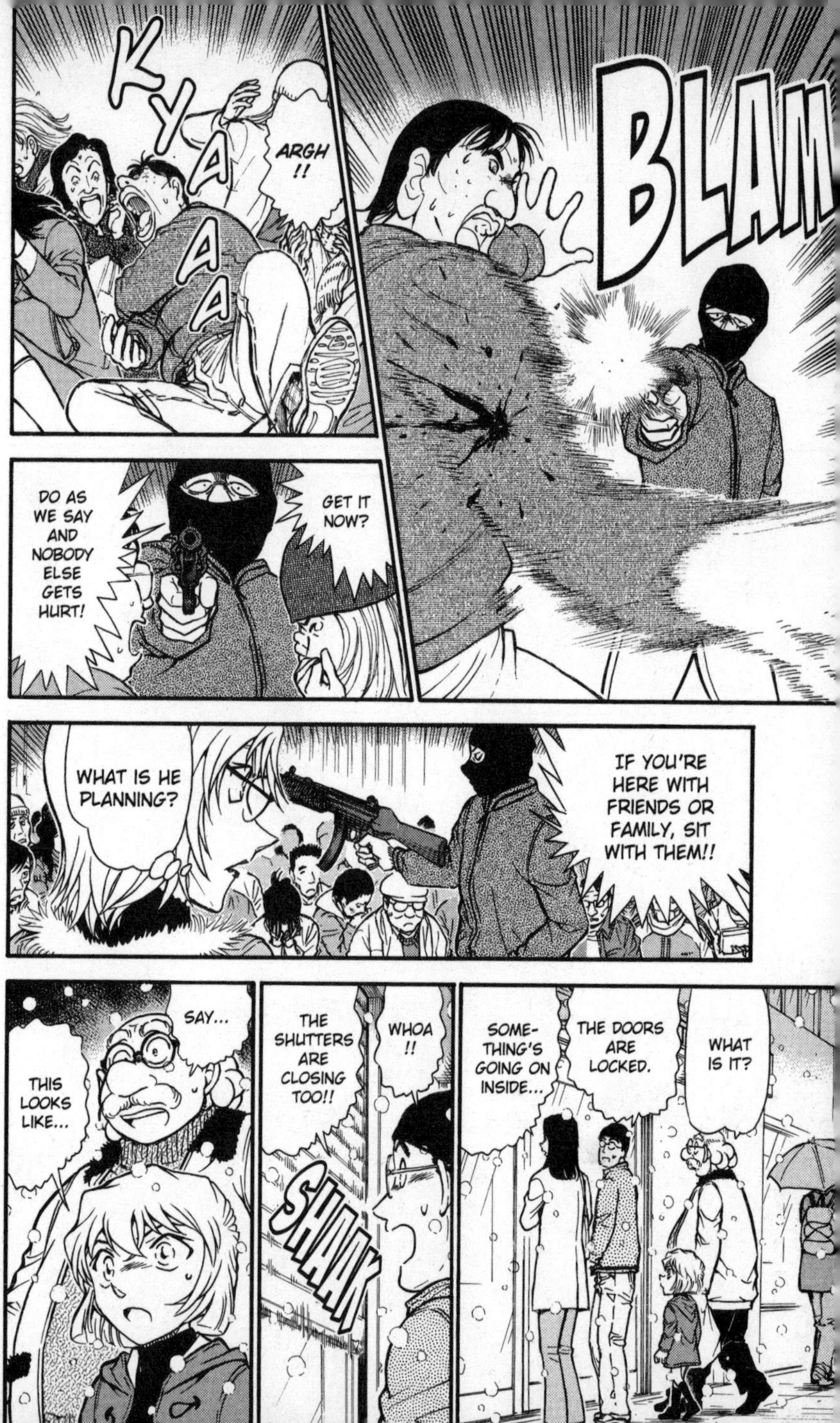
BLAM
ARGH!!
KYAAA
GET IT NOW?
DO AS WE SAY AND NOBODY ELSE GETS HURT!
IF YOU'RE HERE WITH FRIENDS OR FAMILY, SIT WITH THEM!!
WHAT IS HE PLANNING?
WHAT IS IT?
THE DOORS ARE LOCKED.
SOMETHING'S GOING ON INSIDE...
WHOA!!
THE SHUTTERS ARE CLOSING TOO!!
SHAAK
SAY...
THIS LOOKS LIKE...

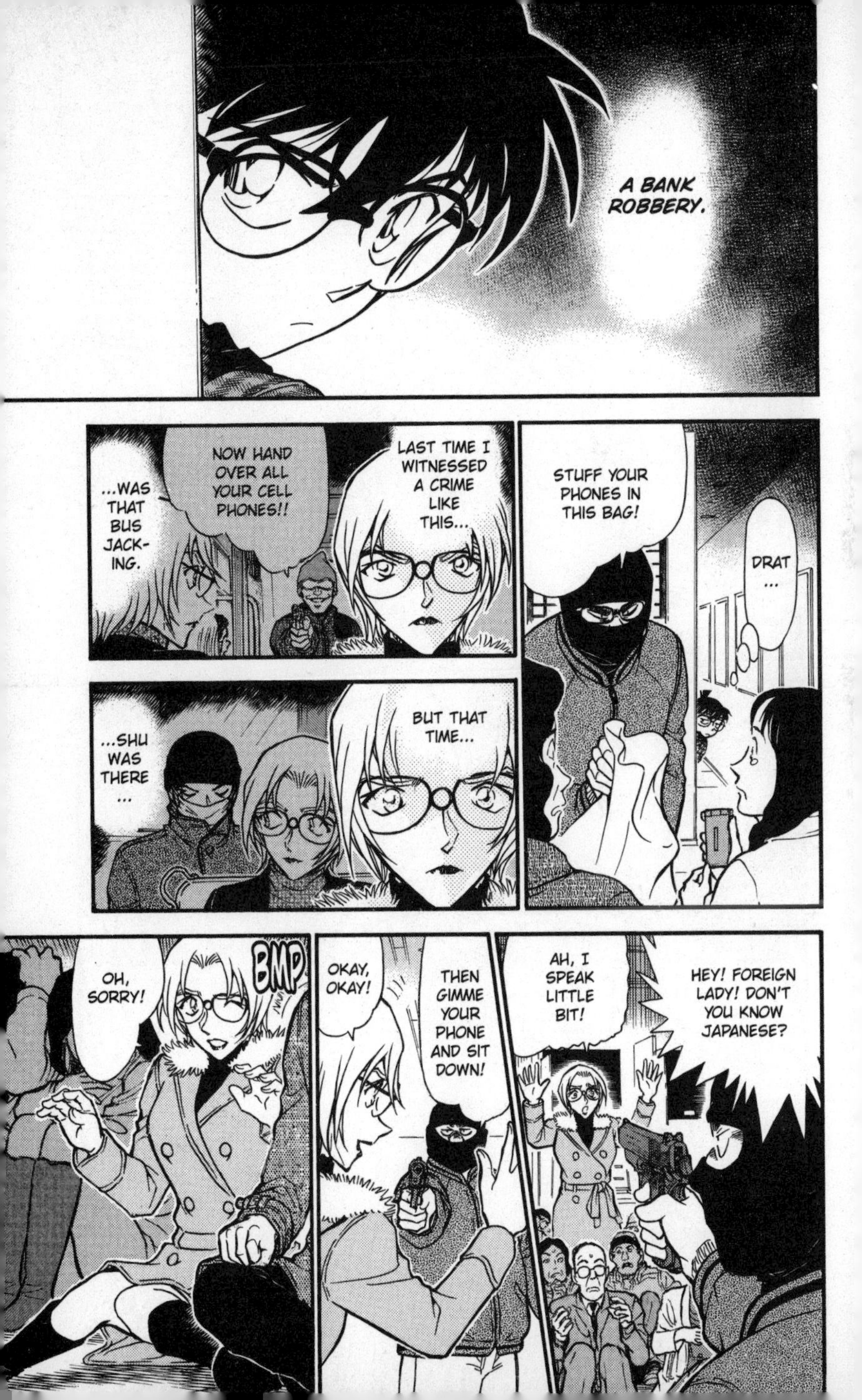
A BANK ROBBERY.
STUFF YOUR PHONES IN THIS BAG!
DRAT ...
LAST TIME I WITNESSED A CRIME LIKE THIS...
NOW HAND OVER ALL YOUR CELL PHONES!!
...WAS THAT BUS JACKING.
BUT THAT TIME...
...SHU WAS THERE ...
HEY! FOREIGN LADY! DON'T YOU KNOW JAPANESE?
AH, I SPEAK LITTLE BIT!
THEN GIMME YOUR PHONE AND SIT DOWN!
OKAY, OKAY!
BMP
OH, SORRY!

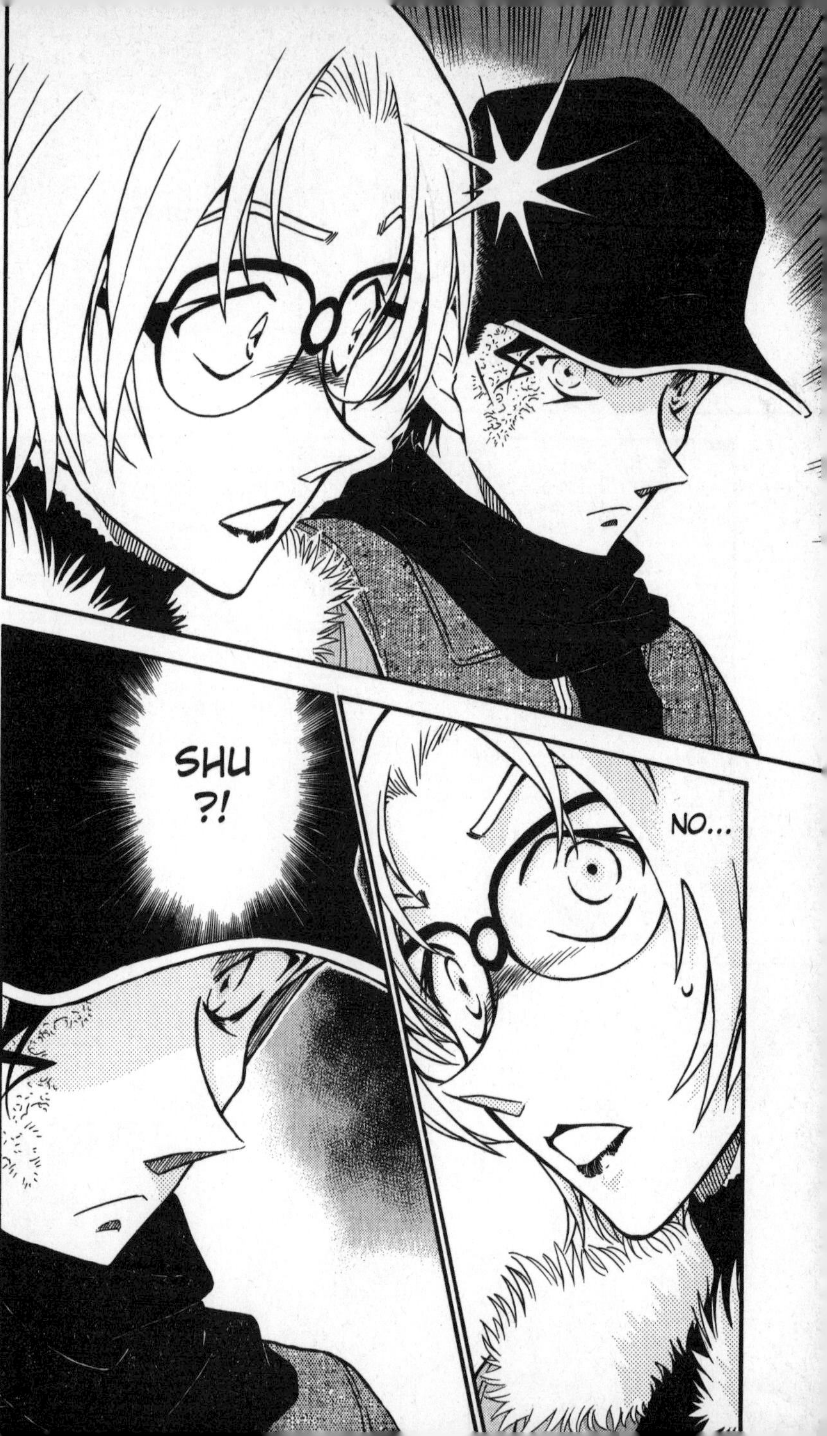
NO...
SHU
?!

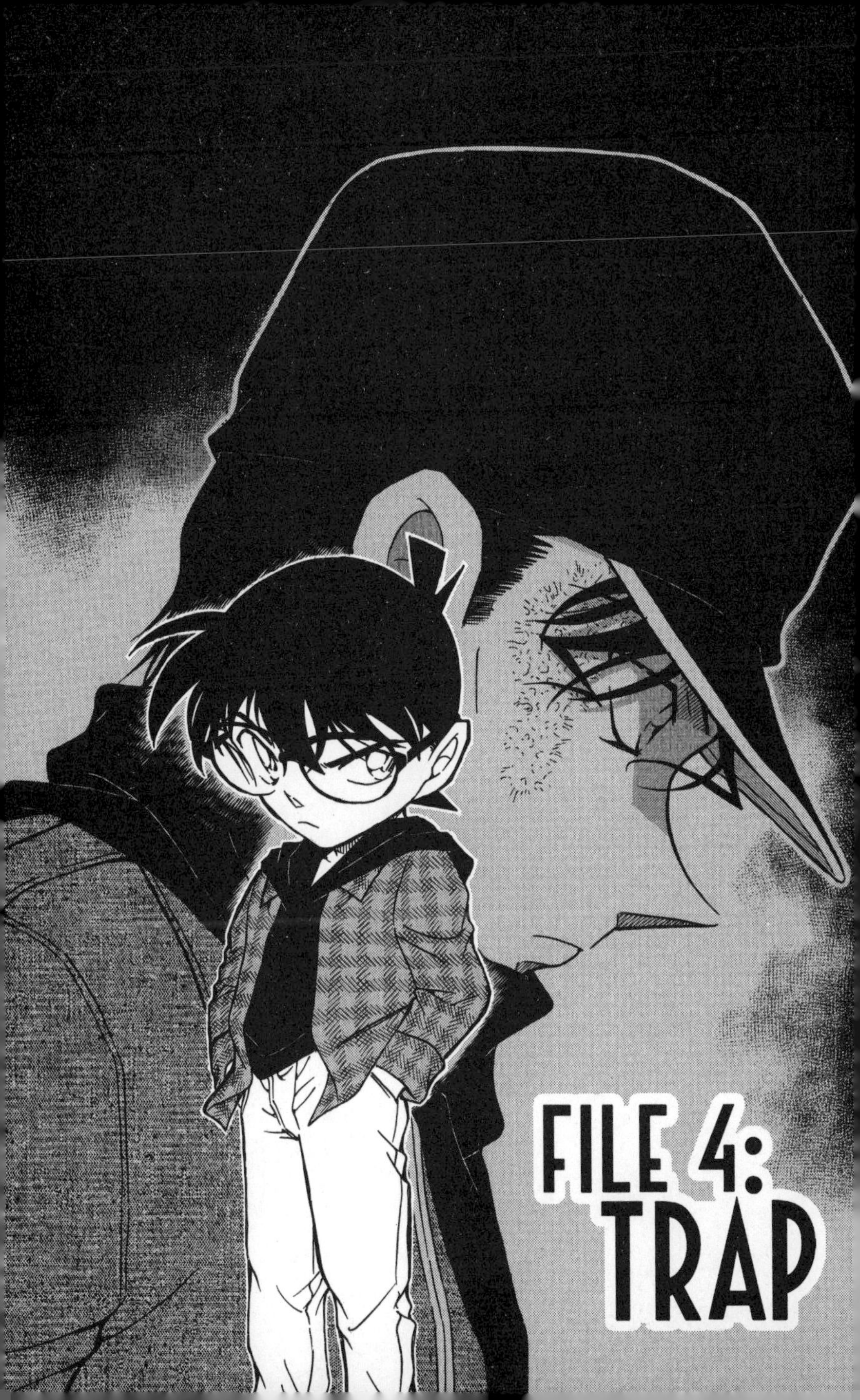
FILE 4:
TRAP

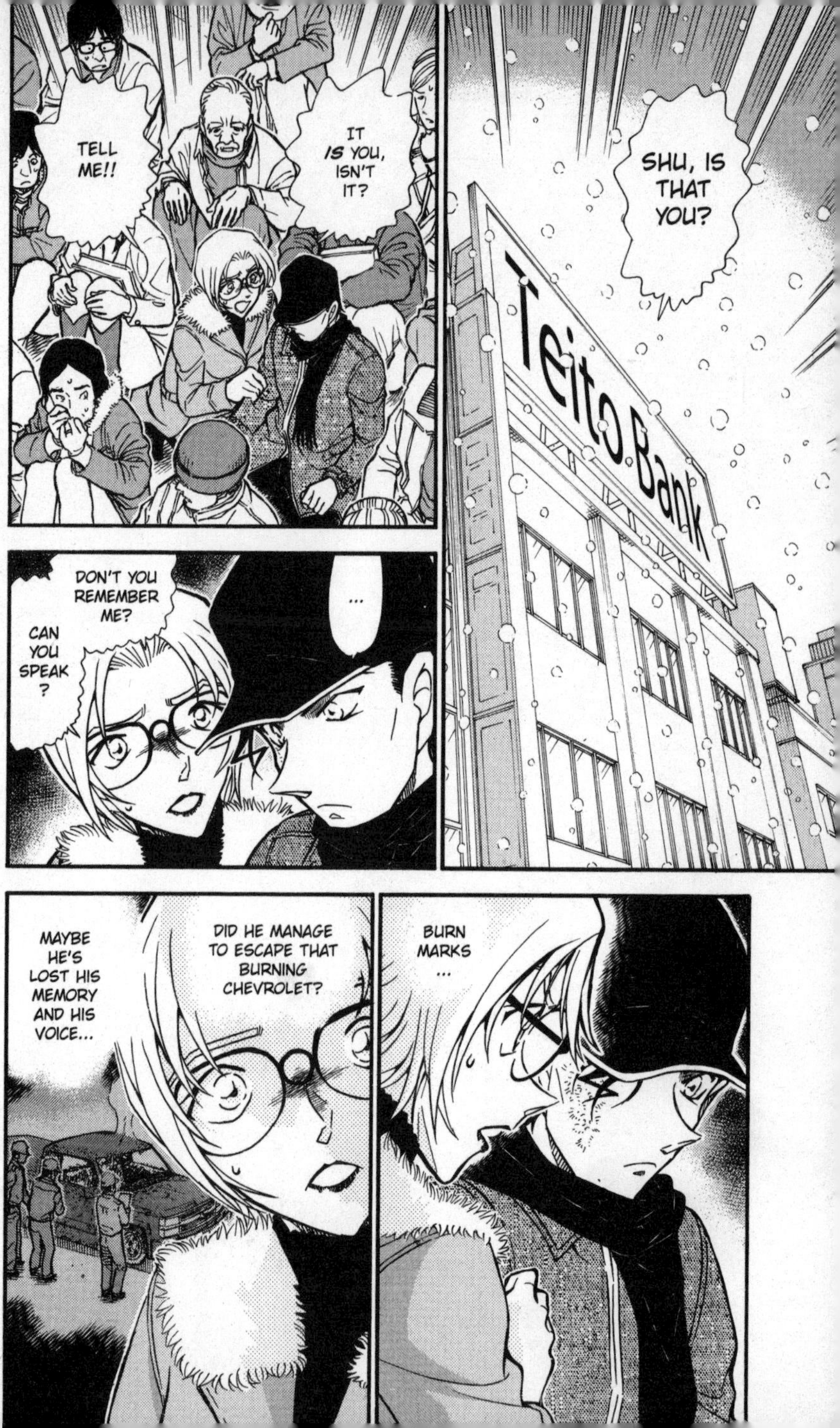
Teito Bank
SHU, IS THAT YOU?
IT IS YOU, ISN'T IT?
TELL ME!!
...
DON'T YOU REMEMBER ME?
CAN YOU SPEAK?
BURN MARKS ...
DID HE MANAGE TO ESCAPE THAT BURNING CHEVROLET?
MAYBE HE'S LOST HIS MEMORY AND HIS VOICE...

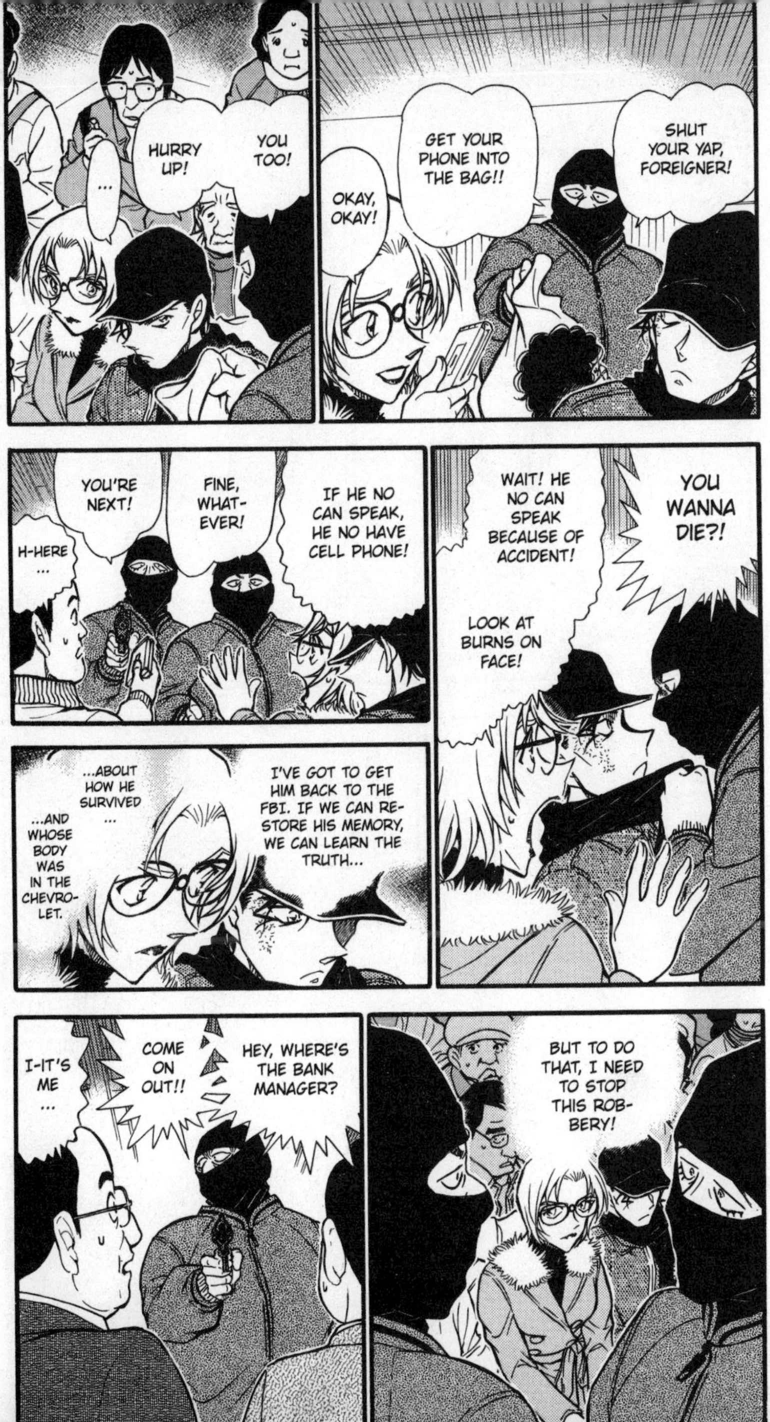
SHUT YOUR YAP, FOREIGNER!
GET YOUR PHONE INTO THE BAG!!
OKAY, OKAY!
YOU TOO!
HURRY UP!
...
YOU WANNA DIE?!
WAIT! HE NO CAN SPEAK BECAUSE OF ACCIDENT!
LOOK AT BURNS ON FACE!
IF HE NO CAN SPEAK, HE NO HAVE CELL PHONE!
FINE, WHATEVER!
YOU'RE NEXT!
H-HERE ...
I'VE GOT TO GET HIM BACK TO THE FBI. IF WE CAN RESTORE HIS MEMORY, WE CAN LEARN THE TRUTH...
...ABOUT HOW HE SURVIVED ...
...AND WHOSE BODY WAS IN THE CHEVROLET.
BUT TO DO THAT, I NEED TO STOP THIS ROBBERY!
HEY, WHERE'S THE BANK MANAGER?
COME ON OUT!!
I-IT'S ME ...

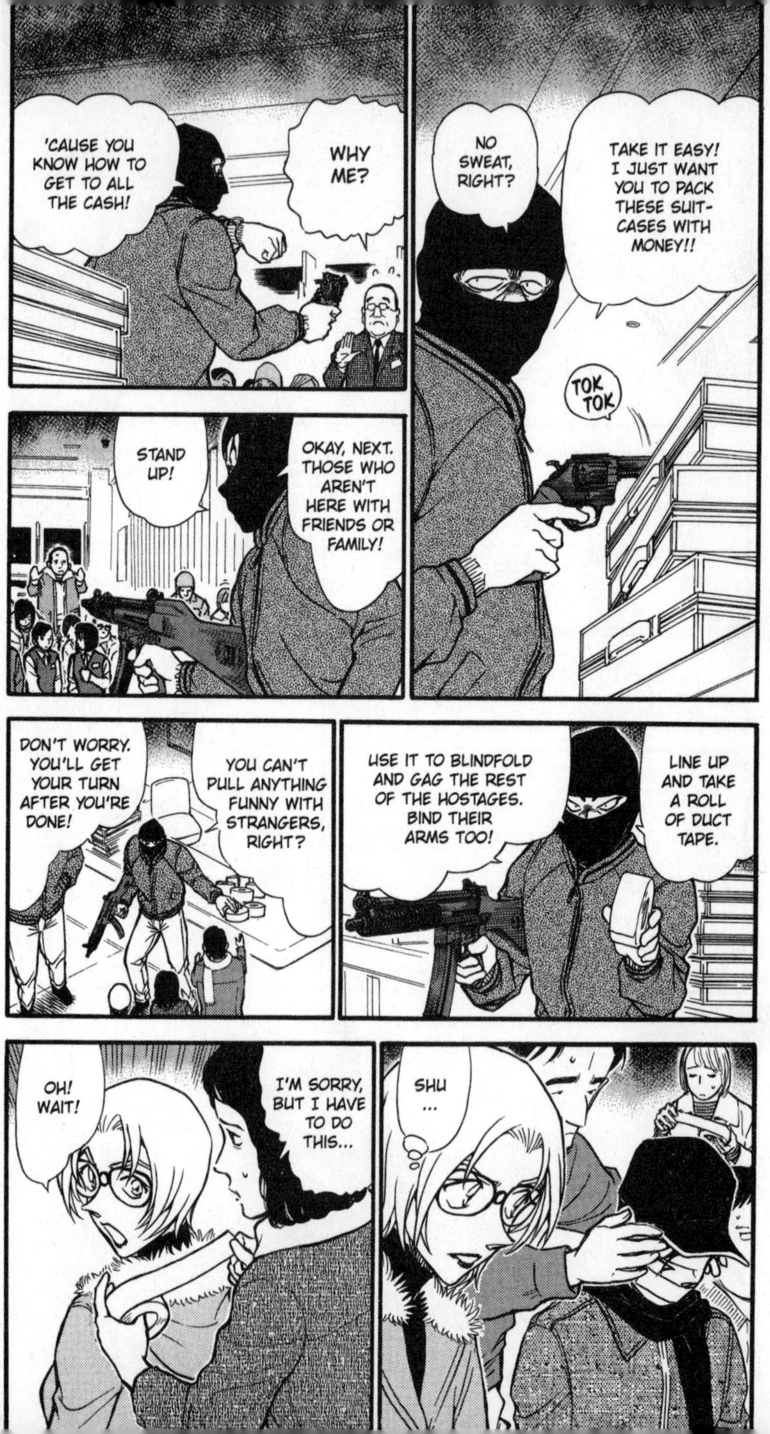
TAKE IT EASY! I JUST WANT YOU TO PACK THESE SUIT-CASES WITH MONEY!!
NO SWEAT, RIGHT?
TOK TOK
WHY ME?
'CAUSE YOU KNOW HOW TO GET TO ALL THE CASH!
OKAY, NEXT. THOSE WHO AREN'T HERE WITH FRIENDS OR FAMILY!
STAND UP!
LINE UP AND TAKE A ROLL OF DUCT TAPE.
USE IT TO BLINDFOLD AND GAG THE REST OF THE HOSTAGES. BIND THEIR ARMS TOO!
YOU CAN'T PULL ANYTHING FUNNY WITH STRANGERS, RIGHT?
DON'T WORRY. YOU'LL GET YOUR TURN AFTER YOU'RE DONE!
SHU ...
I'M SORRY, BUT I HAVE TO DO THIS...
OH! WAIT!

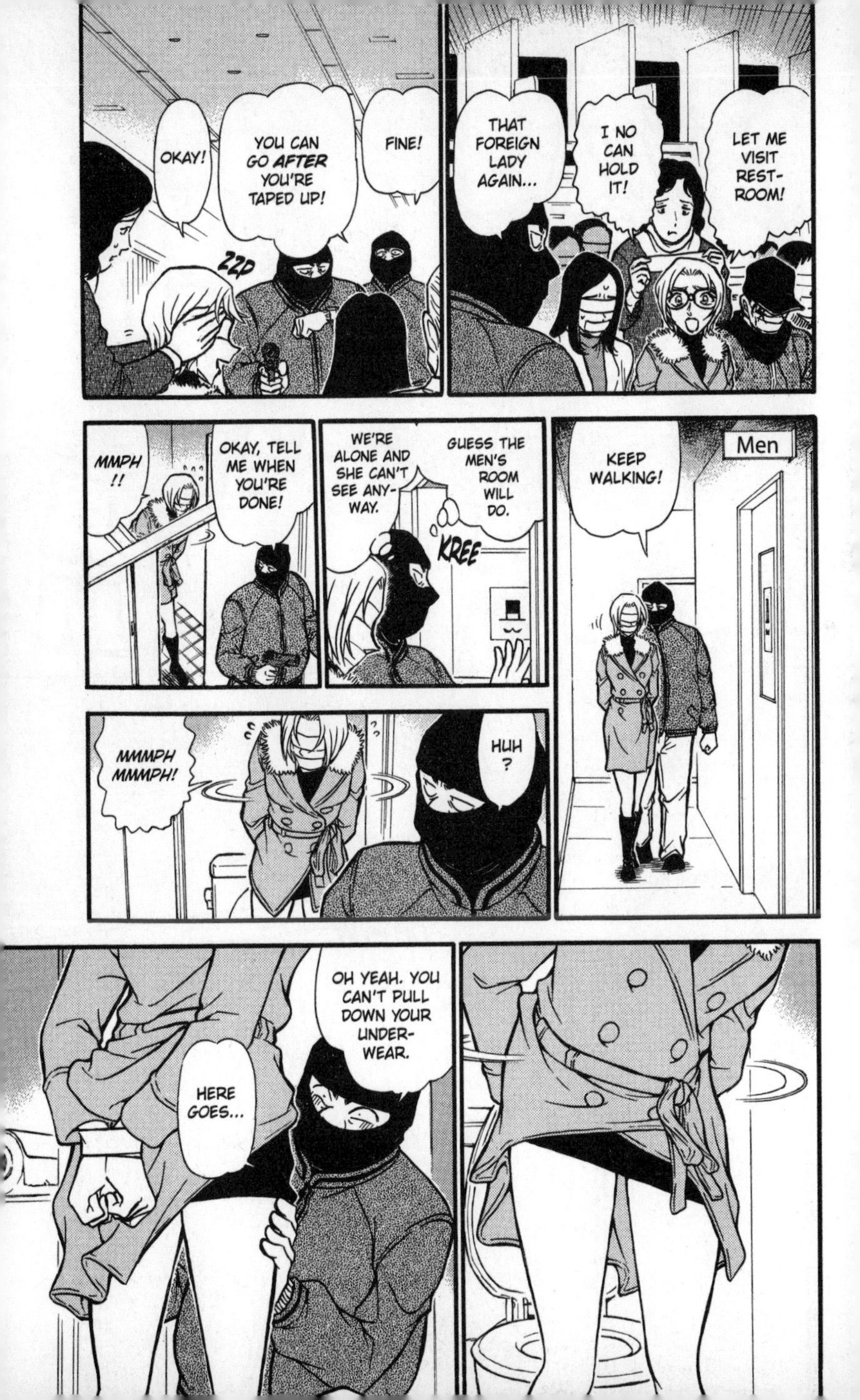
LET ME VISIT REST-ROOM!
I NO CAN HOLD IT!
THAT FOREIGN LADY AGAIN...
FINE!
YOU CAN GO AFTER YOU'RE TAPED UP!
OKAY!
ZZP
Men
KEEP WALKING!
GUESS THE MEN'S ROOM WILL DO.
WE'RE ALONE AND SHE CAN'T SEE ANY-WAY.
KREE
OKAY, TELL ME WHEN YOU'RE DONE!
MMPH !!
HUH ?
MMMPH MMMPH!
OH YEAH. YOU CAN'T PULL DOWN YOUR UNDER-WEAR.
HERE GOES...

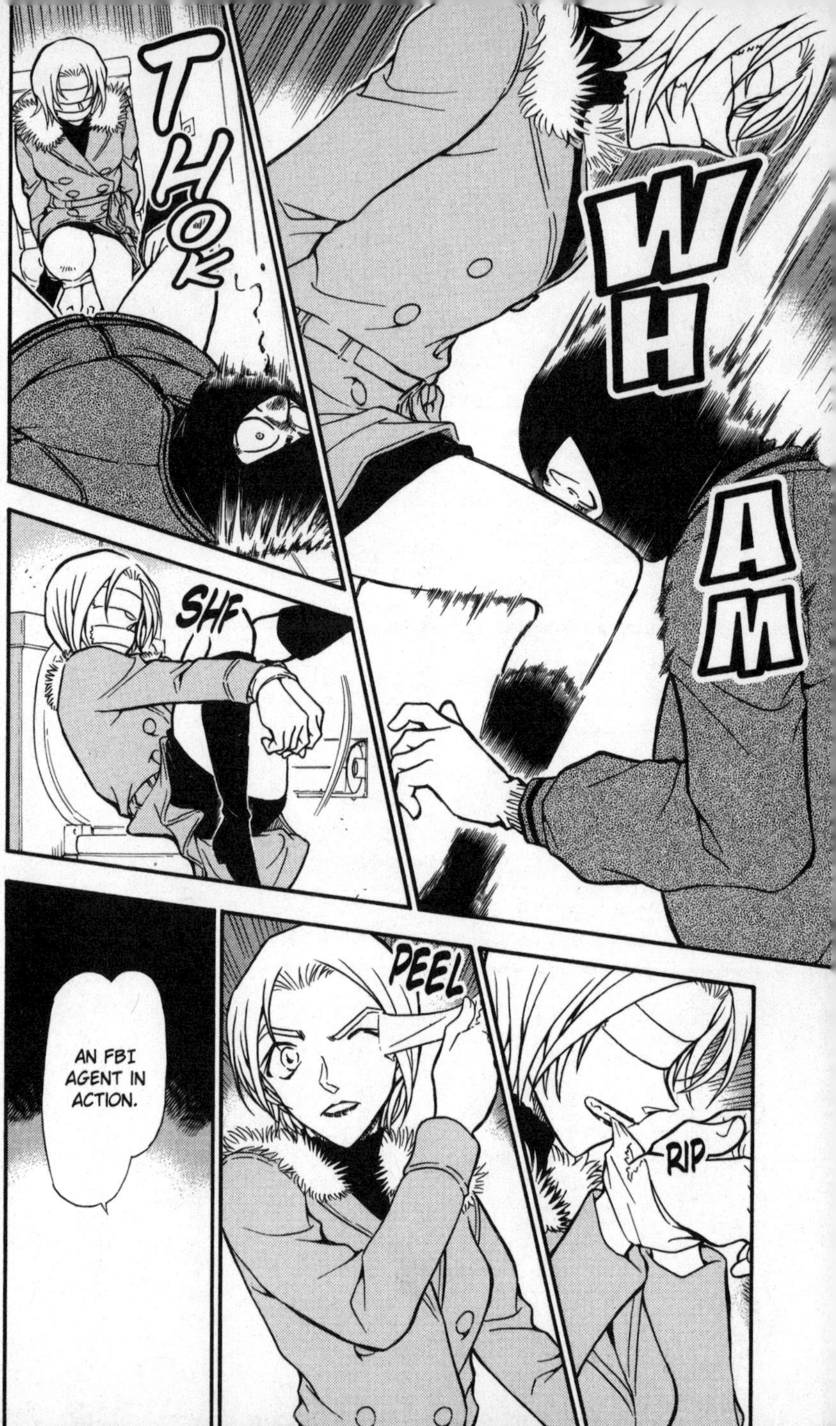
WHAM
THOK
SHF
RIP
PEEL
AN FBI AGENT IN ACTION.

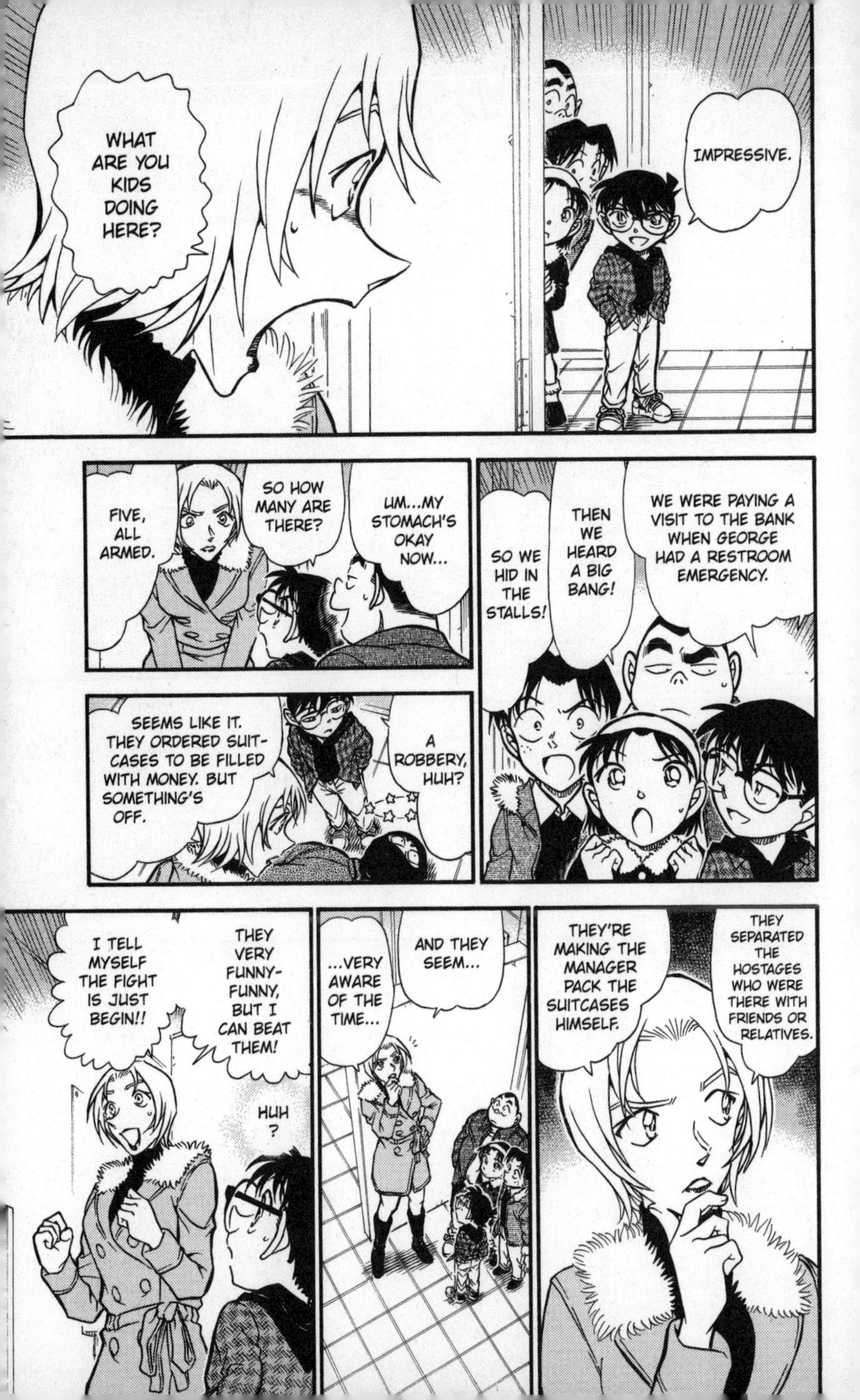
IMPRESSIVE.
WHAT ARE YOU KIDS DOING HERE?
WE WERE PAYING A VISIT TO THE BANK WHEN GEORGE HAD A RESTROOM EMERGENCY.
THEN WE HEARD A BIG BANG!
SO WE HID IN THE STALLS!
UM...MY STOMACH'S OKAY NOW...
SO HOW MANY ARE THERE?
FIVE, ALL ARMED.
A ROBBERY, HUH?
SEEMS LIKE IT. THEY ORDERED SUIT-CASES TO BE FILLED WITH MONEY. BUT SOMETHING'S OFF.
THEY SEPARATED THE HOSTAGES WHO WERE THERE WITH FRIENDS OR RELATIVES.
THEY'RE MAKING THE MANAGER PACK THE SUITCASES HIMSELF.
AND THEY SEEM...
...VERY AWARE OF THE TIME...
THEY VERY FUNNY-FUNNY, BUT I CAN BEAT THEM!
I TELL MYSELF THE FIGHT IS JUST BEGIN!!
HUH?

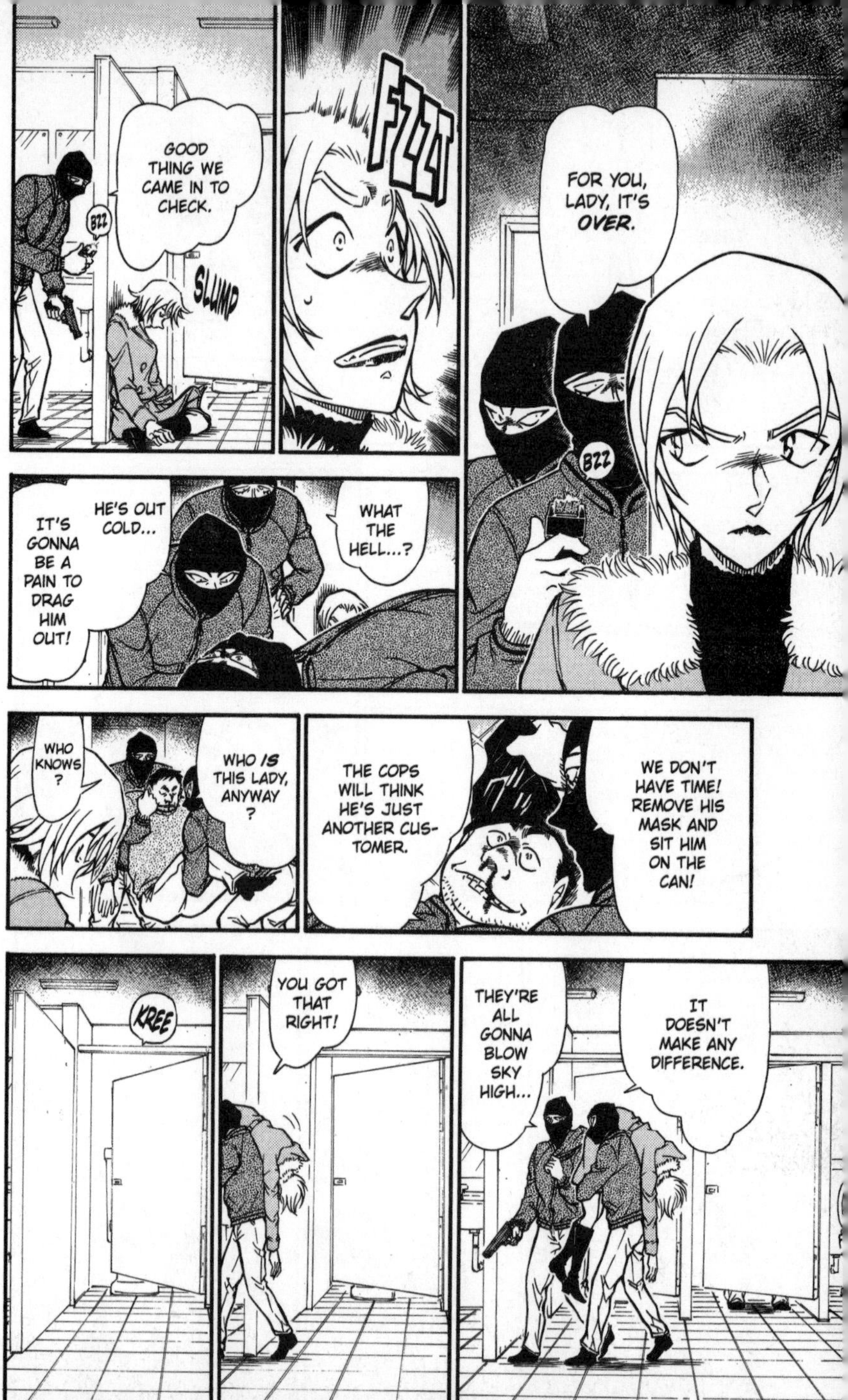

FOR YOU, LADY, IT'S *OVER.*
BZZ
FZZT
GOOD THING WE CAME IN TO CHECK.
BZZ
SLUMP
WHAT THE HELL...?
HE'S OUT COLD...
IT'S GONNA BE A PAIN TO DRAG HIM OUT!
WE DON'T HAVE TIME! REMOVE HIS MASK AND SIT HIM ON THE CAN!
THE COPS WILL THINK HE'S JUST ANOTHER CUS-TOMER.
WHO *IS* THIS LADY, ANYWAY?
WHO KNOWS?
IT DOESN'T MAKE ANY DIFFERENCE.
THEY'RE ALL GONNA BLOW SKY HIGH...
YOU GOT THAT RIGHT!
KREE

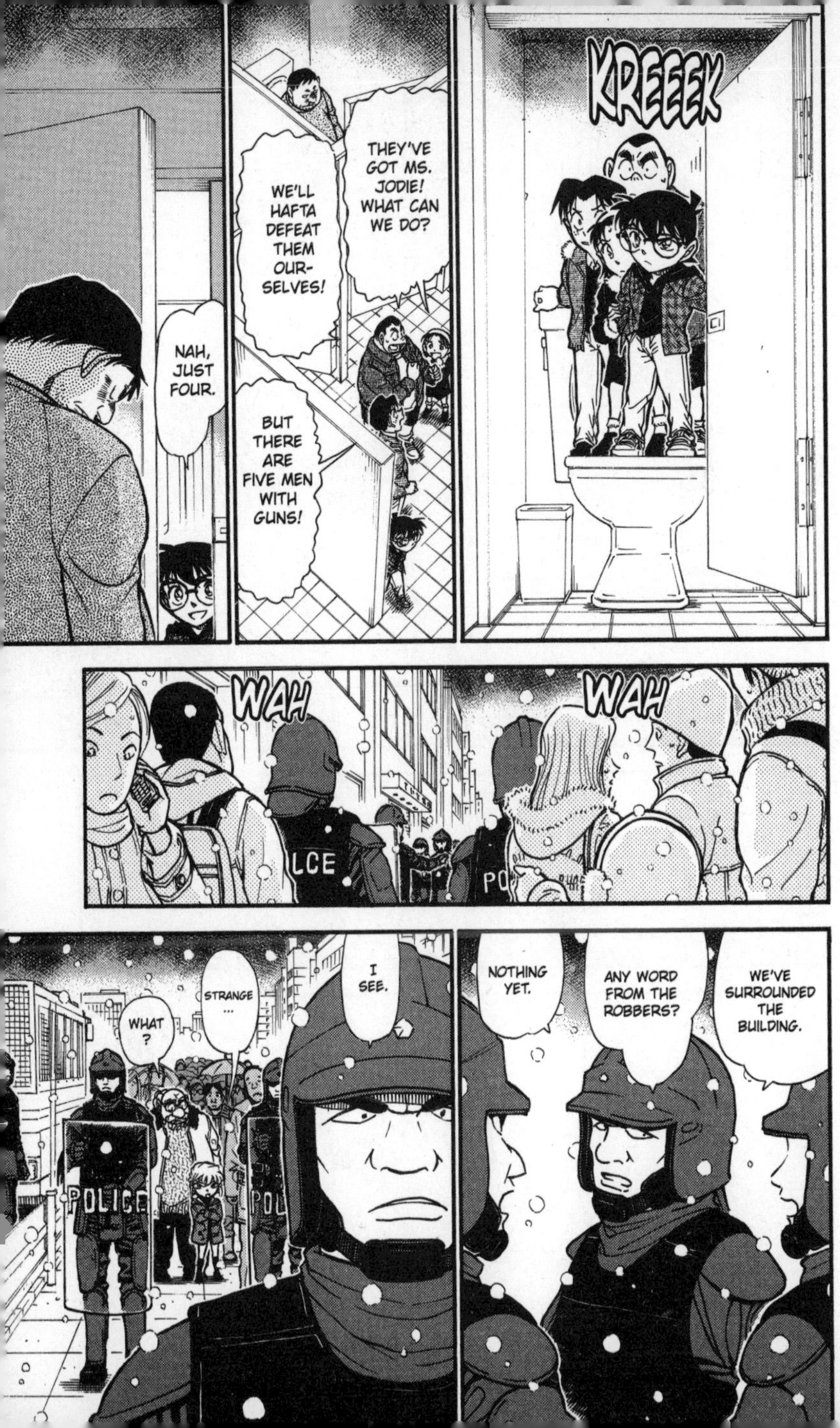
KREEEK
THEY'VE GOT MS. JODIE! WHAT CAN WE DO?
WE'LL HAFTA DEFEAT THEM OURSELVES!
BUT THERE ARE FIVE MEN WITH GUNS!
NAH, JUST FOUR.
WAH
WAH
WE'VE SURROUNDED THE BUILDING.
ANY WORD FROM THE ROBBERS?
NOTHING YET.
I SEE.
STRANGE ...
WHAT ?

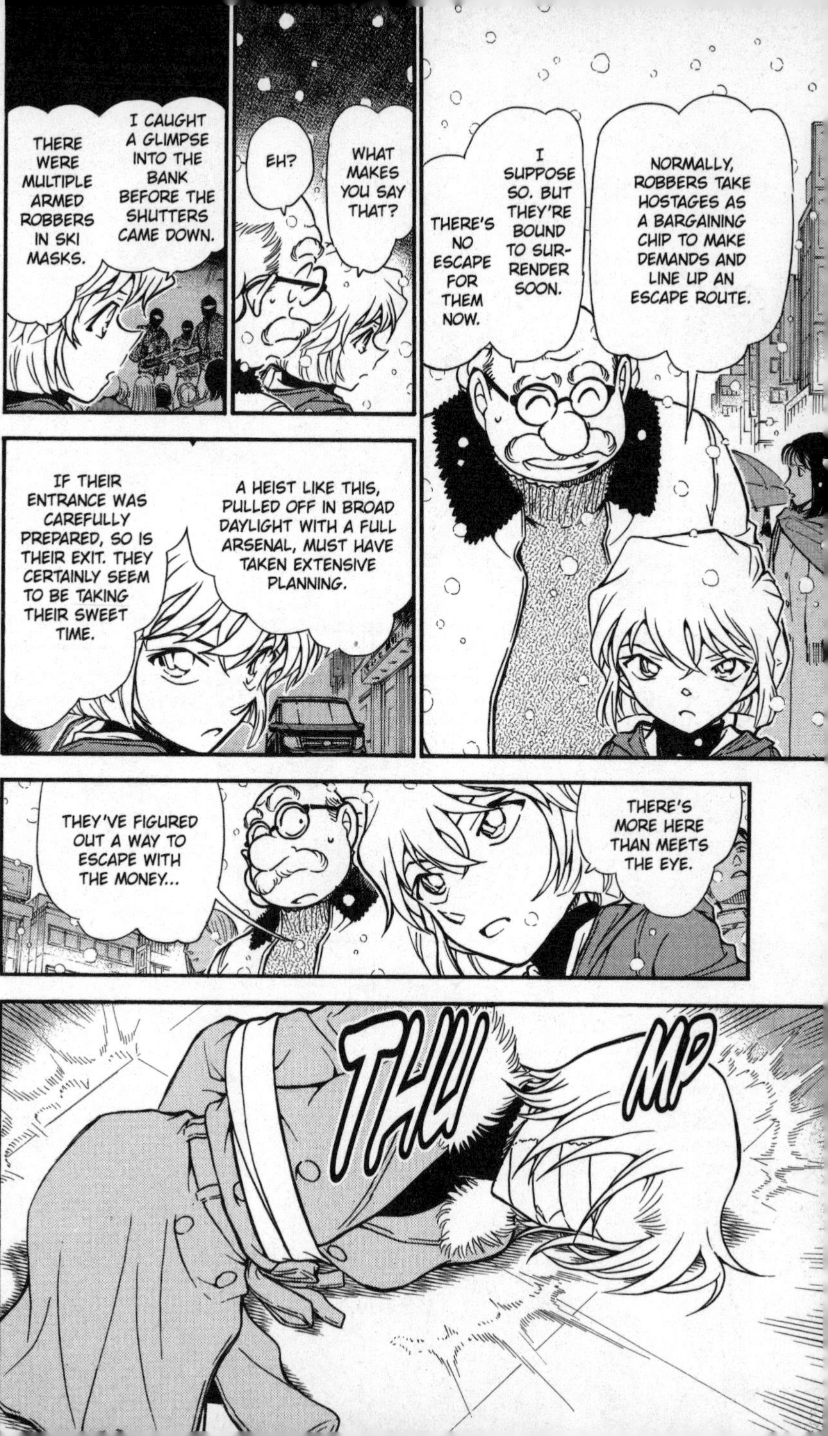
NORMALLY, ROBBERS TAKE HOSTAGES AS A BARGAINING CHIP TO MAKE DEMANDS AND LINE UP AN ESCAPE ROUTE.
I SUPPOSE SO. BUT THEY'RE BOUND TO SUR-RENDER SOON.
THERE'S NO ESCAPE FOR THEM NOW.
WHAT MAKES YOU SAY THAT?
EH?
I CAUGHT A GLIMPSE INTO THE BANK BEFORE THE SHUTTERS CAME DOWN.
THERE WERE MULTIPLE ARMED ROBBERS IN SKI MASKS.
A HEIST LIKE THIS, PULLED OFF IN BROAD DAYLIGHT WITH A FULL ARSENAL, MUST HAVE TAKEN EXTENSIVE PLANNING.
IF THEIR ENTRANCE WAS CAREFULLY PREPARED, SO IS THEIR EXIT. THEY CERTAINLY SEEM TO BE TAKING THEIR SWEET TIME.
THERE'S MORE HERE THAN MEETS THE EYE.
THEY'VE FIGURED OUT A WAY TO ESCAPE WITH THE MONEY...
THUMP

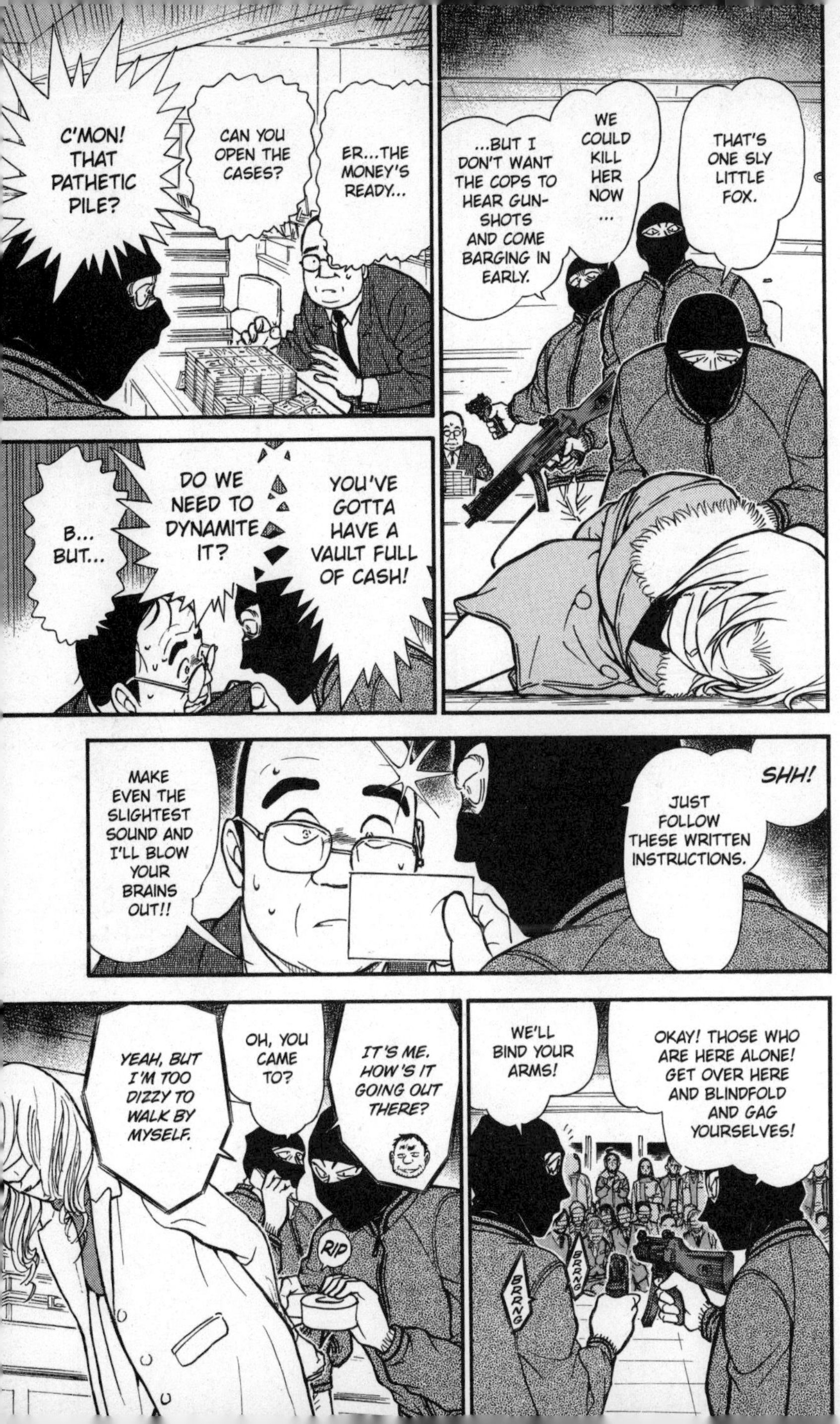
THAT'S ONE SLY LITTLE FOX.
WE COULD KILL HER NOW...
...BUT I DON'T WANT THE COPS TO HEAR GUN-SHOTS AND COME BARGING IN EARLY.
ER...THE MONEY'S READY...
CAN YOU OPEN THE CASES?
C'MON! THAT PATHETIC PILE?
YOU'VE GOTTA HAVE A VAULT FULL OF CASH!
DO WE NEED TO DYNAMITE IT?
B... BUT...
SHH!
JUST FOLLOW THESE WRITTEN INSTRUCTIONS.
MAKE EVEN THE SLIGHTEST SOUND AND I'LL BLOW YOUR BRAINS OUT!!
OKAY! THOSE WHO ARE HERE ALONE! GET OVER HERE AND BLINDFOLD AND GAG YOURSELVES!
WE'LL BIND YOUR ARMS!
BRRNG
BRRNG
IT'S ME. HOW'S IT GOING OUT THERE?
OH, YOU CAME TO?
YEAH, BUT I'M TOO DIZZY TO WALK BY MYSELF.
RIP

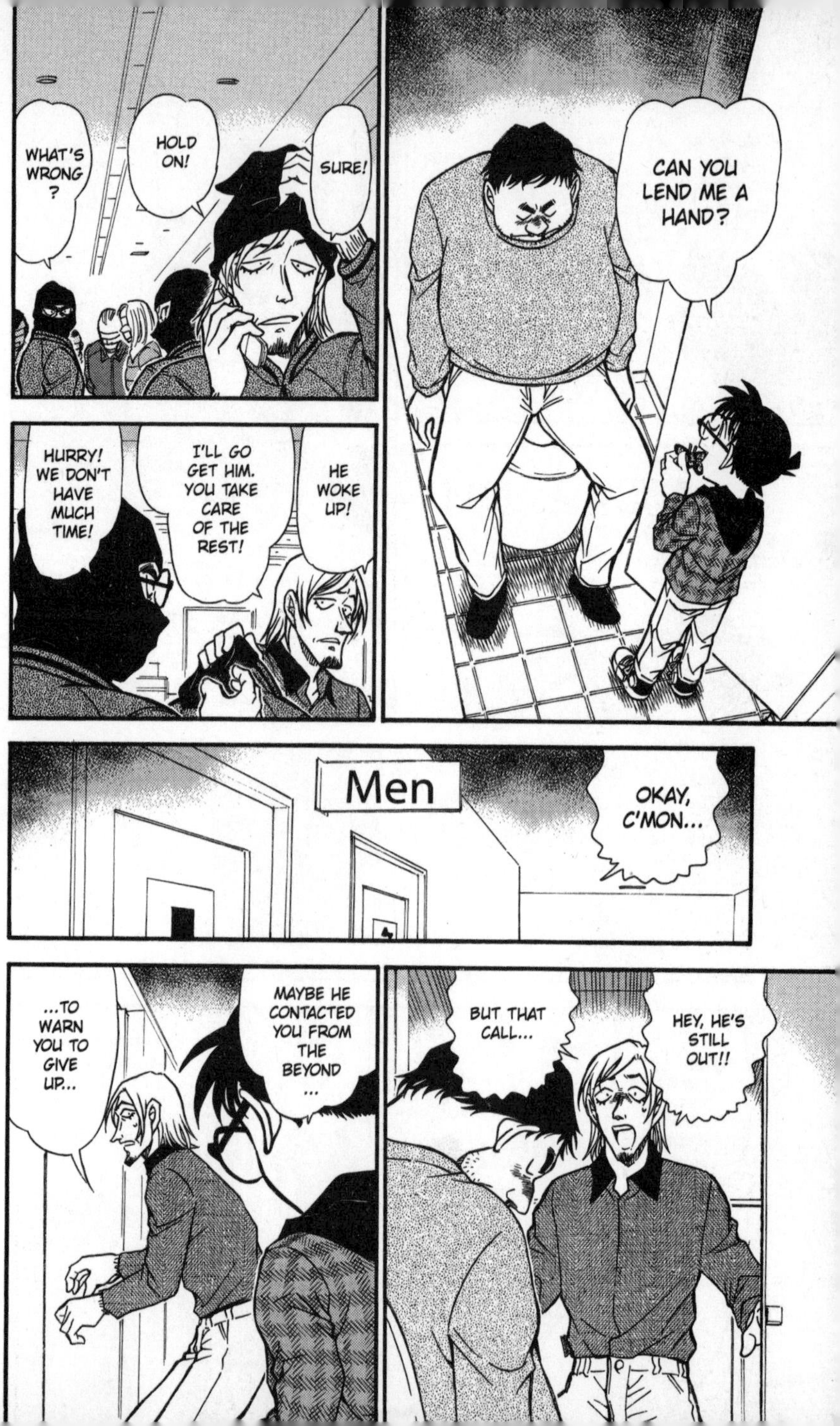
CAN YOU LEND ME A HAND?
SURE!
HOLD ON!
WHAT'S WRONG?
HE WOKE UP!
I'LL GO GET HIM. YOU TAKE CARE OF THE REST!
HURRY! WE DON'T HAVE MUCH TIME!
Men
OKAY, C'MON...
HEY, HE'S STILL OUT!!
BUT THAT CALL...
MAYBE HE CONTACTED YOU FROM THE BEYOND...
...TO WARN YOU TO GIVE UP...

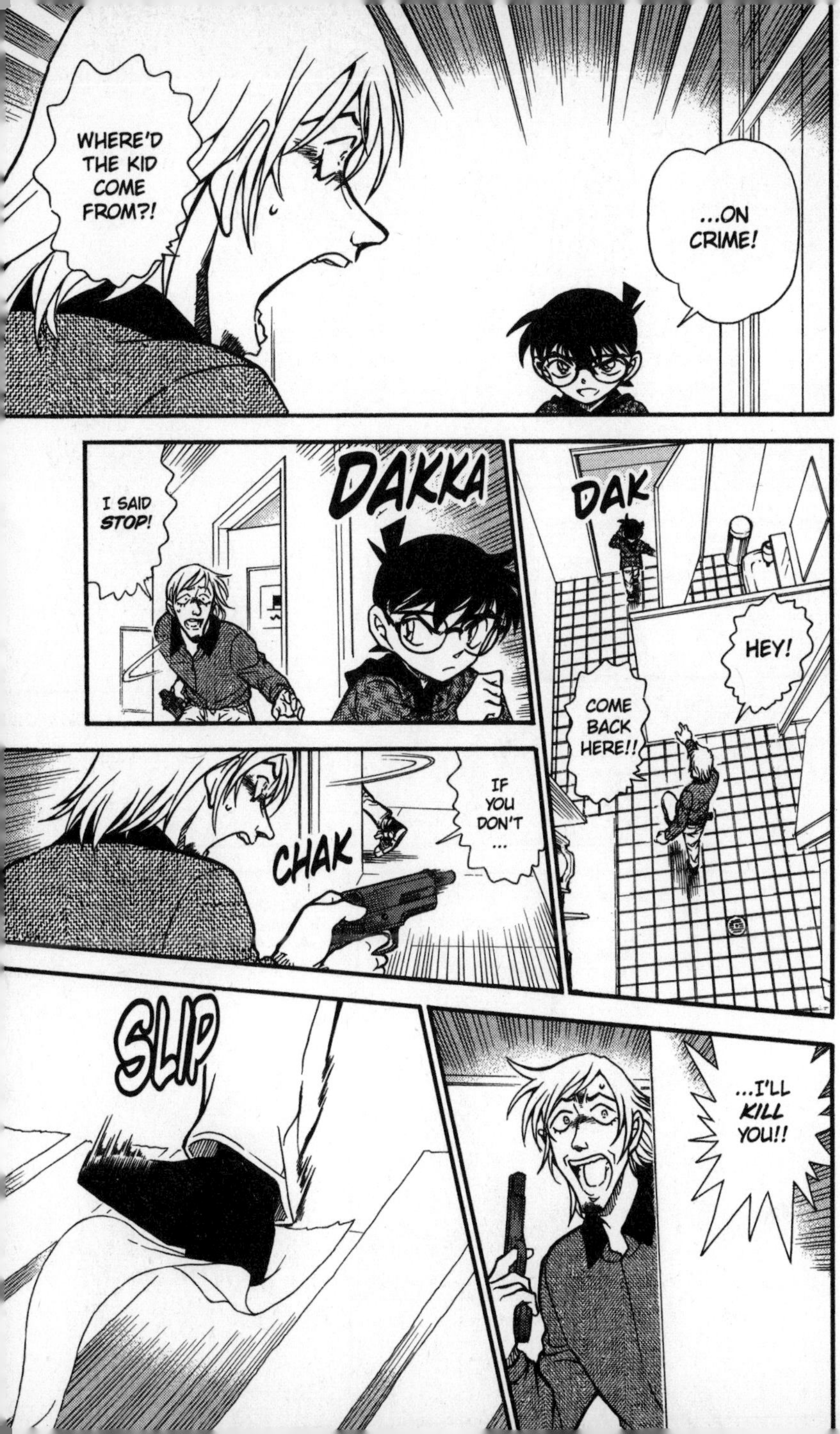
...ON CRIME!
WHERE'D THE KID COME FROM?!
DAK
HEY!
COME BACK HERE!!
DAKKA
I SAID STOP!
IF YOU DON'T ...
CHAK
...I'LL KILL YOU!!
SLIP

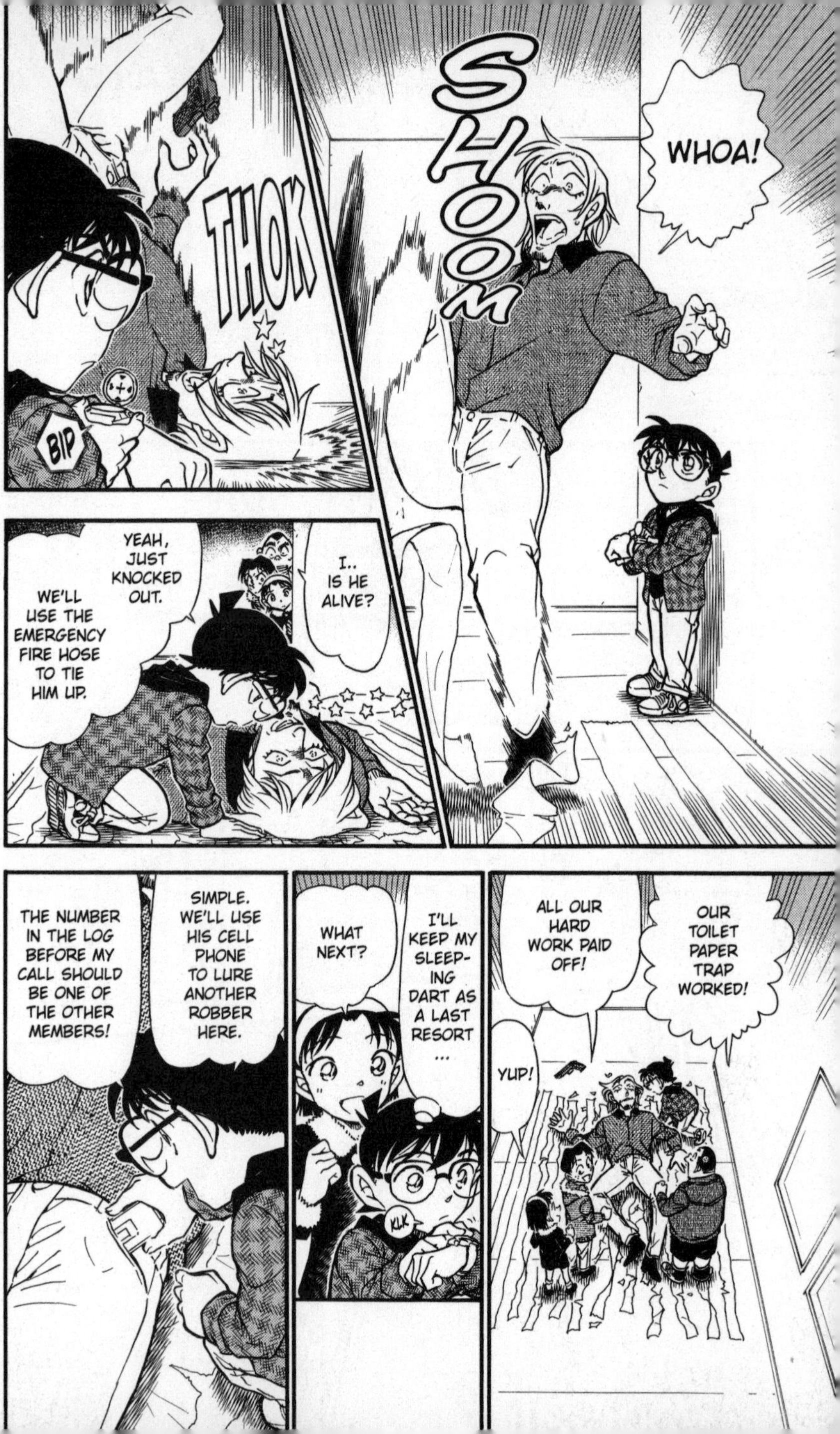
WHOA!
SHOOM
THOK
BIP
I.. IS HE ALIVE?
YEAH, JUST KNOCKED OUT.
WE'LL USE THE EMERGENCY FIRE HOSE TO TIE HIM UP.
OUR TOILET PAPER TRAP WORKED!
ALL OUR HARD WORK PAID OFF!
YUP!
I'LL KEEP MY SLEEP-ING DART AS A LAST RESORT ...
WHAT NEXT?
KLK
SIMPLE. WE'LL USE HIS CELL PHONE TO LURE ANOTHER ROBBER HERE.
THE NUMBER IN THE LOG BEFORE MY CALL SHOULD BE ONE OF THE OTHER MEMBERS!

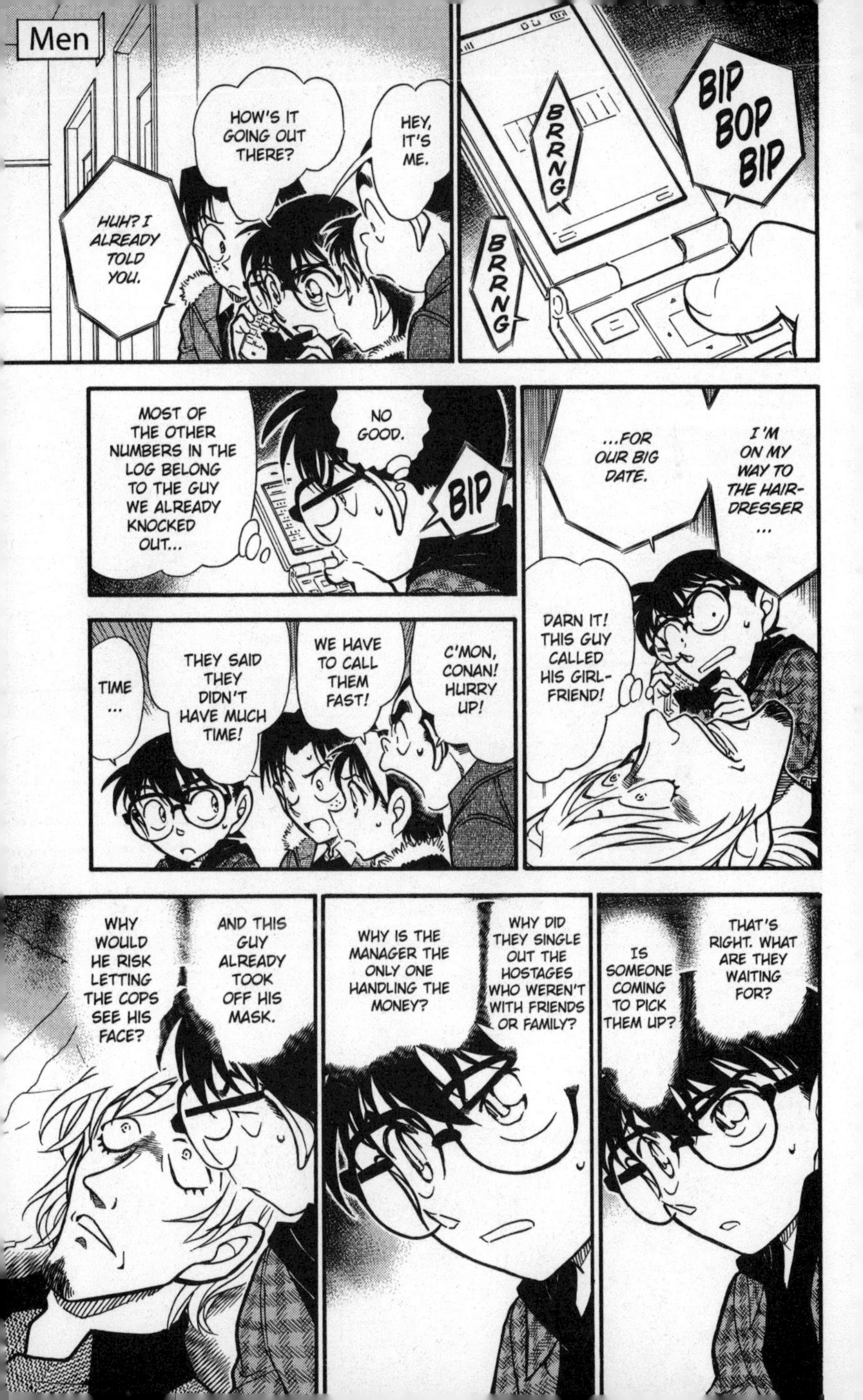
BIP BOP BIP
BRRNG
BRRNG
HEY, IT'S ME.
HOW'S IT GOING OUT THERE?
HUH? I ALREADY TOLD YOU.
Men
I'M ON MY WAY TO THE HAIR-DRESSER...
...FOR OUR BIG DATE.
DARN IT! THIS GUY CALLED HIS GIRL-FRIEND!
BIP
NO GOOD.
MOST OF THE OTHER NUMBERS IN THE LOG BELONG TO THE GUY WE ALREADY KNOCKED OUT...
C'MON, CONAN! HURRY UP!
WE HAVE TO CALL THEM FAST!
THEY SAID THEY DIDN'T HAVE MUCH TIME!
TIME...
THAT'S RIGHT. WHAT ARE THEY WAITING FOR?
IS SOMEONE COMING TO PICK THEM UP?
WHY DID THEY SINGLE OUT THE HOSTAGES WHO WEREN'T WITH FRIENDS OR FAMILY?
WHY IS THE MANAGER THE ONLY ONE HANDLING THE MONEY?
AND THIS GUY ALREADY TOOK OFF HIS MASK.
WHY WOULD HE RISK LETTING THE COPS SEE HIS FACE?

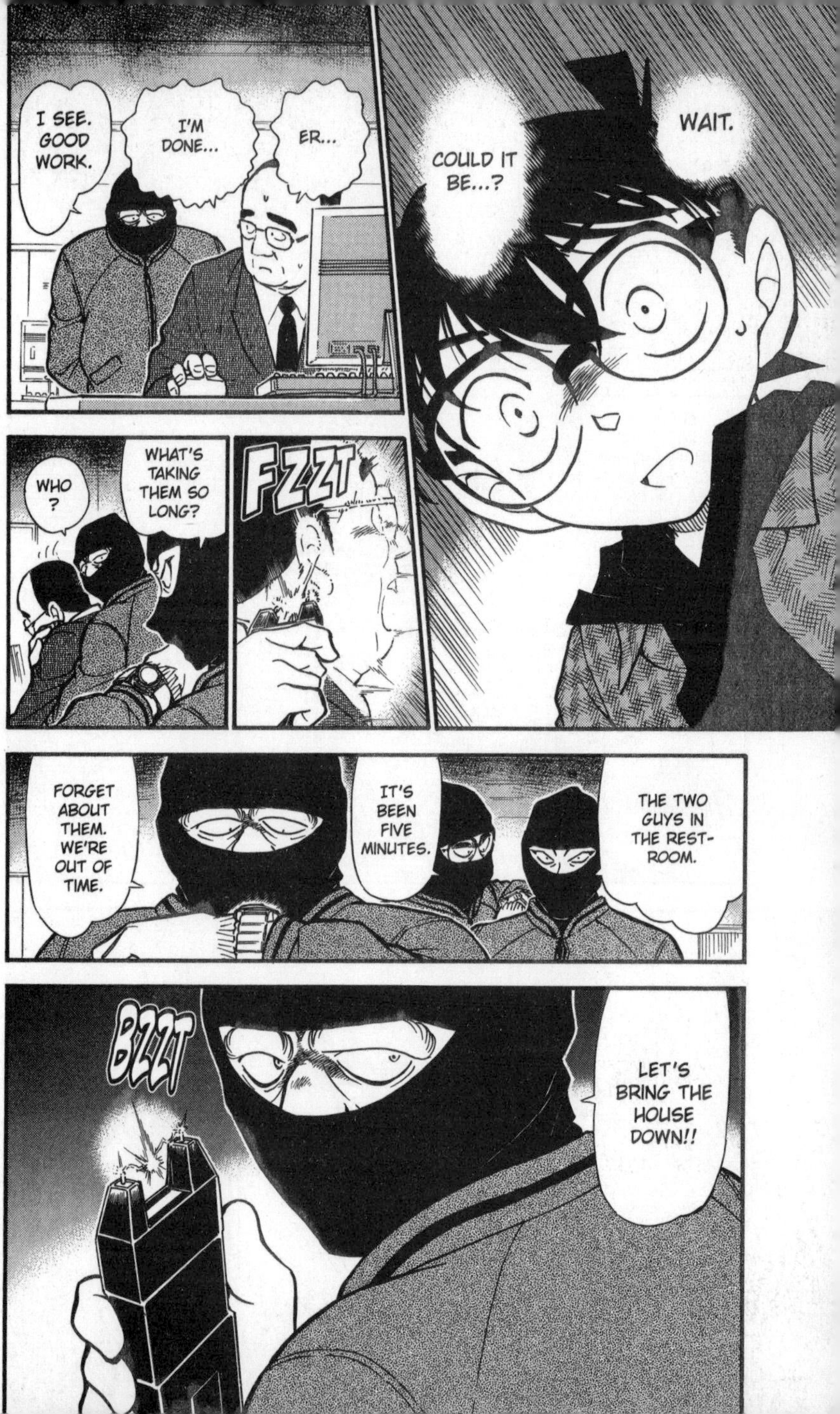
WAIT.
COULD IT BE...?
ER...
I'M DONE...
I SEE. GOOD WORK.
FZZT
WHAT'S TAKING THEM SO LONG?
WHO?
THE TWO GUYS IN THE REST-ROOM.
IT'S BEEN FIVE MINUTES.
FORGET ABOUT THEM. WE'RE OUT OF TIME.
LET'S BRING THE HOUSE DOWN!!
BZZT

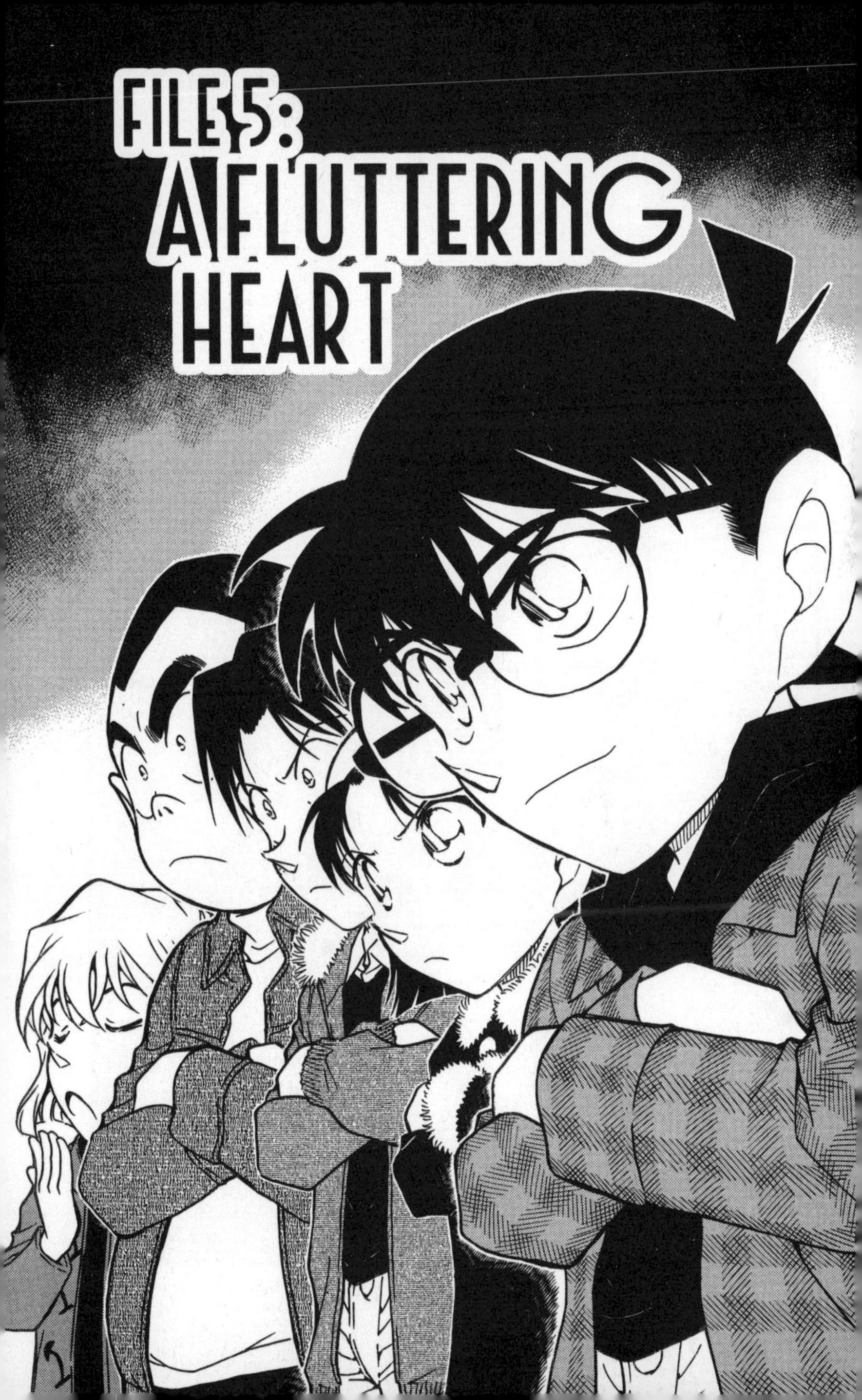
FILE 5:
A FLUTTERING HEART

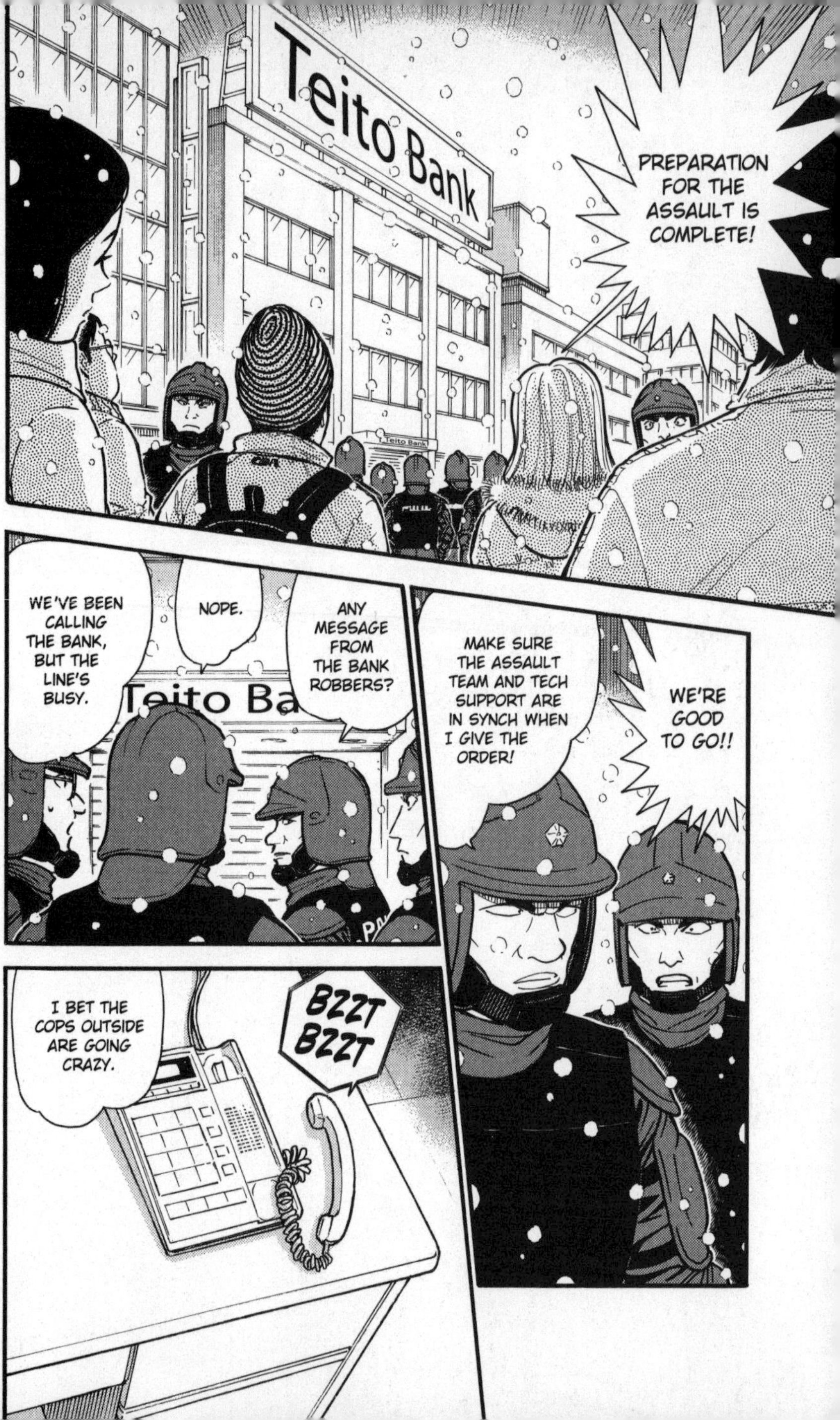
Teito Bank
PREPARATION FOR THE ASSAULT IS COMPLETE!
MAKE SURE THE ASSAULT TEAM AND TECH SUPPORT ARE IN SYNCH WHEN I GIVE THE ORDER!
WE'RE GOOD TO GO!!
ANY MESSAGE FROM THE BANK ROBBERS?
NOPE.
WE'VE BEEN CALLING THE BANK, BUT THE LINE'S BUSY.
BZZT BZZT
I BET THE COPS OUTSIDE ARE GOING CRAZY.

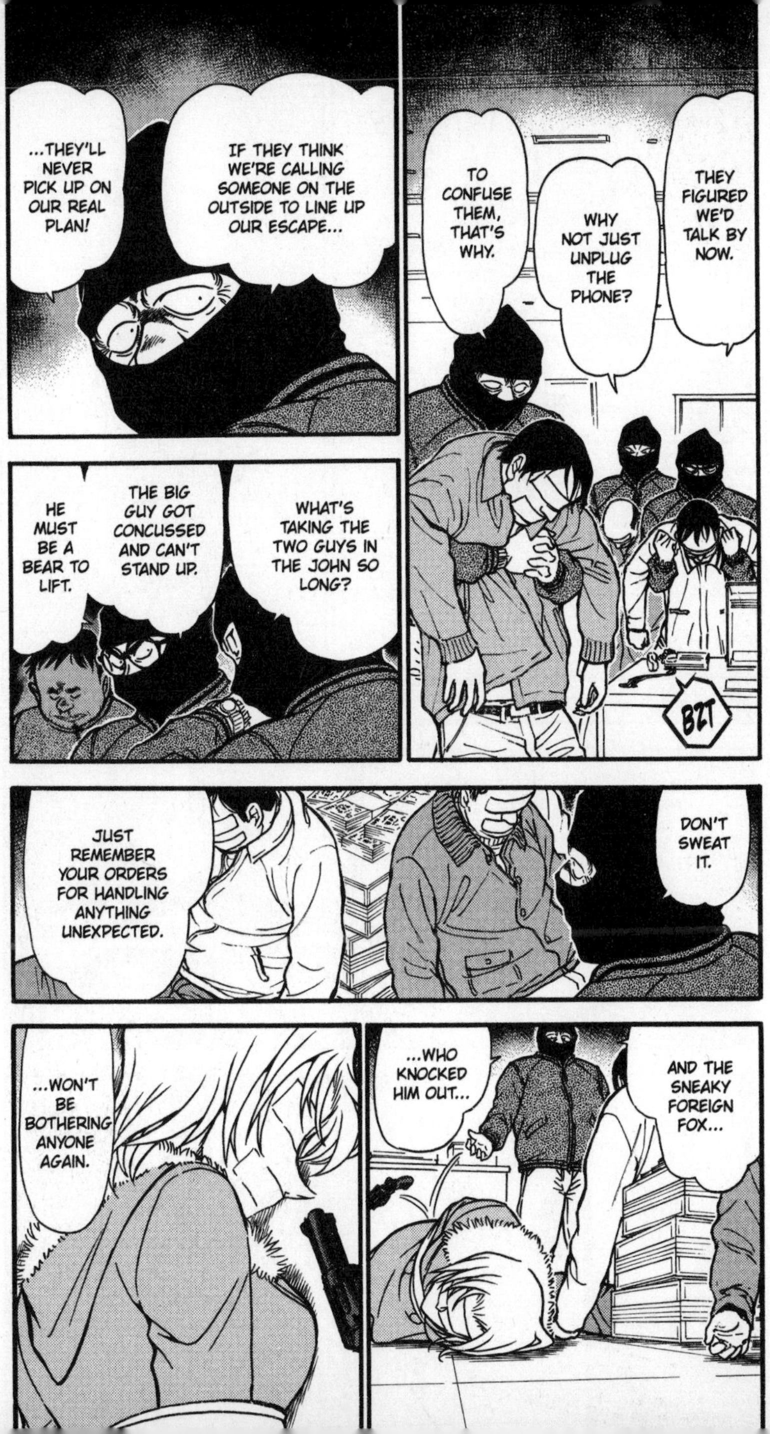
THEY FIGURED WE'D TALK BY NOW.
WHY NOT JUST UNPLUG THE PHONE?
TO CONFUSE THEM, THAT'S WHY.
BZT
IF THEY THINK WE'RE CALLING SOMEONE ON THE OUTSIDE TO LINE UP OUR ESCAPE...
...THEY'LL NEVER PICK UP ON OUR REAL PLAN!
WHAT'S TAKING THE TWO GUYS IN THE JOHN SO LONG?
THE BIG GUY GOT CONCUSSED AND CAN'T STAND UP.
HE MUST BE A BEAR TO LIFT.
DON'T SWEAT IT.
JUST REMEMBER YOUR ORDERS FOR HANDLING ANYTHING UNEXPECTED.
AND THE SNEAKY FOREIGN FOX...
...WHO KNOCKED HIM OUT...
...WON'T BE BOTHERING ANYONE AGAIN.

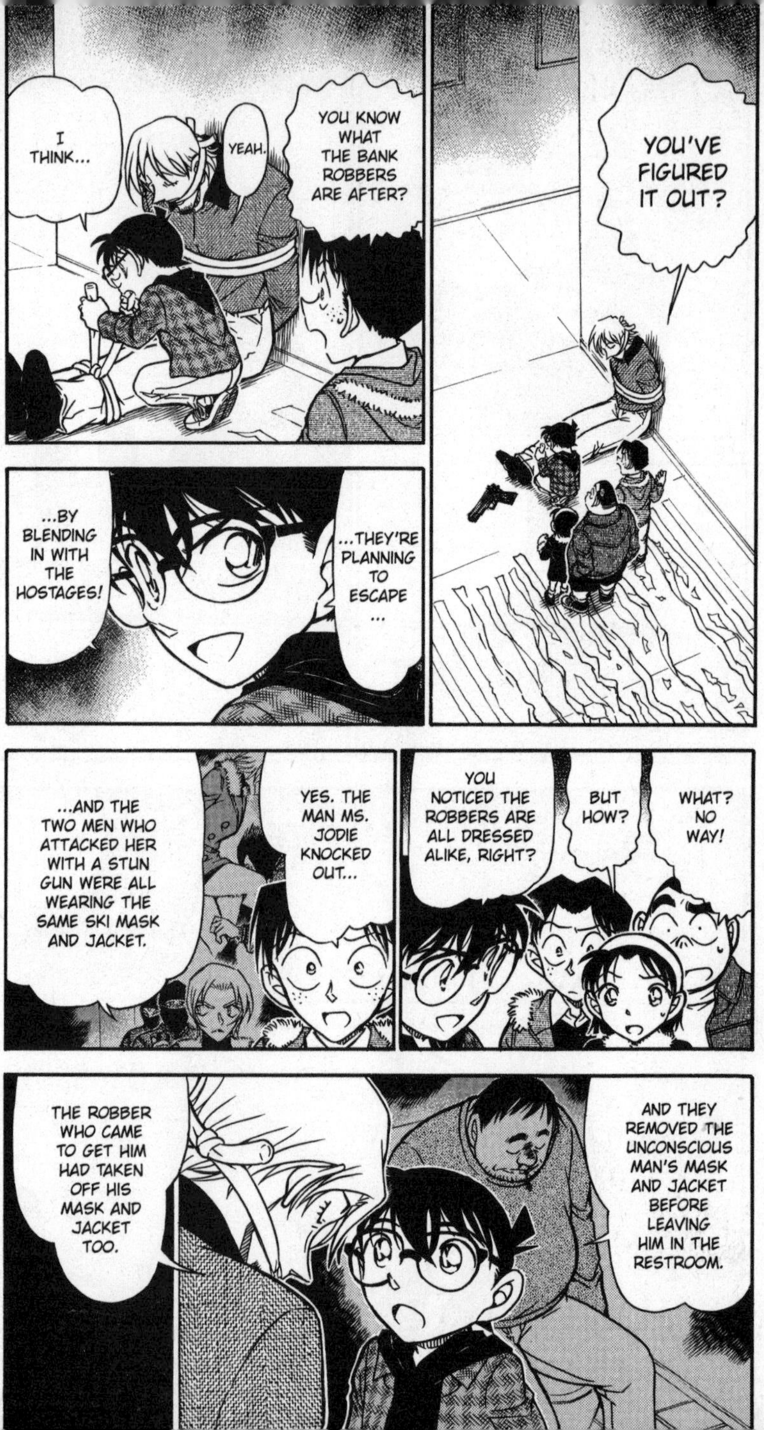
YOU'VE FIGURED IT OUT?
YOU KNOW WHAT THE BANK ROBBERS ARE AFTER?
YEAH.
I THINK...
...THEY'RE PLANNING TO ESCAPE ...
...BY BLENDING IN WITH THE HOSTAGES!
WHAT? NO WAY!
BUT HOW?
YOU NOTICED THE ROBBERS ARE ALL DRESSED ALIKE, RIGHT?
YES. THE MAN MS. JODIE KNOCKED OUT...
...AND THE TWO MEN WHO ATTACKED HER WITH A STUN GUN WERE ALL WEARING THE SAME SKI MASK AND JACKET.
AND THEY REMOVED THE UNCONSCIOUS MAN'S MASK AND JACKET BEFORE LEAVING HIM IN THE RESTROOM.
THE ROBBER WHO CAME TO GET HIM HAD TAKEN OFF HIS MASK AND JACKET TOO.

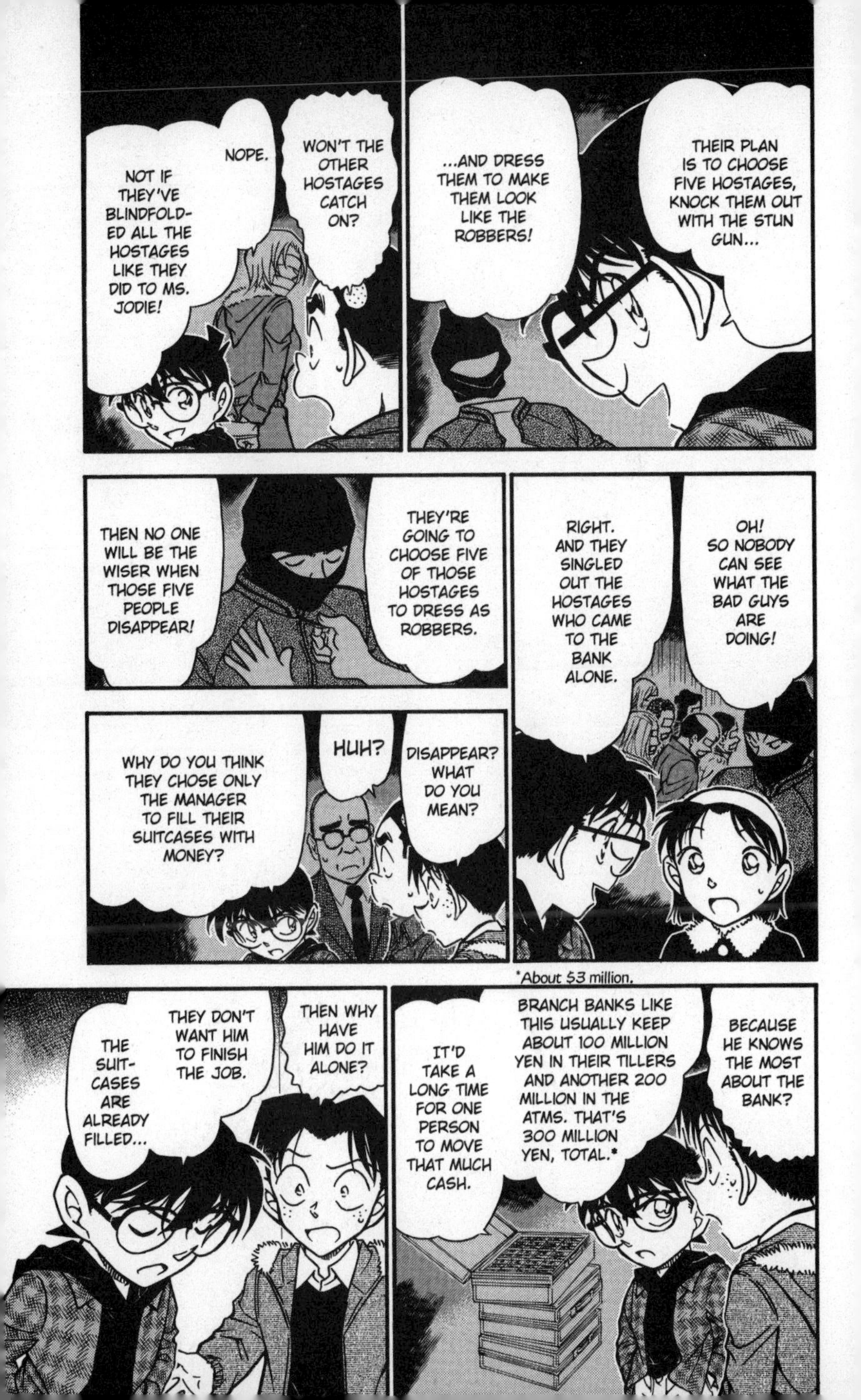
THEIR PLAN IS TO CHOOSE FIVE HOSTAGES, KNOCK THEM OUT WITH THE STUN GUN...
...AND DRESS THEM TO MAKE THEM LOOK LIKE THE ROBBERS!
WON'T THE OTHER HOSTAGES CATCH ON?
NOPE.
NOT IF THEY'VE BLINDFOLDED ALL THE HOSTAGES LIKE THEY DID TO MS. JODIE!
OH! SO NOBODY CAN SEE WHAT THE BAD GUYS ARE DOING!
RIGHT. AND THEY SINGLED OUT THE HOSTAGES WHO CAME TO THE BANK ALONE.
THEY'RE GOING TO CHOOSE FIVE OF THOSE HOSTAGES TO DRESS AS ROBBERS.
THEN NO ONE WILL BE THE WISER WHEN THOSE FIVE PEOPLE DISAPPEAR!
DISAPPEAR? WHAT DO YOU MEAN?
HUH?
WHY DO YOU THINK THEY CHOSE ONLY THE MANAGER TO FILL THEIR SUITCASES WITH MONEY?
BECAUSE HE KNOWS THE MOST ABOUT THE BANK?
BRANCH BANKS LIKE THIS USUALLY KEEP ABOUT 100 MILLION YEN IN THEIR TILLERS AND ANOTHER 200 MILLION IN THE ATMS. THAT'S 300 MILLION YEN, TOTAL.*
IT'D TAKE A LONG TIME FOR ONE PERSON TO MOVE THAT MUCH CASH.
THEN WHY HAVE HIM DO IT ALONE?
THEY DON'T WANT HIM TO FINISH THE JOB.
THE SUITCASES ARE ALREADY FILLED...

*About $3 million.

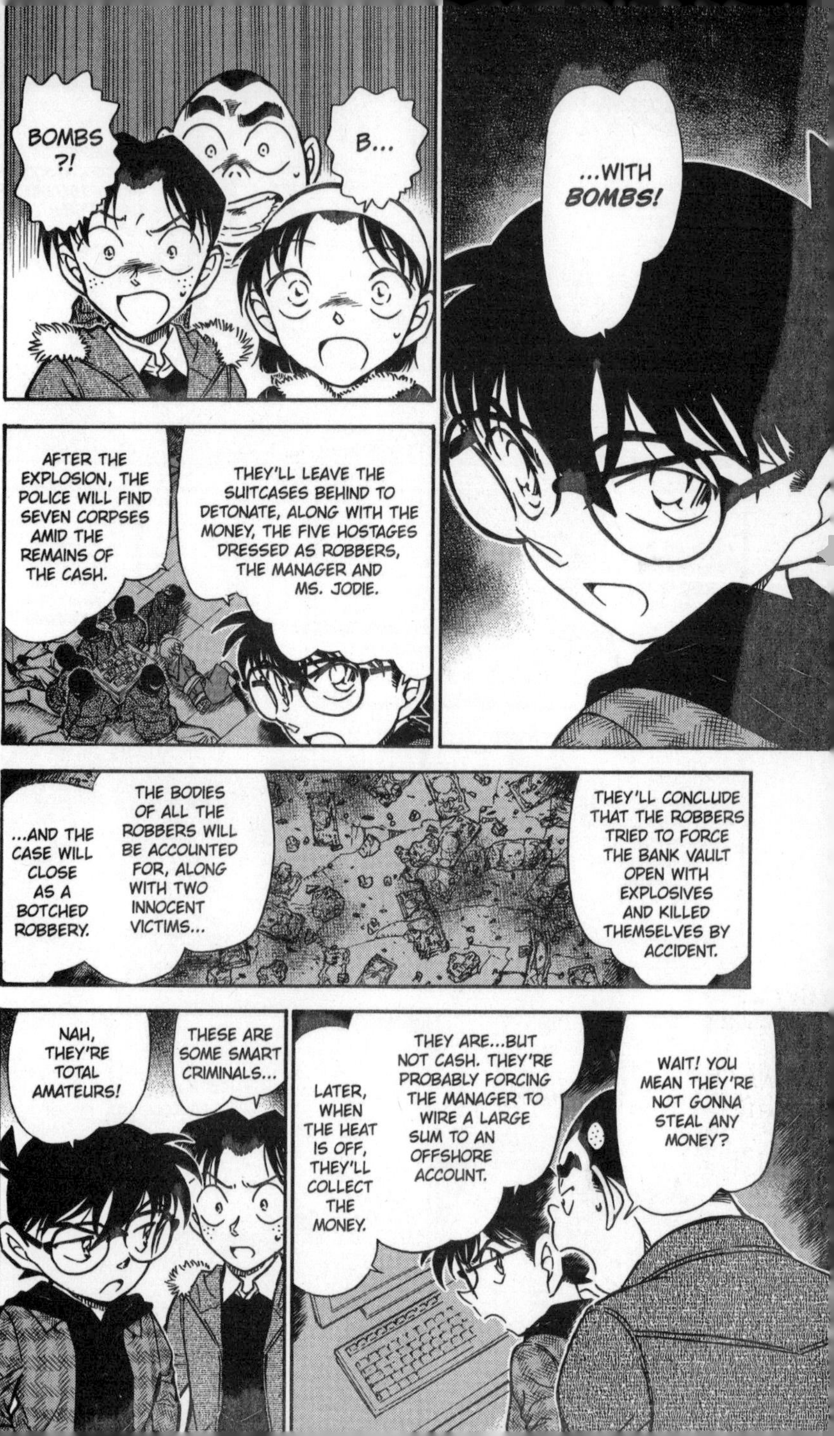
...WITH BOMBS!
B...
BOMBS ?!
THEY'LL LEAVE THE SUITCASES BEHIND TO DETONATE, ALONG WITH THE MONEY, THE FIVE HOSTAGES DRESSED AS ROBBERS, THE MANAGER AND MS. JODIE.
AFTER THE EXPLOSION, THE POLICE WILL FIND SEVEN CORPSES AMID THE REMAINS OF THE CASH.
THEY'LL CONCLUDE THAT THE ROBBERS TRIED TO FORCE THE BANK VAULT OPEN WITH EXPLOSIVES AND KILLED THEMSELVES BY ACCIDENT.
THE BODIES OF ALL THE ROBBERS WILL BE ACCOUNTED FOR, ALONG WITH TWO INNOCENT VICTIMS...
...AND THE CASE WILL CLOSE AS A BOTCHED ROBBERY.
WAIT! YOU MEAN THEY'RE NOT GONNA STEAL ANY MONEY?
THEY ARE...BUT NOT CASH. THEY'RE PROBABLY FORCING THE MANAGER TO WIRE A LARGE SUM TO AN OFFSHORE ACCOUNT.
LATER, WHEN THE HEAT IS OFF, THEY'LL COLLECT THE MONEY.
THESE ARE SOME SMART CRIMINALS...
NAH, THEY'RE TOTAL AMATEURS!

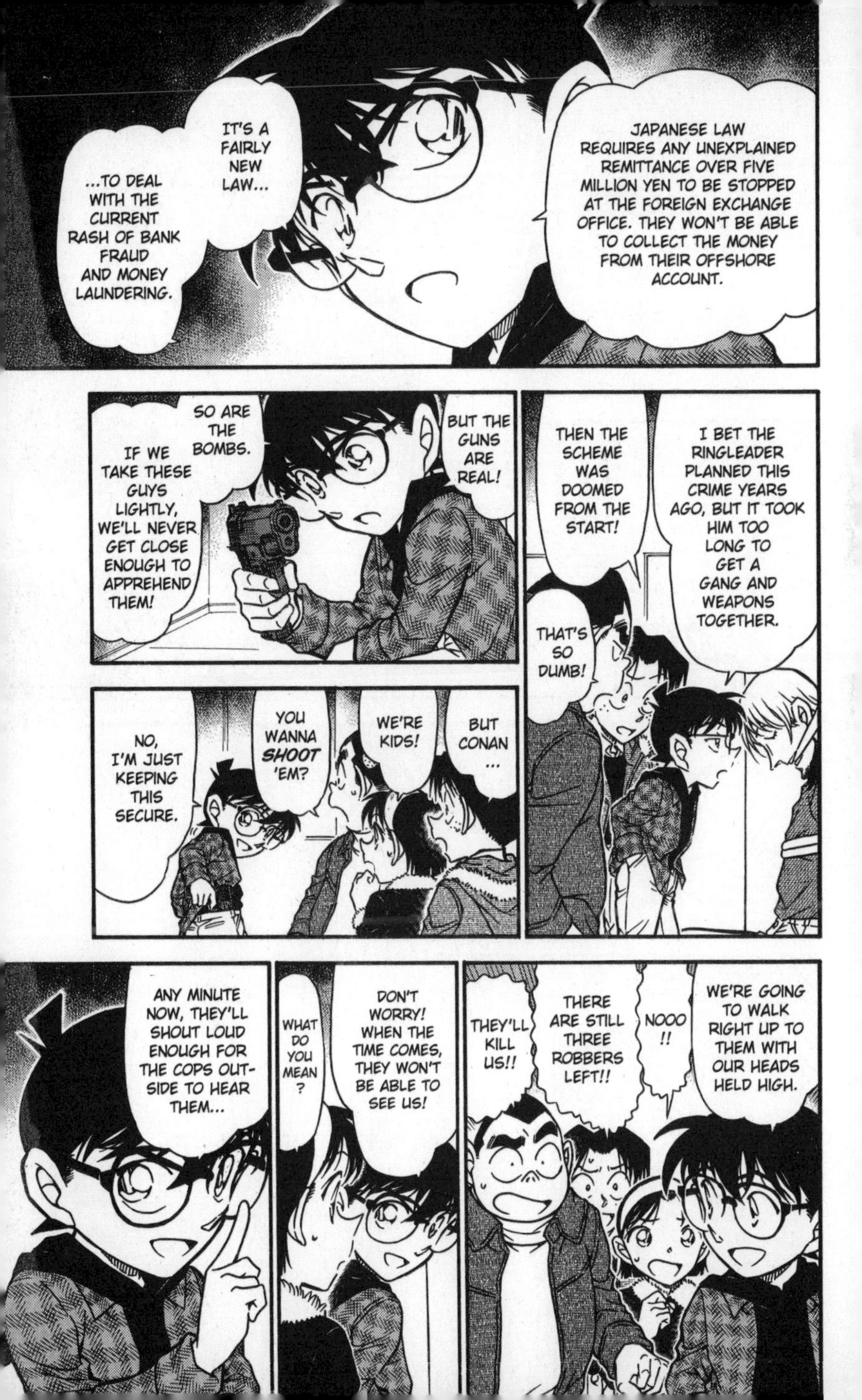
JAPANESE LAW REQUIRES ANY UNEXPLAINED REMITTANCE OVER FIVE MILLION YEN TO BE STOPPED AT THE FOREIGN EXCHANGE OFFICE. THEY WON'T BE ABLE TO COLLECT THE MONEY FROM THEIR OFFSHORE ACCOUNT.
IT'S A FAIRLY NEW LAW...
...TO DEAL WITH THE CURRENT RASH OF BANK FRAUD AND MONEY LAUNDERING.
I BET THE RINGLEADER PLANNED THIS CRIME YEARS AGO, BUT IT TOOK HIM TOO LONG TO GET A GANG AND WEAPONS TOGETHER.
THEN THE SCHEME WAS DOOMED FROM THE START!
THAT'S SO DUMB!
BUT THE GUNS ARE REAL!
SO ARE THE BOMBS.
IF WE TAKE THESE GUYS LIGHTLY, WE'LL NEVER GET CLOSE ENOUGH TO APPREHEND THEM!
BUT CONAN ...
WE'RE KIDS!
YOU WANNA *SHOOT* 'EM?
NO, I'M JUST KEEPING THIS SECURE.
WE'RE GOING TO WALK RIGHT UP TO THEM WITH OUR HEADS HELD HIGH.
NOOO !!
THERE ARE STILL THREE ROBBERS LEFT!!
THEY'LL KILL US!!
DON'T WORRY! WHEN THE TIME COMES, THEY WON'T BE ABLE TO SEE US!
WHAT DO YOU MEAN ?
ANY MINUTE NOW, THEY'LL SHOUT LOUD ENOUGH FOR THE COPS OUT-SIDE TO HEAR THEM...

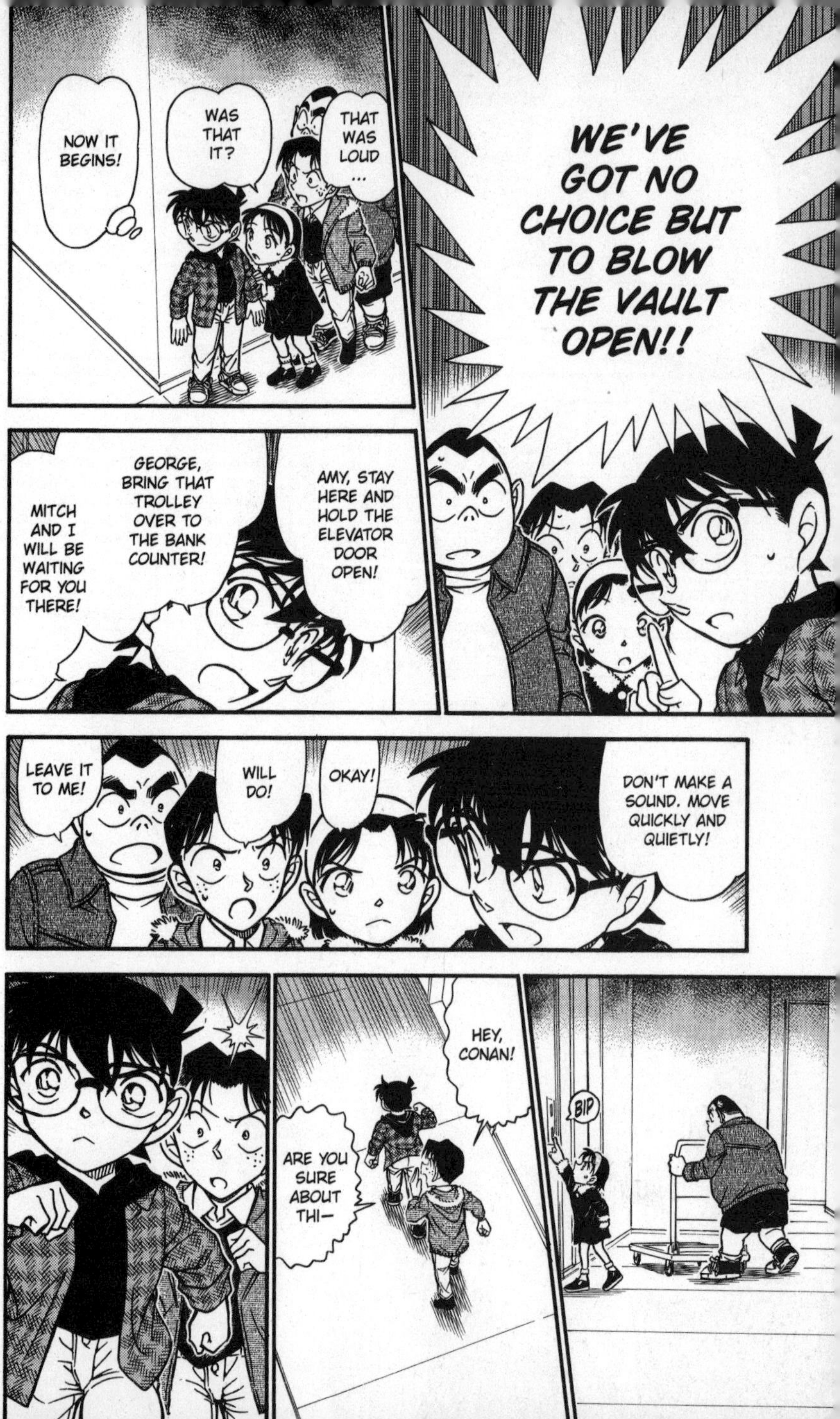
WE'VE GOT NO CHOICE BUT TO BLOW THE VAULT OPEN!!
THAT WAS LOUD ...
WAS THAT IT?
NOW IT BEGINS!
AMY, STAY HERE AND HOLD THE ELEVATOR DOOR OPEN!
GEORGE, BRING THAT TROLLEY OVER TO THE BANK COUNTER!
MITCH AND I WILL BE WAITING FOR YOU THERE!
DON'T MAKE A SOUND. MOVE QUICKLY AND QUIETLY!
OKAY!
WILL DO!
LEAVE IT TO ME!
BIP
HEY, CONAN!
ARE YOU SURE ABOUT THI—

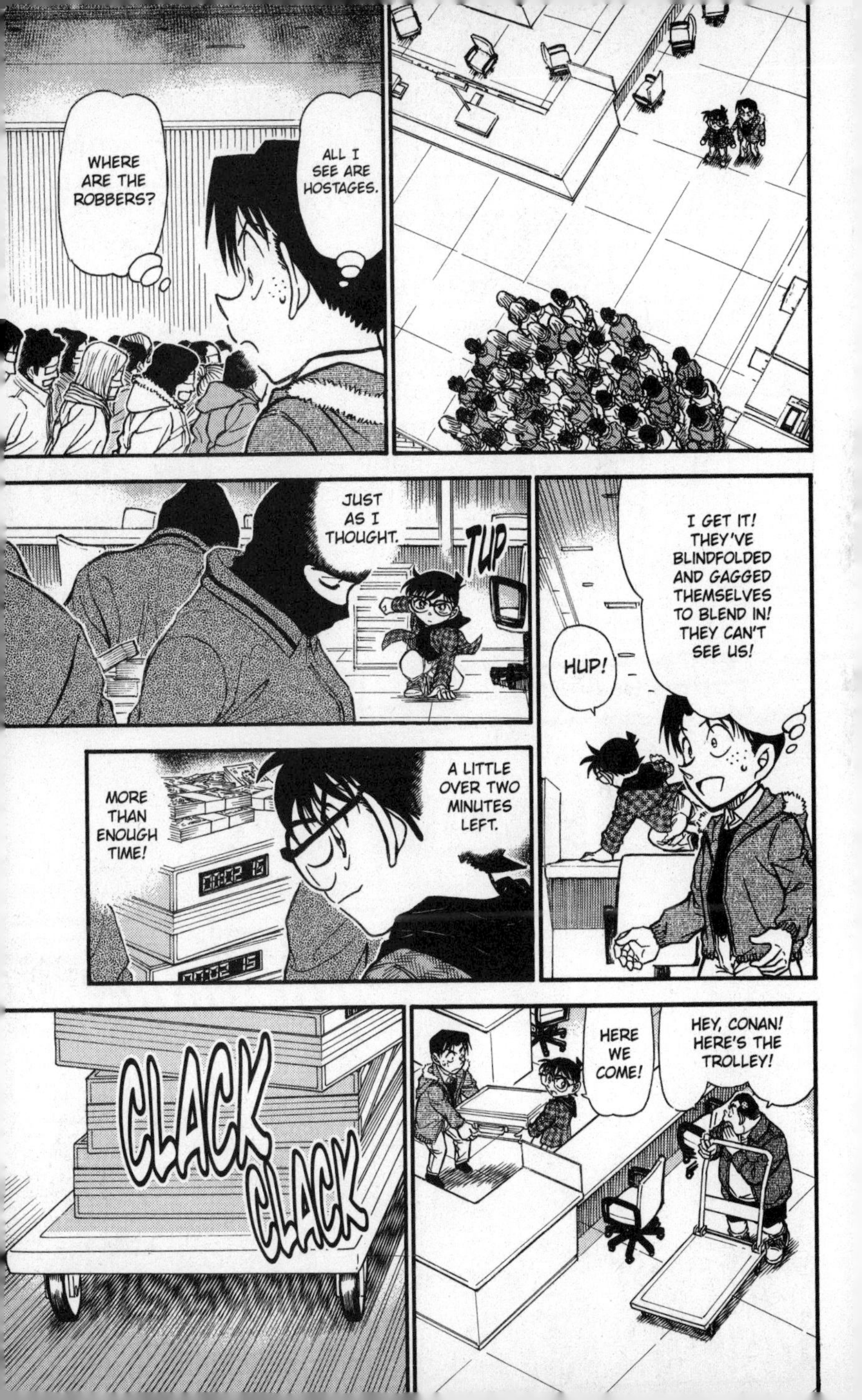
ALL I SEE ARE HOSTAGES.
WHERE ARE THE ROBBERS?
I GET IT! THEY'VE BLINDFOLDED AND GAGGED THEMSELVES TO BLEND IN! THEY CAN'T SEE US!
HUP!
JUST AS I THOUGHT.
TUP
A LITTLE OVER TWO MINUTES LEFT.
MORE THAN ENOUGH TIME!
HEY, CONAN! HERE'S THE TROLLEY!
HERE WE COME!
CLACK
CLACK

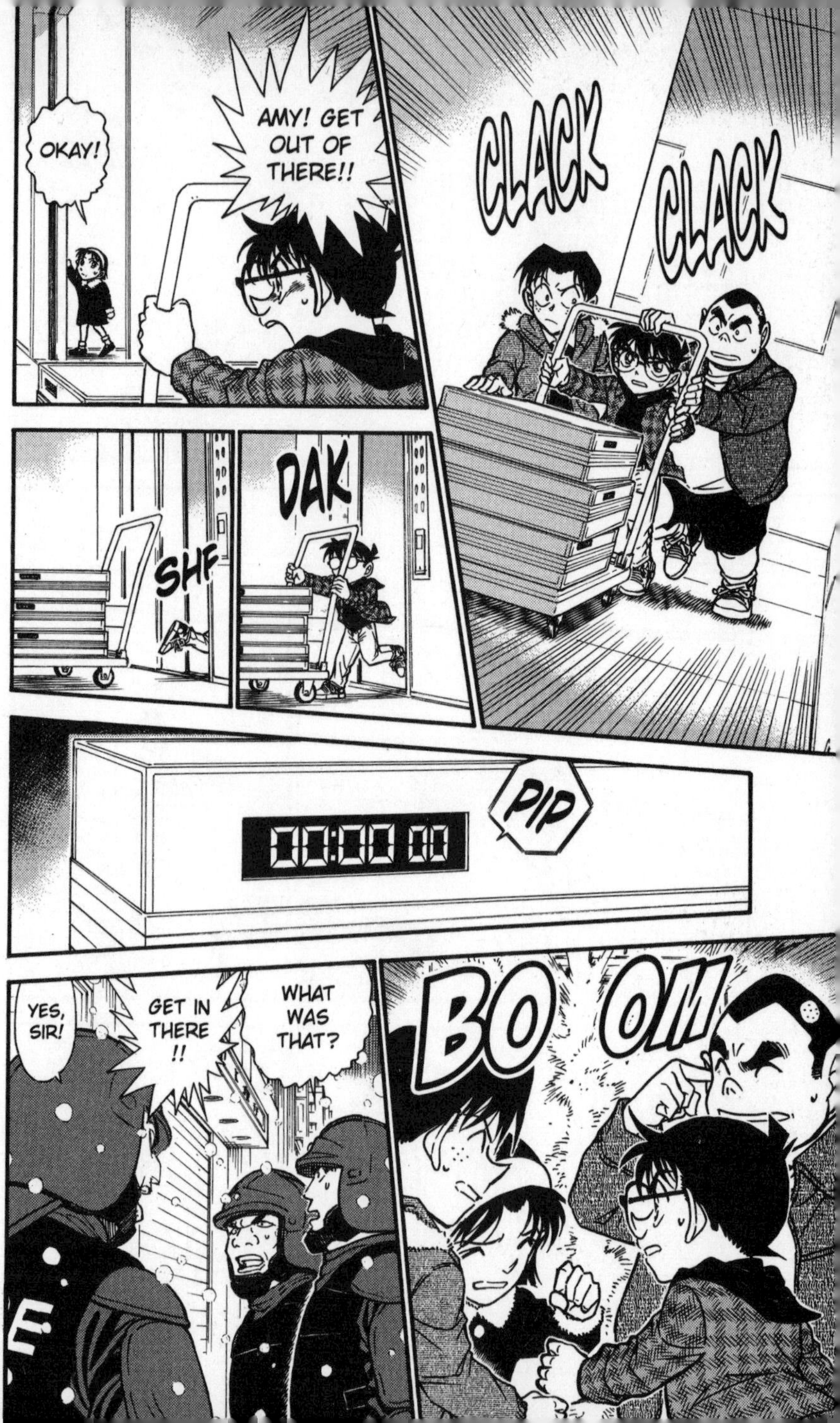
CLACK
CLACK
AMY! GET OUT OF THERE!!
OKAY!
DAK
SHF
00:00 00
PIP
BOOM
WHAT WAS THAT?
GET IN THERE !!
YES, SIR!

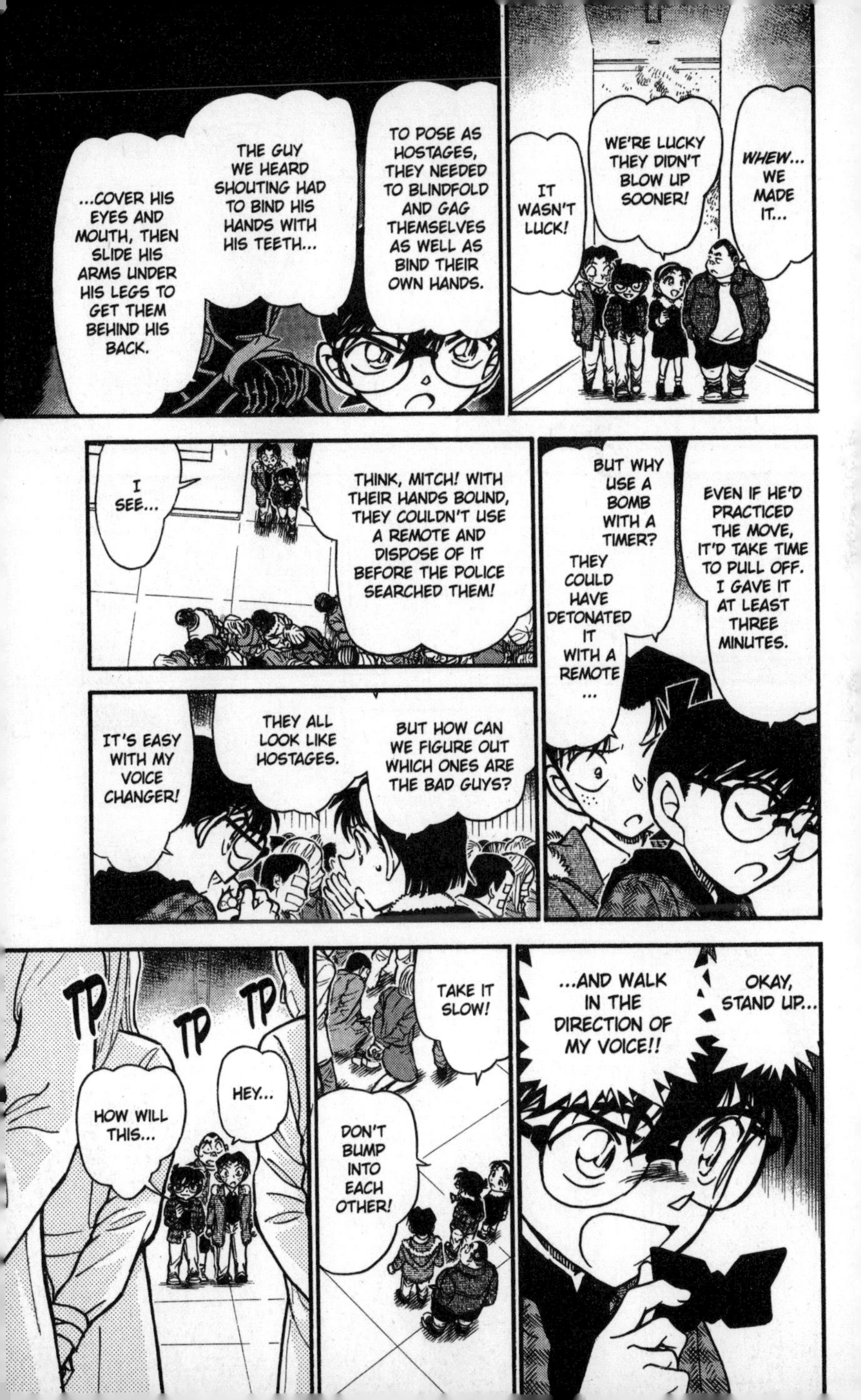
WHEW... WE MADE IT...
WE'RE LUCKY THEY DIDN'T BLOW UP SOONER!
IT WASN'T LUCK!
TO POSE AS HOSTAGES, THEY NEEDED TO BLINDFOLD AND GAG THEMSELVES AS WELL AS BIND THEIR OWN HANDS.
THE GUY WE HEARD SHOUTING HAD TO BIND HIS HANDS WITH HIS TEETH...
...COVER HIS EYES AND MOUTH, THEN SLIDE HIS ARMS UNDER HIS LEGS TO GET THEM BEHIND HIS BACK.
EVEN IF HE'D PRACTICED THE MOVE, IT'D TAKE TIME TO PULL OFF. I GAVE IT AT LEAST THREE MINUTES.
BUT WHY USE A BOMB WITH A TIMER?
THEY COULD HAVE DETONATED IT WITH A REMOTE...
THINK, MITCH! WITH THEIR HANDS BOUND, THEY COULDN'T USE A REMOTE AND DISPOSE OF IT BEFORE THE POLICE SEARCHED THEM!
I SEE...
BUT HOW CAN WE FIGURE OUT WHICH ONES ARE THE BAD GUYS?
THEY ALL LOOK LIKE HOSTAGES.
IT'S EASY WITH MY VOICE CHANGER!
OKAY, STAND UP...
...AND WALK IN THE DIRECTION OF MY VOICE!!
TAKE IT SLOW!
DON'T BUMP INTO EACH OTHER!
TP
TP
TP
HEY...
HOW WILL THIS...

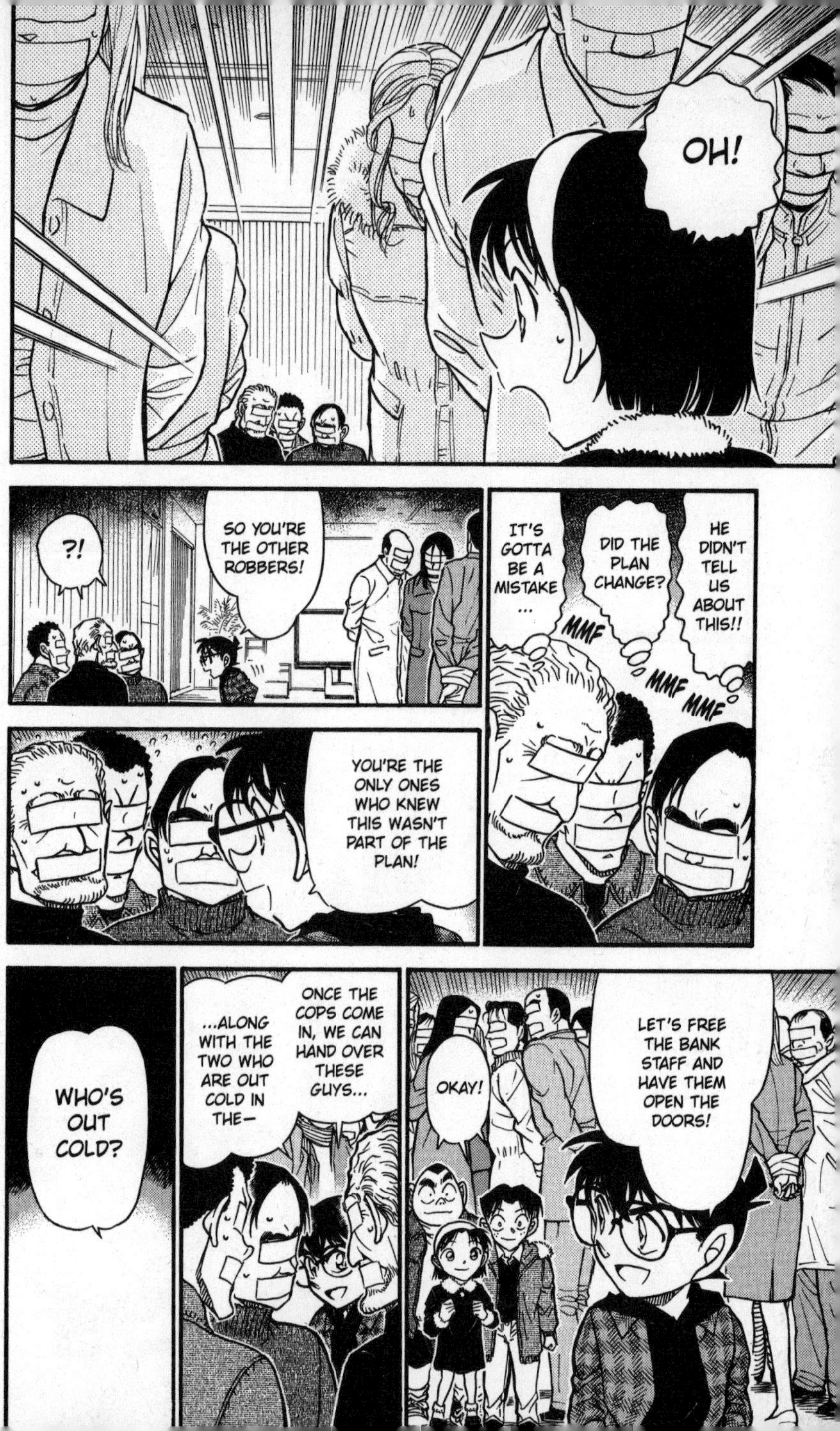
OH!
HE DIDN'T TELL US ABOUT THIS!!
DID THE PLAN CHANGE?
IT'S GOTTA BE A MISTAKE ...
MMF
MMF
MMF
SO YOU'RE THE OTHER ROBBERS!
?!
YOU'RE THE ONLY ONES WHO KNEW THIS WASN'T PART OF THE PLAN!
LET'S FREE THE BANK STAFF AND HAVE THEM OPEN THE DOORS!
OKAY!
ONCE THE COPS COME IN, WE CAN HAND OVER THESE GUYS...
...ALONG WITH THE TWO WHO ARE OUT COLD IN THE—
WHO'S OUT COLD?

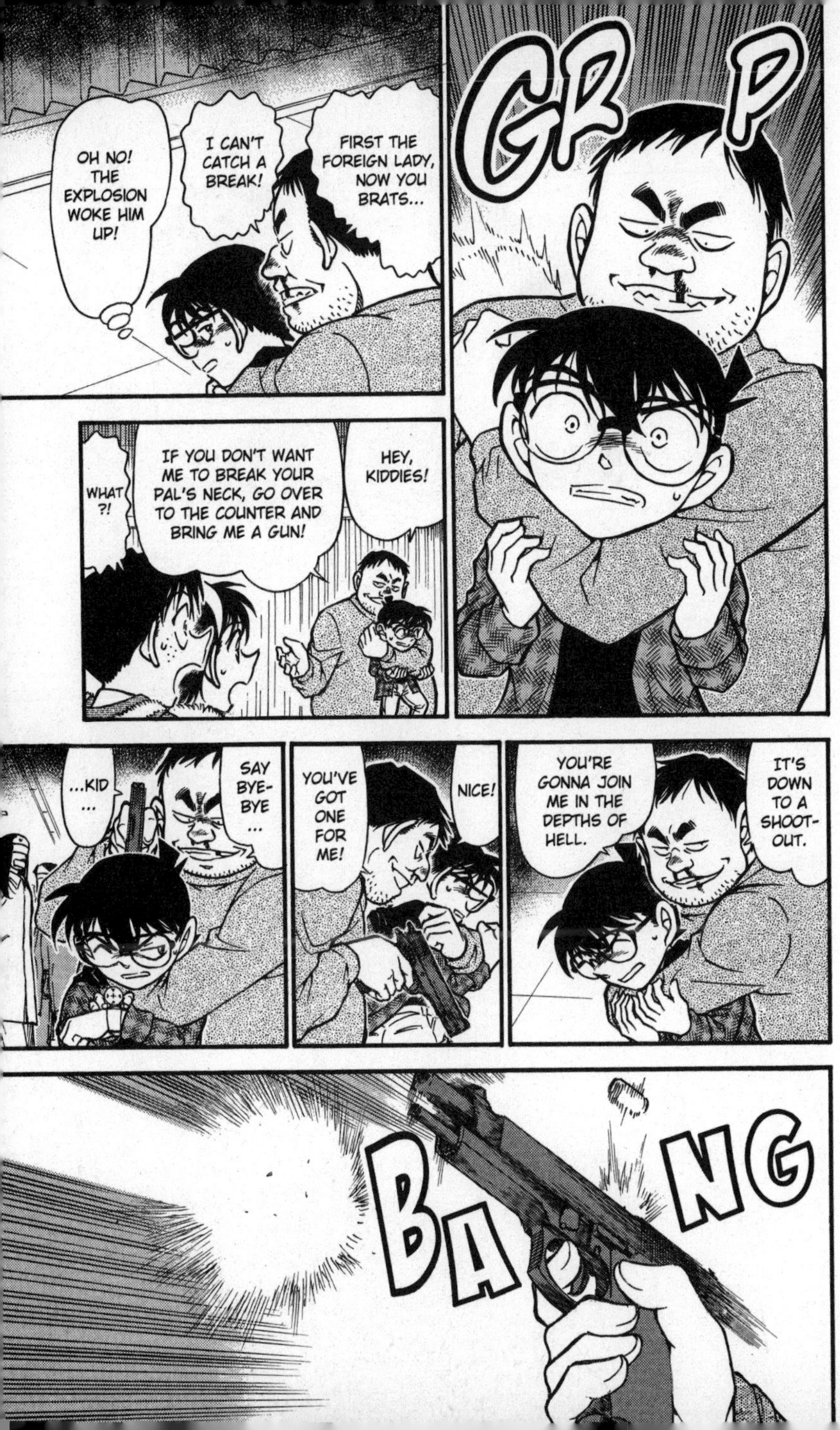
GRIP
FIRST THE FOREIGN LADY, NOW YOU BRATS...
I CAN'T CATCH A BREAK!
OH NO! THE EXPLOSION WOKE HIM UP!
HEY, KIDDIES!
IF YOU DON'T WANT ME TO BREAK YOUR PAL'S NECK, GO OVER TO THE COUNTER AND BRING ME A GUN!
WHAT ?!
IT'S DOWN TO A SHOOT-OUT.
YOU'RE GONNA JOIN ME IN THE DEPTHS OF HELL.
NICE!
YOU'VE GOT ONE FOR ME!
SAY BYE-BYE ...
...KID ...
BANG

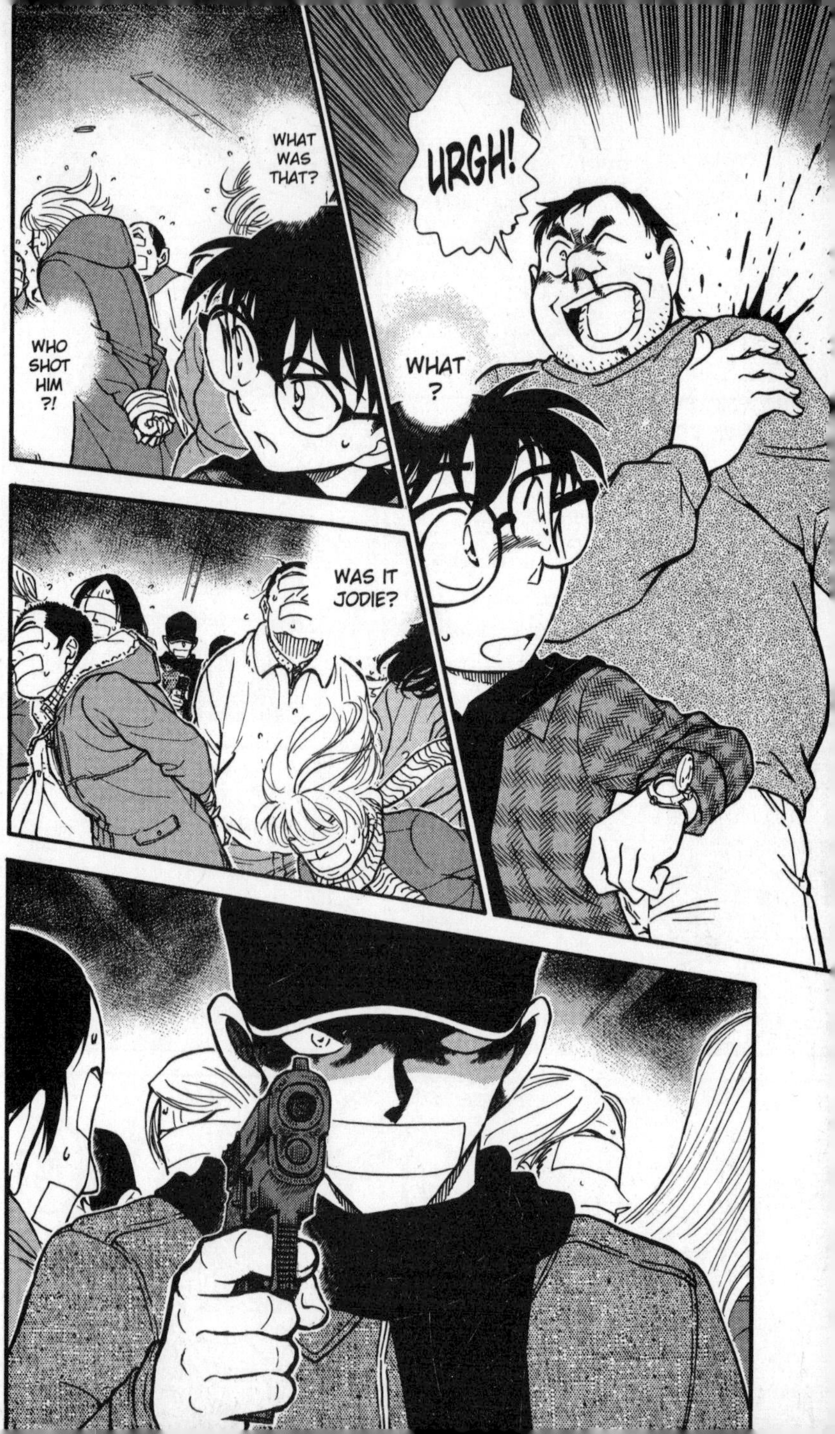
URGH!
WHAT ?
WHAT WAS THAT?
WHO SHOT HIM ?!
WAS IT JODIE?

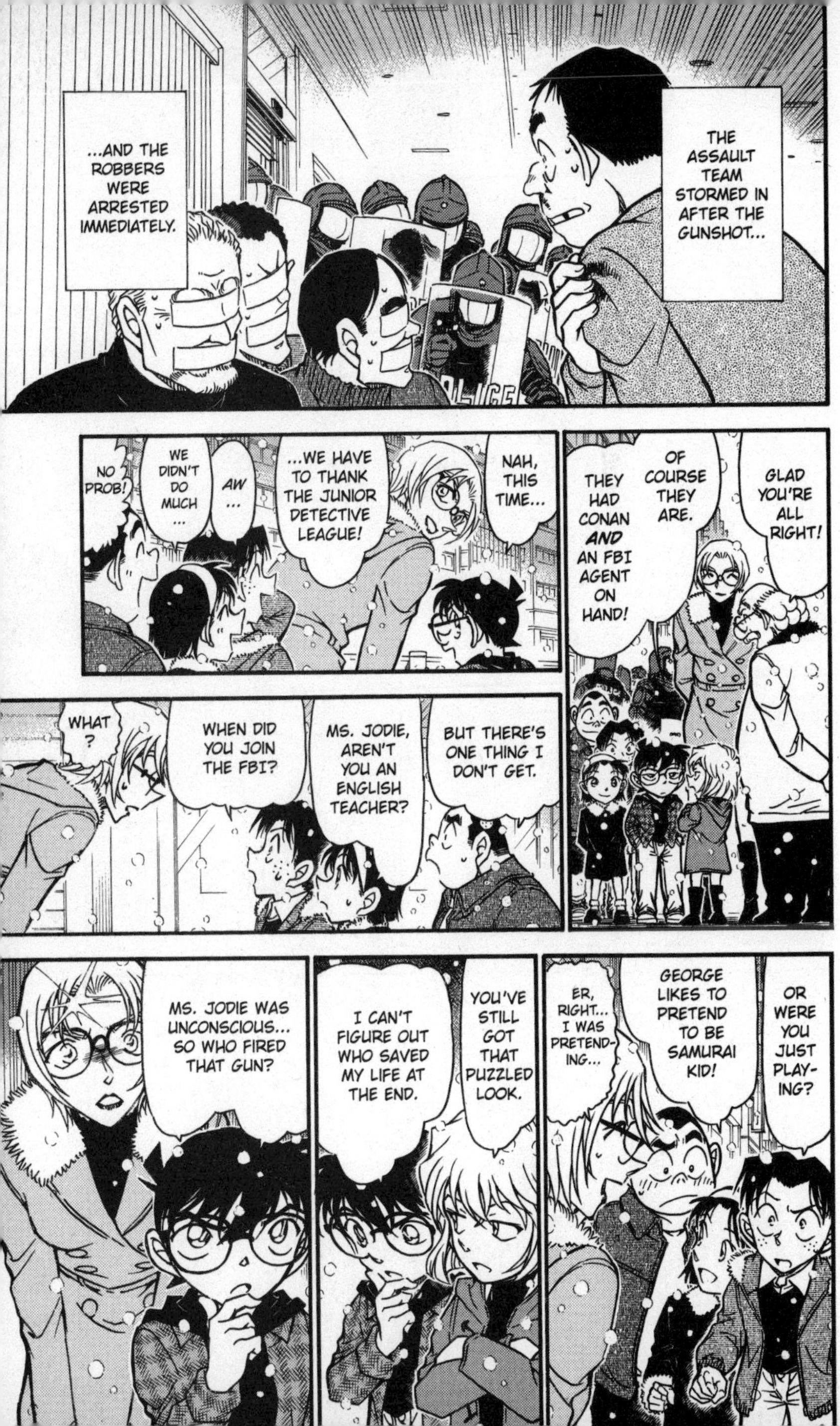
THE ASSAULT TEAM STORMED IN AFTER THE GUNSHOT...
...AND THE ROBBERS WERE ARRESTED IMMEDIATELY.
POLICE
GLAD YOU'RE ALL RIGHT!
OF COURSE THEY ARE.
THEY HAD CONAN AND AN FBI AGENT ON HAND!
NAH, THIS TIME...
...WE HAVE TO THANK THE JUNIOR DETECTIVE LEAGUE!
AW...
WE DIDN'T DO MUCH...
NO PROB!
BUT THERE'S ONE THING I DON'T GET.
MS. JODIE, AREN'T YOU AN ENGLISH TEACHER?
WHEN DID YOU JOIN THE FBI?
WHAT?
OR WERE YOU JUST PLAYING?
GEORGE LIKES TO PRETEND TO BE SAMURAI KID!
ER, RIGHT... I WAS PRETENDING...
YOU'VE STILL GOT THAT PUZZLED LOOK.
I CAN'T FIGURE OUT WHO SAVED MY LIFE AT THE END.
MS. JODIE WAS UNCONSCIOUS... SO WHO FIRED THAT GUN?

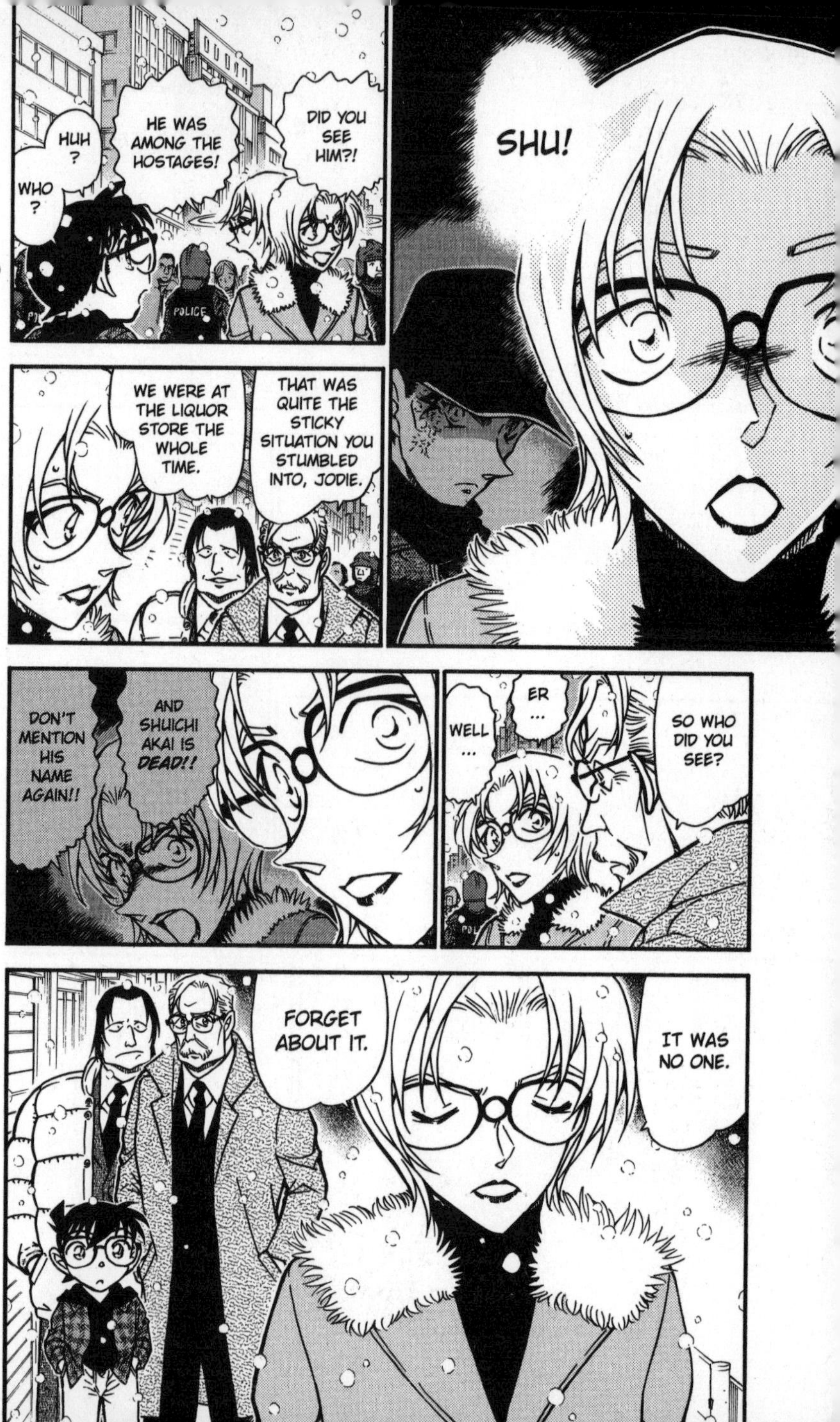
SHU!
DID YOU SEE HIM?!
HE WAS AMONG THE HOSTAGES!
HUH?
WHO?
THAT WAS QUITE THE STICKY SITUATION YOU STUMBLED INTO, JODIE.
WE WERE AT THE LIQUOR STORE THE WHOLE TIME.
SO WHO DID YOU SEE?
ER...
WELL...
AND SHUICHI AKAI IS *DEAD!!*
DON'T MENTION HIS NAME AGAIN!!
IT WAS NO ONE.
FORGET ABOUT IT.

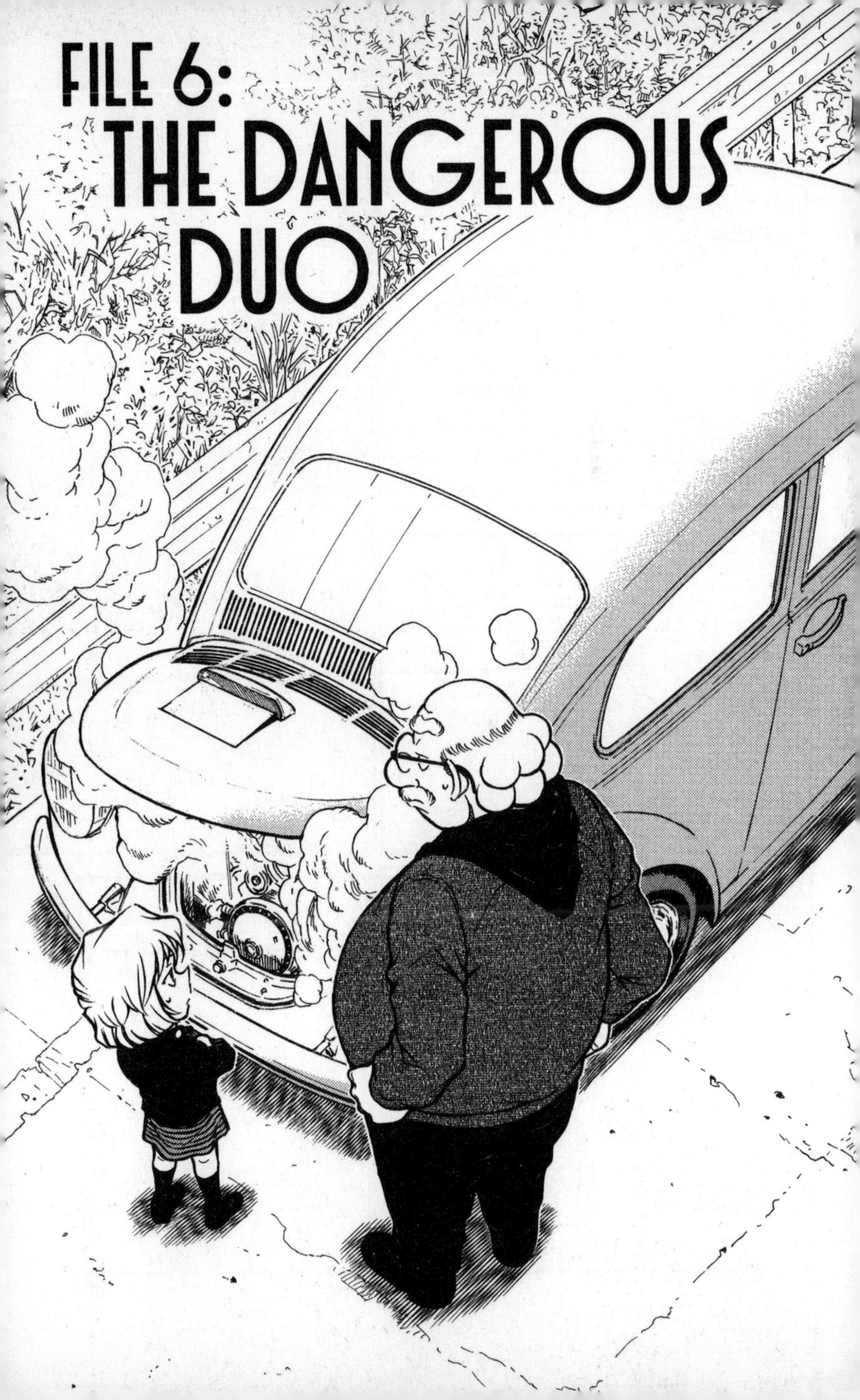
FILE 6:
THE DANGEROUS DUO

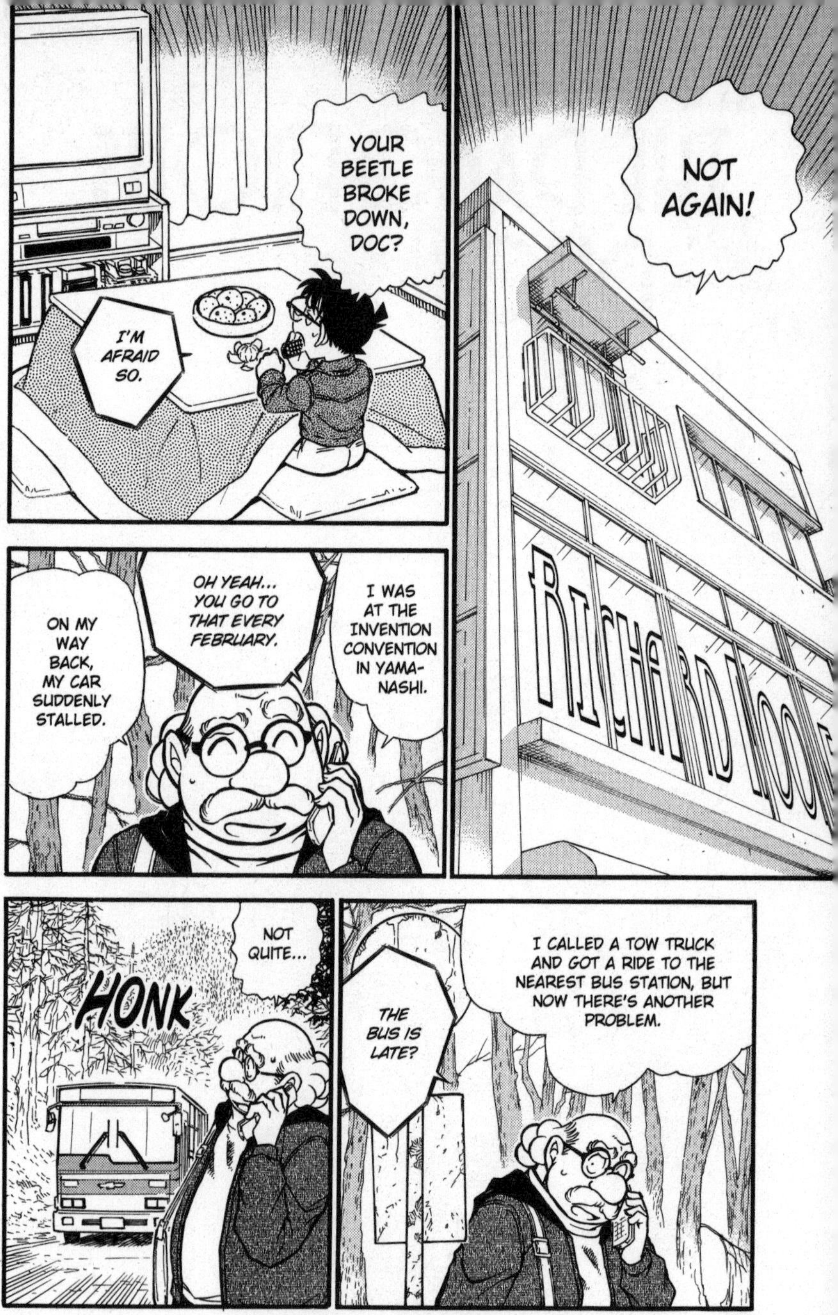
NOT AGAIN!
YOUR BEETLE BROKE DOWN, DOC?
I'M AFRAID SO.
I WAS AT THE INVENTION CONVENTION IN YAMA-NASHI.
OH YEAH... YOU GO TO THAT EVERY FEBRUARY.
ON MY WAY BACK, MY CAR SUDDENLY STALLED.
I CALLED A TOW TRUCK AND GOT A RIDE TO THE NEAREST BUS STATION, BUT NOW THERE'S ANOTHER PROBLEM.
THE BUS IS LATE?
NOT QUITE...
HONK

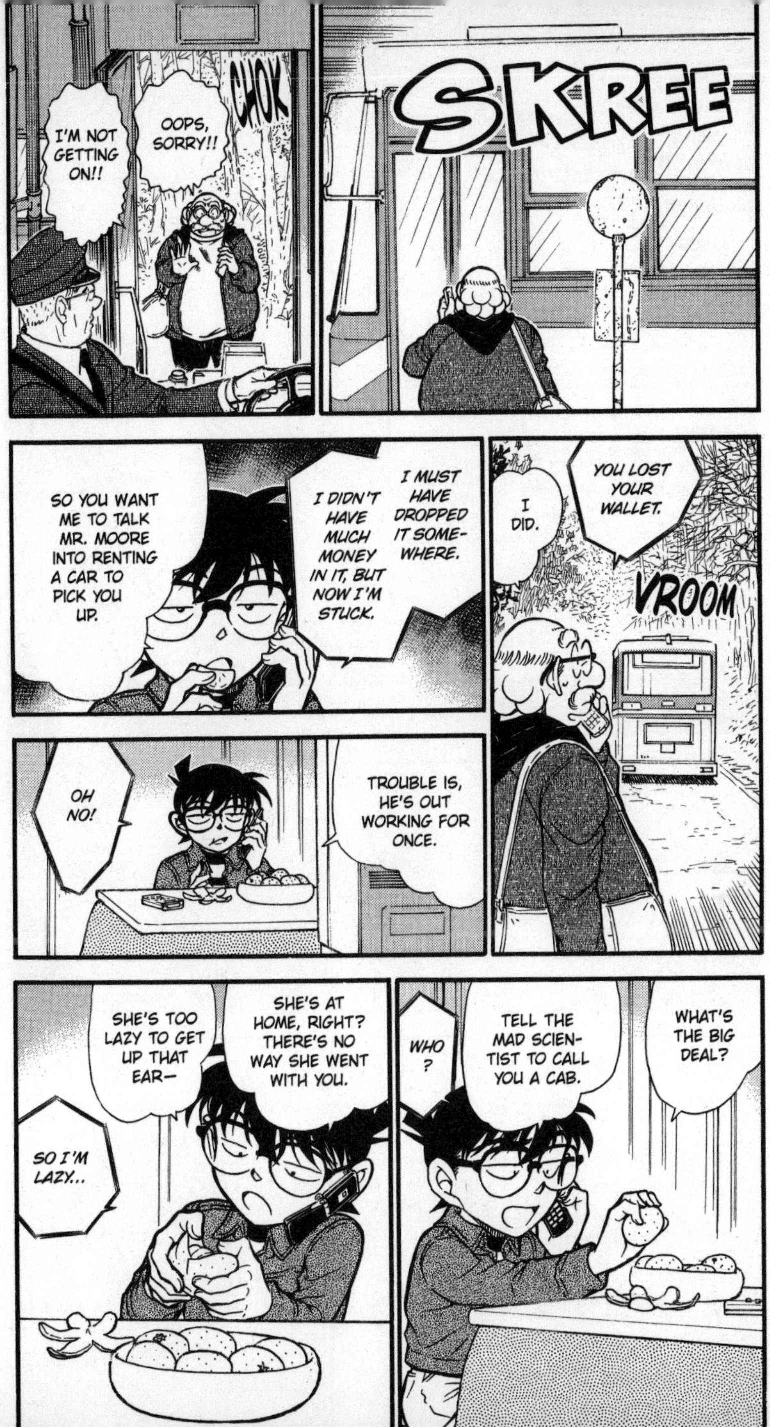
SKREE
CHOK
OOPS, SORRY!!
I'M NOT GETTING ON!!
YOU LOST YOUR WALLET.
I DID.
VROOM
I MUST HAVE DROPPED IT SOME-WHERE.
I DIDN'T HAVE MUCH MONEY IN IT, BUT NOW I'M STUCK.
SO YOU WANT ME TO TALK MR. MOORE INTO RENTING A CAR TO PICK YOU UP.
TROUBLE IS, HE'S OUT WORKING FOR ONCE.
OH NO!
WHAT'S THE BIG DEAL?
TELL THE MAD SCIEN-TIST TO CALL YOU A CAB.
WHO?
SHE'S AT HOME, RIGHT? THERE'S NO WAY SHE WENT WITH YOU.
SHE'S TOO LAZY TO GET UP THAT EAR—
SO I'M LAZY...

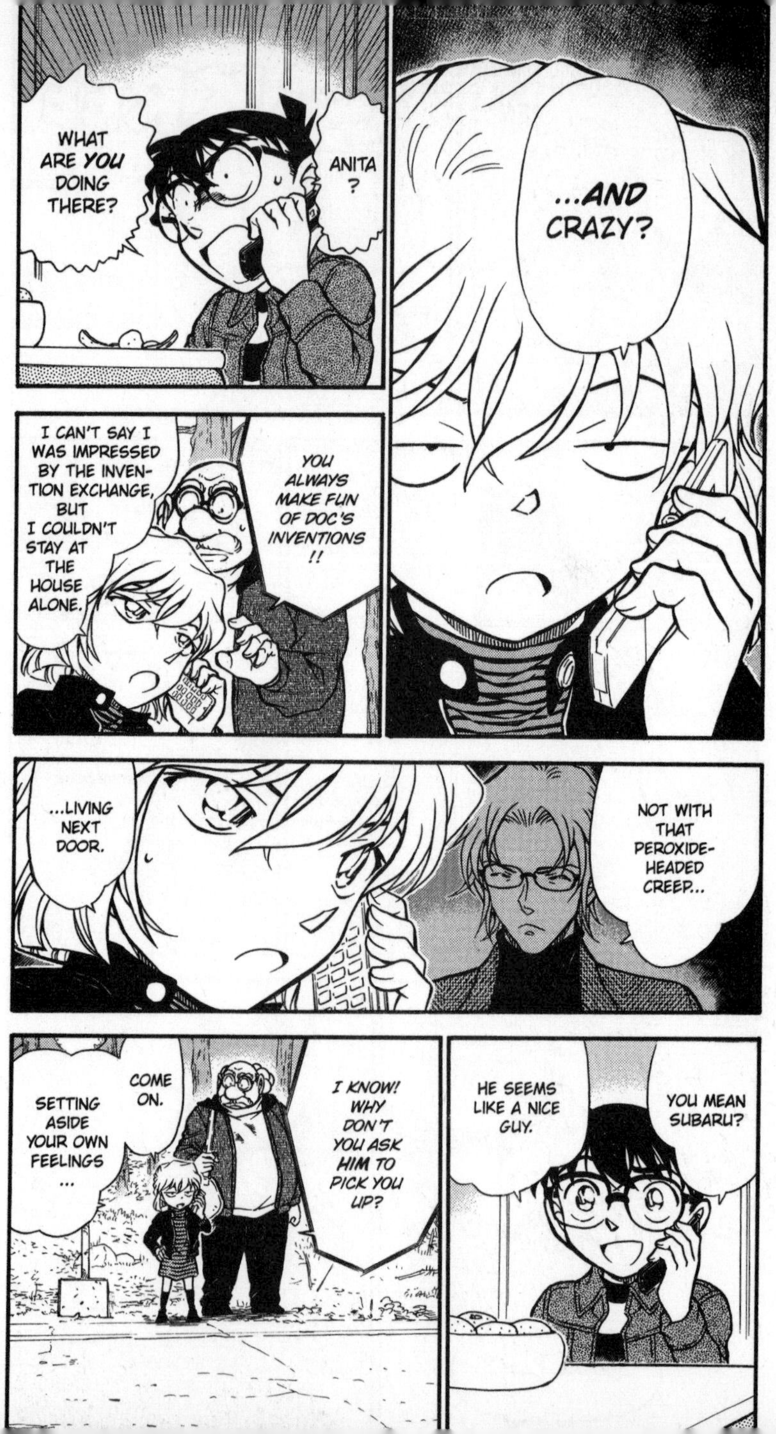
...AND CRAZY?
ANITA ?
WHAT ARE YOU DOING THERE?
YOU ALWAYS MAKE FUN OF DOC'S INVENTIONS !!
I CAN'T SAY I WAS IMPRESSED BY THE INVENTION EXCHANGE, BUT I COULDN'T STAY AT THE HOUSE ALONE.
NOT WITH THAT PEROXIDE-HEADED CREEP...
...LIVING NEXT DOOR.
YOU MEAN SUBARU?
HE SEEMS LIKE A NICE GUY.
I KNOW! WHY DON'T YOU ASK HIM TO PICK YOU UP?
COME ON.
SETTING ASIDE YOUR OWN FEELINGS ...

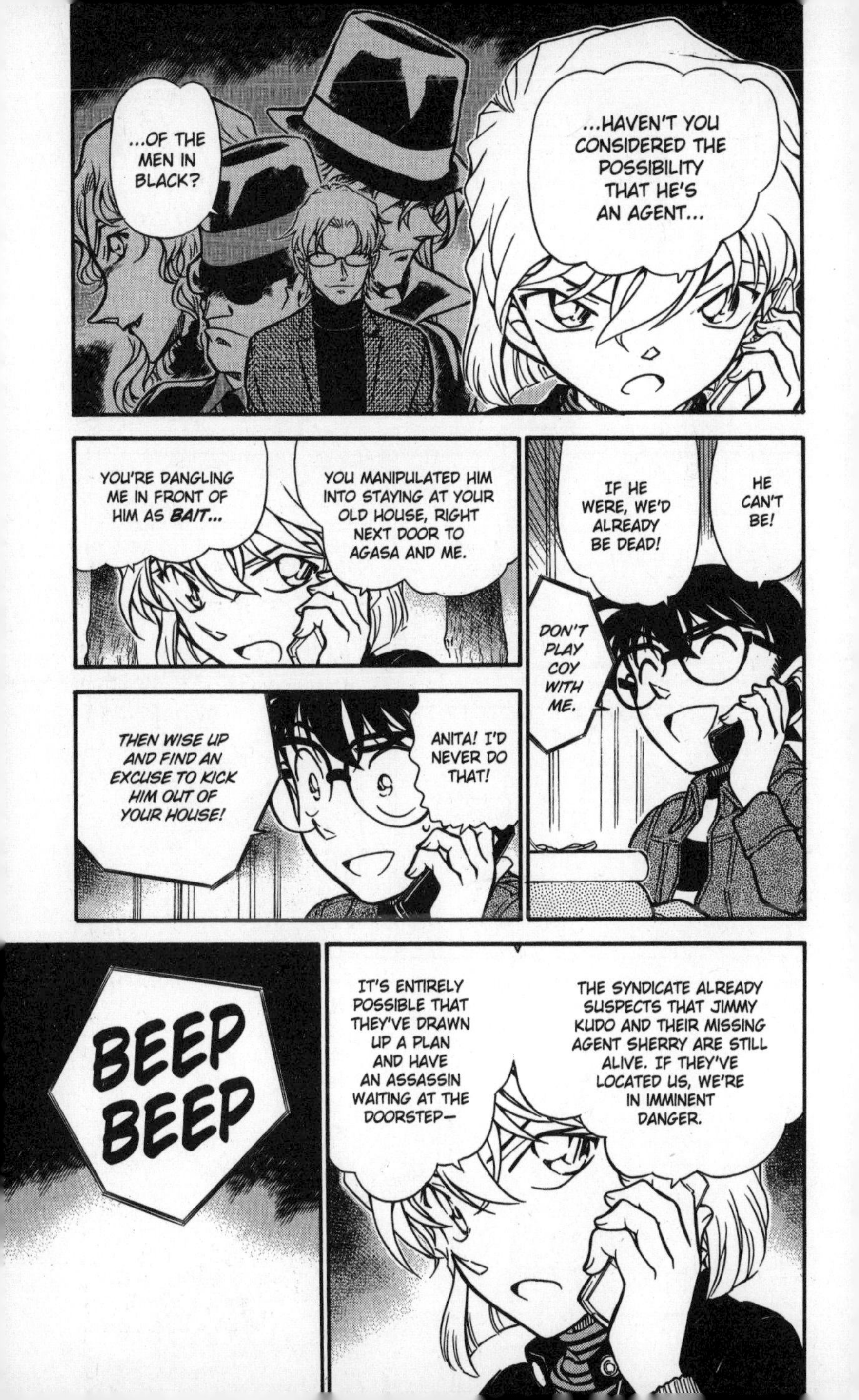
...HAVEN'T YOU CONSIDERED THE POSSIBILITY THAT HE'S AN AGENT...
...OF THE MEN IN BLACK?
HE CAN'T BE!
IF HE WERE, WE'D ALREADY BE DEAD!
DON'T PLAY COY WITH ME.
YOU MANIPULATED HIM INTO STAYING AT YOUR OLD HOUSE, RIGHT NEXT DOOR TO AGASA AND ME.
YOU'RE DANGLING ME IN FRONT OF HIM AS *BAIT*...
ANITA! I'D NEVER DO THAT!
THEN WISE UP AND FIND AN EXCUSE TO KICK HIM OUT OF YOUR HOUSE!
THE SYNDICATE ALREADY SUSPECTS THAT JIMMY KUDO AND THEIR MISSING AGENT SHERRY ARE STILL ALIVE. IF THEY'VE LOCATED US, WE'RE IN IMMINENT DANGER.
IT'S ENTIRELY POSSIBLE THAT THEY'VE DRAWN UP A PLAN AND HAVE AN ASSASSIN WAITING AT THE DOORSTEP—
BEEP BEEP

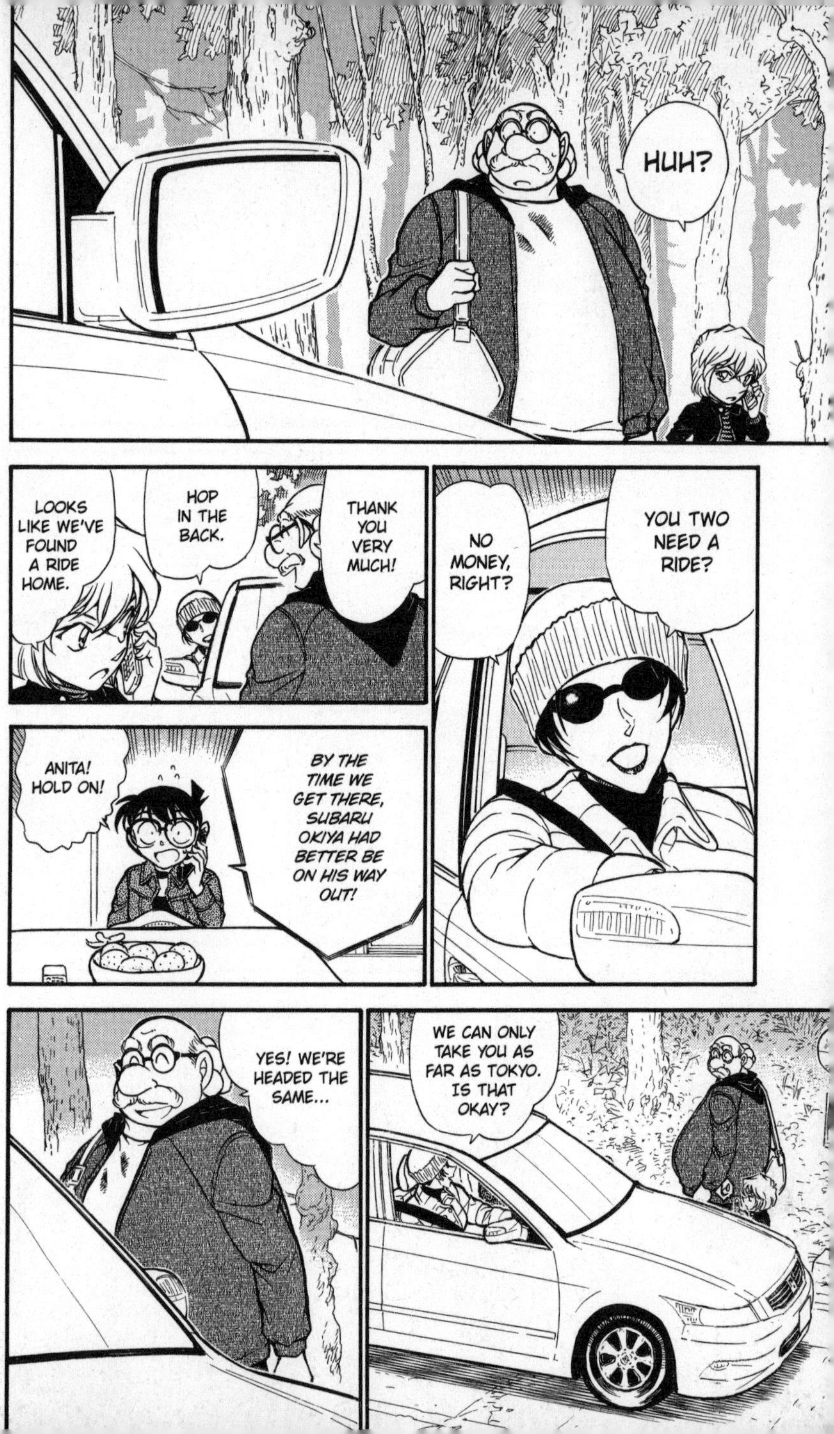
HUH?
YOU TWO NEED A RIDE?
NO MONEY, RIGHT?
THANK YOU VERY MUCH!
HOP IN THE BACK.
LOOKS LIKE WE'VE FOUND A RIDE HOME.
BY THE TIME WE GET THERE, SUBARU OKIYA HAD BETTER BE ON HIS WAY OUT!
ANITA! HOLD ON!
WE CAN ONLY TAKE YOU AS FAR AS TOKYO. IS THAT OKAY?
YES! WE'RE HEADED THE SAME...

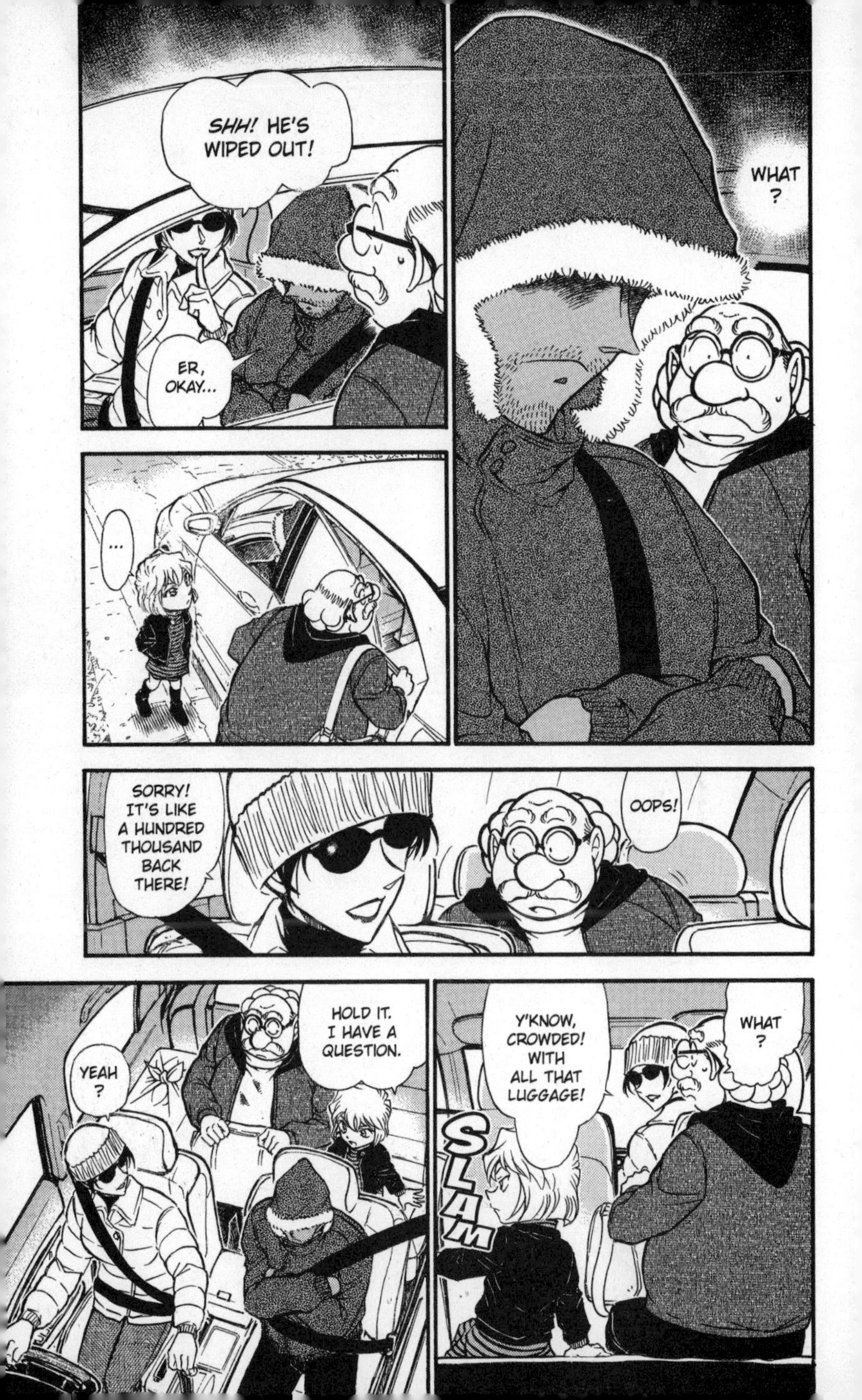
WHAT ?
SHH! HE'S WIPED OUT!
ER, OKAY...
...
OOPS!
SORRY! IT'S LIKE A HUNDRED THOUSAND BACK THERE!
WHAT ?
Y'KNOW, CROWDED! WITH ALL THAT LUGGAGE!
SLAM
HOLD IT. I HAVE A QUESTION.
YEAH ?

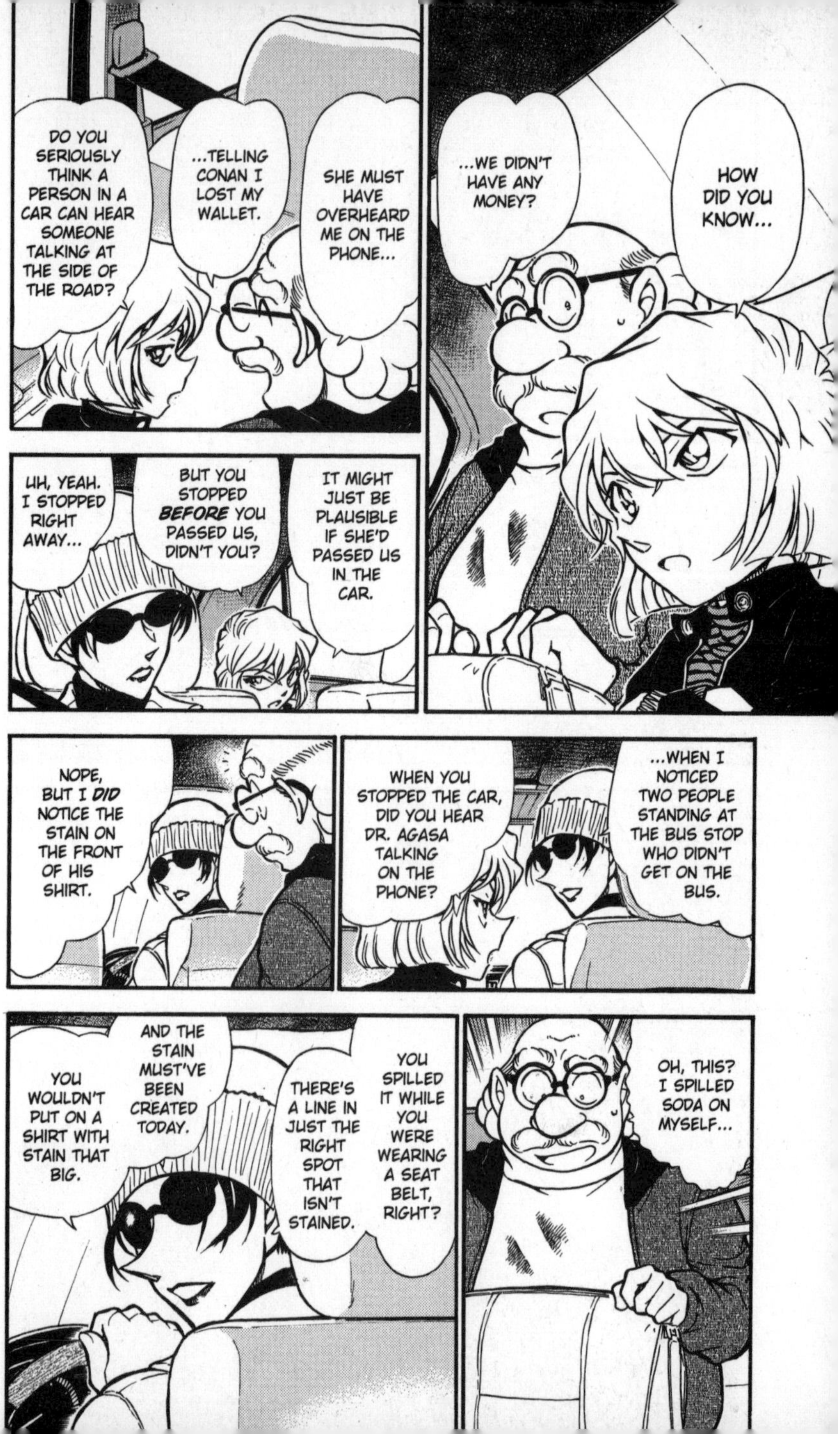
HOW DID YOU KNOW...
...WE DIDN'T HAVE ANY MONEY?
SHE MUST HAVE OVERHEARD ME ON THE PHONE...
...TELLING CONAN I LOST MY WALLET.
DO YOU SERIOUSLY THINK A PERSON IN A CAR CAN HEAR SOMEONE TALKING AT THE SIDE OF THE ROAD?
IT MIGHT JUST BE PLAUSIBLE IF SHE'D PASSED US IN THE CAR.
BUT YOU STOPPED *BEFORE* YOU PASSED US, DIDN'T YOU?
UH, YEAH. I STOPPED RIGHT AWAY...
...WHEN I NOTICED TWO PEOPLE STANDING AT THE BUS STOP WHO DIDN'T GET ON THE BUS.
WHEN YOU STOPPED THE CAR, DID YOU HEAR DR. AGASA TALKING ON THE PHONE?
NOPE, BUT I *DID* NOTICE THE STAIN ON THE FRONT OF HIS SHIRT.
OH, THIS? I SPILLED SODA ON MYSELF...
YOU SPILLED IT WHILE YOU WERE WEARING A SEAT BELT, RIGHT?
THERE'S A LINE IN JUST THE RIGHT SPOT THAT ISN'T STAINED.
AND THE STAIN MUST'VE BEEN CREATED TODAY.
YOU WOULDN'T PUT ON A SHIRT WITH STAIN THAT BIG.

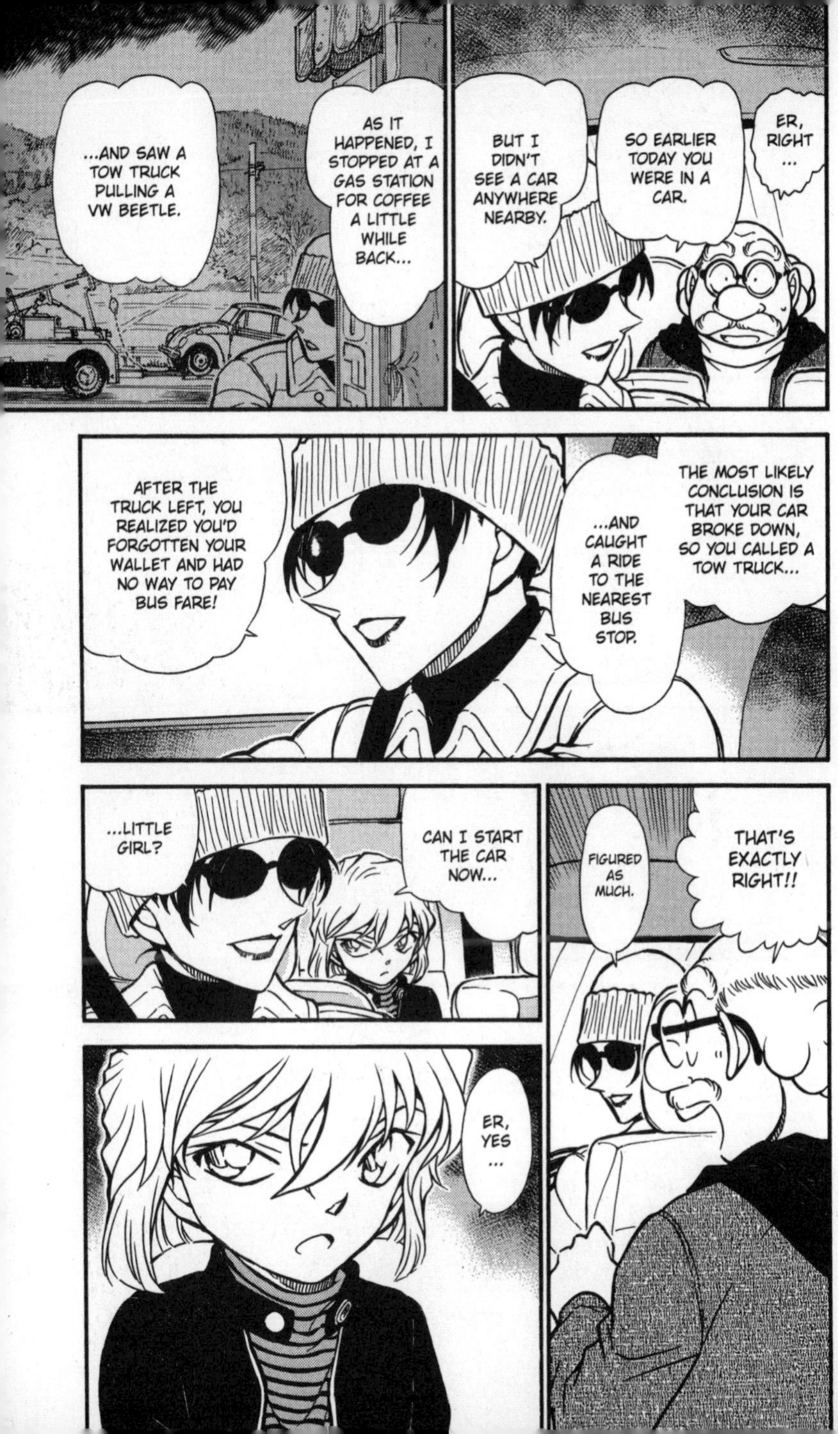
ER, RIGHT ...
SO EARLIER TODAY YOU WERE IN A CAR.
BUT I DIDN'T SEE A CAR ANYWHERE NEARBY.
AS IT HAPPENED, I STOPPED AT A GAS STATION FOR COFFEE A LITTLE WHILE BACK...
...AND SAW A TOW TRUCK PULLING A VW BEETLE.
THE MOST LIKELY CONCLUSION IS THAT YOUR CAR BROKE DOWN, SO YOU CALLED A TOW TRUCK...
...AND CAUGHT A RIDE TO THE NEAREST BUS STOP.
AFTER THE TRUCK LEFT, YOU REALIZED YOU'D FORGOTTEN YOUR WALLET AND HAD NO WAY TO PAY BUS FARE!
THAT'S EXACTLY RIGHT!!
FIGURED AS MUCH.
CAN I START THE CAR NOW...
...LITTLE GIRL?
ER, YES ...

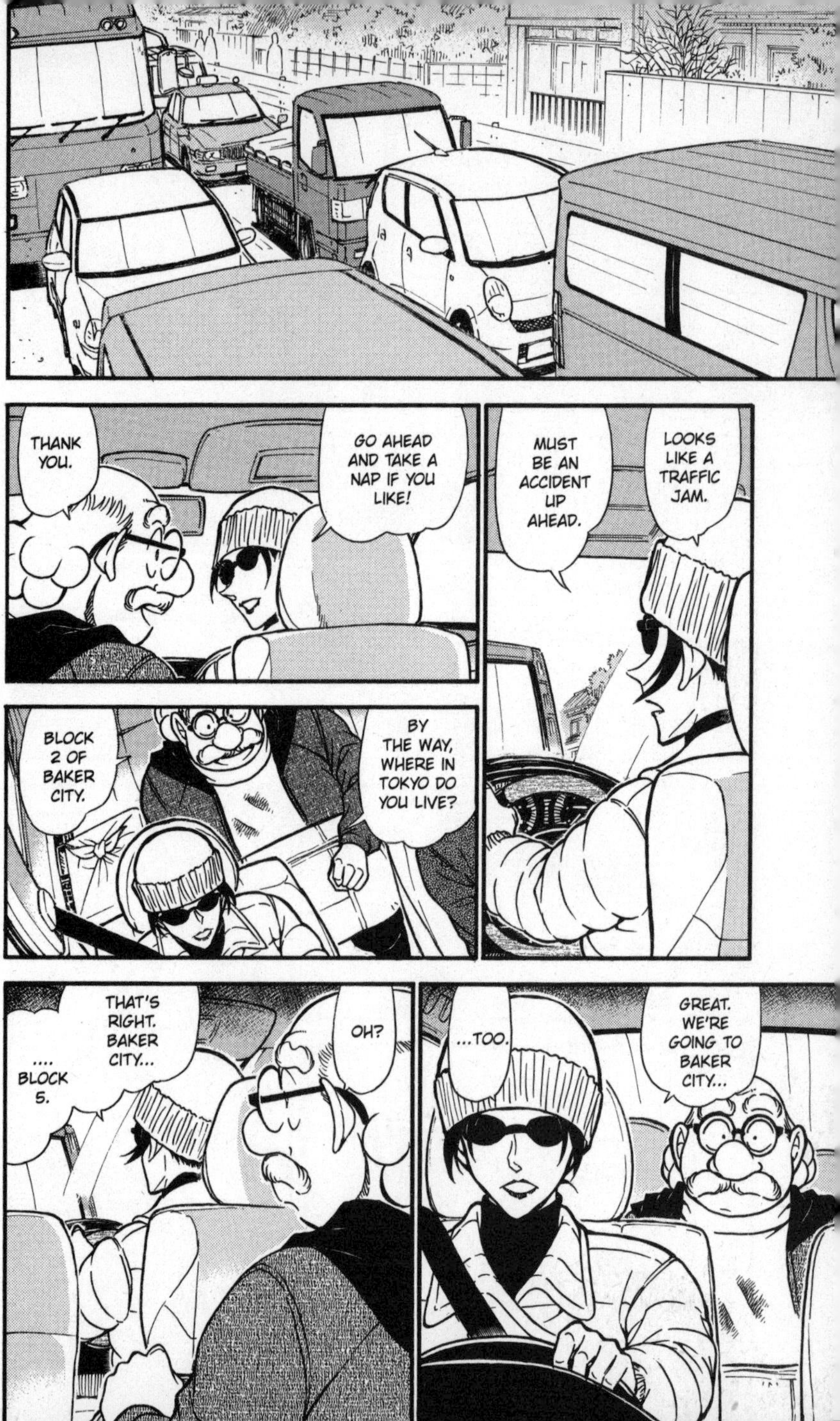
LOOKS LIKE A TRAFFIC JAM.
MUST BE AN ACCIDENT UP AHEAD.
GO AHEAD AND TAKE A NAP IF YOU LIKE!
THANK YOU.
BY THE WAY, WHERE IN TOKYO DO YOU LIVE?
BLOCK 2 OF BAKER CITY.
GREAT. WE'RE GOING TO BAKER CITY...
...TOO.
OH?
THAT'S RIGHT. BAKER CITY...
.... BLOCK 5.

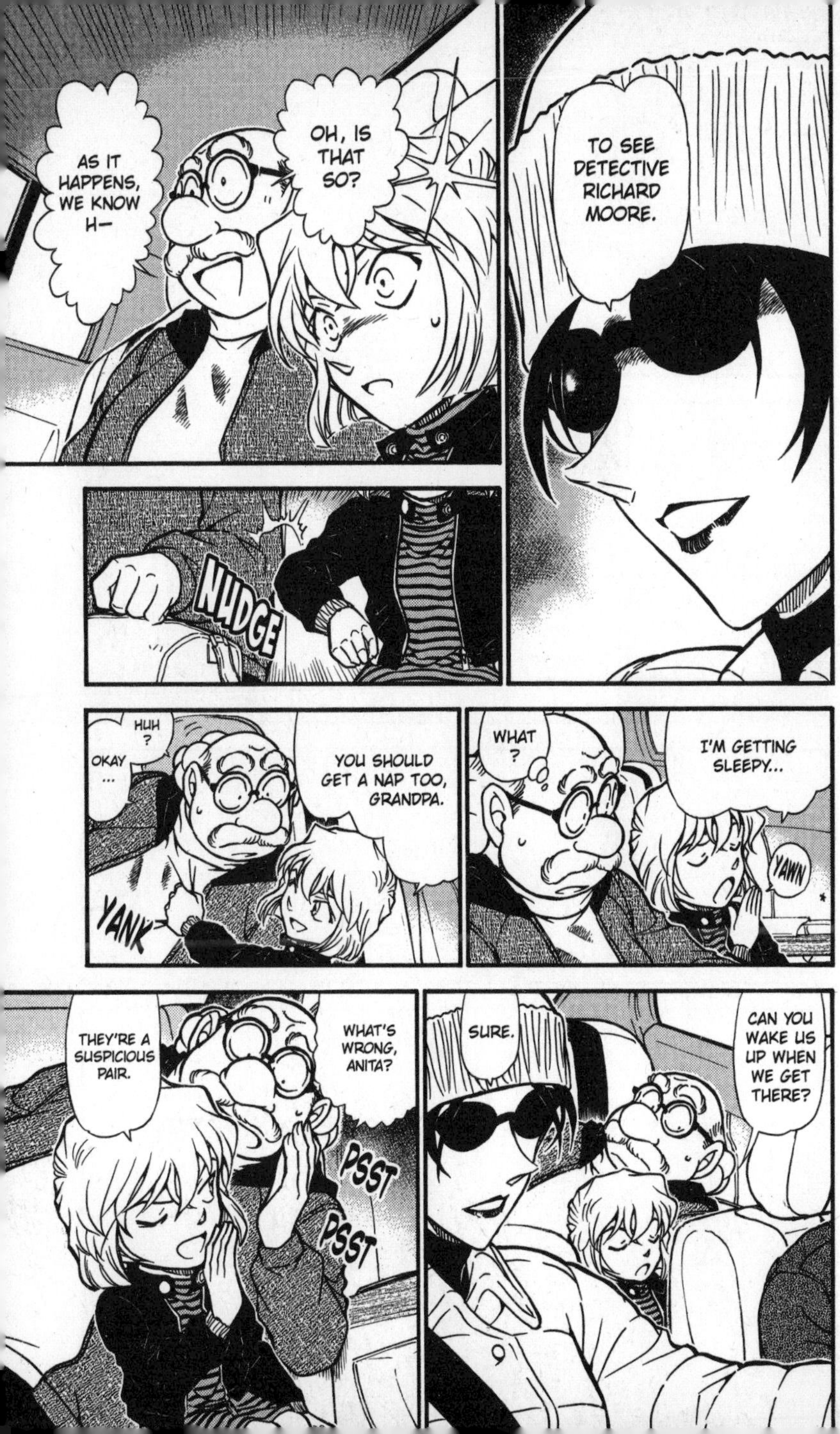
TO SEE DETECTIVE RICHARD MOORE.
OH, IS THAT SO?
AS IT HAPPENS, WE KNOW H—
NUDGE
I'M GETTING SLEEPY...
YAWN
WHAT?
YOU SHOULD GET A NAP TOO, GRANDPA.
YANK
HUH? OKAY...
CAN YOU WAKE US UP WHEN WE GET THERE?
SURE.
WHAT'S WRONG, ANITA?
THEY'RE A SUSPICIOUS PAIR.
PSST
PSST

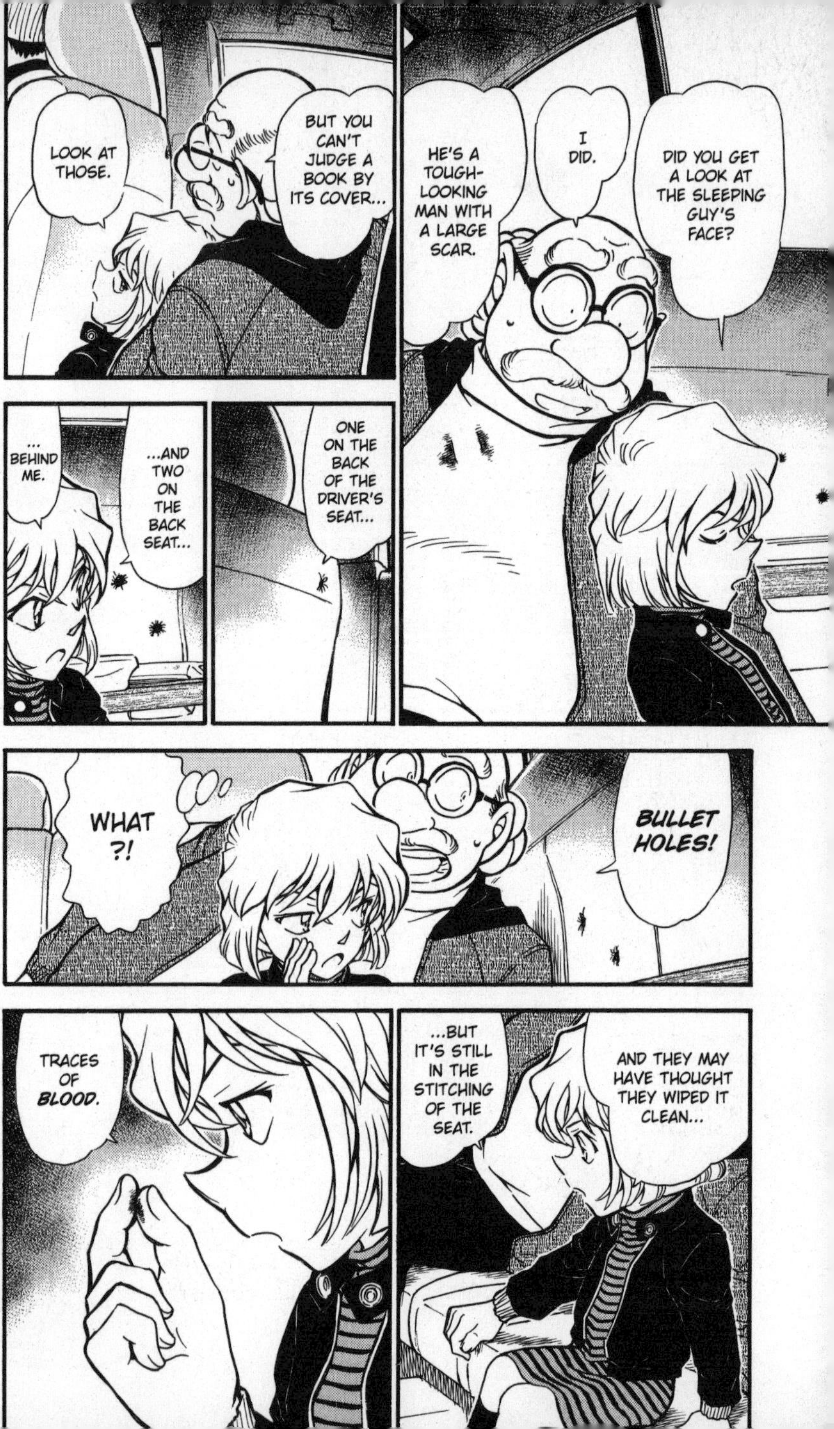
DID YOU GET A LOOK AT THE SLEEPING GUY'S FACE?
I DID.
HE'S A TOUGH-LOOKING MAN WITH A LARGE SCAR.
BUT YOU CAN'T JUDGE A BOOK BY ITS COVER...
LOOK AT THOSE.
ONE ON THE BACK OF THE DRIVER'S SEAT...
...AND TWO ON THE BACK SEAT...
... BEHIND ME.
BULLET HOLES!
WHAT ?!
AND THEY MAY HAVE THOUGHT THEY WIPED IT CLEAN...
...BUT IT'S STILL IN THE STITCHING OF THE SEAT.
TRACES OF BLOOD.

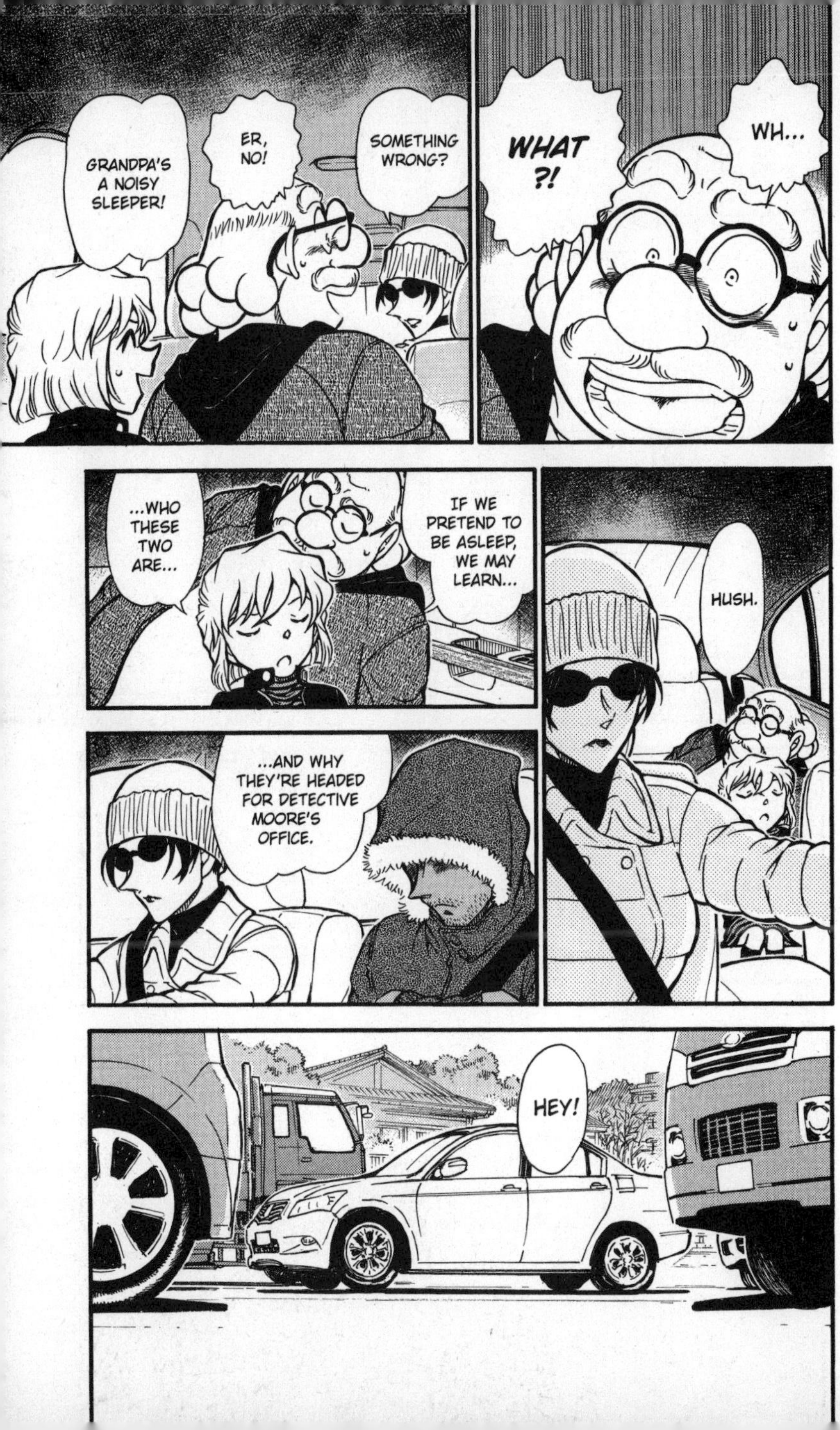
WH...
WHAT ?!
SOMETHING WRONG?
ER, NO!
GRANDPA'S A NOISY SLEEPER!
HUSH.
IF WE PRETEND TO BE ASLEEP, WE MAY LEARN...
...WHO THESE TWO ARE...
...AND WHY THEY'RE HEADED FOR DETECTIVE MOORE'S OFFICE.
HEY!

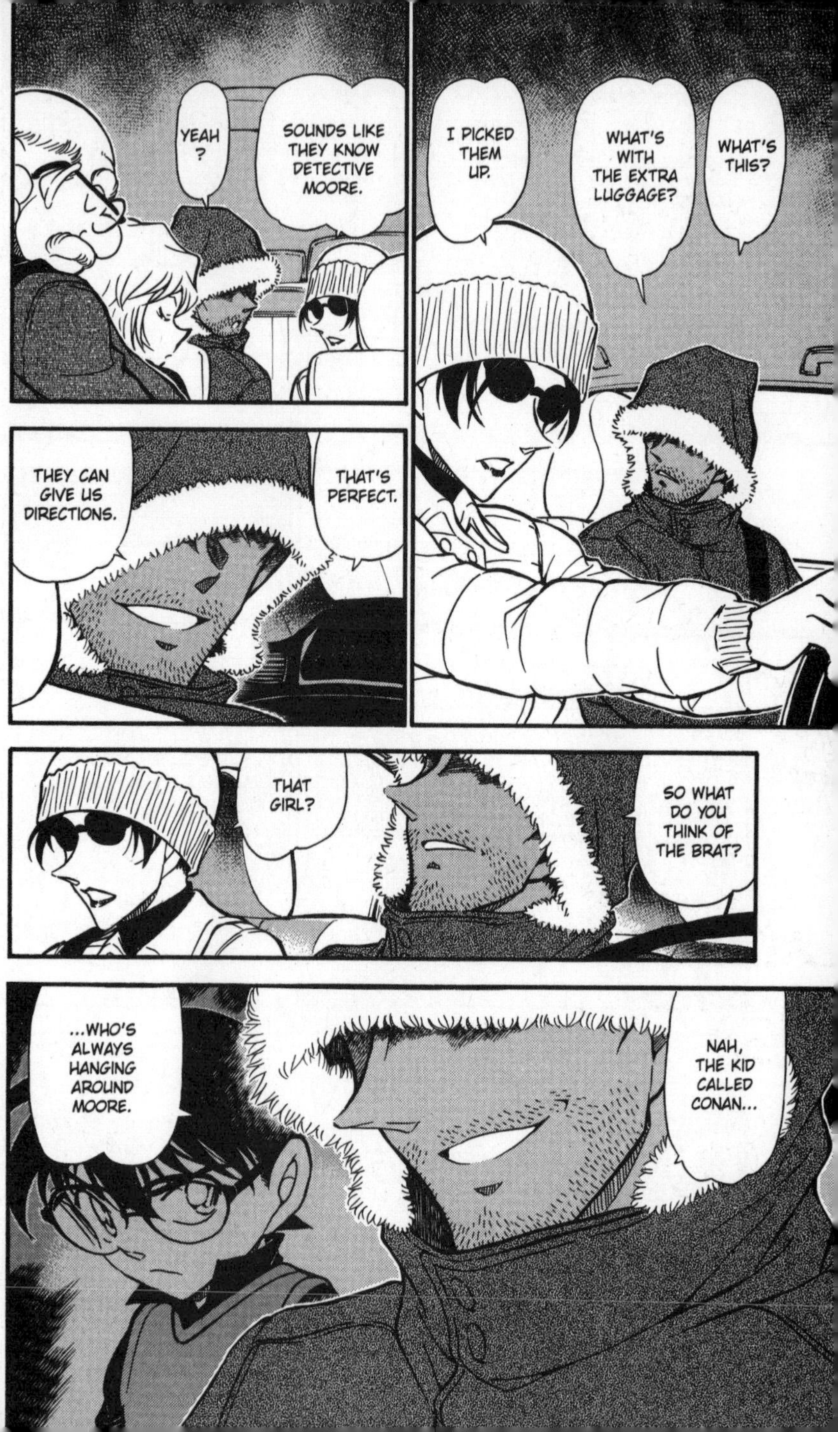
WHAT'S THIS?
WHAT'S WITH THE EXTRA LUGGAGE?
I PICKED THEM UP.
SOUNDS LIKE THEY KNOW DETECTIVE MOORE.
YEAH?
THAT'S PERFECT.
THEY CAN GIVE US DIRECTIONS.
SO WHAT DO YOU THINK OF THE BRAT?
THAT GIRL?
NAH, THE KID CALLED CONAN...
...WHO'S ALWAYS HANGING AROUND MOORE.

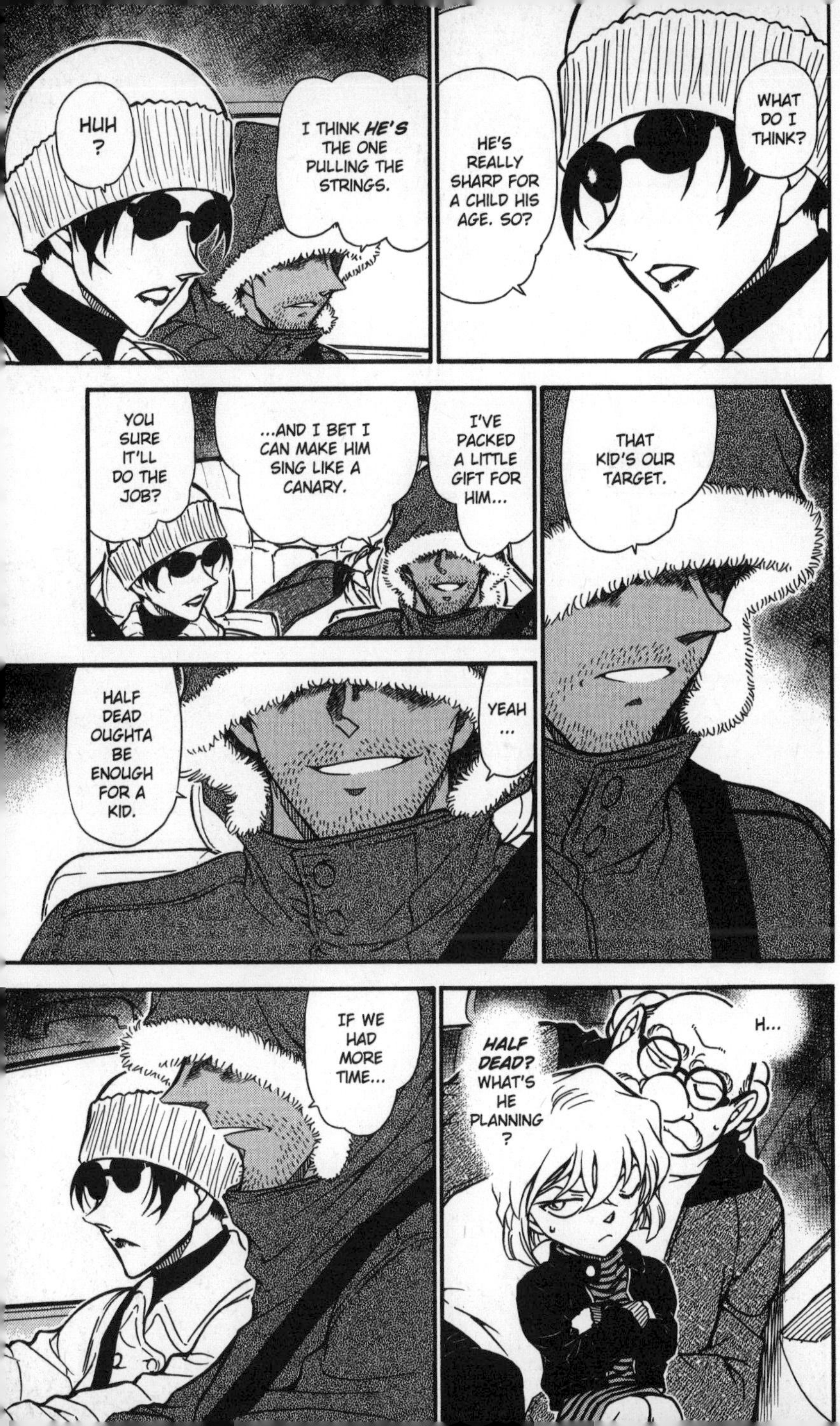
WHAT DO I THINK?
HE'S REALLY SHARP FOR A CHILD HIS AGE. SO?
I THINK **HE'S** THE ONE PULLING THE STRINGS.
HUH?
THAT KID'S OUR TARGET.
I'VE PACKED A LITTLE GIFT FOR HIM...
...AND I BET I CAN MAKE HIM SING LIKE A CANARY.
YOU SURE IT'LL DO THE JOB?
YEAH...
HALF DEAD OUGHTA BE ENOUGH FOR A KID.
H...
HALF DEAD? WHAT'S HE PLANNING?
IF WE HAD MORE TIME...

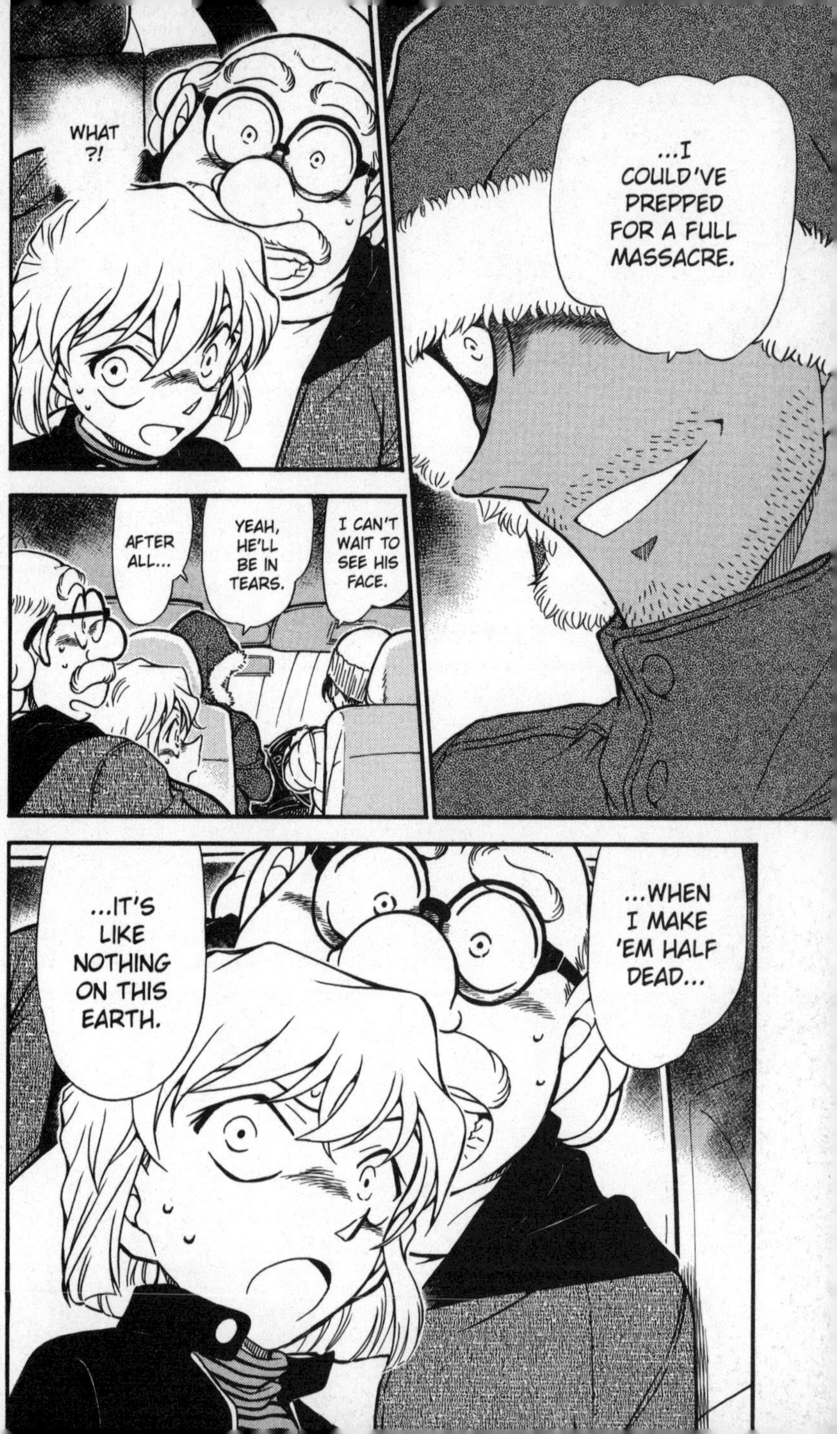
...I COULD'VE PREPPED FOR A FULL MASSACRE.
WHAT ?!
I CAN'T WAIT TO SEE HIS FACE.
YEAH, HE'LL BE IN TEARS.
AFTER ALL...
...WHEN I MAKE 'EM HALF DEAD...
...IT'S LIKE NOTHING ON THIS EARTH.

FILE 7: HALF DEAD

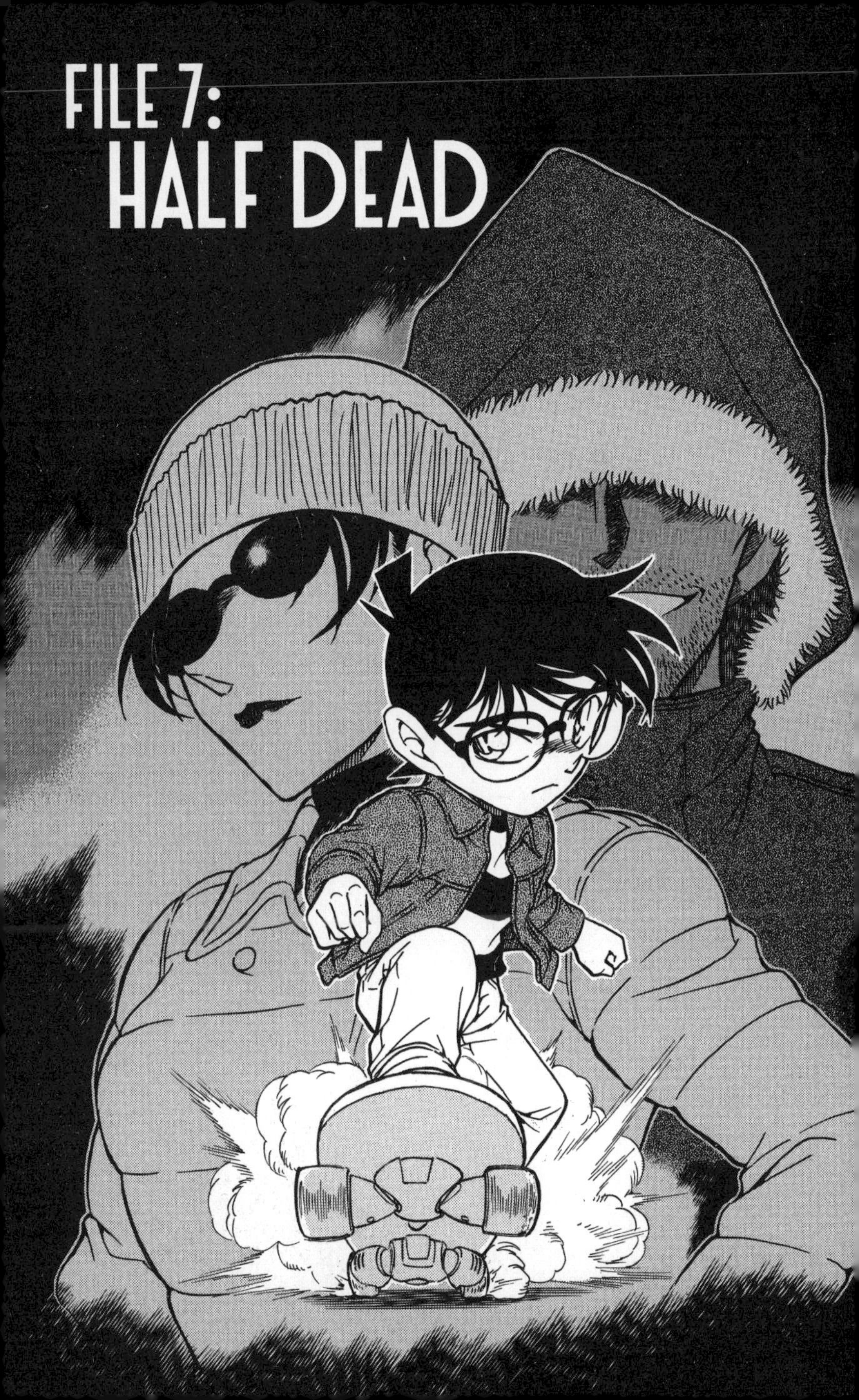

...TO SEE HIS FACE.

YEAH...

I CAN'T WAIT...

AFTER ALL...

...HE'LL BE IN TEARS.

...IT'S LIKE NOTHING ON THIS EARTH.

...WHEN I MAKE 'EM HALF DEAD...

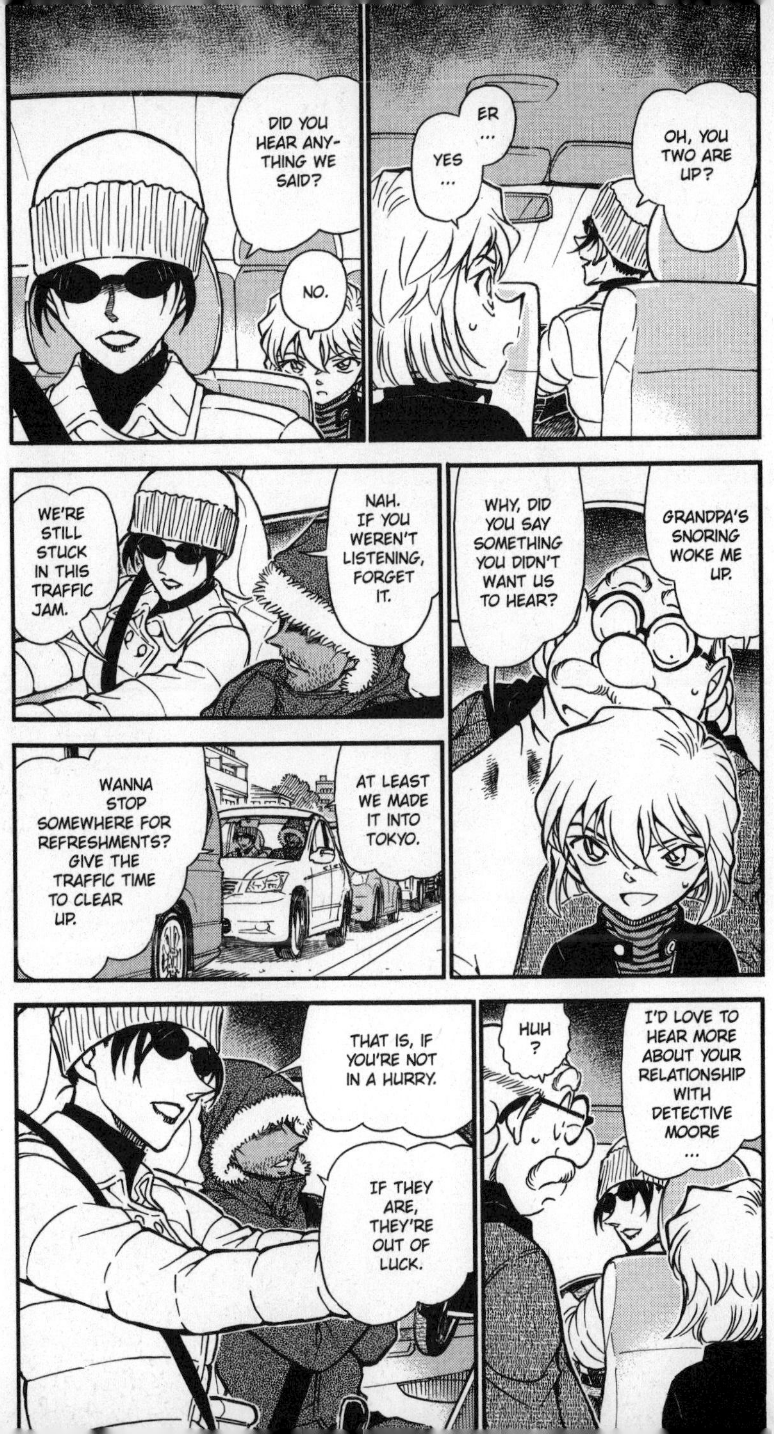
OH, YOU TWO ARE UP?
ER ...
YES ...
DID YOU HEAR ANY-THING WE SAID?
NO.
GRANDPA'S SNORING WOKE ME UP.
WHY, DID YOU SAY SOMETHING YOU DIDN'T WANT US TO HEAR?
NAH. IF YOU WEREN'T LISTENING, FORGET IT.
WE'RE STILL STUCK IN THIS TRAFFIC JAM.
AT LEAST WE MADE IT INTO TOKYO.
WANNA STOP SOMEWHERE FOR REFRESHMENTS? GIVE THE TRAFFIC TIME TO CLEAR UP.
I'D LOVE TO HEAR MORE ABOUT YOUR RELATIONSHIP WITH DETECTIVE MOORE ...
HUH ?
THAT IS, IF YOU'RE NOT IN A HURRY.
IF THEY ARE, THEY'RE OUT OF LUCK.

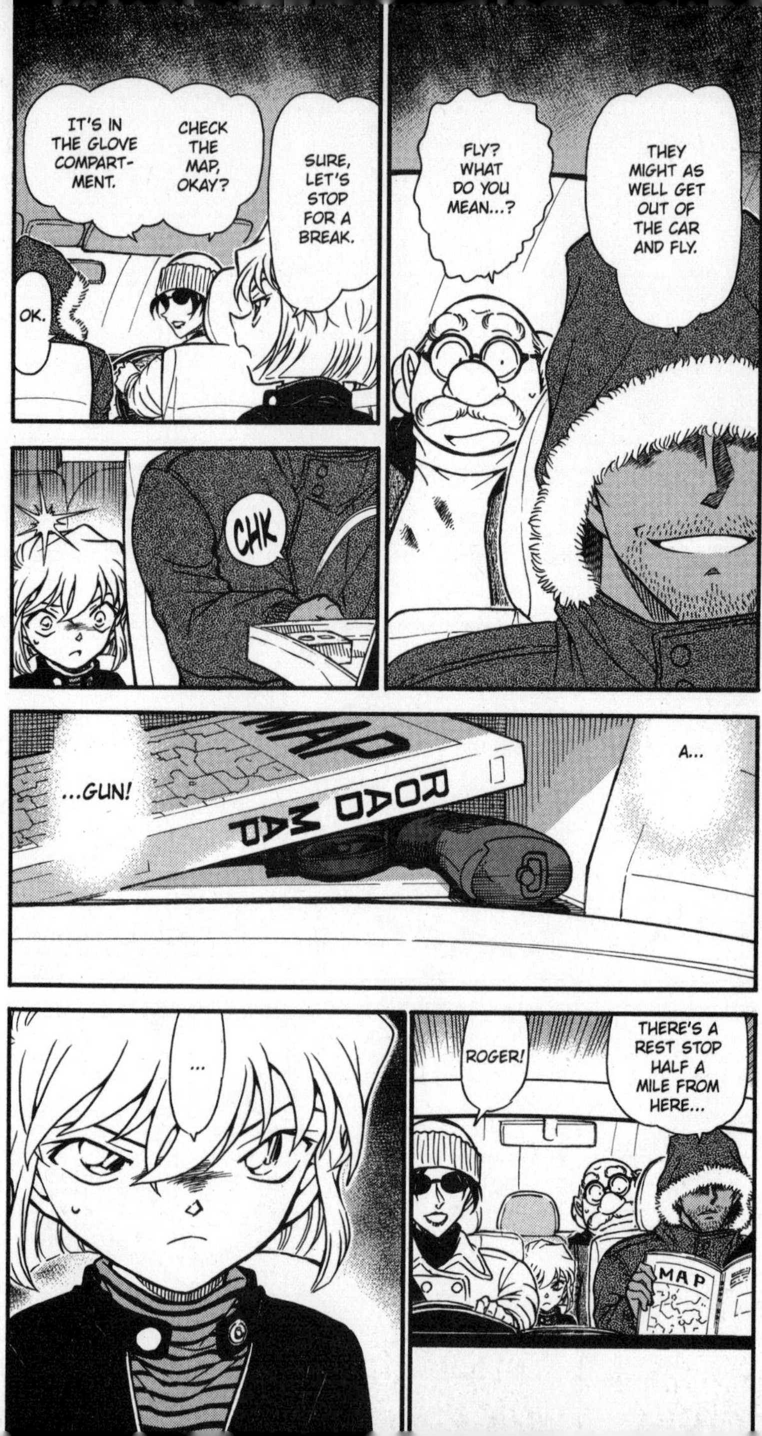

THEY MIGHT AS WELL GET OUT OF THE CAR AND FLY.
FLY? WHAT DO YOU MEAN...?
SURE, LET'S STOP FOR A BREAK.
CHECK THE MAP, OKAY?
IT'S IN THE GLOVE COMPARTMENT.
OK.
CHK
A...
ROAD MAP
...GUN!
THERE'S A REST STOP HALF A MILE FROM HERE...
ROGER!
MAP
...

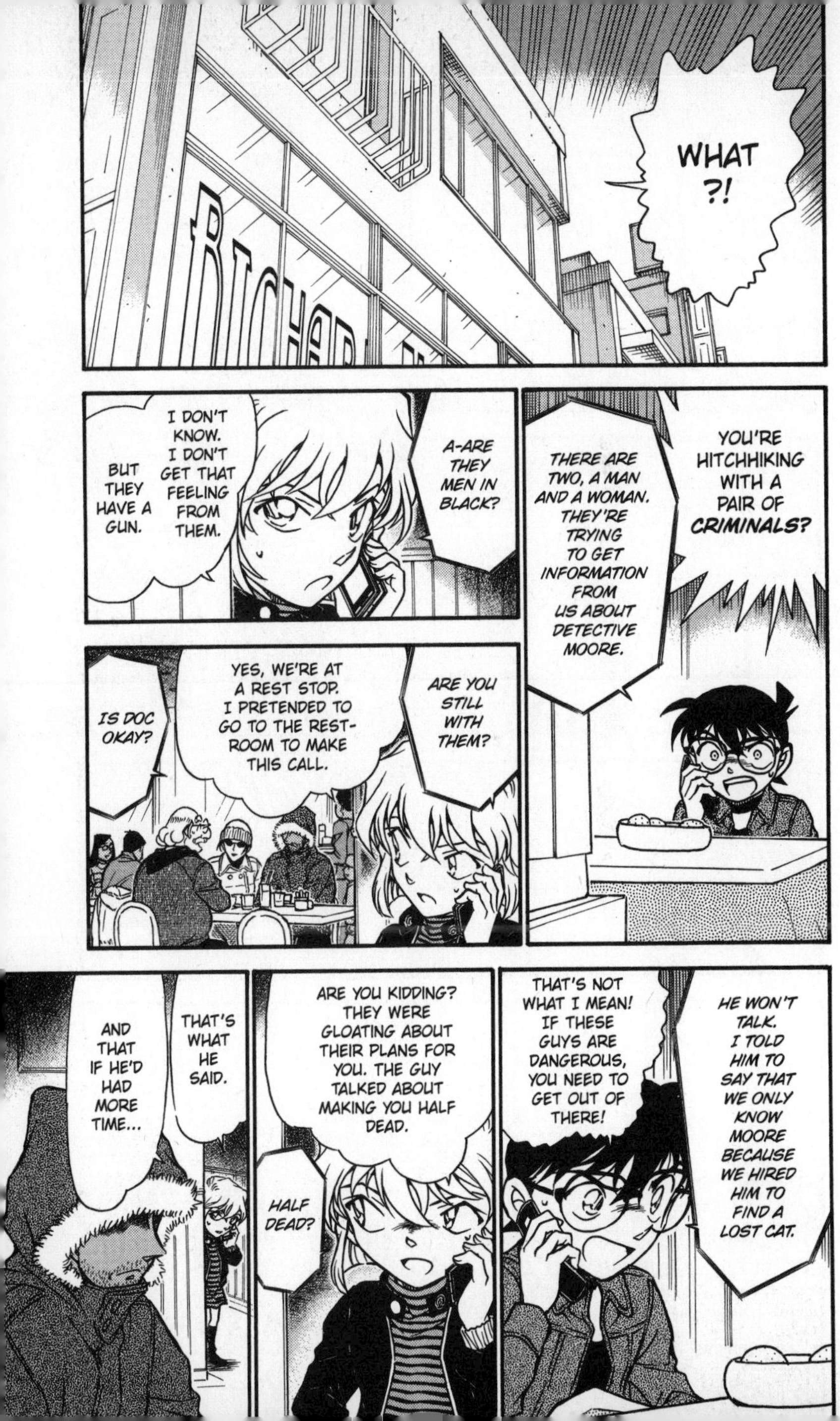
WHAT ?!
YOU'RE HITCHHIKING WITH A PAIR OF CRIMINALS?
THERE ARE TWO, A MAN AND A WOMAN. THEY'RE TRYING TO GET INFORMATION FROM US ABOUT DETECTIVE MOORE.
A-ARE THEY MEN IN BLACK?
I DON'T KNOW. I DON'T GET THAT FEELING FROM THEM.
BUT THEY HAVE A GUN.
ARE YOU STILL WITH THEM?
YES, WE'RE AT A REST STOP. I PRETENDED TO GO TO THE REST-ROOM TO MAKE THIS CALL.
IS DOC OKAY?
HE WON'T TALK. I TOLD HIM TO SAY THAT WE ONLY KNOW MOORE BECAUSE WE HIRED HIM TO FIND A LOST CAT.
THAT'S NOT WHAT I MEAN! IF THESE GUYS ARE DANGEROUS, YOU NEED TO GET OUT OF THERE!
ARE YOU KIDDING? THEY WERE GLOATING ABOUT THEIR PLANS FOR YOU. THE GUY TALKED ABOUT MAKING YOU HALF DEAD.
HALF DEAD?
THAT'S WHAT HE SAID.
AND THAT IF HE'D HAD MORE TIME...

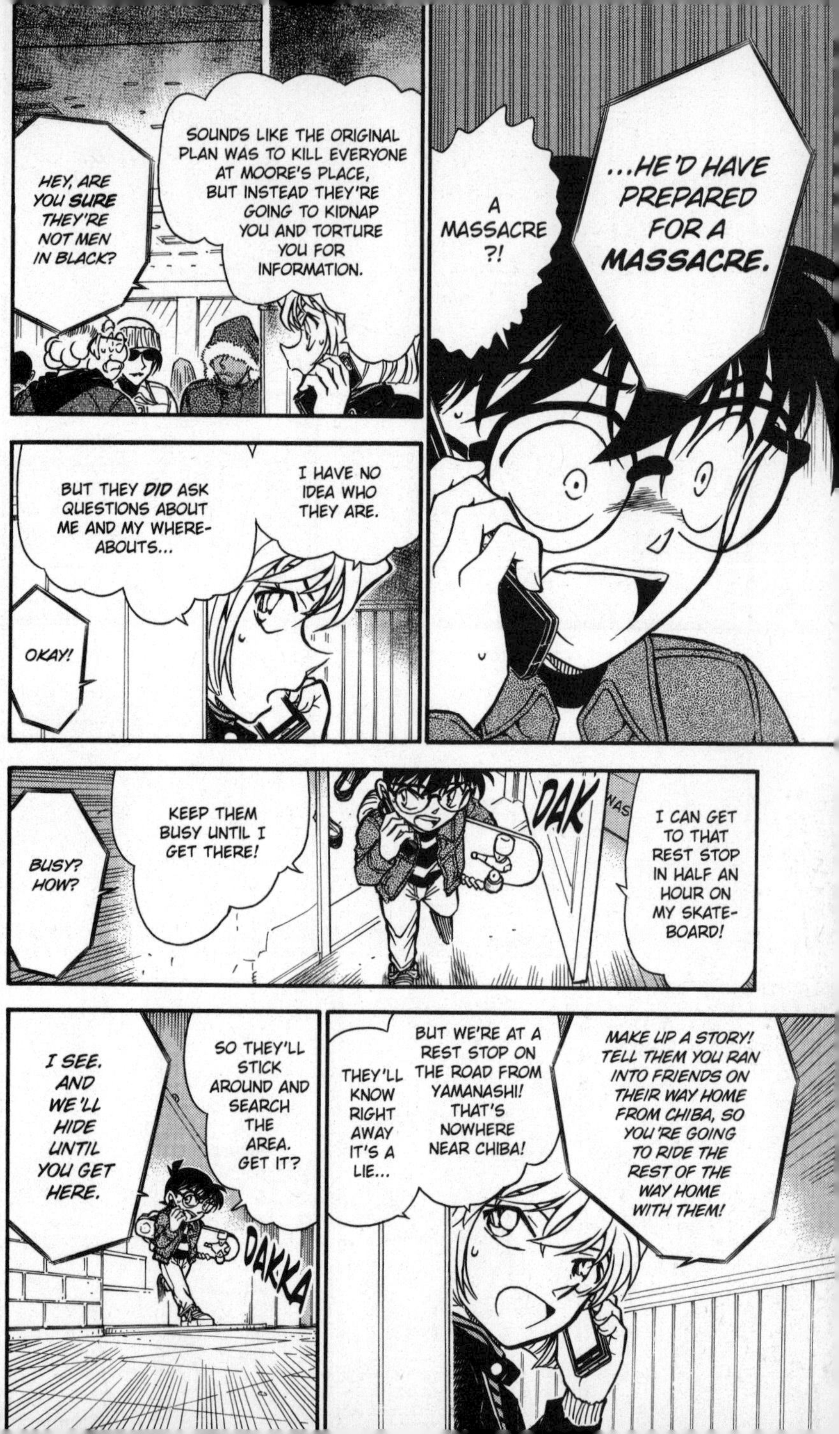
...HE'D HAVE PREPARED FOR A MASSACRE.
A MASSACRE ?!
SOUNDS LIKE THE ORIGINAL PLAN WAS TO KILL EVERYONE AT MOORE'S PLACE, BUT INSTEAD THEY'RE GOING TO KIDNAP YOU AND TORTURE YOU FOR INFORMATION.
HEY, ARE YOU SURE THEY'RE NOT MEN IN BLACK?
I HAVE NO IDEA WHO THEY ARE.
BUT THEY DID ASK QUESTIONS ABOUT ME AND MY WHERE-ABOUTS...
OKAY!
I CAN GET TO THAT REST STOP IN HALF AN HOUR ON MY SKATE-BOARD!
DAK
KEEP THEM BUSY UNTIL I GET THERE!
BUSY? HOW?
MAKE UP A STORY! TELL THEM YOU RAN INTO FRIENDS ON THEIR WAY HOME FROM CHIBA, SO YOU'RE GOING TO RIDE THE REST OF THE WAY HOME WITH THEM!
BUT WE'RE AT A REST STOP ON THE ROAD FROM YAMANASHI! THAT'S NOWHERE NEAR CHIBA!
THEY'LL KNOW RIGHT AWAY IT'S A LIE...
SO THEY'LL STICK AROUND AND SEARCH THE AREA. GET IT?
I SEE. AND WE'LL HIDE UNTIL YOU GET HERE.
DAKKA

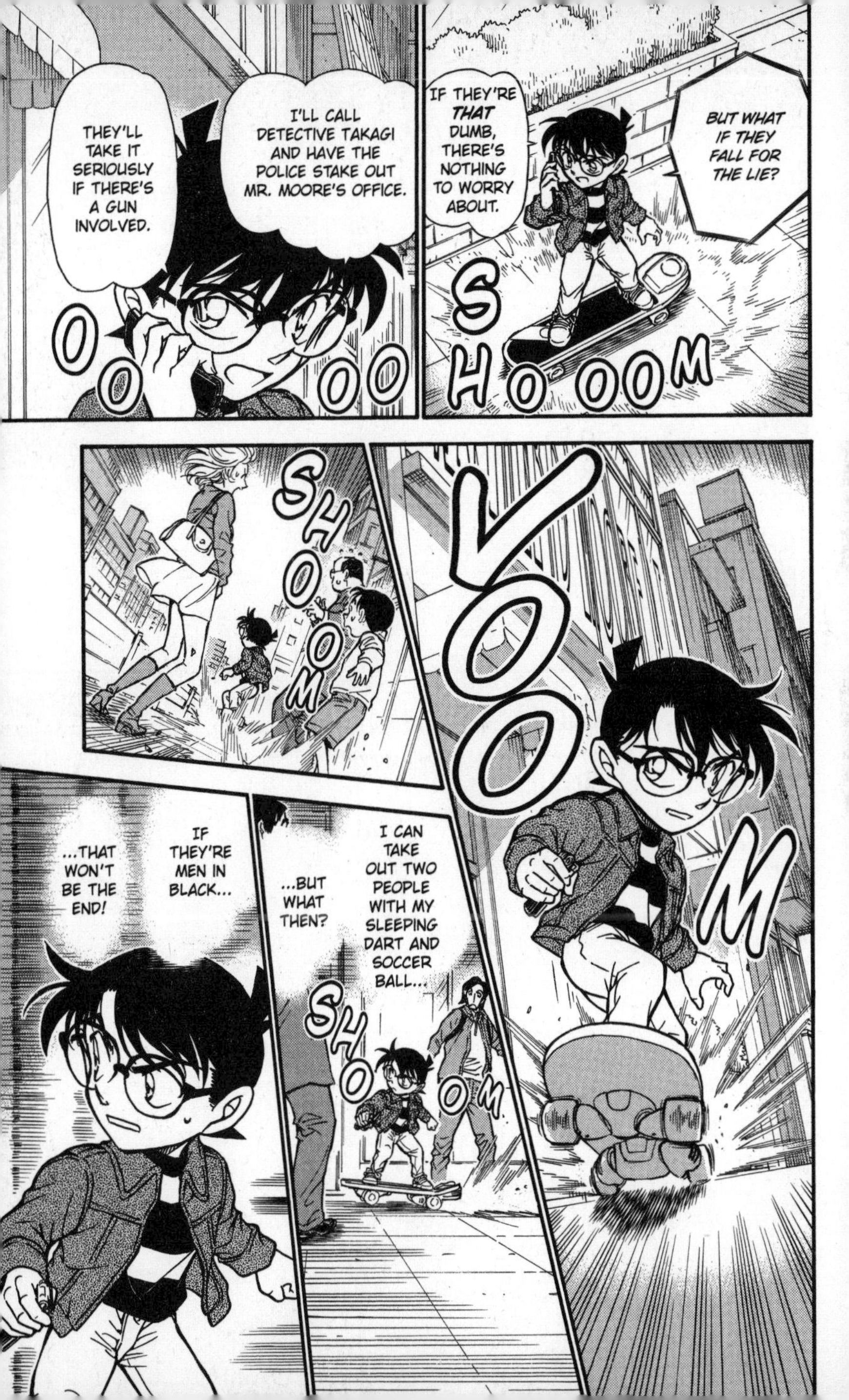

BUT WHAT IF THEY FALL FOR THE LIE?
IF THEY'RE *THAT* DUMB, THERE'S NOTHING TO WORRY ABOUT.
SHOOOM
I'LL CALL DETECTIVE TAKAGI AND HAVE THE POLICE STAKE OUT MR. MOORE'S OFFICE.
THEY'LL TAKE IT SERIOUSLY IF THERE'S A GUN INVOLVED.
OOOO
VOOOM
SHOOOM
I CAN TAKE OUT TWO PEOPLE WITH MY SLEEPING DART AND SOCCER BALL...
...BUT WHAT THEN?
SHOOOM
IF THEY'RE MEN IN BLACK...
...THAT WON'T BE THE END!

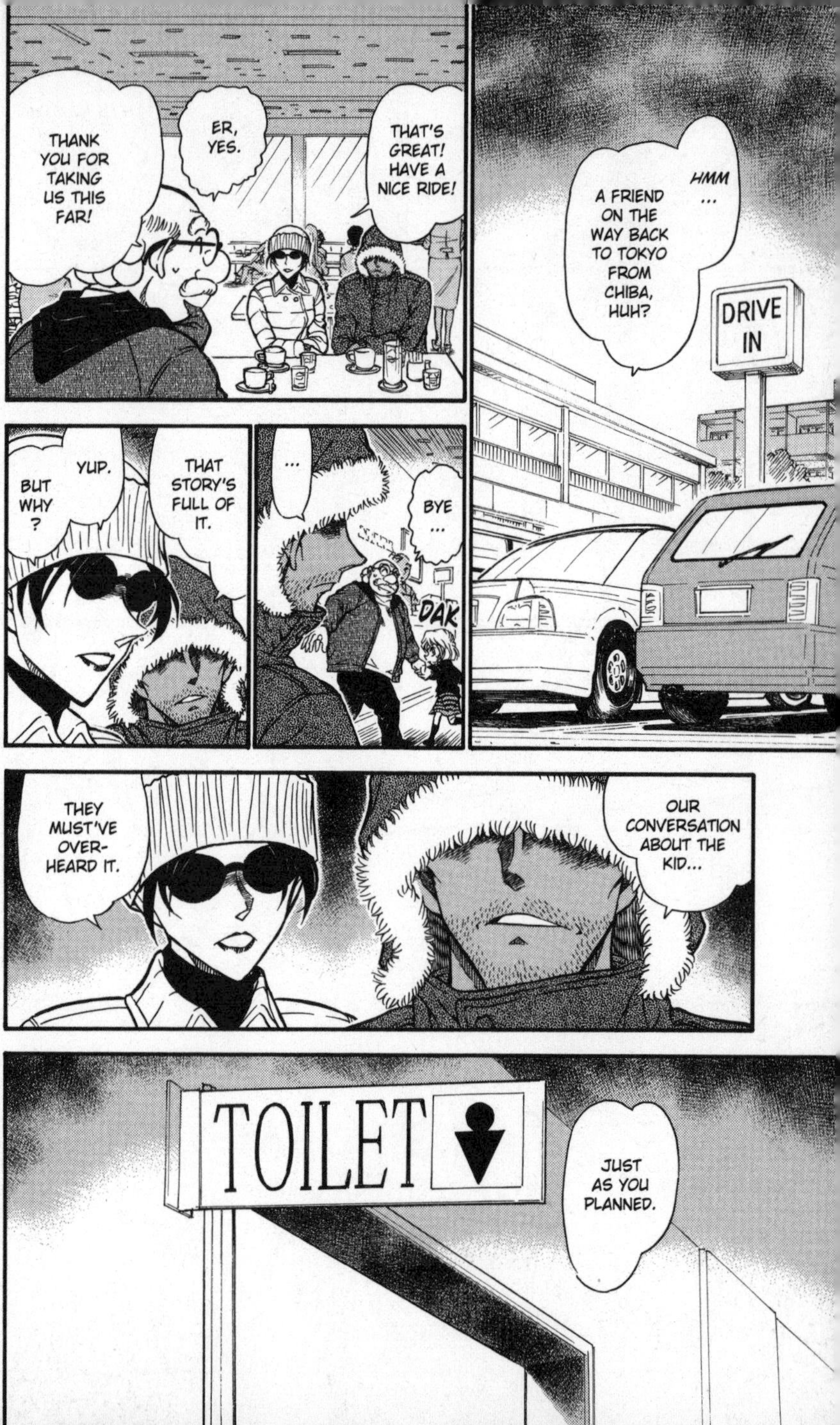
HMM ...
A FRIEND ON THE WAY BACK TO TOKYO FROM CHIBA, HUH?
DRIVE IN
THAT'S GREAT! HAVE A NICE RIDE!
ER, YES.
THANK YOU FOR TAKING US THIS FAR!
...
BYE ...
DAK
THAT STORY'S FULL OF IT.
YUP.
BUT WHY ?
OUR CONVERSATION ABOUT THE KID...
THEY MUST'VE OVER-HEARD IT.
TOILET
JUST AS YOU PLANNED.

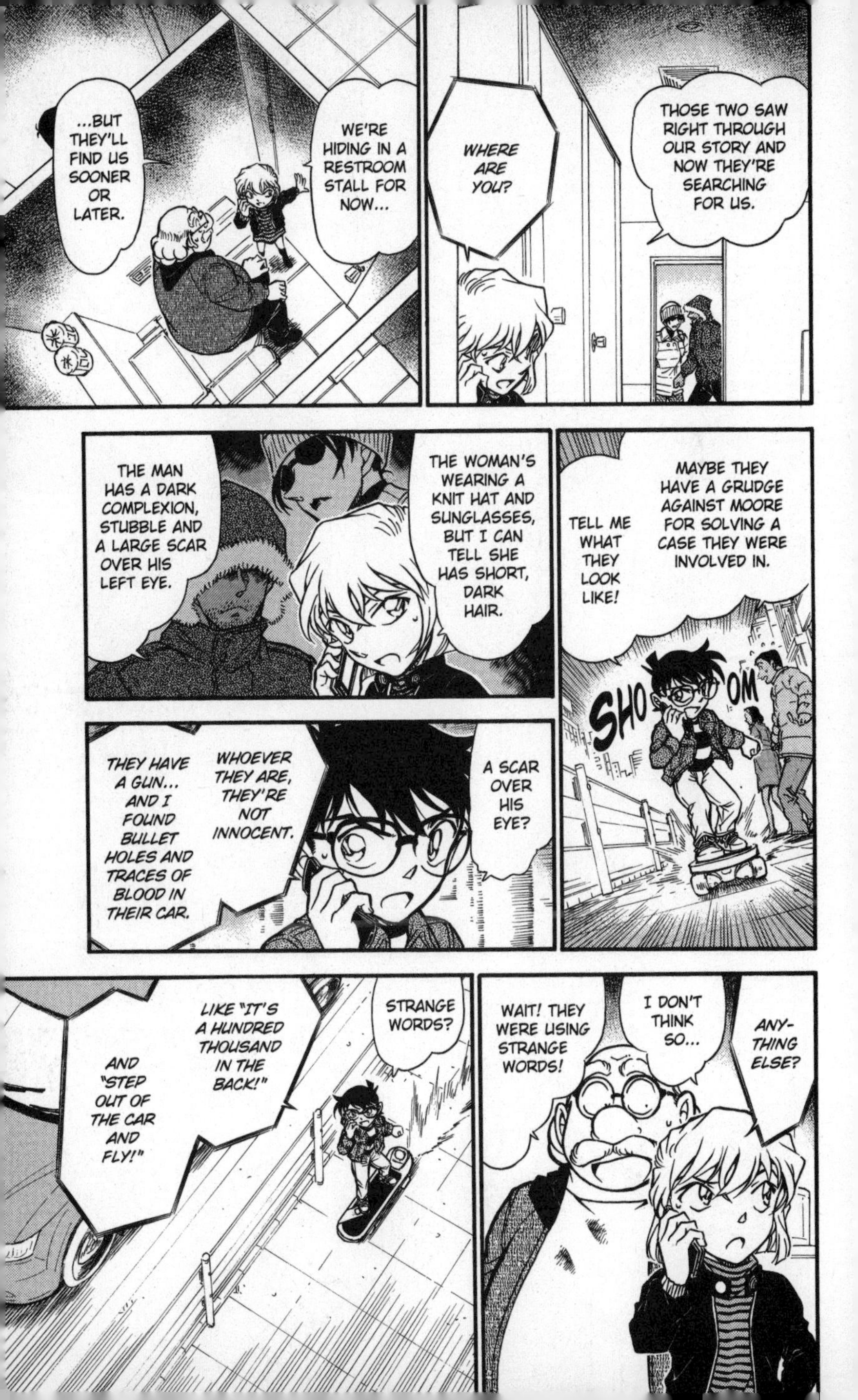
THOSE TWO SAW RIGHT THROUGH OUR STORY AND NOW THEY'RE SEARCHING FOR US.
WHERE ARE YOU?
WE'RE HIDING IN A RESTROOM STALL FOR NOW...
...BUT THEY'LL FIND US SOONER OR LATER.
MAYBE THEY HAVE A GRUDGE AGAINST MOORE FOR SOLVING A CASE THEY WERE INVOLVED IN.
TELL ME WHAT THEY LOOK LIKE!
SHO OM
THE WOMAN'S WEARING A KNIT HAT AND SUNGLASSES, BUT I CAN TELL SHE HAS SHORT, DARK HAIR.
THE MAN HAS A DARK COMPLEXION, STUBBLE AND A LARGE SCAR OVER HIS LEFT EYE.
A SCAR OVER HIS EYE?
WHOEVER THEY ARE, THEY'RE NOT INNOCENT.
THEY HAVE A GUN... AND I FOUND BULLET HOLES AND TRACES OF BLOOD IN THEIR CAR.
ANY-THING ELSE?
I DON'T THINK SO...
WAIT! THEY WERE USING STRANGE WORDS!
STRANGE WORDS?
LIKE "IT'S A HUNDRED THOUSAND IN THE BACK!"
AND "STEP OUT OF THE CAR AND FLY!"

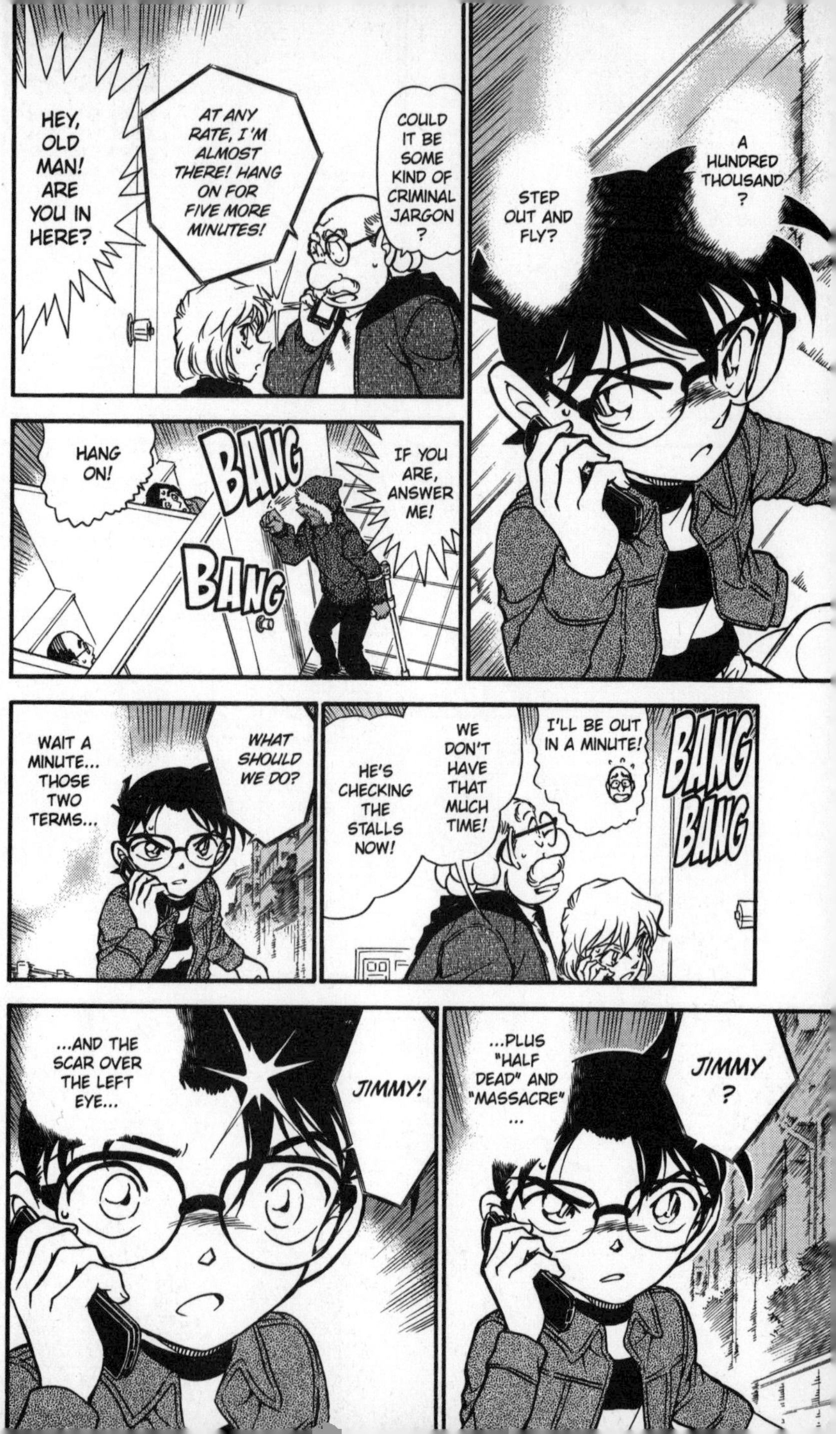
A HUNDRED THOUSAND?
STEP OUT AND FLY?
COULD IT BE SOME KIND OF CRIMINAL JARGON?
AT ANY RATE, I'M ALMOST THERE! HANG ON FOR FIVE MORE MINUTES!
HEY, OLD MAN! ARE YOU IN HERE?
IF YOU ARE, ANSWER ME!
BANG
BANG
HANG ON!
BANG BANG
I'LL BE OUT IN A MINUTE!
WE DON'T HAVE THAT MUCH TIME!
HE'S CHECKING THE STALLS NOW!
WHAT SHOULD WE DO?
WAIT A MINUTE... THOSE TWO TERMS...
JIMMY?
...PLUS "HALF DEAD" AND "MASSACRE"...
JIMMY!
...AND THE SCAR OVER THE LEFT EYE...

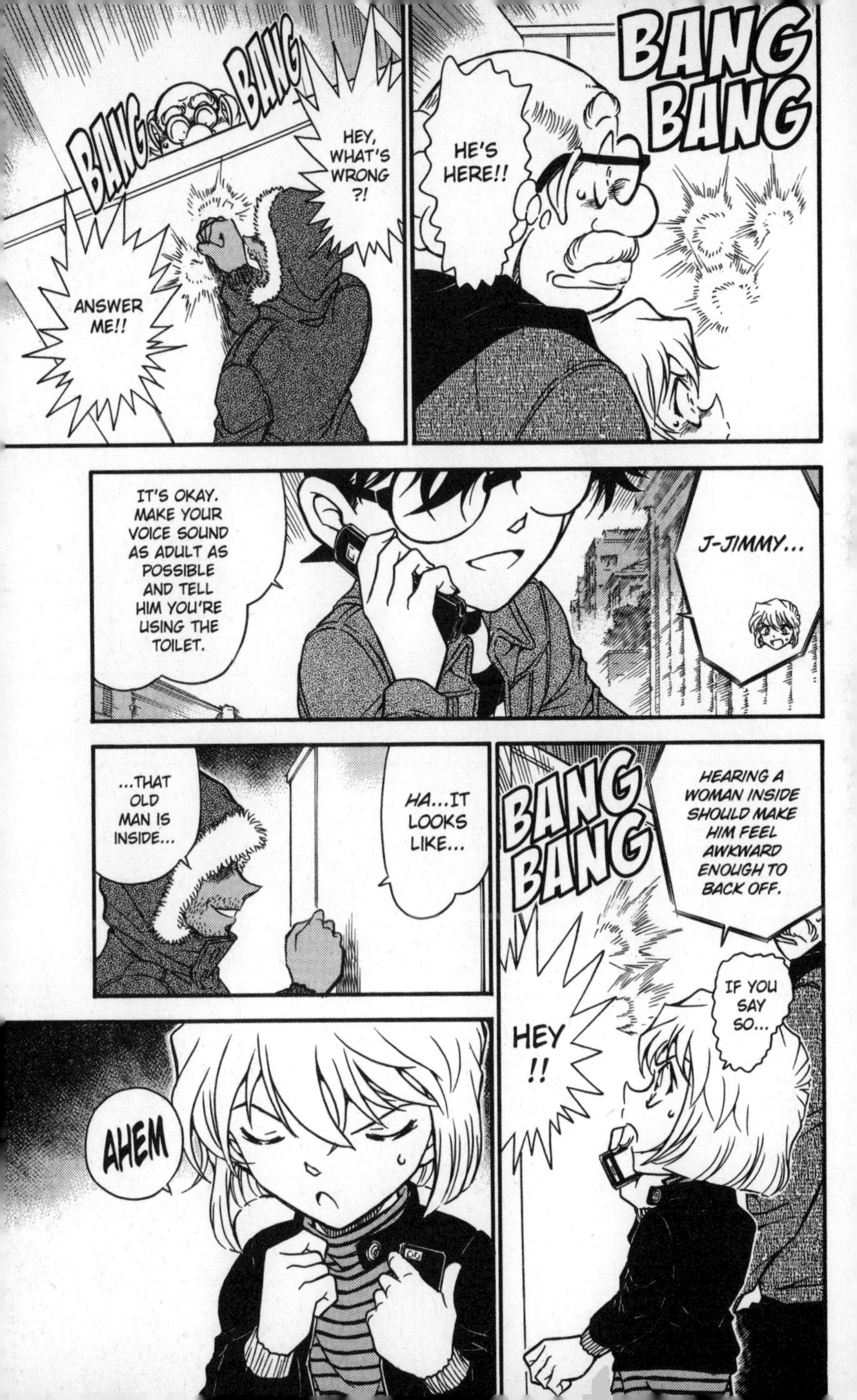
BANG
BANG
HE'S HERE!!
BANG
BANG
HEY, WHAT'S WRONG ?!
ANSWER ME!!
J-JIMMY...
IT'S OKAY. MAKE YOUR VOICE SOUND AS ADULT AS POSSIBLE AND TELL HIM YOU'RE USING THE TOILET.
HEARING A WOMAN INSIDE SHOULD MAKE HIM FEEL AWKWARD ENOUGH TO BACK OFF.
BANG
BANG
IF YOU SAY SO...
HEY !!
HA...IT LOOKS LIKE...
...THAT OLD MAN IS INSIDE...
AHEM

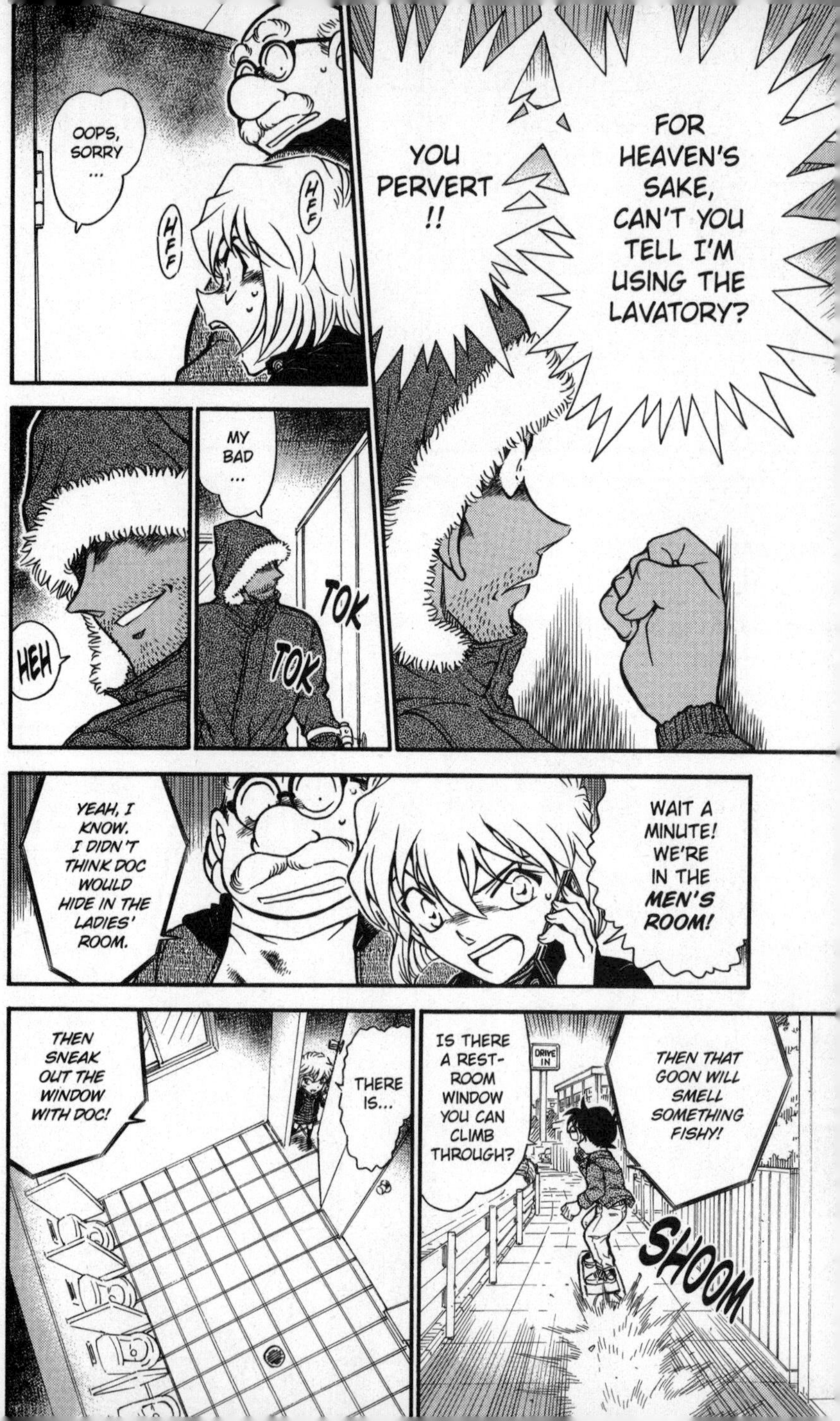
FOR HEAVEN'S SAKE, CAN'T YOU TELL I'M USING THE LAVATORY?
YOU PERVERT !!
HEFF
HEFF
OOPS, SORRY ...
TOK
TOK
MY BAD ...
HEH
WAIT A MINUTE! WE'RE IN THE MEN'S ROOM!
YEAH, I KNOW. I DIDN'T THINK DOC WOULD HIDE IN THE LADIES' ROOM.
THEN THAT GOON WILL SMELL SOMETHING FISHY!
DRIVE IN
IS THERE A REST-ROOM WINDOW YOU CAN CLIMB THROUGH?
SHOOM
THERE IS...
THEN SNEAK OUT THE WINDOW WITH DOC!

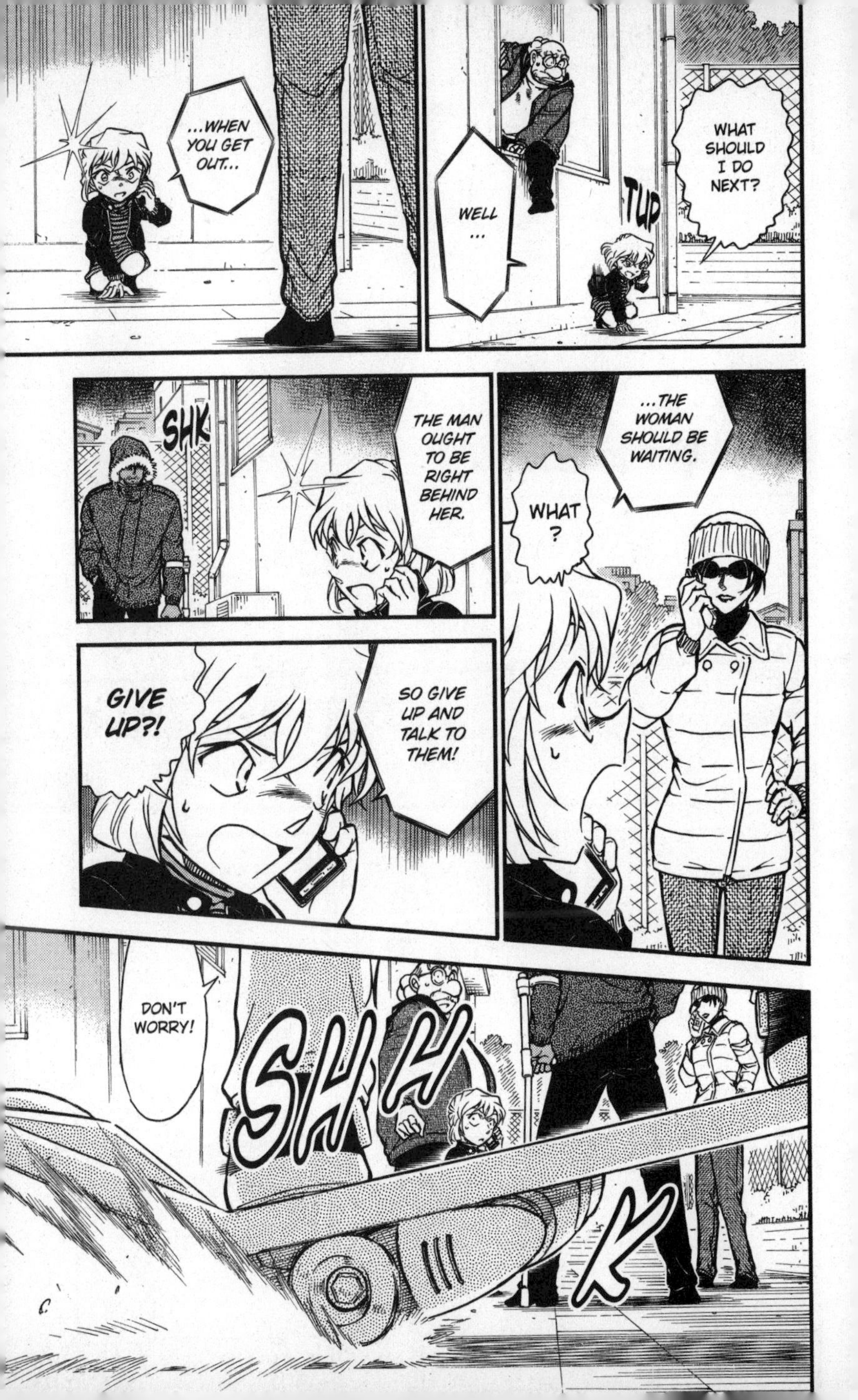
WHAT SHOULD I DO NEXT?
TUP
WELL ...
...WHEN YOU GET OUT...
...THE WOMAN SHOULD BE WAITING.
WHAT ?
THE MAN OUGHT TO BE RIGHT BEHIND HER.
SHK
SO GIVE UP AND TALK TO THEM!
GIVE UP?!
DON'T WORRY!
SHHK

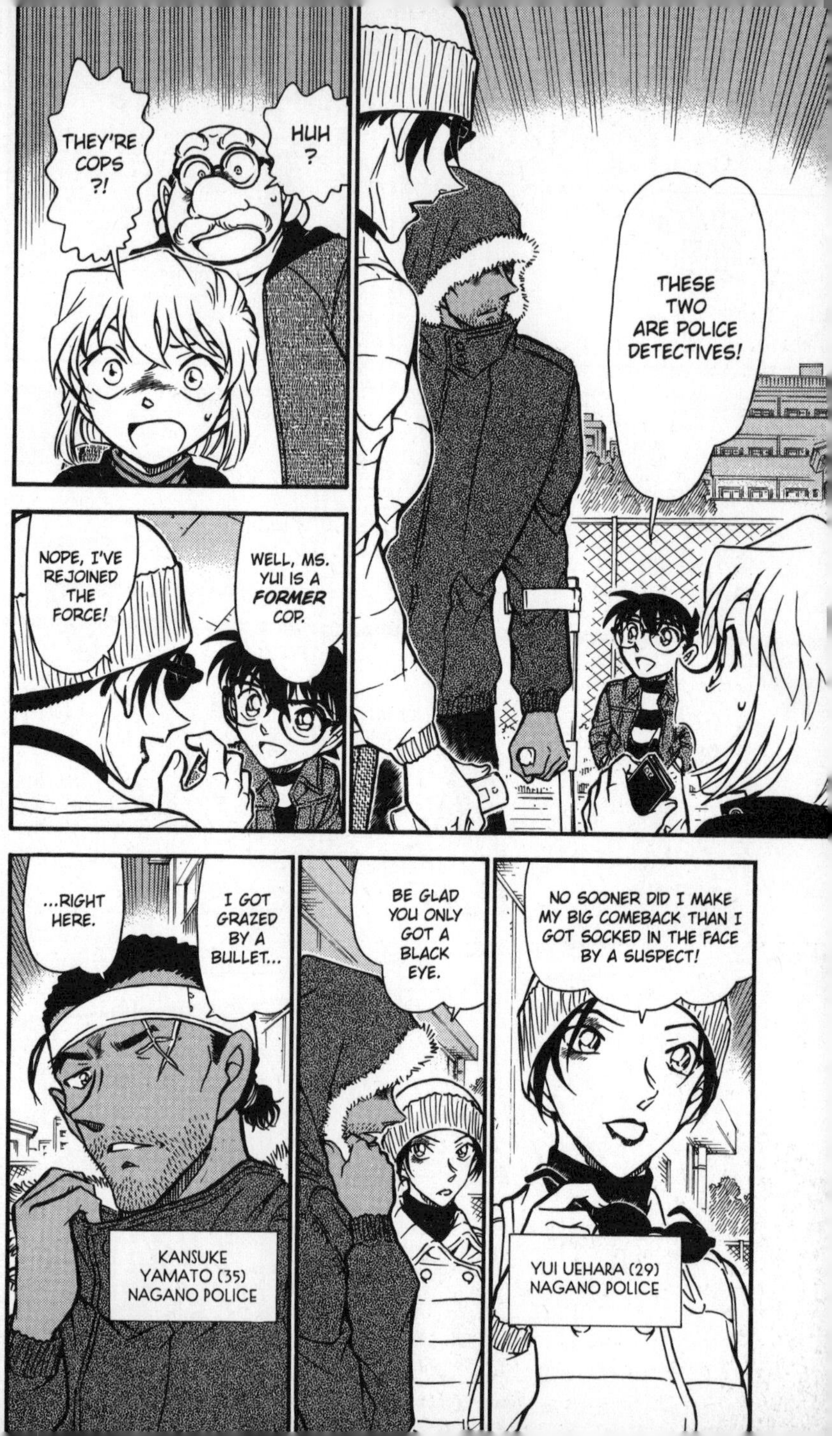
THESE TWO ARE POLICE DETECTIVES!
HUH?
THEY'RE COPS?!
WELL, MS. YUI IS A *FORMER* COP.
NOPE, I'VE REJOINED THE FORCE!
NO SOONER DID I MAKE MY BIG COMEBACK THAN I GOT SOCKED IN THE FACE BY A SUSPECT!
YUI UEHARA (29) NAGANO POLICE
BE GLAD YOU ONLY GOT A BLACK EYE.
I GOT GRAZED BY A BULLET...
...RIGHT HERE.
KANSUKE YAMATO (35) NAGANO POLICE

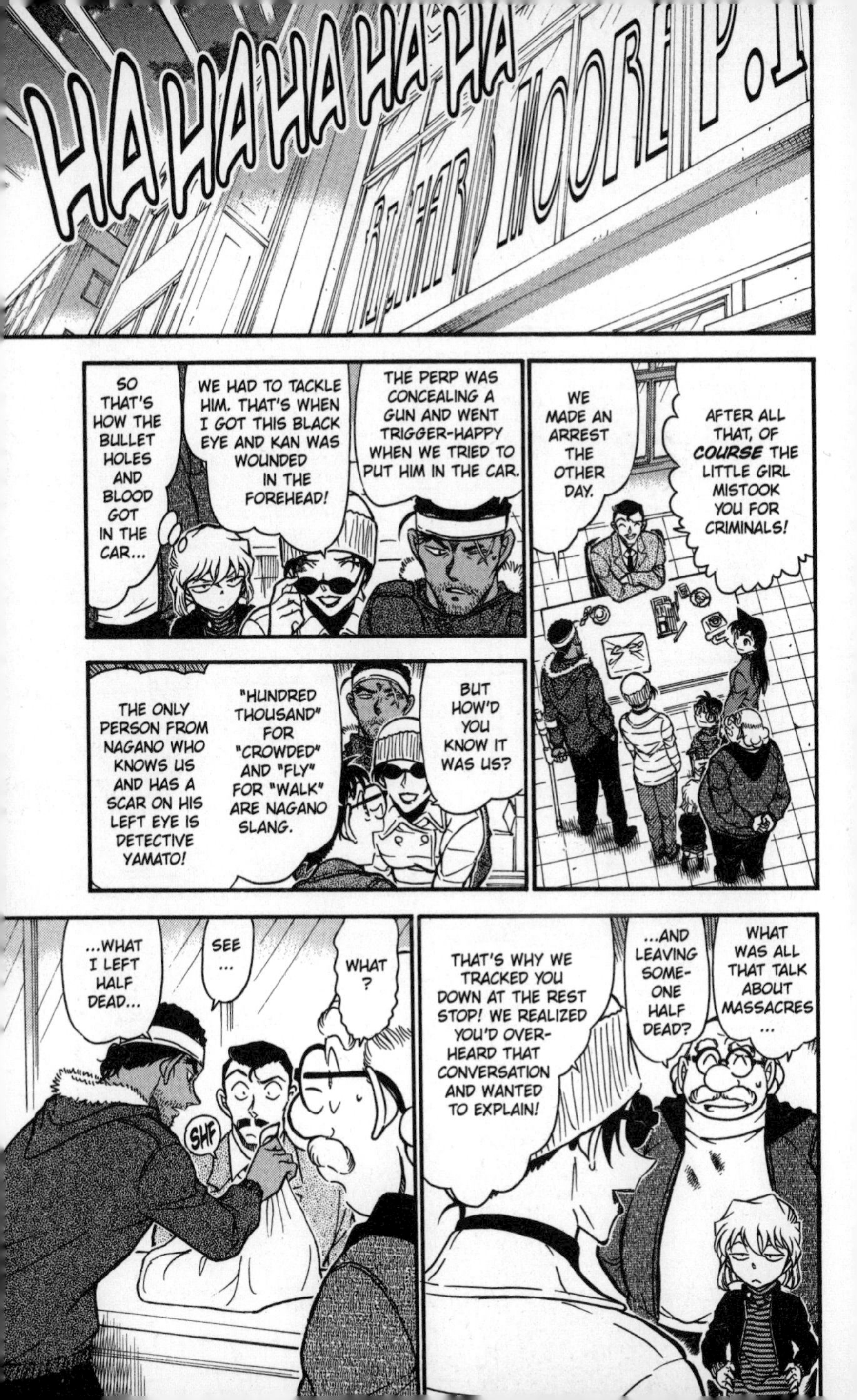

HA HA HA HA HA HA
AFTER ALL THAT, OF COURSE THE LITTLE GIRL MISTOOK YOU FOR CRIMINALS!
WE MADE AN ARREST THE OTHER DAY.
THE PERP WAS CONCEALING A GUN AND WENT TRIGGER-HAPPY WHEN WE TRIED TO PUT HIM IN THE CAR.
WE HAD TO TACKLE HIM. THAT'S WHEN I GOT THIS BLACK EYE AND KAN WAS WOUNDED IN THE FOREHEAD!
SO THAT'S HOW THE BULLET HOLES AND BLOOD GOT IN THE CAR...
BUT HOW'D YOU KNOW IT WAS US?
"HUNDRED THOUSAND" FOR "CROWDED" AND "FLY" FOR "WALK" ARE NAGANO SLANG.
THE ONLY PERSON FROM NAGANO WHO KNOWS US AND HAS A SCAR ON HIS LEFT EYE IS DETECTIVE YAMATO!
WHAT WAS ALL THAT TALK ABOUT MASSACRES...
...AND LEAVING SOME-ONE HALF DEAD?
THAT'S WHY WE TRACKED YOU DOWN AT THE REST STOP! WE REALIZED YOU'D OVER-HEARD THAT CONVERSATION AND WANTED TO EXPLAIN!
WHAT?
SEE...
...WHAT I LEFT HALF DEAD...
SHF

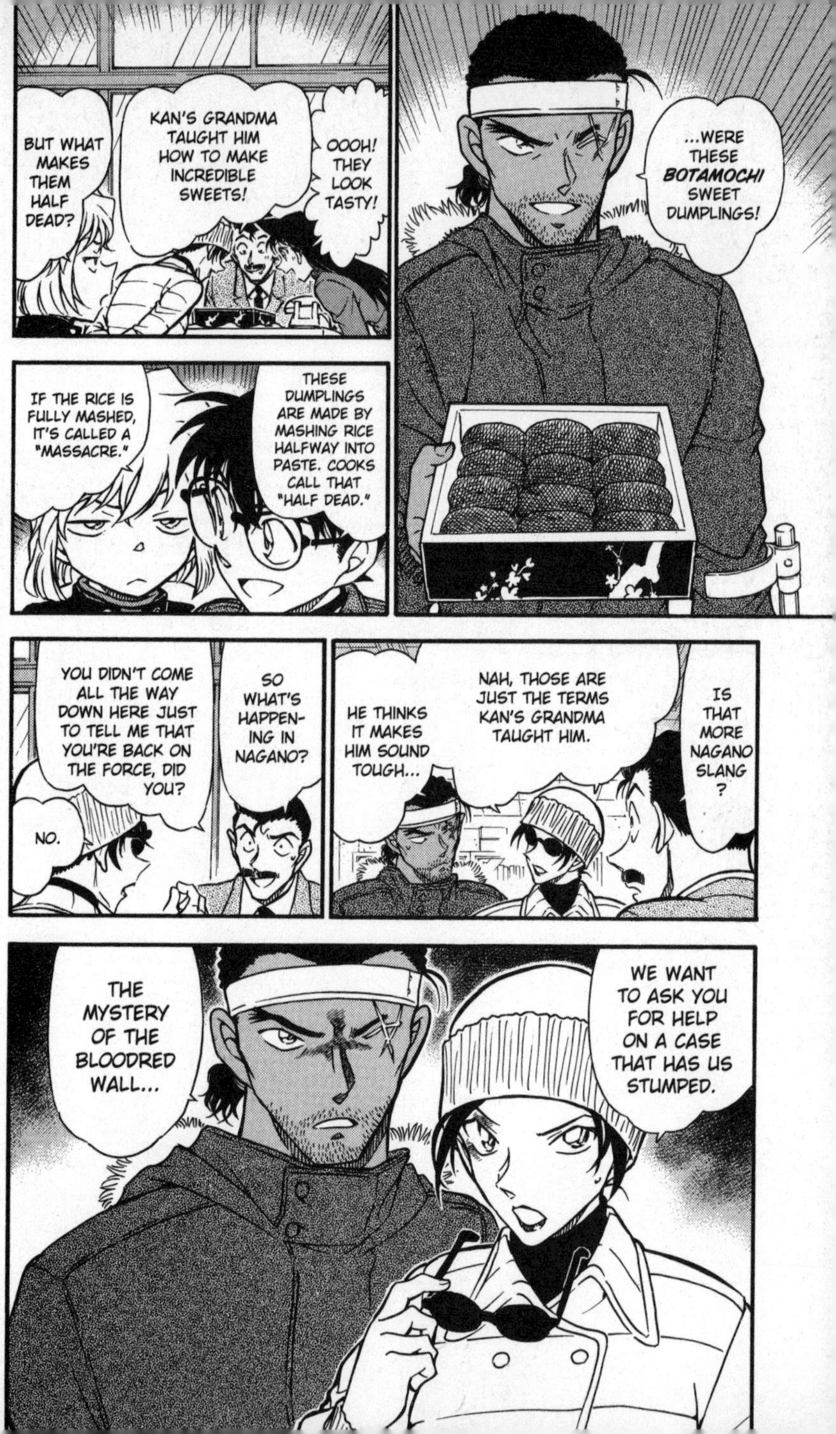
...WERE THESE ***BOTAMOCHI*** SWEET DUMPLINGS!
OOOH! THEY LOOK TASTY!
KAN'S GRANDMA TAUGHT HIM HOW TO MAKE INCREDIBLE SWEETS!
BUT WHAT MAKES THEM HALF DEAD?
THESE DUMPLINGS ARE MADE BY MASHING RICE HALFWAY INTO PASTE. COOKS CALL THAT "HALF DEAD."
IF THE RICE IS FULLY MASHED, IT'S CALLED A "MASSACRE."
IS THAT MORE NAGANO SLANG?
NAH, THOSE ARE JUST THE TERMS KAN'S GRANDMA TAUGHT HIM.
HE THINKS IT MAKES HIM SOUND TOUGH...
SO WHAT'S HAPPEN-ING IN NAGANO?
YOU DIDN'T COME ALL THE WAY DOWN HERE JUST TO TELL ME THAT YOU'RE BACK ON THE FORCE, DID YOU?
NO.
WE WANT TO ASK YOU FOR HELP ON A CASE THAT HAS US STUMPED.
THE MYSTERY OF THE BLOODRED WALL...

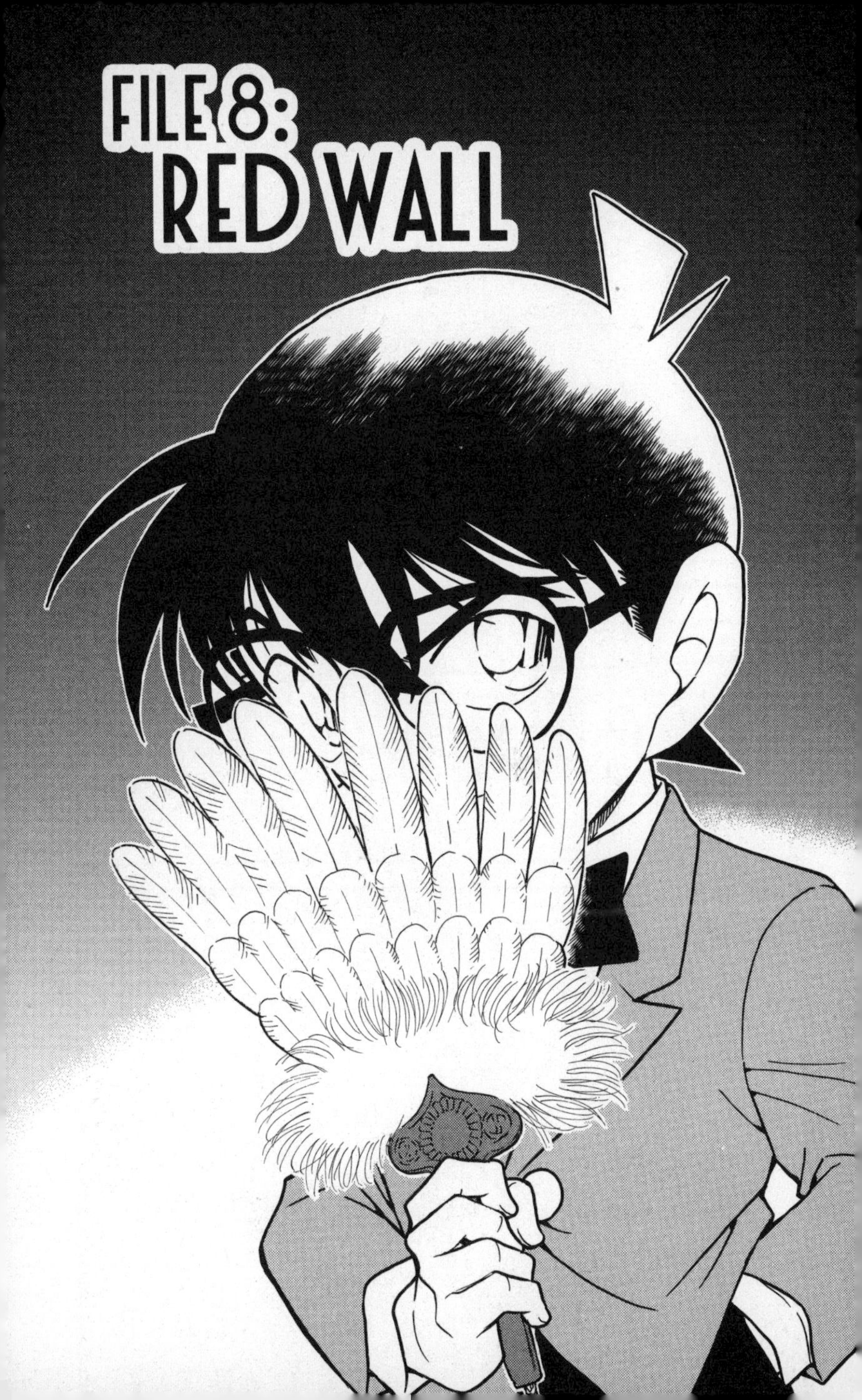
FILE 8:
RED WALL

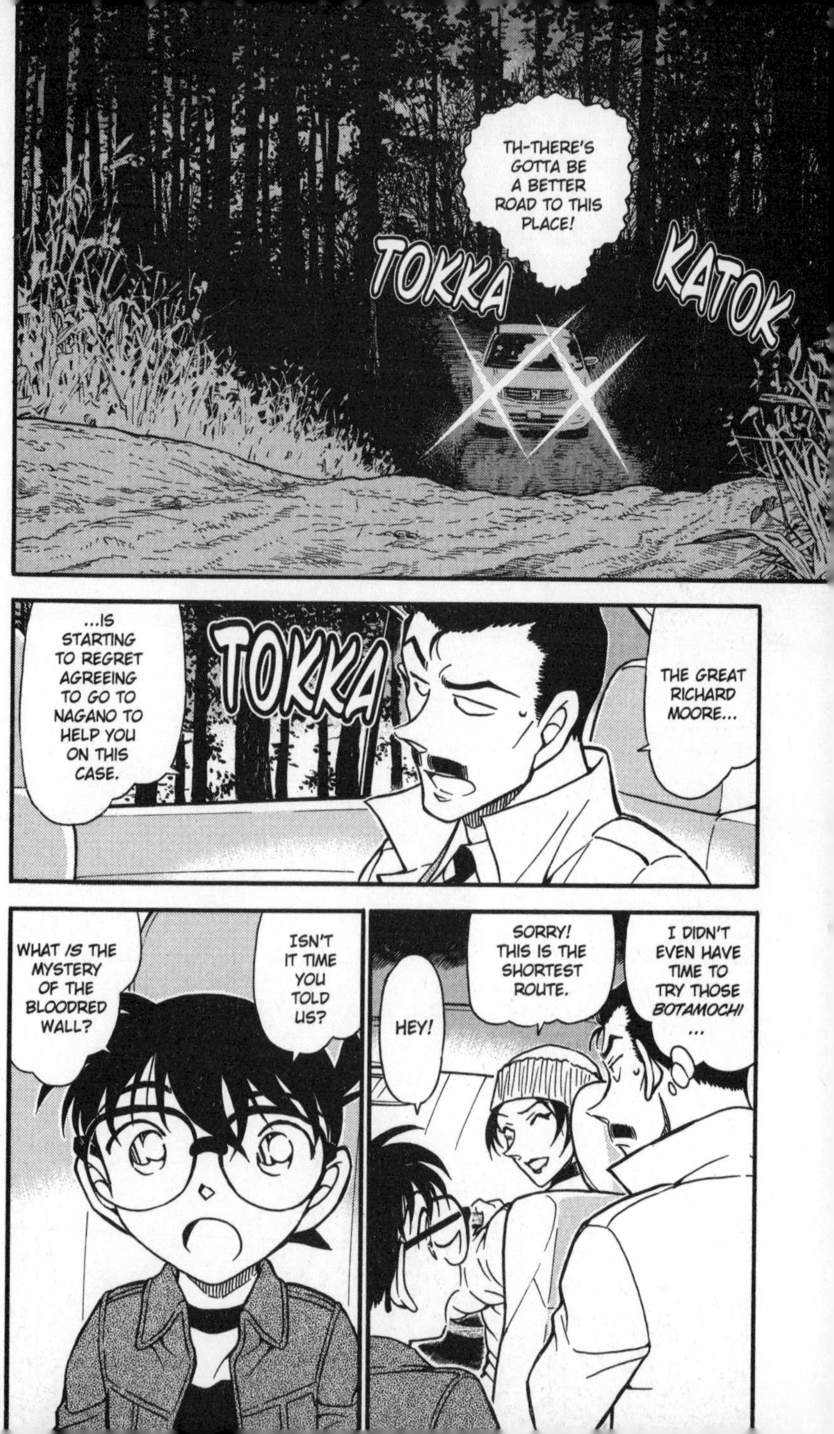
TH-THERE'S GOTTA BE A BETTER ROAD TO THIS PLACE!
TOKKA
KATOK
THE GREAT RICHARD MOORE...
...IS STARTING TO REGRET AGREEING TO GO TO NAGANO TO HELP YOU ON THIS CASE.
TOKKA
I DIDN'T EVEN HAVE TIME TO TRY THOSE *BOTAMOCHI* ...
SORRY! THIS IS THE SHORTEST ROUTE.
HEY!
ISN'T IT TIME YOU TOLD US?
WHAT *IS* THE MYSTERY OF THE BLOODRED WALL?

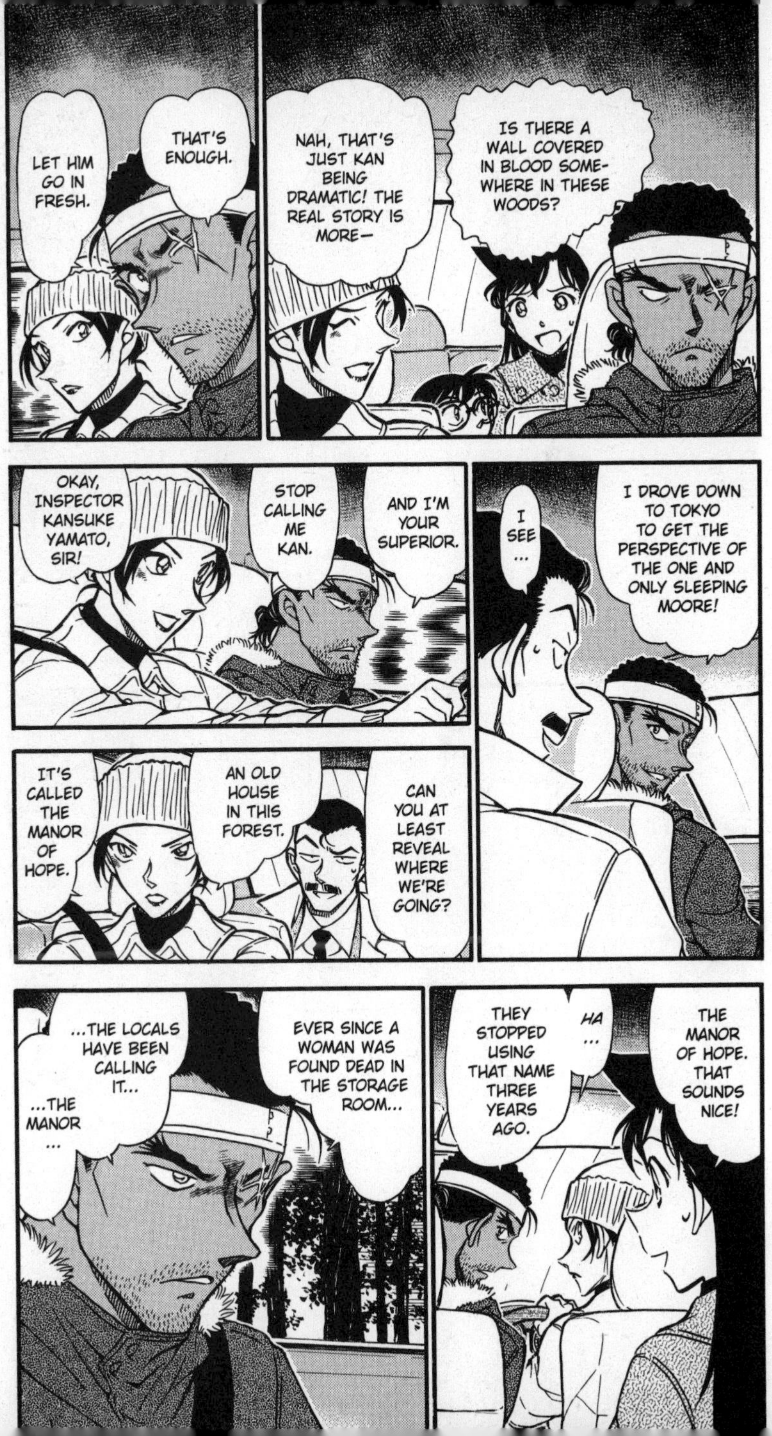
IS THERE A WALL COVERED IN BLOOD SOME-WHERE IN THESE WOODS?
NAH, THAT'S JUST KAN BEING DRAMATIC! THE REAL STORY IS MORE—
THAT'S ENOUGH.
LET HIM GO IN FRESH.
I DROVE DOWN TO TOKYO TO GET THE PERSPECTIVE OF THE ONE AND ONLY SLEEPING MOORE!
I SEE...
AND I'M YOUR SUPERIOR.
STOP CALLING ME KAN.
OKAY, INSPECTOR KANSUKE YAMATO, SIR!
CAN YOU AT LEAST REVEAL WHERE WE'RE GOING?
AN OLD HOUSE IN THIS FOREST.
IT'S CALLED THE MANOR OF HOPE.
THE MANOR OF HOPE. THAT SOUNDS NICE!
HA...
THEY STOPPED USING THAT NAME THREE YEARS AGO.
EVER SINCE A WOMAN WAS FOUND DEAD IN THE STORAGE ROOM...
...THE LOCALS HAVE BEEN CALLING IT...
...THE MANOR...

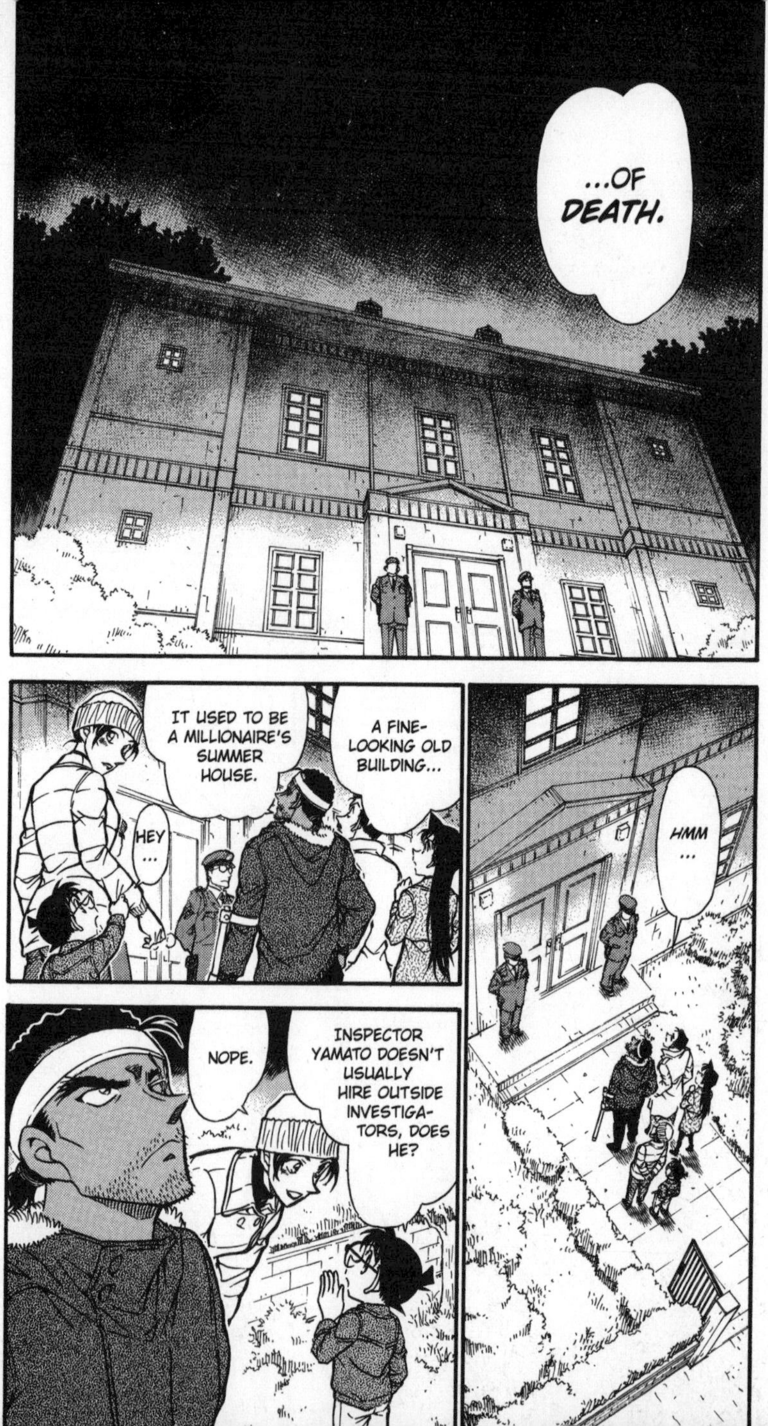
...OF DEATH.
HMM...
A FINE-LOOKING OLD BUILDING...
IT USED TO BE A MILLIONAIRE'S SUMMER HOUSE.
HEY...
INSPECTOR YAMATO DOESN'T USUALLY HIRE OUTSIDE INVESTIGA-TORS, DOES HE?
NOPE.

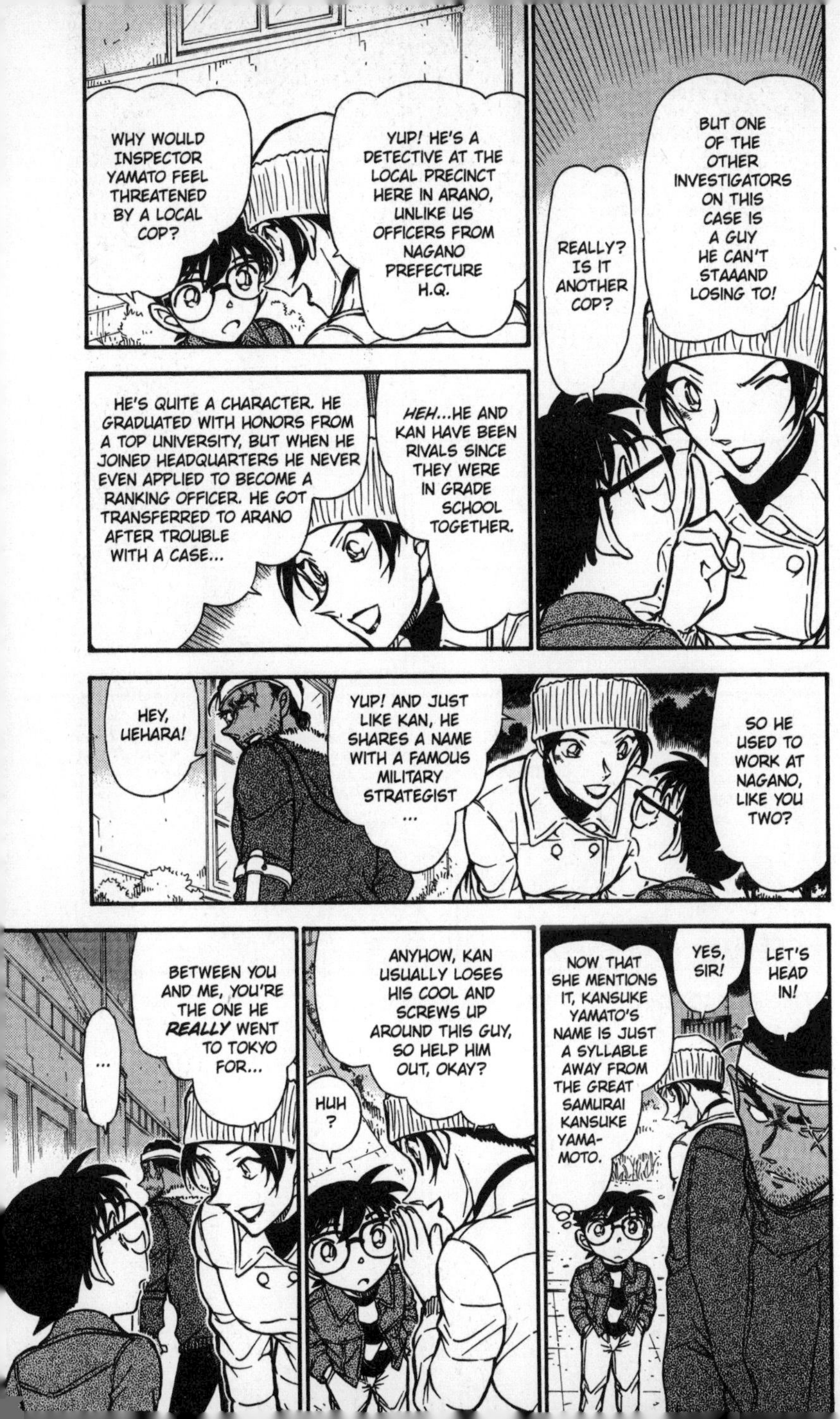

BUT ONE OF THE OTHER INVESTIGATORS ON THIS CASE IS A GUY HE CAN'T STAAAND LOSING TO!
REALLY? IS IT ANOTHER COP?
YUP! HE'S A DETECTIVE AT THE LOCAL PRECINCT HERE IN ARANO, UNLIKE US OFFICERS FROM NAGANO PREFECTURE H.Q.
WHY WOULD INSPECTOR YAMATO FEEL THREATENED BY A LOCAL COP?
HEH...HE AND KAN HAVE BEEN RIVALS SINCE THEY WERE IN GRADE SCHOOL TOGETHER.
HE'S QUITE A CHARACTER. HE GRADUATED WITH HONORS FROM A TOP UNIVERSITY, BUT WHEN HE JOINED HEADQUARTERS HE NEVER EVEN APPLIED TO BECOME A RANKING OFFICER. HE GOT TRANSFERRED TO ARANO AFTER TROUBLE WITH A CASE...
SO HE USED TO WORK AT NAGANO, LIKE YOU TWO?
YUP! AND JUST LIKE KAN, HE SHARES A NAME WITH A FAMOUS MILITARY STRATEGIST...
HEY, UEHARA!
LET'S HEAD IN!
YES, SIR!
NOW THAT SHE MENTIONS IT, KANSUKE YAMATO'S NAME IS JUST A SYLLABLE AWAY FROM THE GREAT SAMURAI KANSUKE YAMAMOTO.
ANYHOW, KAN USUALLY LOSES HIS COOL AND SCREWS UP AROUND THIS GUY, SO HELP HIM OUT, OKAY?
HUH?
BETWEEN YOU AND ME, YOU'RE THE ONE HE *REALLY* WENT TO TOKYO FOR...
...

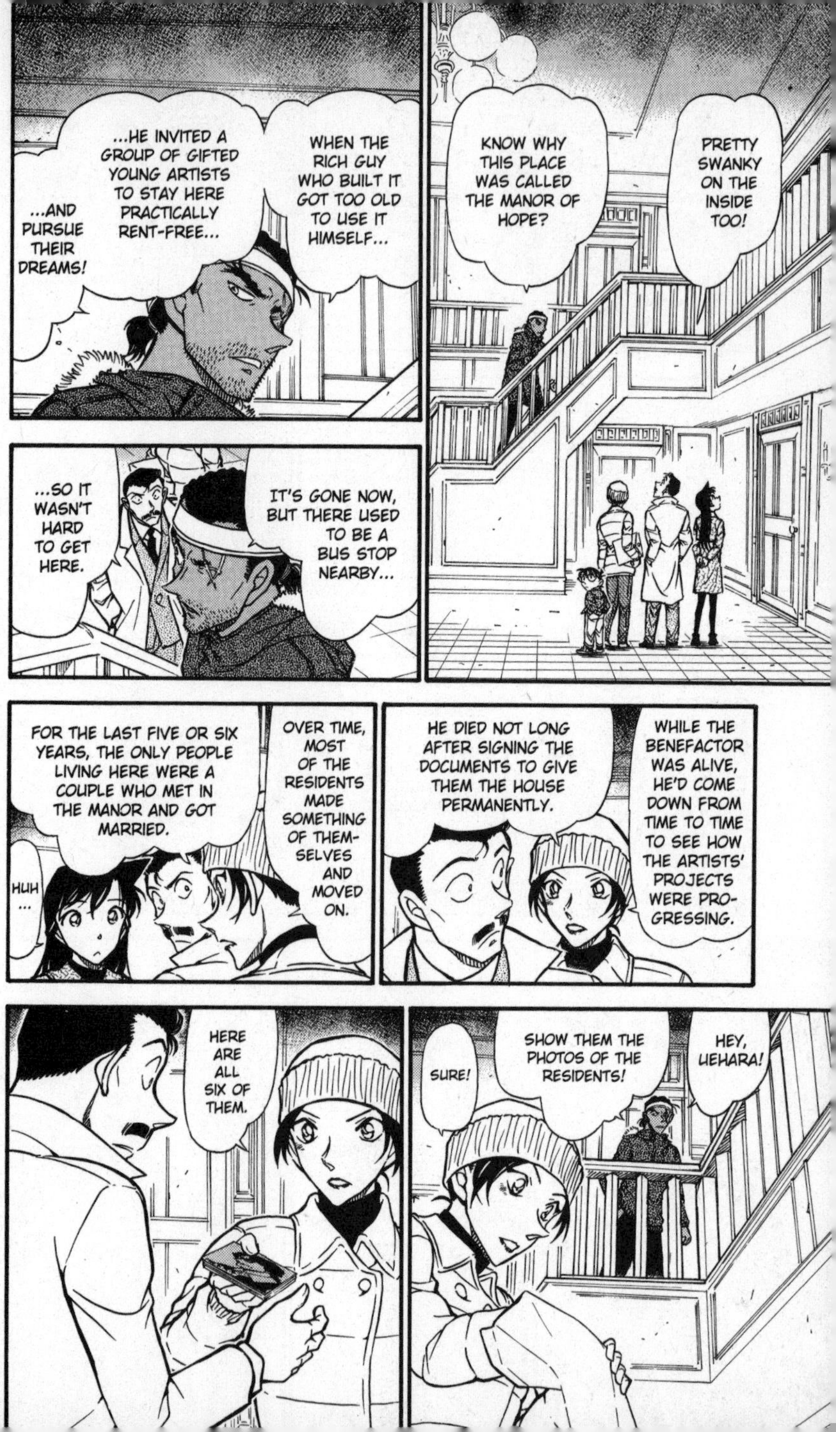
PRETTY SWANKY ON THE INSIDE TOO!
KNOW WHY THIS PLACE WAS CALLED THE MANOR OF HOPE?
WHEN THE RICH GUY WHO BUILT IT GOT TOO OLD TO USE IT HIMSELF...
...HE INVITED A GROUP OF GIFTED YOUNG ARTISTS TO STAY HERE PRACTICALLY RENT-FREE...
...AND PURSUE THEIR DREAMS!
IT'S GONE NOW, BUT THERE USED TO BE A BUS STOP NEARBY...
...SO IT WASN'T HARD TO GET HERE.
WHILE THE BENEFACTOR WAS ALIVE, HE'D COME DOWN FROM TIME TO TIME TO SEE HOW THE ARTISTS' PROJECTS WERE PROGRESSING.
HE DIED NOT LONG AFTER SIGNING THE DOCUMENTS TO GIVE THEM THE HOUSE PERMANENTLY.
OVER TIME, MOST OF THE RESIDENTS MADE SOMETHING OF THEMSELVES AND MOVED ON.
FOR THE LAST FIVE OR SIX YEARS, THE ONLY PEOPLE LIVING HERE WERE A COUPLE WHO MET IN THE MANOR AND GOT MARRIED.
HUH...
HEY, UEHARA!
SHOW THEM THE PHOTOS OF THE RESIDENTS!
SURE!
HERE ARE ALL SIX OF THEM.

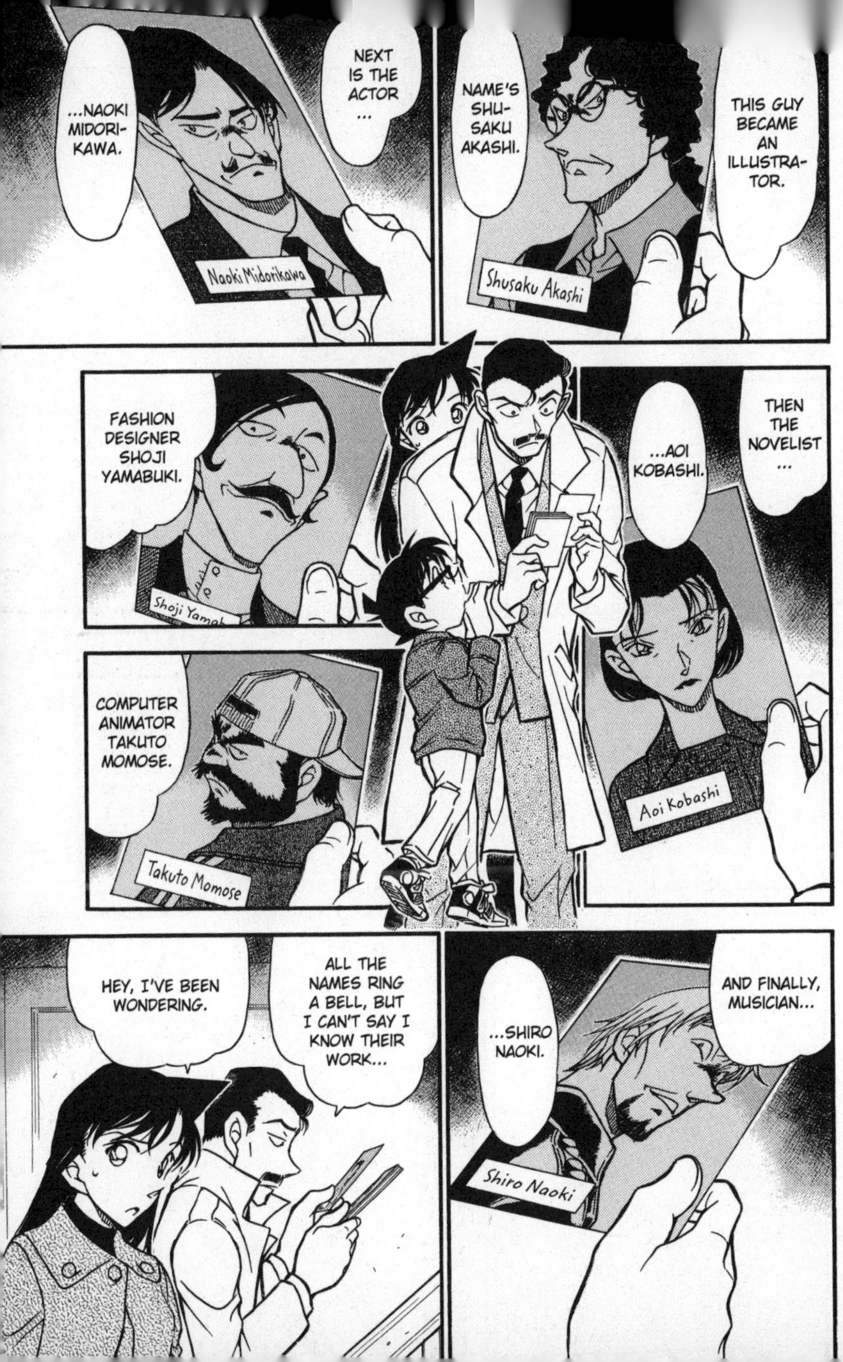
THIS GUY BECAME AN ILLUSTRATOR.
NAME'S SHUSAKU AKASHI.
Shusaku Akashi
NEXT IS THE ACTOR...
...NAOKI MIDORIKAWA.
Naoki Midorikawa
THEN THE NOVELIST...
...AOI KOBASHI.
Aoi Kobashi
FASHION DESIGNER SHOJI YAMABUKI.
COMPUTER ANIMATOR TAKUTO MOMOSE.
Takuto Momose
AND FINALLY, MUSICIAN...
...SHIRO NAOKI.
Shiro Naoki
ALL THE NAMES RING A BELL, BUT I CAN'T SAY I KNOW THEIR WORK...
HEY, I'VE BEEN WONDERING.

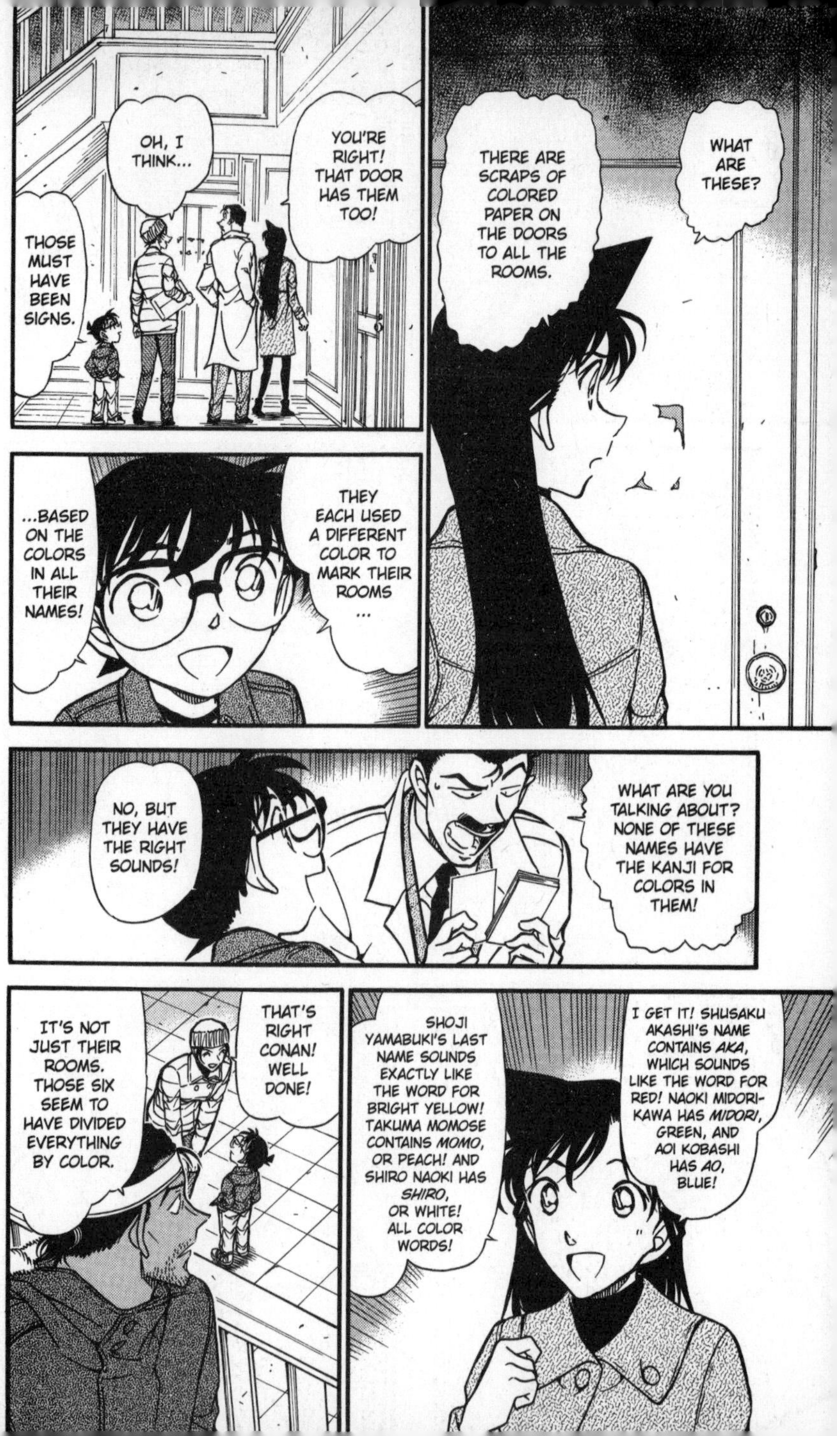
WHAT ARE THESE?
THERE ARE SCRAPS OF COLORED PAPER ON THE DOORS TO ALL THE ROOMS.
YOU'RE RIGHT! THAT DOOR HAS THEM TOO!
OH, I THINK...
THOSE MUST HAVE BEEN SIGNS.
THEY EACH USED A DIFFERENT COLOR TO MARK THEIR ROOMS ...
...BASED ON THE COLORS IN ALL THEIR NAMES!
WHAT ARE YOU TALKING ABOUT? NONE OF THESE NAMES HAVE THE KANJI FOR COLORS IN THEM!
NO, BUT THEY HAVE THE RIGHT SOUNDS!
I GET IT! SHUSAKU AKASHI'S NAME CONTAINS *AKA*, WHICH SOUNDS LIKE THE WORD FOR RED! NAOKI MIDORI-KAWA HAS *MIDORI*, GREEN, AND AOI KOBASHI HAS *AO*, BLUE!
SHOJI YAMABUKI'S LAST NAME SOUNDS EXACTLY LIKE THE WORD FOR BRIGHT YELLOW! TAKUMA MOMOSE CONTAINS *MOMO*, OR PEACH! AND SHIRO NAOKI HAS *SHIRO*, OR WHITE! ALL COLOR WORDS!
THAT'S RIGHT CONAN! WELL DONE!
IT'S NOT JUST THEIR ROOMS. THOSE SIX SEEM TO HAVE DIVIDED EVERYTHING BY COLOR.

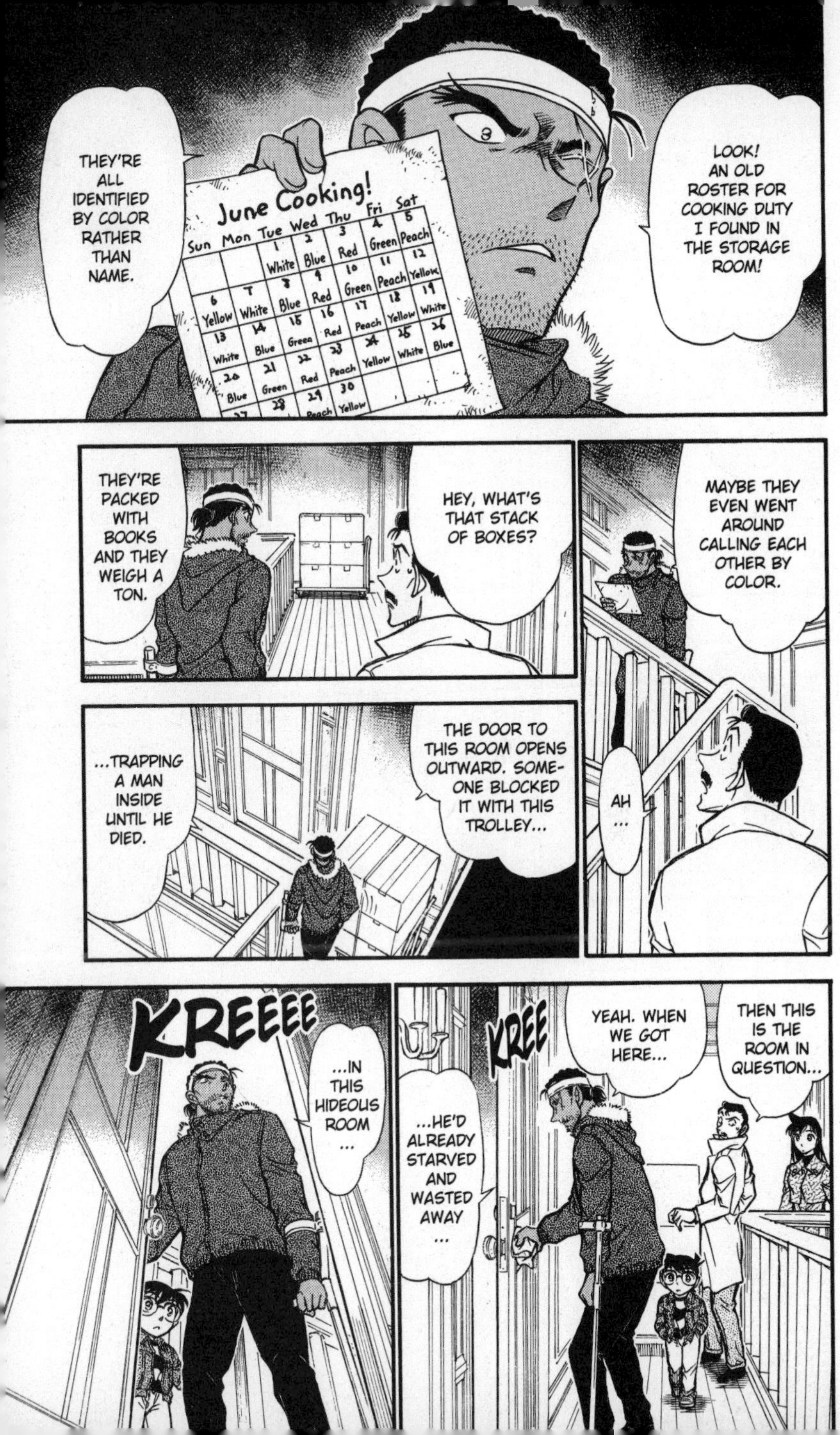
LOOK! AN OLD ROSTER FOR COOKING DUTY I FOUND IN THE STORAGE ROOM!
June Cooking!
Sun Mon Tue Wed Thu Fri Sat
THEY'RE ALL IDENTIFIED BY COLOR RATHER THAN NAME.
MAYBE THEY EVEN WENT AROUND CALLING EACH OTHER BY COLOR.
AH ...
HEY, WHAT'S THAT STACK OF BOXES?
THEY'RE PACKED WITH BOOKS AND THEY WEIGH A TON.
THE DOOR TO THIS ROOM OPENS OUTWARD. SOME-ONE BLOCKED IT WITH THIS TROLLEY...
...TRAPPING A MAN INSIDE UNTIL HE DIED.
THEN THIS IS THE ROOM IN QUESTION...
YEAH. WHEN WE GOT HERE...
KREE
...HE'D ALREADY STARVED AND WASTED AWAY ...
KREEEE
...IN THIS HIDEOUS ROOM ...

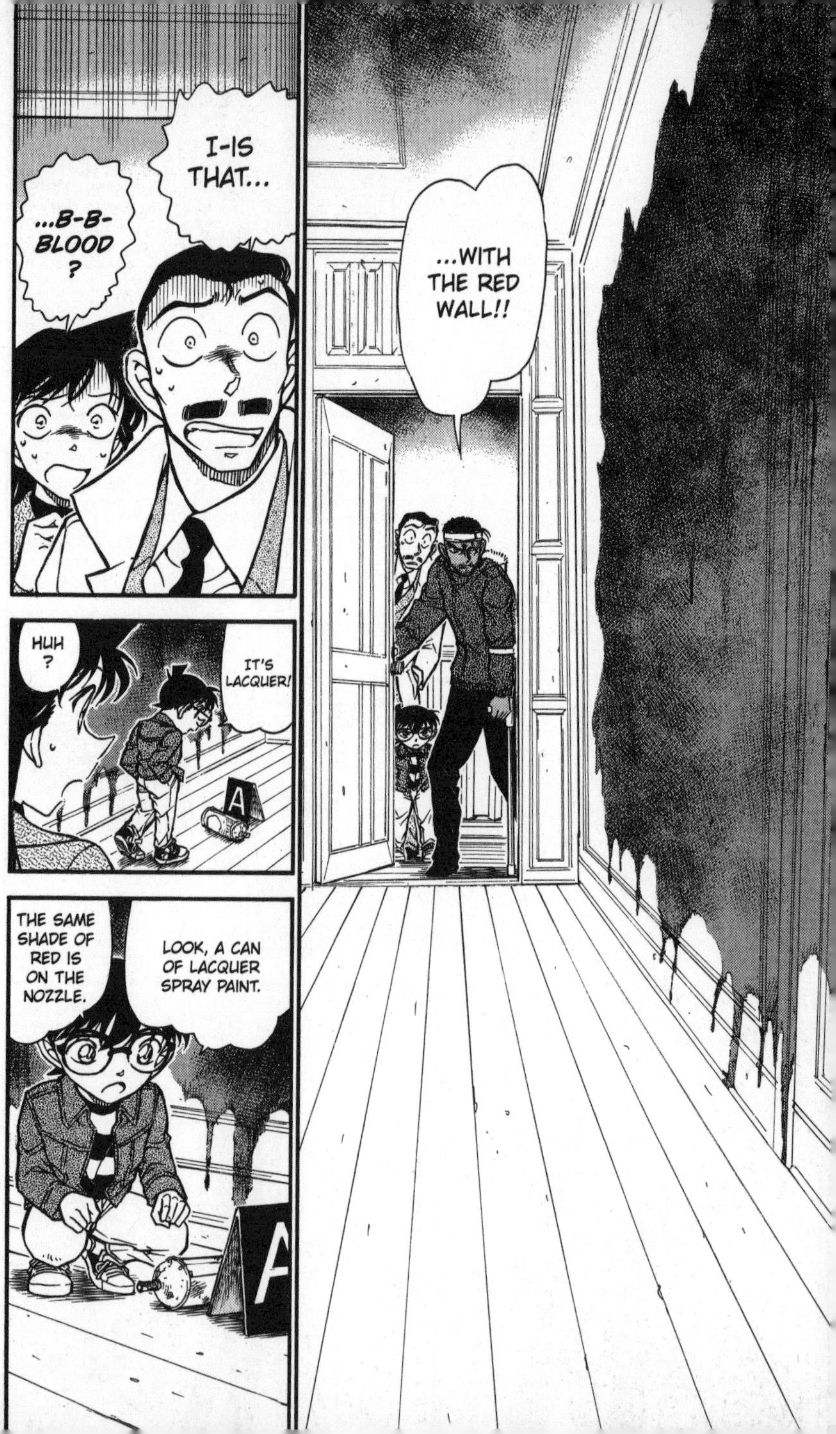
...WITH THE RED WALL!!
I-IS THAT...
...B-B-BLOOD ?
IT'S LACQUER!
HUH ?
LOOK, A CAN OF LACQUER SPRAY PAINT.
THE SAME SHADE OF RED IS ON THE NOZZLE.

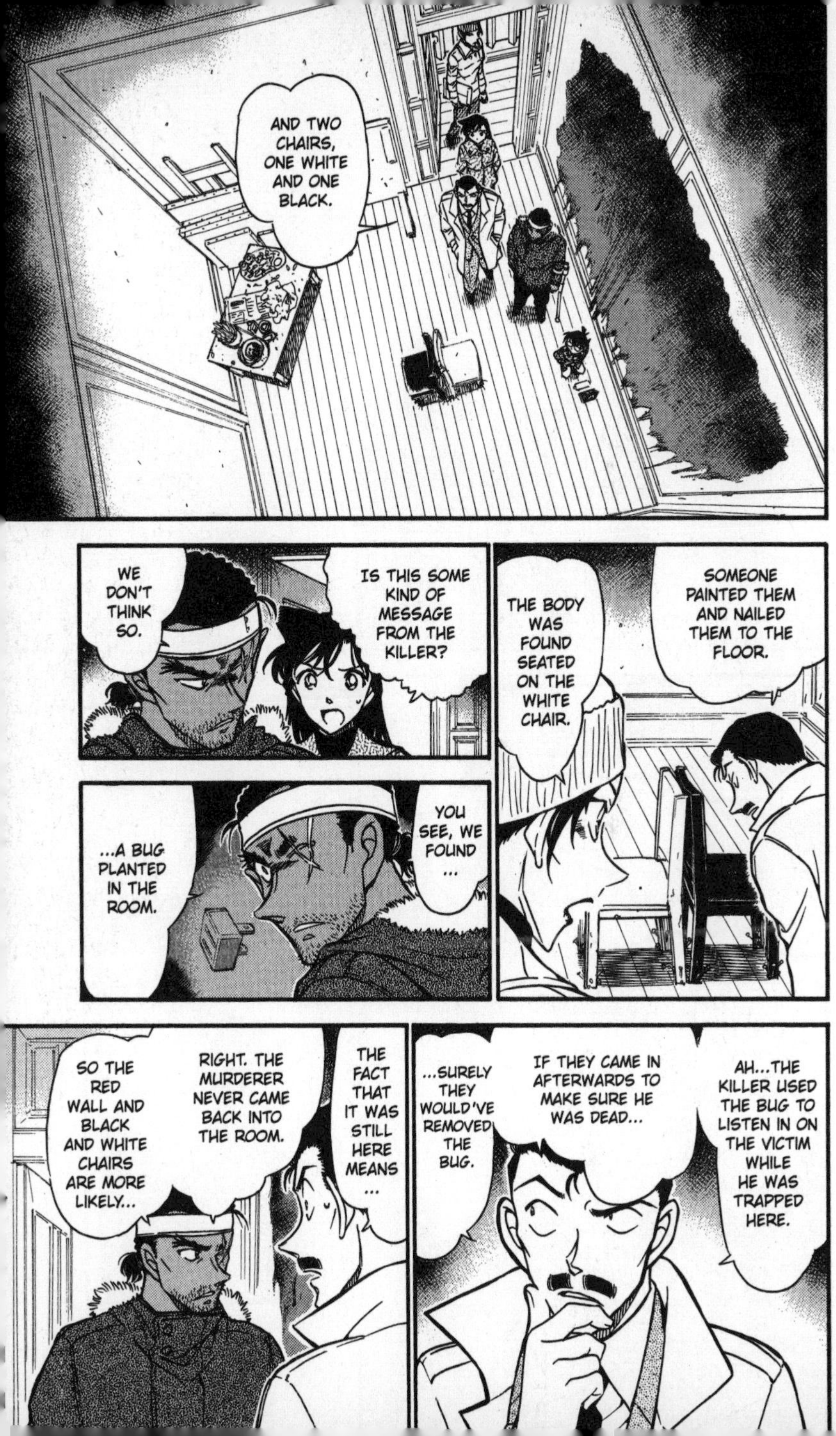
AND TWO CHAIRS, ONE WHITE AND ONE BLACK.
SOMEONE PAINTED THEM AND NAILED THEM TO THE FLOOR.
THE BODY WAS FOUND SEATED ON THE WHITE CHAIR.
IS THIS SOME KIND OF MESSAGE FROM THE KILLER?
WE DON'T THINK SO.
YOU SEE, WE FOUND ...
...A BUG PLANTED IN THE ROOM.
AH...THE KILLER USED THE BUG TO LISTEN IN ON THE VICTIM WHILE HE WAS TRAPPED HERE.
IF THEY CAME IN AFTERWARDS TO MAKE SURE HE WAS DEAD...
...SURELY THEY WOULD'VE REMOVED THE BUG.
THE FACT THAT IT WAS STILL HERE MEANS ...
RIGHT. THE MURDERER NEVER CAME BACK INTO THE ROOM.
SO THE RED WALL AND BLACK AND WHITE CHAIRS ARE MORE LIKELY...

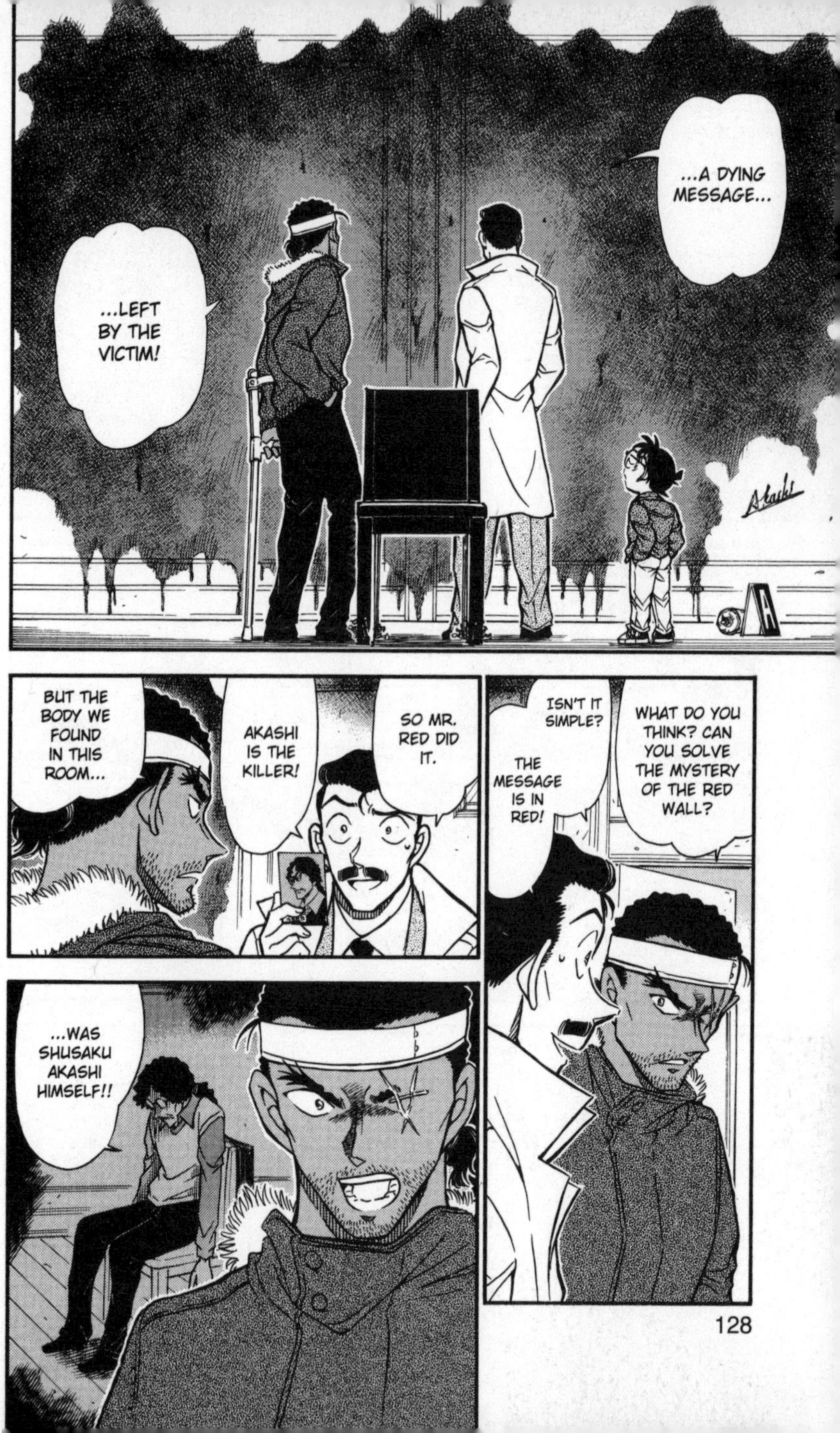
...A DYING MESSAGE...
...LEFT BY THE VICTIM!
Akashi
WHAT DO YOU THINK? CAN YOU SOLVE THE MYSTERY OF THE RED WALL?
ISN'T IT SIMPLE?
THE MESSAGE IS IN RED!
SO MR. RED DID IT.
AKASHI IS THE KILLER!
BUT THE BODY WE FOUND IN THIS ROOM...
...WAS SHUSAKU AKASHI HIMSELF!!

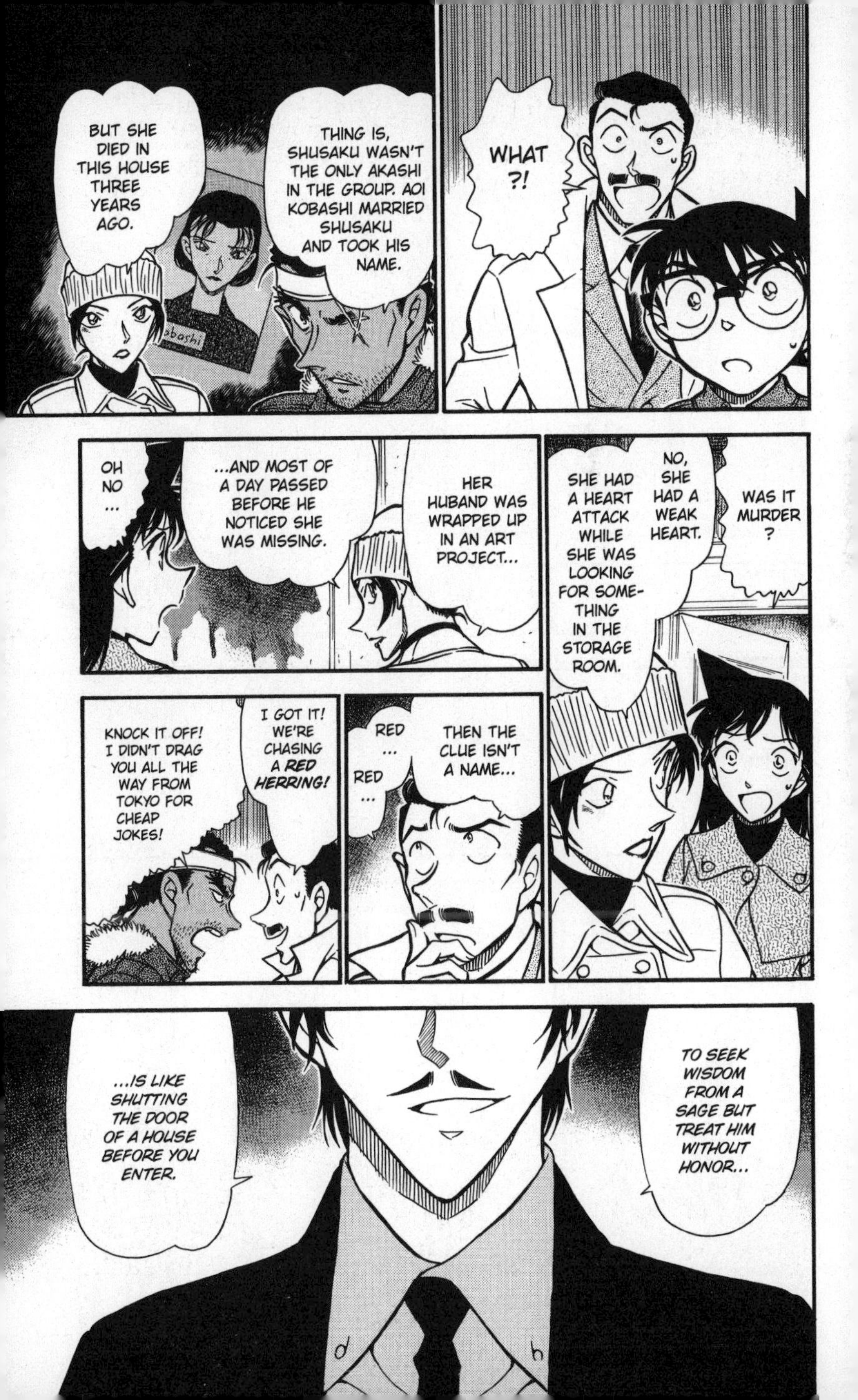
WHAT ?!
THING IS, SHUSAKU WASN'T THE ONLY AKASHI IN THE GROUP. AOI KOBASHI MARRIED SHUSAKU AND TOOK HIS NAME.
BUT SHE DIED IN THIS HOUSE THREE YEARS AGO.
kobashi
WAS IT MURDER ?
NO, SHE HAD A WEAK HEART.
SHE HAD A HEART ATTACK WHILE SHE WAS LOOKING FOR SOME-THING IN THE STORAGE ROOM.
HER HUBAND WAS WRAPPED UP IN AN ART PROJECT...
...AND MOST OF A DAY PASSED BEFORE HE NOTICED SHE WAS MISSING.
OH NO ...
THEN THE CLUE ISN'T A NAME...
RED ... RED ...
I GOT IT! WE'RE CHASING A *RED HERRING!*
KNOCK IT OFF! I DIDN'T DRAG YOU ALL THE WAY FROM TOKYO FOR CHEAP JOKES!
TO SEEK WISDOM FROM A SAGE BUT TREAT HIM WITHOUT HONOR...
...IS LIKE SHUTTING THE DOOR OF A HOUSE BEFORE YOU ENTER.

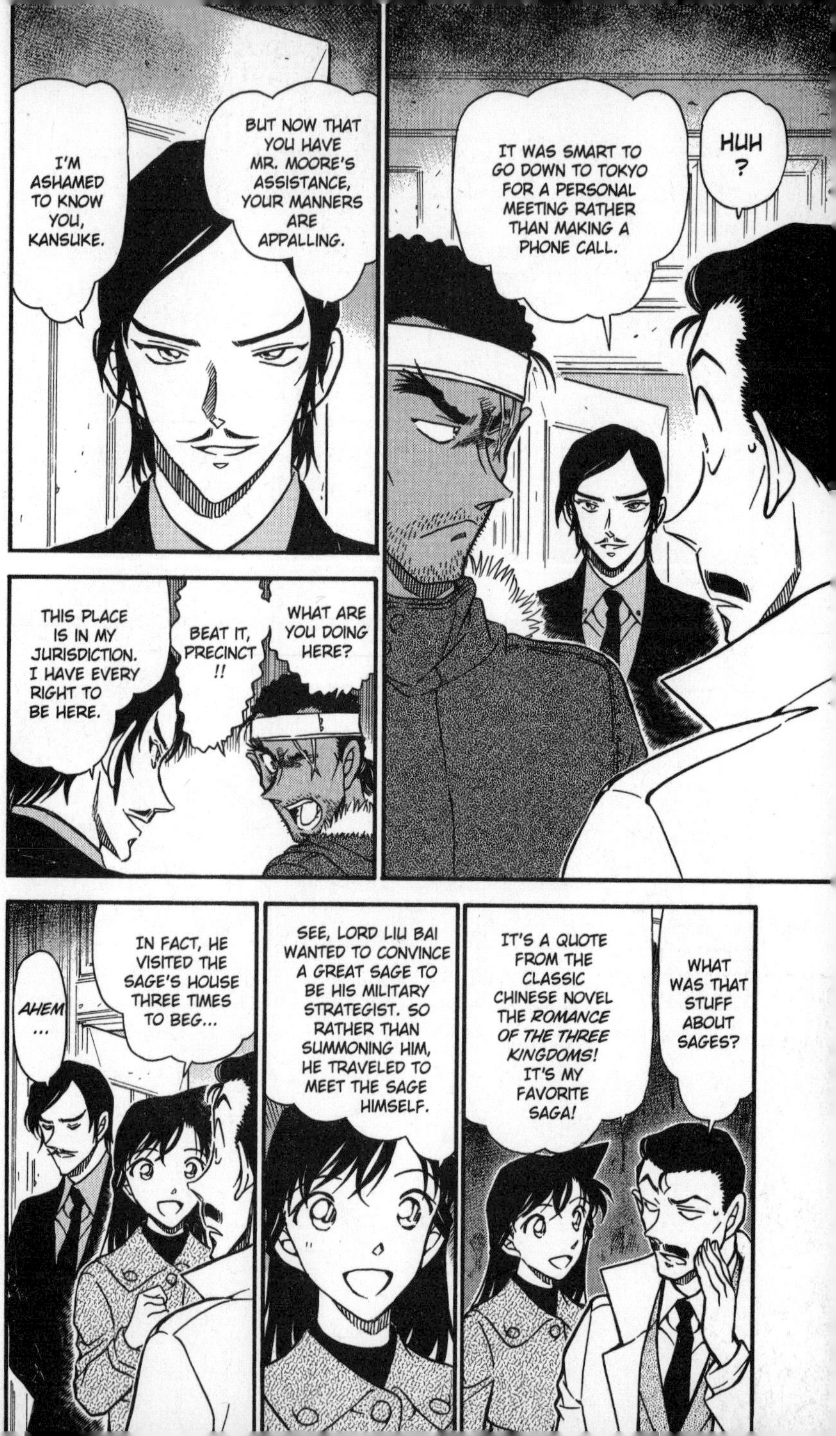
HUH?
IT WAS SMART TO GO DOWN TO TOKYO FOR A PERSONAL MEETING RATHER THAN MAKING A PHONE CALL.
BUT NOW THAT YOU HAVE MR. MOORE'S ASSISTANCE, YOUR MANNERS ARE APPALLING.
I'M ASHAMED TO KNOW YOU, KANSUKE.
WHAT ARE YOU DOING HERE?
BEAT IT, PRECINCT!!
THIS PLACE IS IN MY JURISDICTION. I HAVE EVERY RIGHT TO BE HERE.
WHAT WAS THAT STUFF ABOUT SAGES?
IT'S A QUOTE FROM THE CLASSIC CHINESE NOVEL THE *ROMANCE OF THE THREE KINGDOMS*! IT'S MY FAVORITE SAGA!
SEE, LORD LIU BAI WANTED TO CONVINCE A GREAT SAGE TO BE HIS MILITARY STRATEGIST. SO RATHER THAN SUMMONING HIM, HE TRAVELED TO MEET THE SAGE HIMSELF.
IN FACT, HE VISITED THE SAGE'S HOUSE THREE TIMES TO BEG...
AHEM...

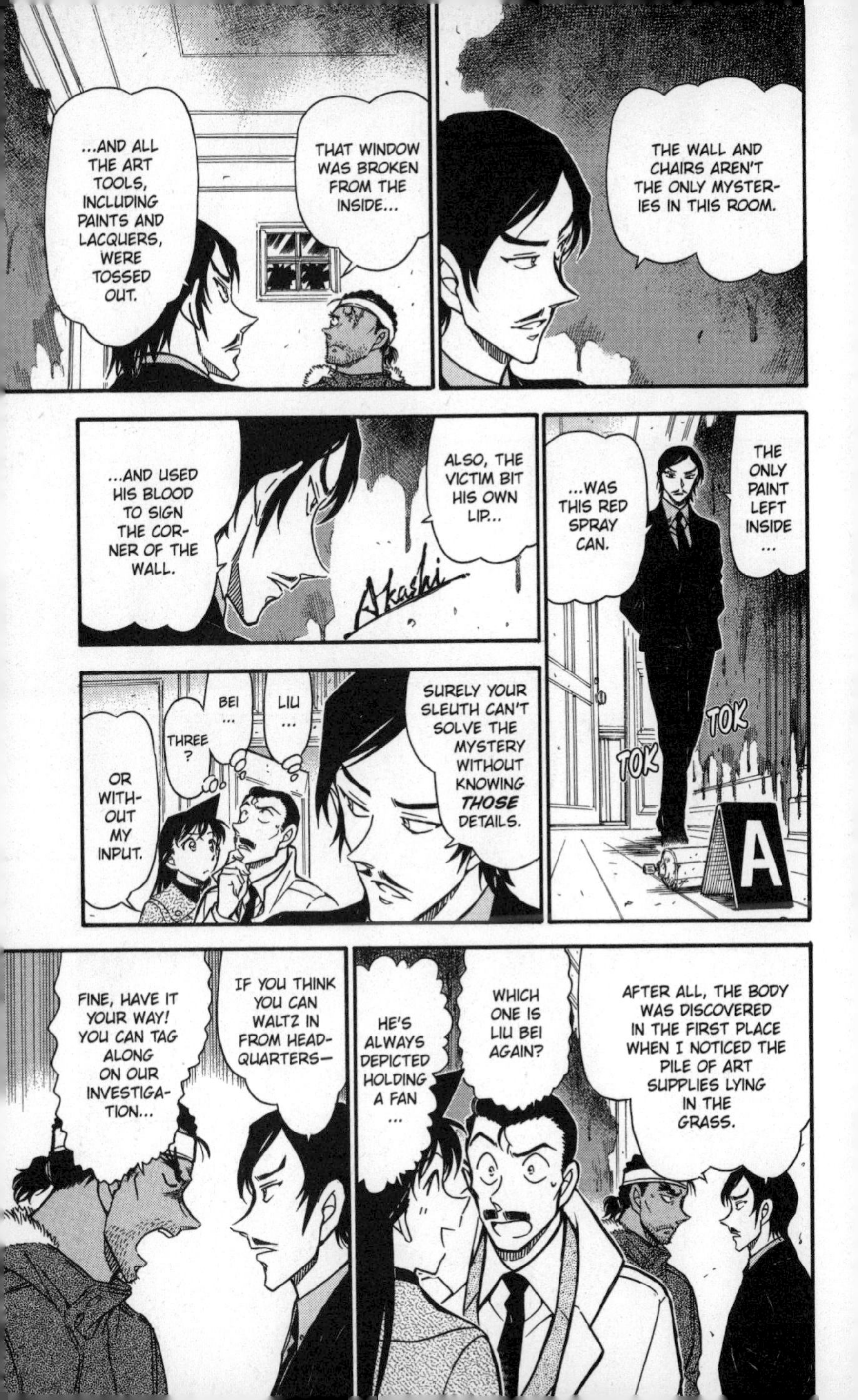
THE WALL AND CHAIRS AREN'T THE ONLY MYSTERIES IN THIS ROOM.
THAT WINDOW WAS BROKEN FROM THE INSIDE...
...AND ALL THE ART TOOLS, INCLUDING PAINTS AND LACQUERS, WERE TOSSED OUT.
THE ONLY PAINT LEFT INSIDE ...
...WAS THIS RED SPRAY CAN.
TOK
TOK
A
ALSO, THE VICTIM BIT HIS OWN LIP...
...AND USED HIS BLOOD TO SIGN THE CORNER OF THE WALL.
Akashi
SURELY YOUR SLEUTH CAN'T SOLVE THE MYSTERY WITHOUT KNOWING *THOSE* DETAILS.
LIU ...
BEI ...
THREE ?
OR WITHOUT MY INPUT.
AFTER ALL, THE BODY WAS DISCOVERED IN THE FIRST PLACE WHEN I NOTICED THE PILE OF ART SUPPLIES LYING IN THE GRASS.
WHICH ONE IS LIU BEI AGAIN?
HE'S ALWAYS DEPICTED HOLDING A FAN ...
IF YOU THINK YOU CAN WALTZ IN FROM HEADQUARTERS—
FINE, HAVE IT YOUR WAY! YOU CAN TAG ALONG ON OUR INVESTIGATION...

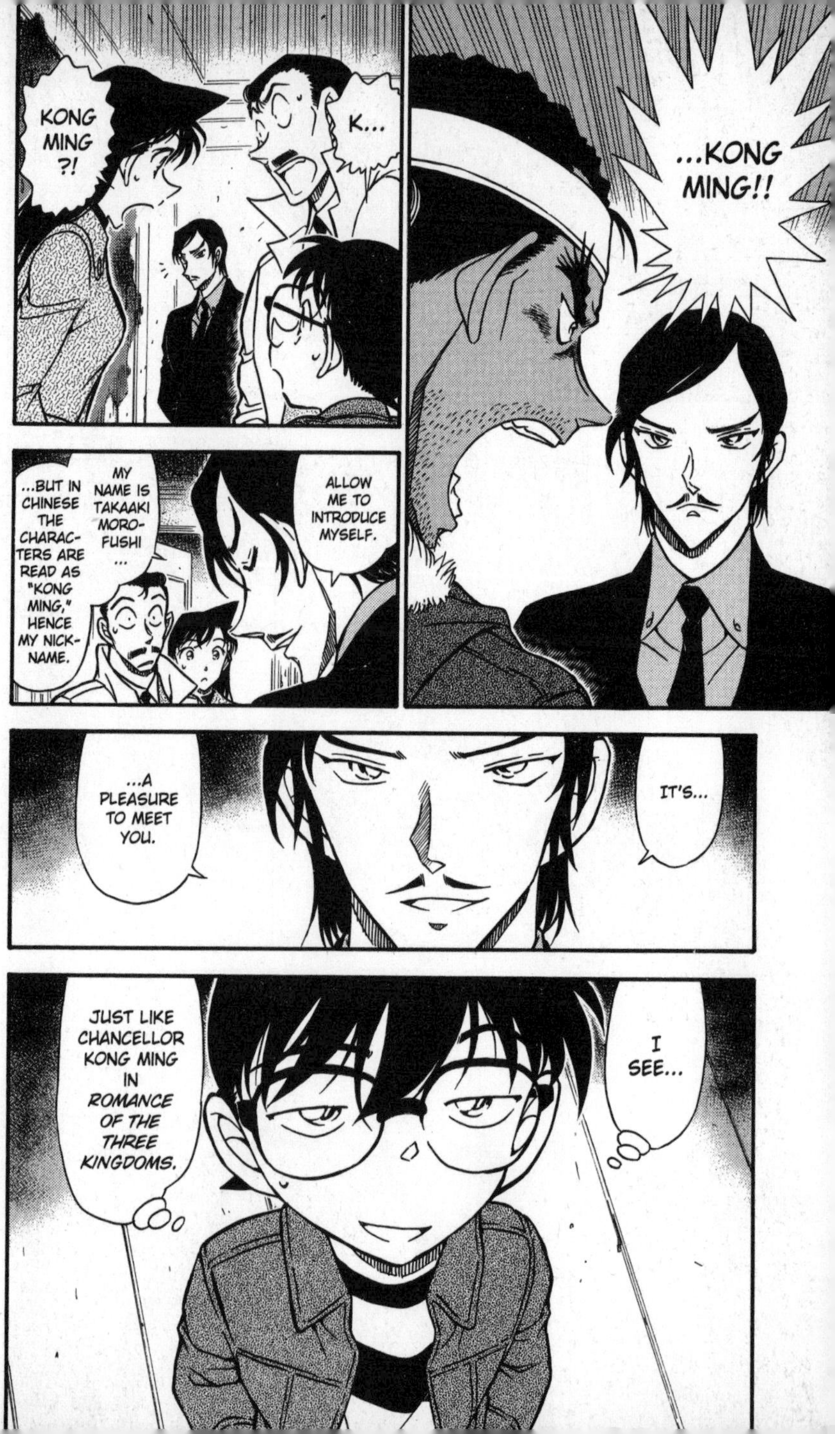

...KONG MING!!
K...
KONG MING ?!
ALLOW ME TO INTRODUCE MYSELF.
MY NAME IS TAKAAKI MORO-FUSHI ...
...BUT IN CHINESE THE CHARAC-TERS ARE READ AS "KONG MING," HENCE MY NICK-NAME.
IT'S...
...A PLEASURE TO MEET YOU.
I SEE...
JUST LIKE CHANCELLOR KONG MING IN *ROMANCE OF THE THREE KINGDOMS.*

FILE 9:
IN ONE'S GRASP

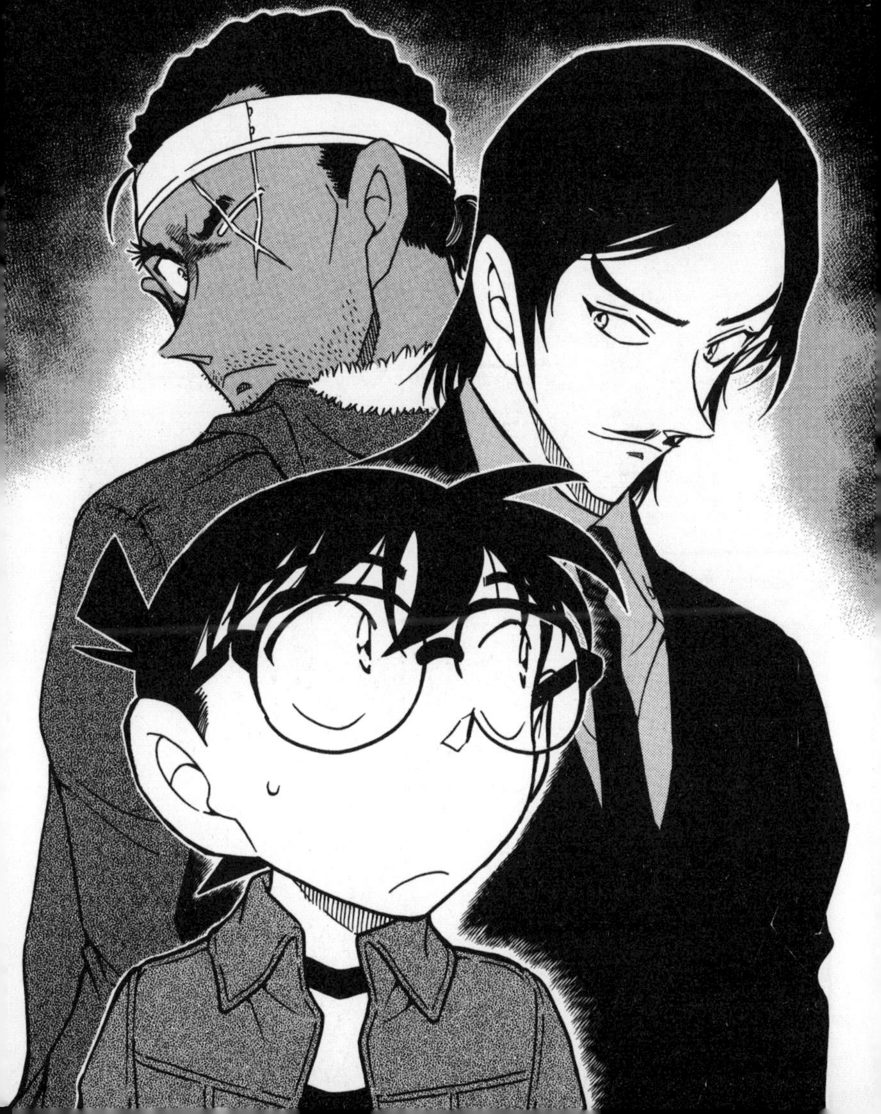

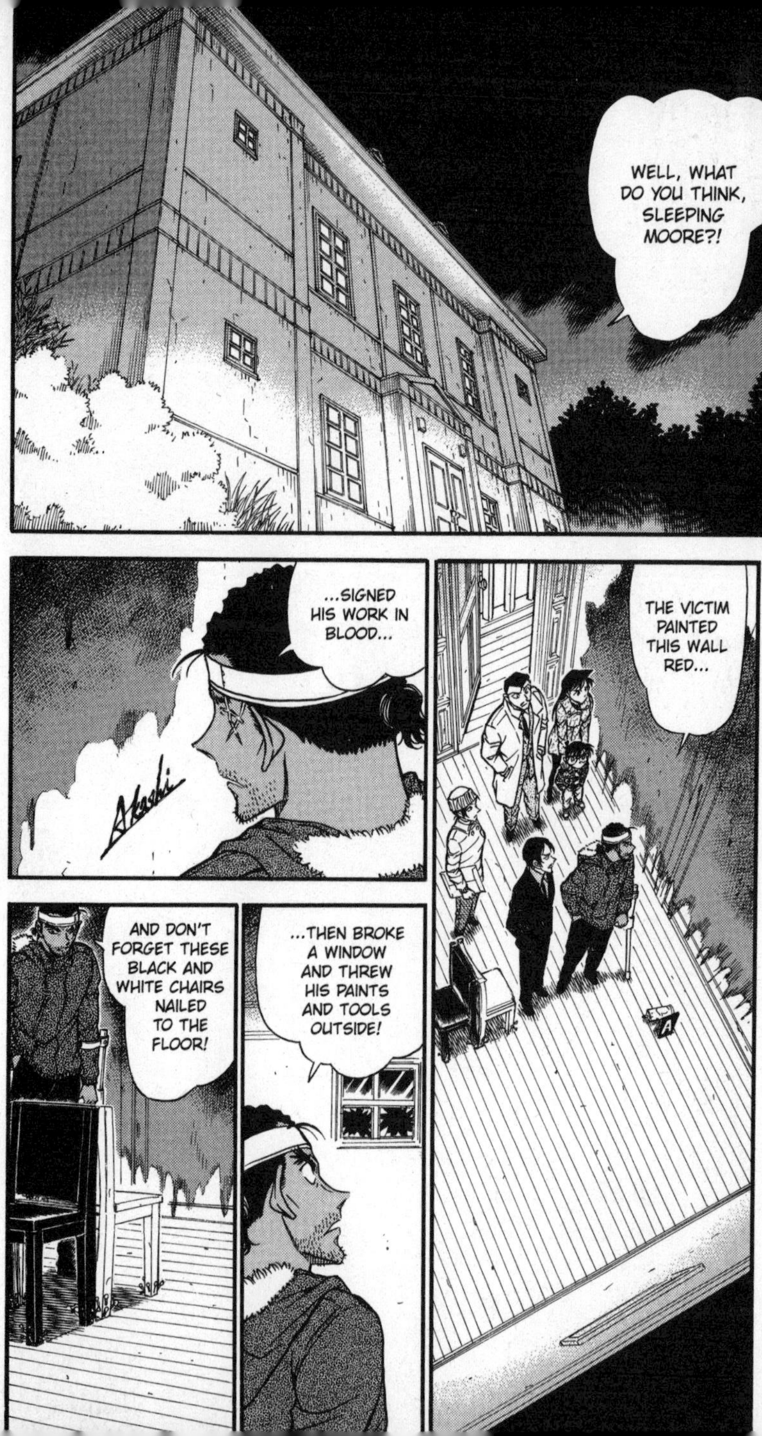
WELL, WHAT DO YOU THINK, SLEEPING MOORE?!
THE VICTIM PAINTED THIS WALL RED...
...SIGNED HIS WORK IN BLOOD...
Akashi
...THEN BROKE A WINDOW AND THREW HIS PAINTS AND TOOLS OUTSIDE!
AND DON'T FORGET THESE BLACK AND WHITE CHAIRS NAILED TO THE FLOOR!

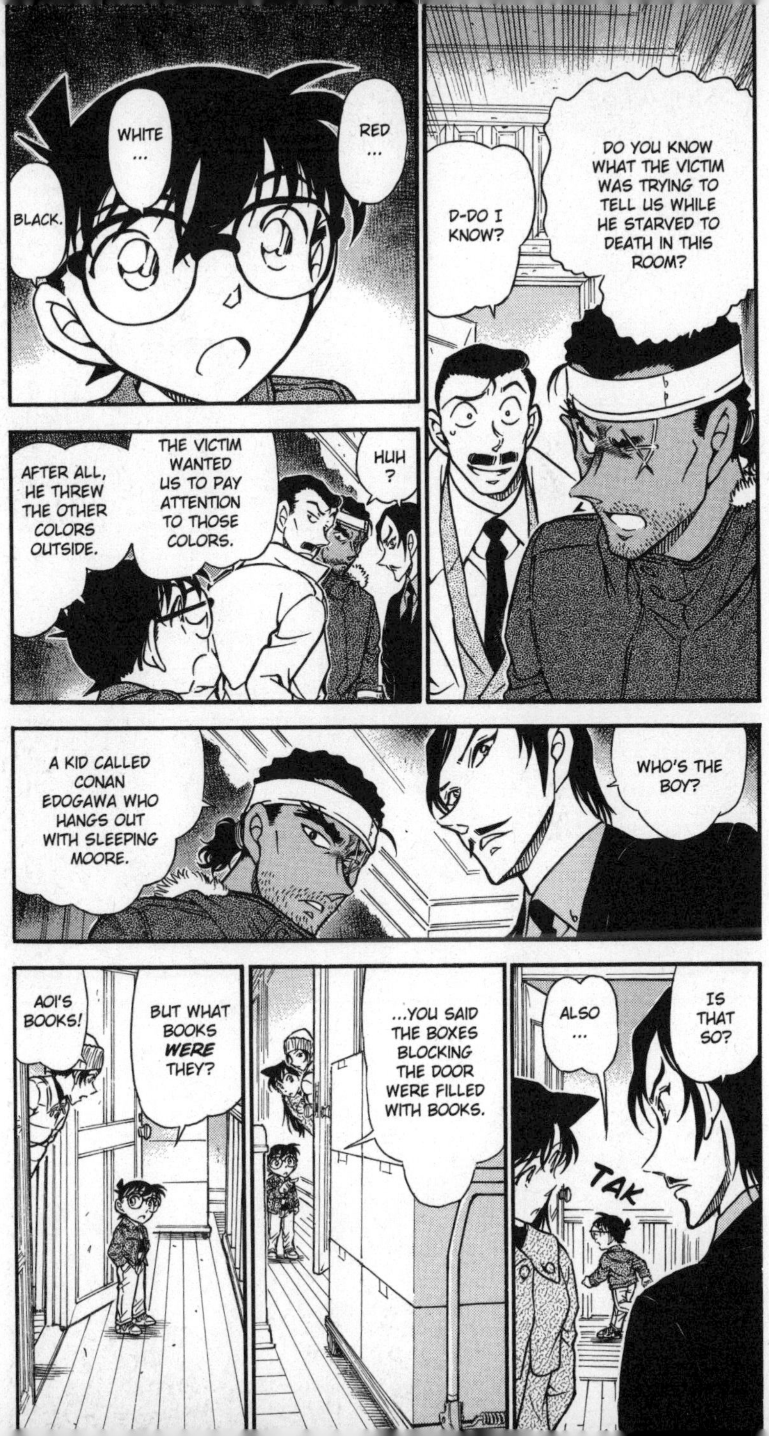

DO YOU KNOW WHAT THE VICTIM WAS TRYING TO TELL US WHILE HE STARVED TO DEATH IN THIS ROOM?
D-DO I KNOW?
RED ...
WHITE ...
BLACK.
HUH ?
THE VICTIM WANTED US TO PAY ATTENTION TO THOSE COLORS.
AFTER ALL, HE THREW THE OTHER COLORS OUTSIDE.
WHO'S THE BOY?
A KID CALLED CONAN EDOGAWA WHO HANGS OUT WITH SLEEPING MOORE.
IS THAT SO?
ALSO ...
TAK
...YOU SAID THE BOXES BLOCKING THE DOOR WERE FILLED WITH BOOKS.
BUT WHAT BOOKS *WERE* THEY?
AOI'S BOOKS!

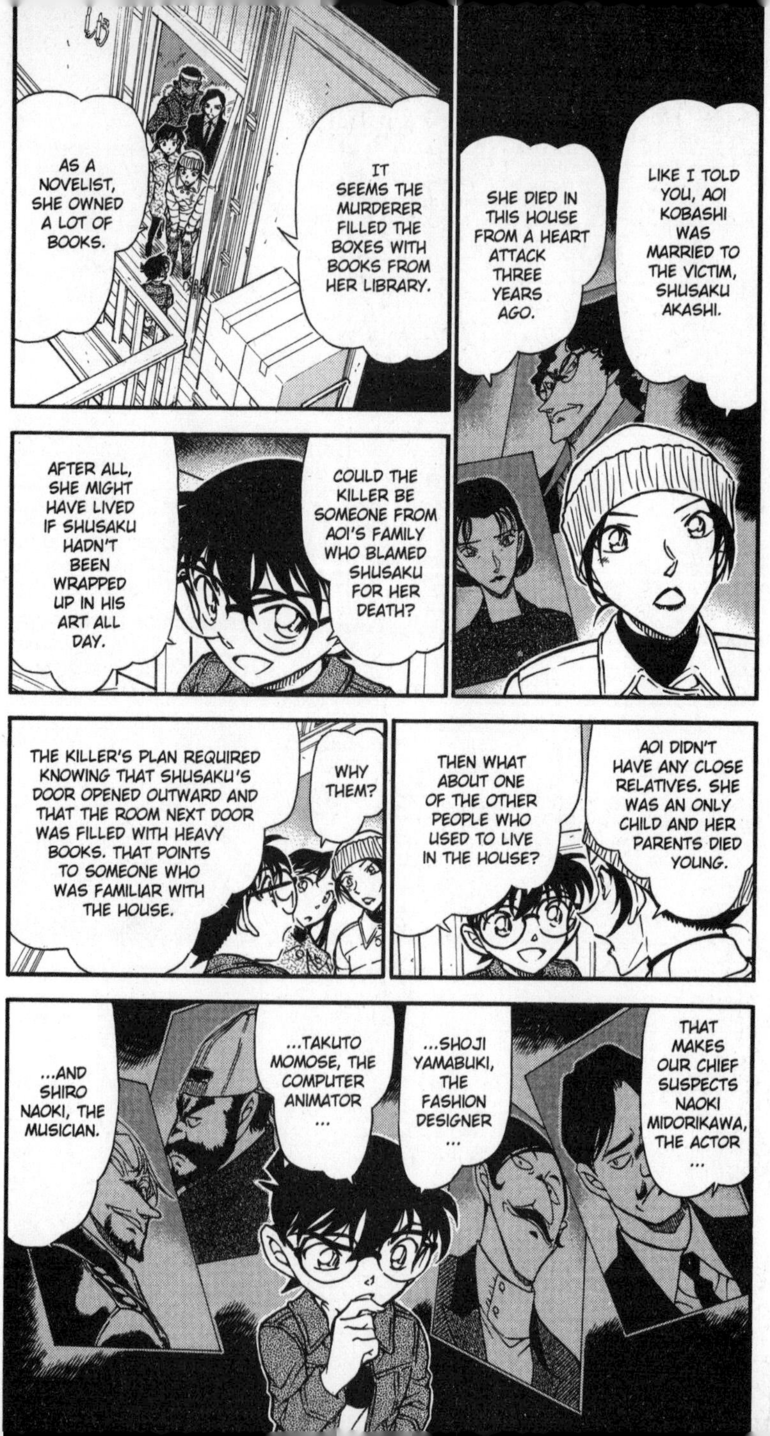
LIKE I TOLD YOU, AOI KOBASHI WAS MARRIED TO THE VICTIM, SHUSAKU AKASHI.
SHE DIED IN THIS HOUSE FROM A HEART ATTACK THREE YEARS AGO.
IT SEEMS THE MURDERER FILLED THE BOXES WITH BOOKS FROM HER LIBRARY.
AS A NOVELIST, SHE OWNED A LOT OF BOOKS.
COULD THE KILLER BE SOMEONE FROM AOI'S FAMILY WHO BLAMED SHUSAKU FOR HER DEATH?
AFTER ALL, SHE MIGHT HAVE LIVED IF SHUSAKU HADN'T BEEN WRAPPED UP IN HIS ART ALL DAY.
AOI DIDN'T HAVE ANY CLOSE RELATIVES. SHE WAS AN ONLY CHILD AND HER PARENTS DIED YOUNG.
THEN WHAT ABOUT ONE OF THE OTHER PEOPLE WHO USED TO LIVE IN THE HOUSE?
WHY THEM?
THE KILLER'S PLAN REQUIRED KNOWING THAT SHUSAKU'S DOOR OPENED OUTWARD AND THAT THE ROOM NEXT DOOR WAS FILLED WITH HEAVY BOOKS. THAT POINTS TO SOMEONE WHO WAS FAMILIAR WITH THE HOUSE.
THAT MAKES OUR CHIEF SUSPECTS NAOKI MIDORIKAWA, THE ACTOR ...
...SHOJI YAMABUKI, THE FASHION DESIGNER ...
...TAKUTO MOMOSE, THE COMPUTER ANIMATOR ...
...AND SHIRO NAOKI, THE MUSICIAN.

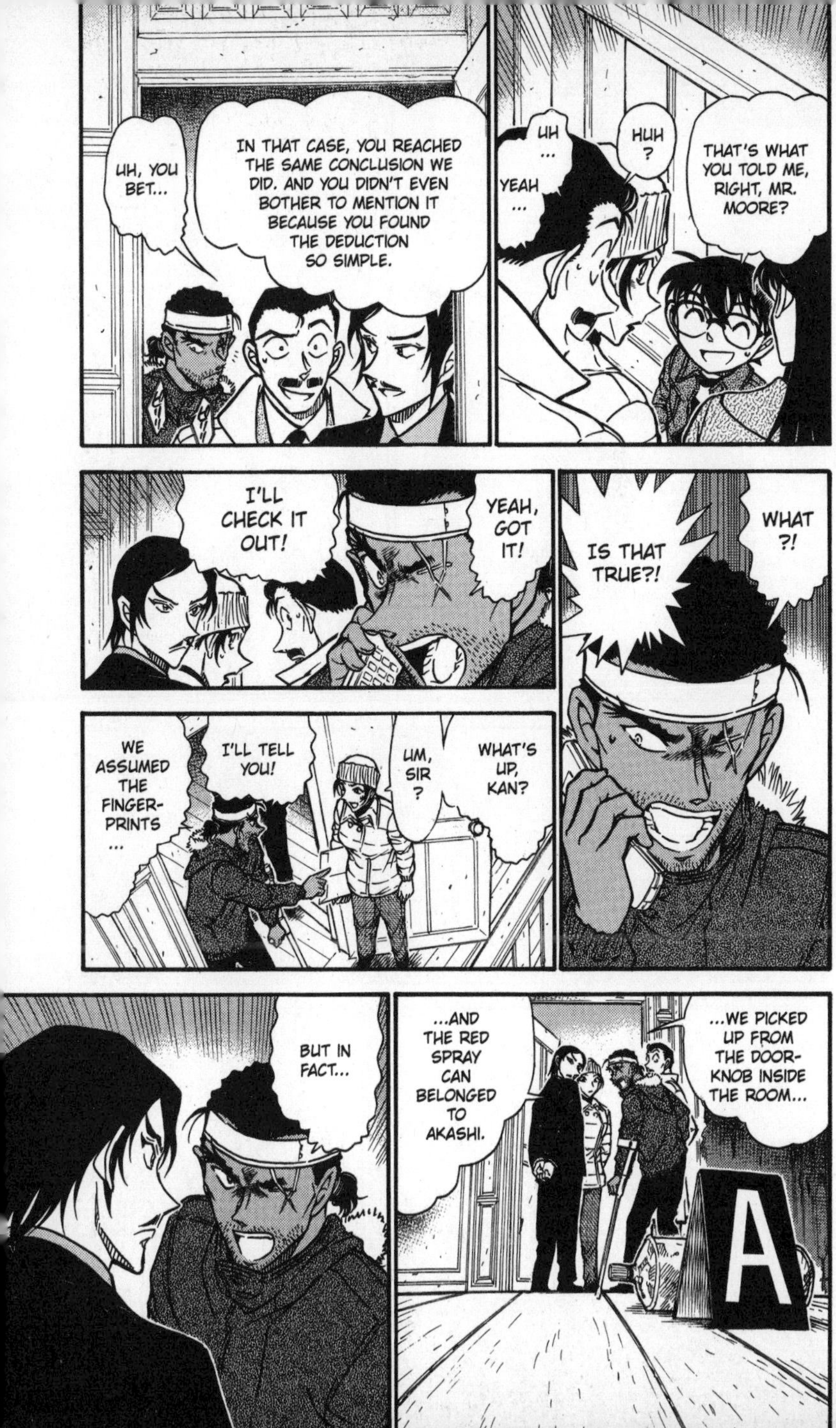
THAT'S WHAT YOU TOLD ME, RIGHT, MR. MOORE?
HUH?
UH... YEAH...
IN THAT CASE, YOU REACHED THE SAME CONCLUSION WE DID. AND YOU DIDN'T EVEN BOTHER TO MENTION IT BECAUSE YOU FOUND THE DEDUCTION SO SIMPLE.
UH, YOU BET...
WHAT?!
IS THAT TRUE?!
YEAH, GOT IT!
I'LL CHECK IT OUT!
WHAT'S UP, KAN?
UM, SIR?
I'LL TELL YOU!
WE ASSUMED THE FINGER-PRINTS...
...WE PICKED UP FROM THE DOOR-KNOB INSIDE THE ROOM...
...AND THE RED SPRAY CAN BELONGED TO AKASHI.
BUT IN FACT...

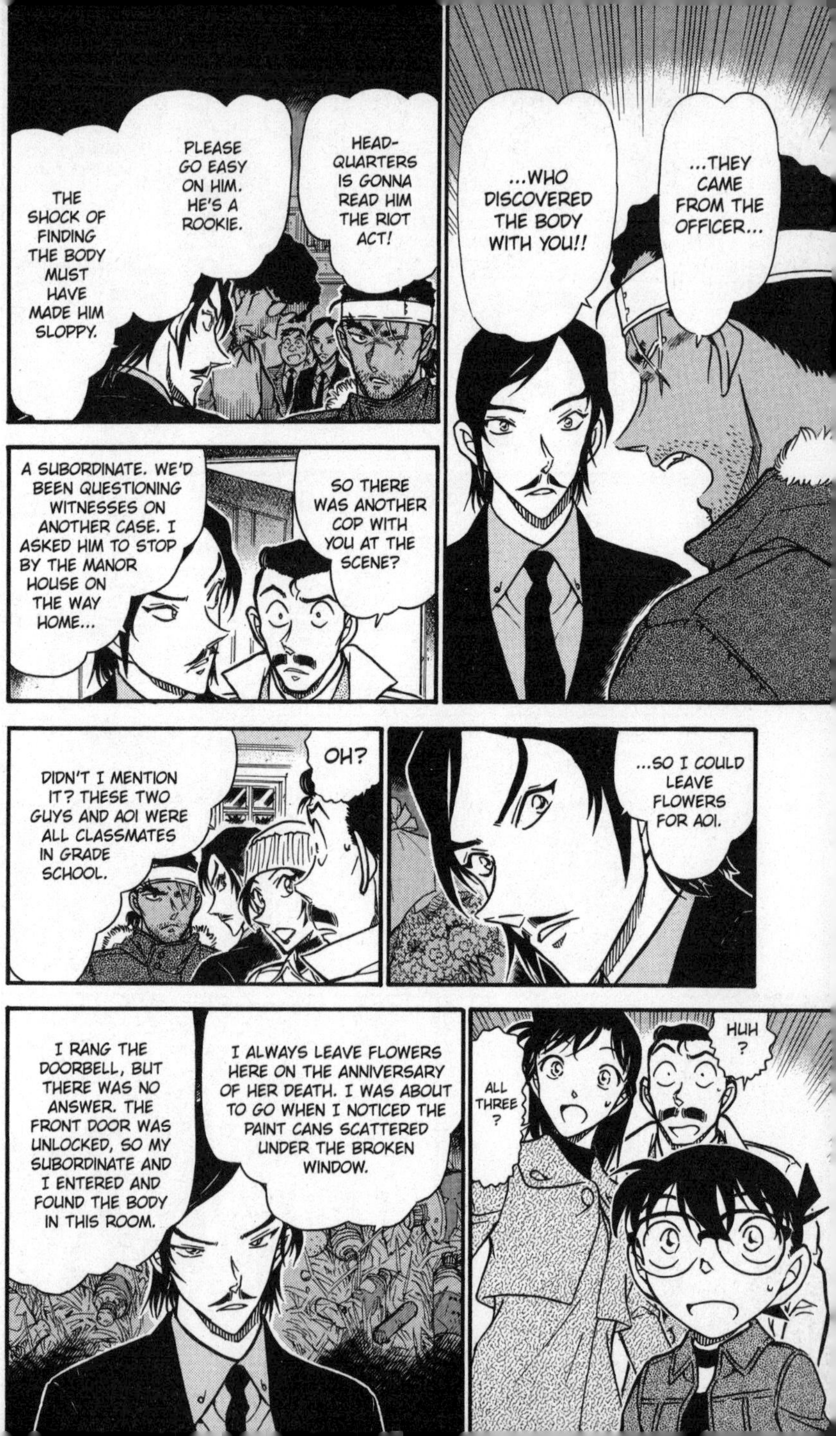
...THEY CAME FROM THE OFFICER...
...WHO DISCOVERED THE BODY WITH YOU!!
HEAD-QUARTERS IS GONNA READ HIM THE RIOT ACT!
PLEASE GO EASY ON HIM. HE'S A ROOKIE.
THE SHOCK OF FINDING THE BODY MUST HAVE MADE HIM SLOPPY.
SO THERE WAS ANOTHER COP WITH YOU AT THE SCENE?
A SUBORDINATE. WE'D BEEN QUESTIONING WITNESSES ON ANOTHER CASE. I ASKED HIM TO STOP BY THE MANOR HOUSE ON THE WAY HOME...
...SO I COULD LEAVE FLOWERS FOR AOI.
OH?
DIDN'T I MENTION IT? THESE TWO GUYS AND AOI WERE ALL CLASSMATES IN GRADE SCHOOL.
HUH?
ALL THREE?
I ALWAYS LEAVE FLOWERS HERE ON THE ANNIVERSARY OF HER DEATH. I WAS ABOUT TO GO WHEN I NOTICED THE PAINT CANS SCATTERED UNDER THE BROKEN WINDOW.
I RANG THE DOORBELL, BUT THERE WAS NO ANSWER. THE FRONT DOOR WAS UNLOCKED, SO MY SUBORDINATE AND I ENTERED AND FOUND THE BODY IN THIS ROOM.

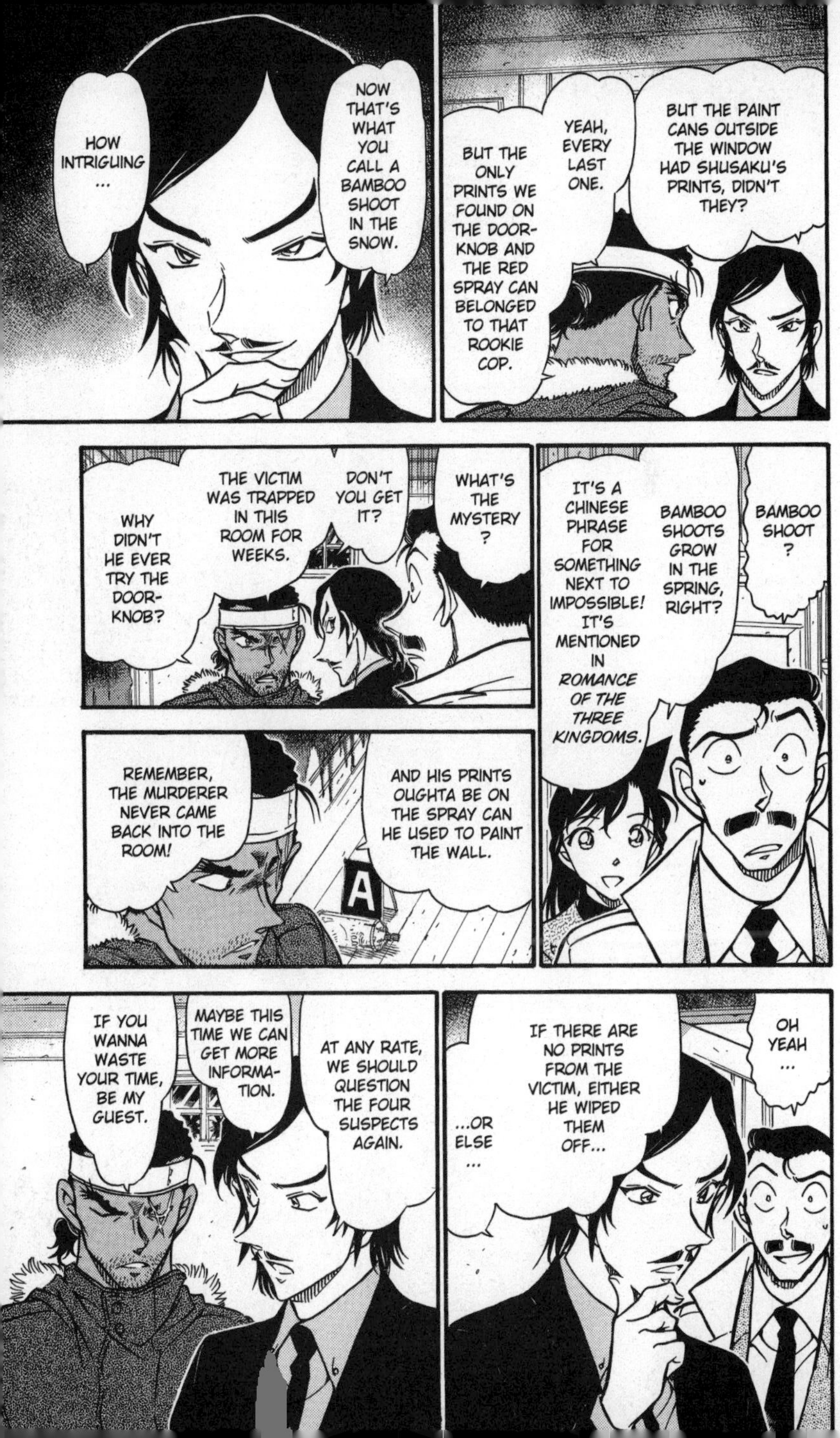
BUT THE PAINT CANS OUTSIDE THE WINDOW HAD SHUSAKU'S PRINTS, DIDN'T THEY?
YEAH, EVERY LAST ONE.
BUT THE ONLY PRINTS WE FOUND ON THE DOORKNOB AND THE RED SPRAY CAN BELONGED TO THAT ROOKIE COP.
NOW THAT'S WHAT YOU CALL A BAMBOO SHOOT IN THE SNOW.
HOW INTRIGUING...
BAMBOO SHOOT?
BAMBOO SHOOTS GROW IN THE SPRING, RIGHT?
IT'S A CHINESE PHRASE FOR SOMETHING NEXT TO IMPOSSIBLE! IT'S MENTIONED IN *ROMANCE OF THE THREE KINGDOMS.*
WHAT'S THE MYSTERY?
DON'T YOU GET IT?
THE VICTIM WAS TRAPPED IN THIS ROOM FOR WEEKS.
WHY DIDN'T HE EVER TRY THE DOORKNOB?
AND HIS PRINTS OUGHTA BE ON THE SPRAY CAN HE USED TO PAINT THE WALL.
REMEMBER, THE MURDERER NEVER CAME BACK INTO THE ROOM!
A
OH YEAH...
IF THERE ARE NO PRINTS FROM THE VICTIM, EITHER HE WIPED THEM OFF...
...OR ELSE...
AT ANY RATE, WE SHOULD QUESTION THE FOUR SUSPECTS AGAIN.
MAYBE THIS TIME WE CAN GET MORE INFORMATION.
IF YOU WANNA WASTE YOUR TIME, BE MY GUEST.

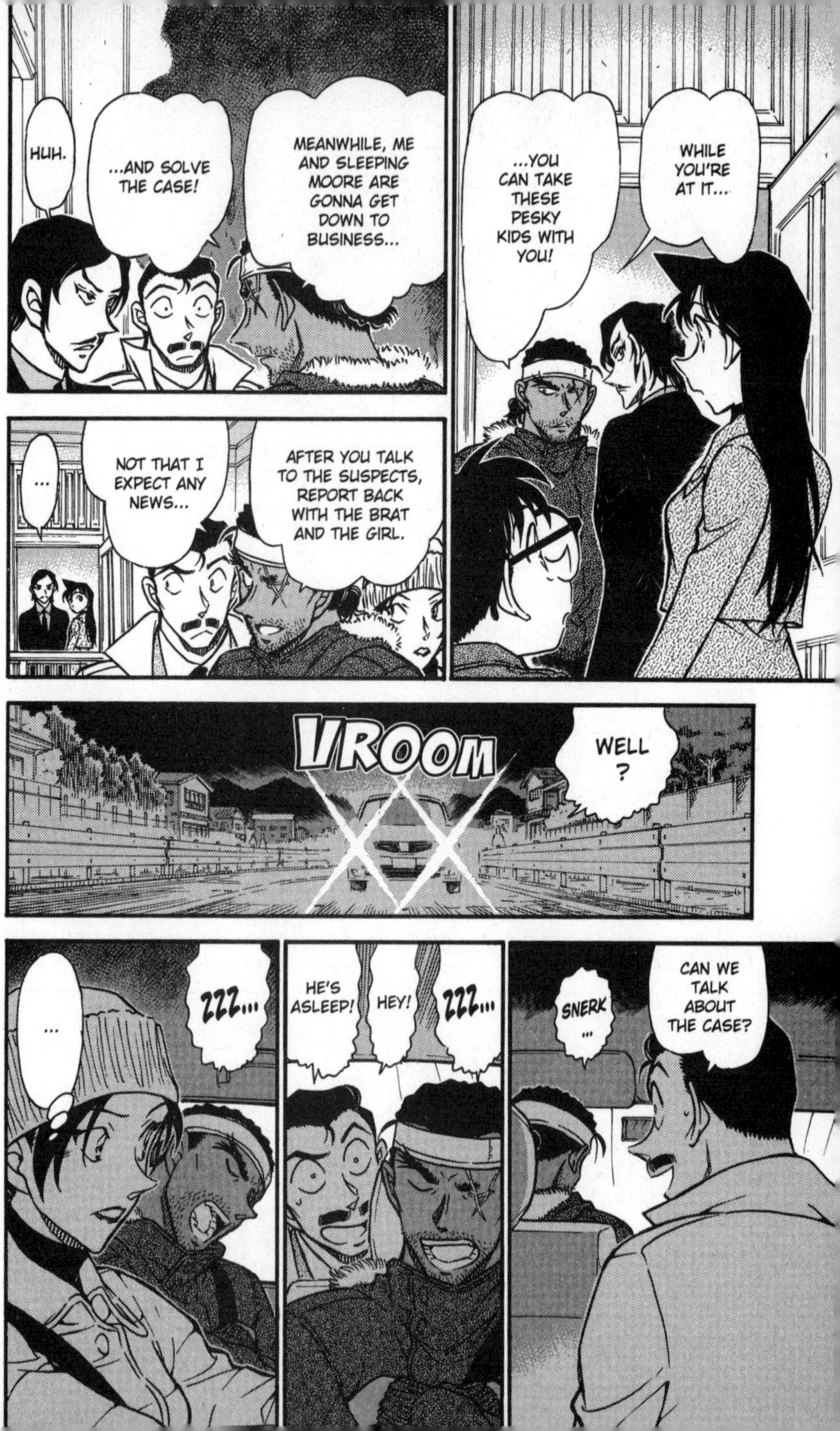
WHILE YOU'RE AT IT...
...YOU CAN TAKE THESE PESKY KIDS WITH YOU!
MEANWHILE, ME AND SLEEPING MOORE ARE GONNA GET DOWN TO BUSINESS...
...AND SOLVE THE CASE!
HUH.
AFTER YOU TALK TO THE SUSPECTS, REPORT BACK WITH THE BRAT AND THE GIRL.
NOT THAT I EXPECT ANY NEWS...
...
VROOM
WELL ?
CAN WE TALK ABOUT THE CASE?
SNERK ...
ZZZ...
HEY!
HE'S ASLEEP!
ZZZ...
...

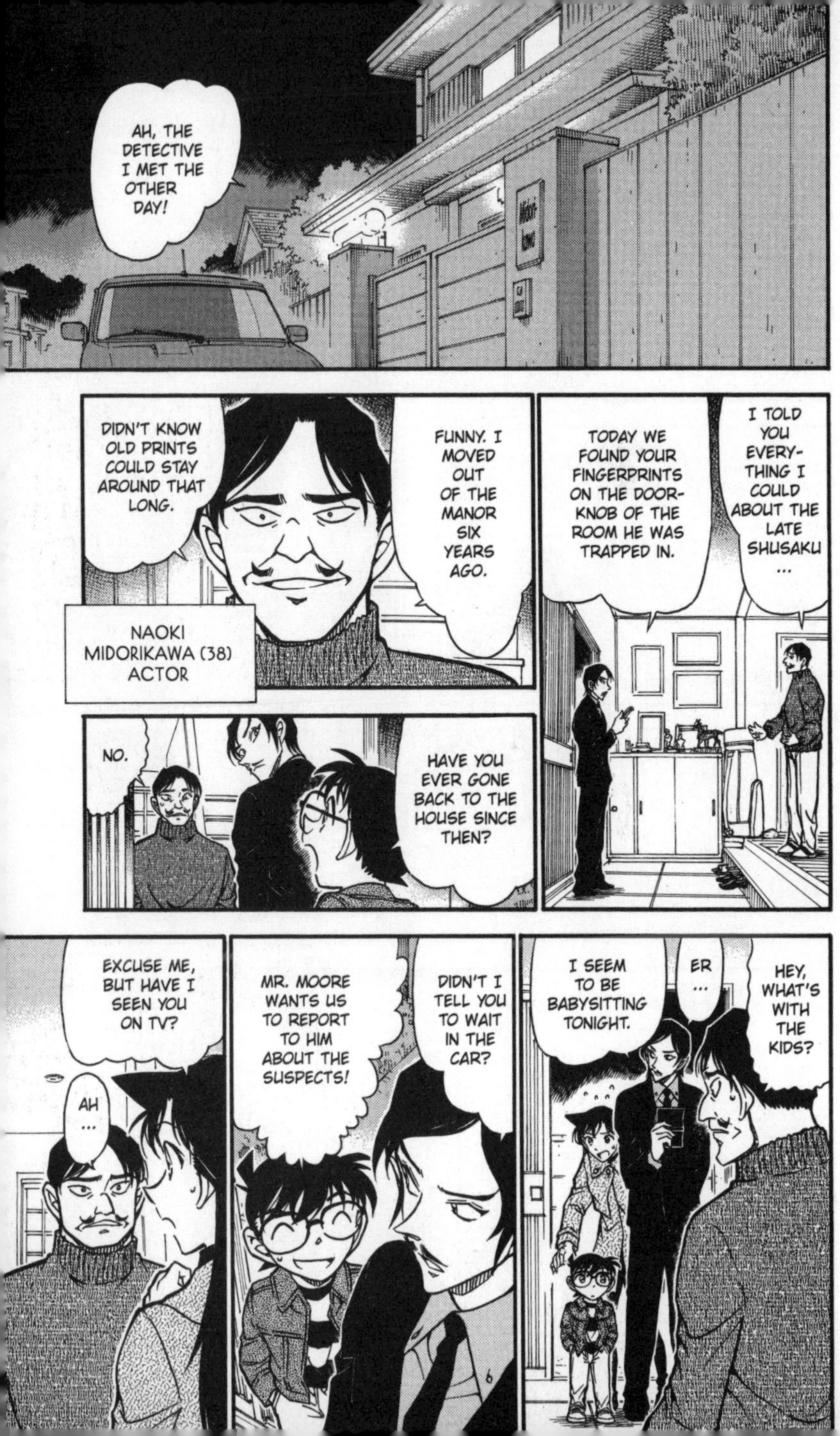
AH, THE DETECTIVE I MET THE OTHER DAY!
I TOLD YOU EVERY-THING I COULD ABOUT THE LATE SHUSAKU ...
TODAY WE FOUND YOUR FINGERPRINTS ON THE DOOR-KNOB OF THE ROOM HE WAS TRAPPED IN.
FUNNY. I MOVED OUT OF THE MANOR SIX YEARS AGO.
DIDN'T KNOW OLD PRINTS COULD STAY AROUND THAT LONG.
NAOKI MIDORIKAWA (38) ACTOR
HAVE YOU EVER GONE BACK TO THE HOUSE SINCE THEN?
NO.
HEY, WHAT'S WITH THE KIDS?
ER ...
I SEEM TO BE BABYSITTING TONIGHT.
DIDN'T I TELL YOU TO WAIT IN THE CAR?
MR. MOORE WANTS US TO REPORT TO HIM ABOUT THE SUSPECTS!
EXCUSE ME, BUT HAVE I SEEN YOU ON TV?
AH ...

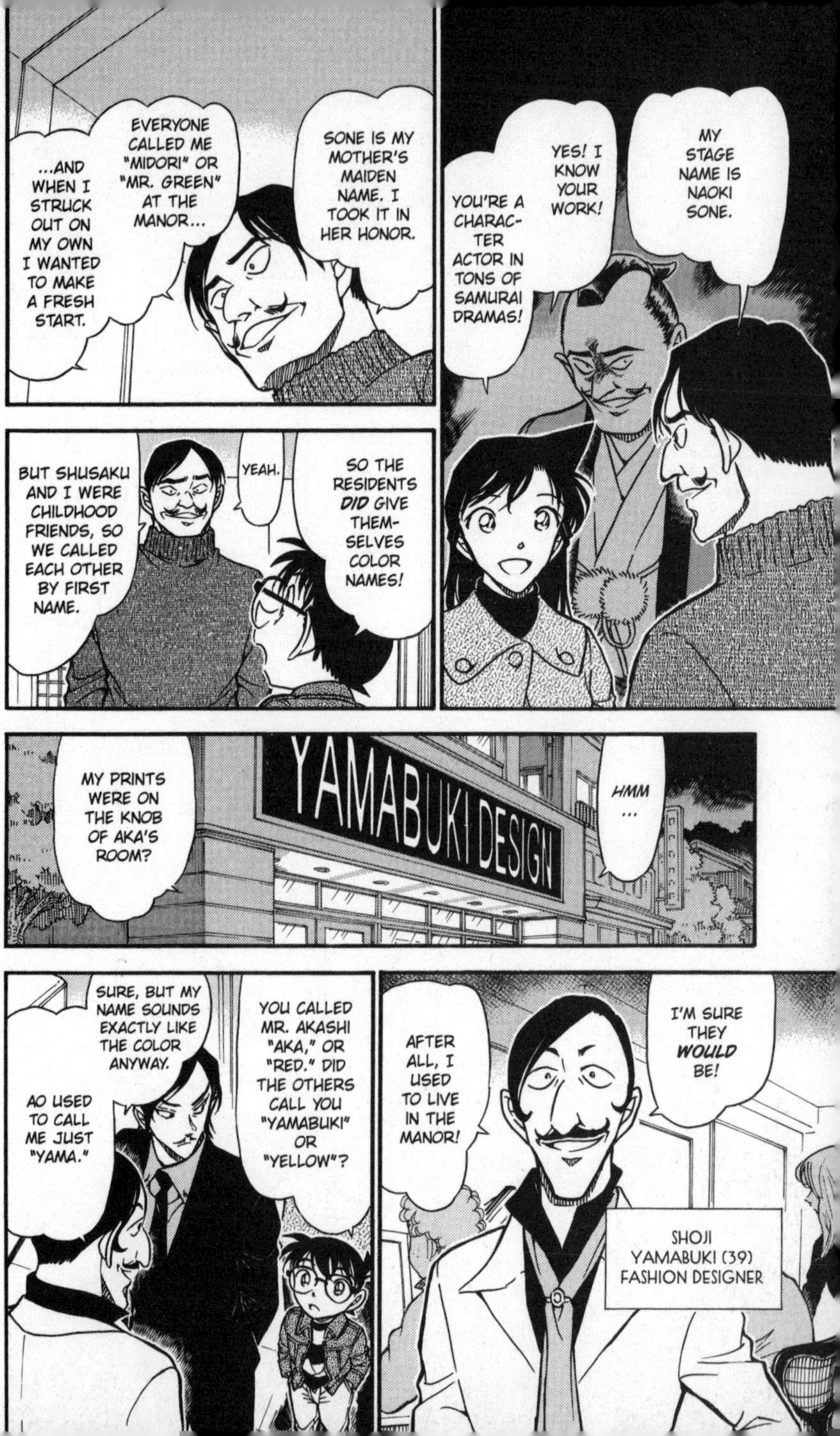
MY STAGE NAME IS NAOKI SONE.
YES! I KNOW YOUR WORK!
YOU'RE A CHARACTER ACTOR IN TONS OF SAMURAI DRAMAS!
SONE IS MY MOTHER'S MAIDEN NAME. I TOOK IT IN HER HONOR.
EVERYONE CALLED ME "MIDORI" OR "MR. GREEN" AT THE MANOR...
...AND WHEN I STRUCK OUT ON MY OWN I WANTED TO MAKE A FRESH START.
SO THE RESIDENTS *DID* GIVE THEMSELVES COLOR NAMES!
YEAH.
BUT SHUSAKU AND I WERE CHILDHOOD FRIENDS, SO WE CALLED EACH OTHER BY FIRST NAME.
YAMABUKI DESIGN
HMM ...
MY PRINTS WERE ON THE KNOB OF AKA'S ROOM?
I'M SURE THEY *WOULD* BE!
AFTER ALL, I USED TO LIVE IN THE MANOR!
SHOJI YAMABUKI (39) FASHION DESIGNER
YOU CALLED MR. AKASHI "AKA," OR "RED." DID THE OTHERS CALL YOU "YAMABUKI" OR "YELLOW"?
SURE, BUT MY NAME SOUNDS EXACTLY LIKE THE COLOR ANYWAY.
AO USED TO CALL ME JUST "YAMA."

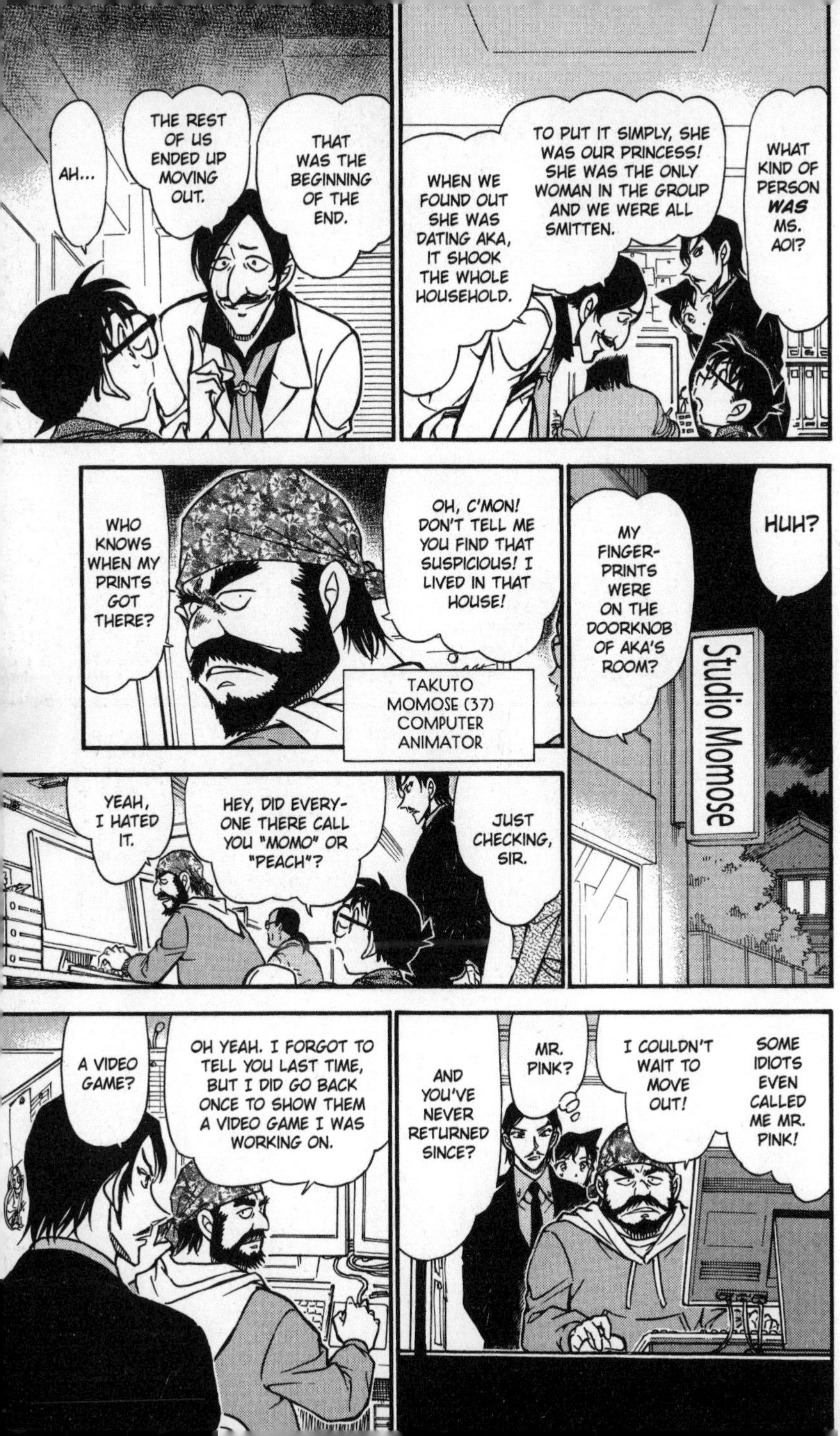
WHAT KIND OF PERSON WAS MS. AOI?
TO PUT IT SIMPLY, SHE WAS OUR PRINCESS! SHE WAS THE ONLY WOMAN IN THE GROUP AND WE WERE ALL SMITTEN.
WHEN WE FOUND OUT SHE WAS DATING AKA, IT SHOOK THE WHOLE HOUSEHOLD.
THAT WAS THE BEGINNING OF THE END.
THE REST OF US ENDED UP MOVING OUT.
AH...
HUH?
MY FINGER-PRINTS WERE ON THE DOORKNOB OF AKA'S ROOM?
Studio Momose
OH, C'MON! DON'T TELL ME YOU FIND THAT SUSPICIOUS! I LIVED IN THAT HOUSE!
WHO KNOWS WHEN MY PRINTS GOT THERE?
TAKUTO MOMOSE (37) COMPUTER ANIMATOR
JUST CHECKING, SIR.
HEY, DID EVERY-ONE THERE CALL YOU "MOMO" OR "PEACH"?
YEAH, I HATED IT.
SOME IDIOTS EVEN CALLED ME MR. PINK!
I COULDN'T WAIT TO MOVE OUT!
MR. PINK?
AND YOU'VE NEVER RETURNED SINCE?
OH YEAH. I FORGOT TO TELL YOU LAST TIME, BUT I DID GO BACK ONCE TO SHOW THEM A VIDEO GAME I WAS WORKING ON.
A VIDEO GAME?

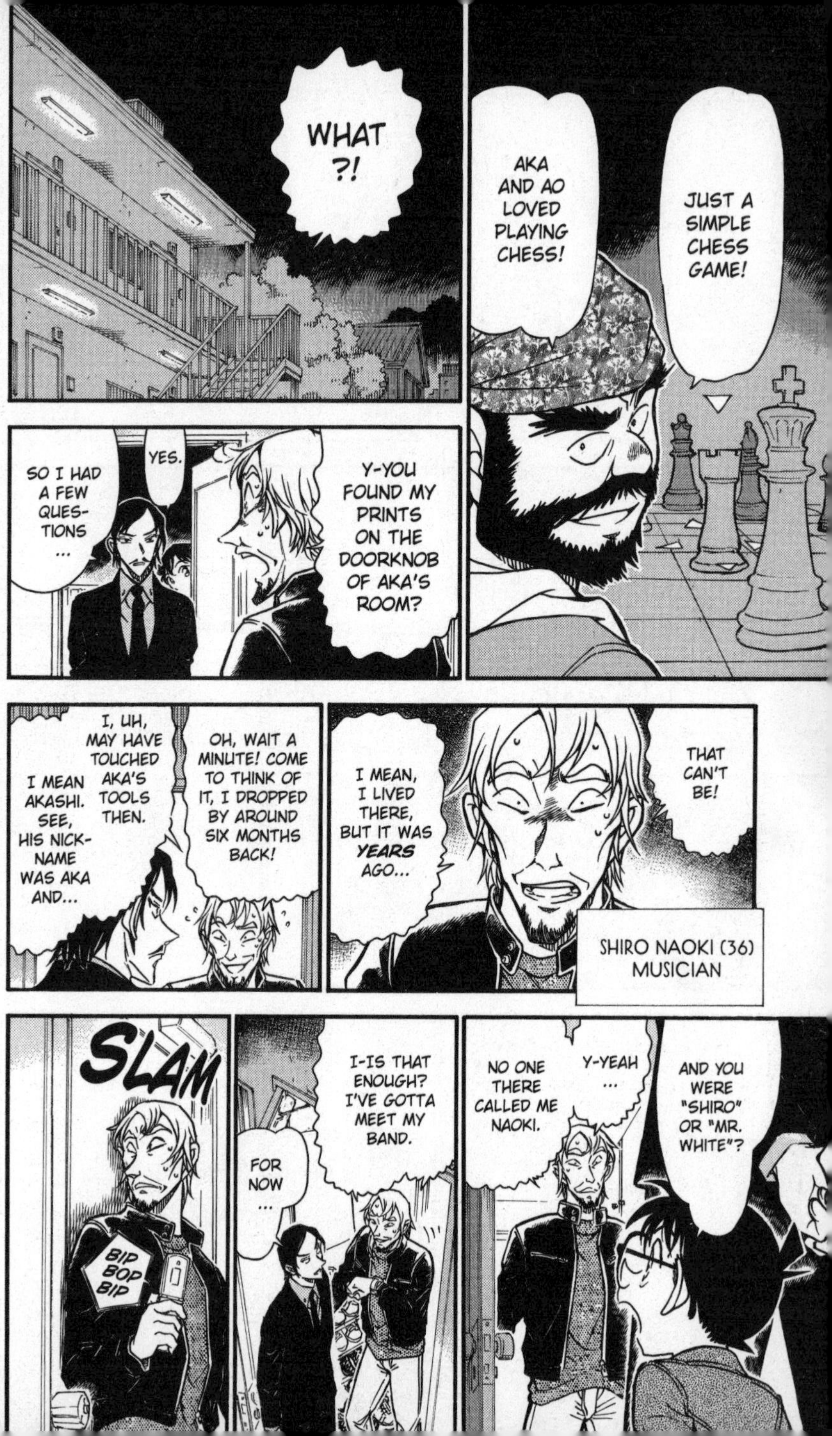
JUST A SIMPLE CHESS GAME!
AKA AND AO LOVED PLAYING CHESS!
WHAT ?!
Y-YOU FOUND MY PRINTS ON THE DOORKNOB OF AKA'S ROOM?
YES.
SO I HAD A FEW QUES-TIONS ...
THAT CAN'T BE!
I MEAN, I LIVED THERE, BUT IT WAS *YEARS* AGO...
SHIRO NAOKI (36) MUSICIAN
OH, WAIT A MINUTE! COME TO THINK OF IT, I DROPPED BY AROUND SIX MONTHS BACK!
I, UH, MAY HAVE TOUCHED AKA'S TOOLS THEN.
I MEAN AKASHI. SEE, HIS NICK-NAME WAS AKA AND...
AND YOU WERE "SHIRO" OR "MR. WHITE"?
Y-YEAH ...
NO ONE THERE CALLED ME NAOKI.
I-IS THAT ENOUGH? I'VE GOTTA MEET MY BAND.
FOR NOW ...
SLAM
BIP BOP BIP

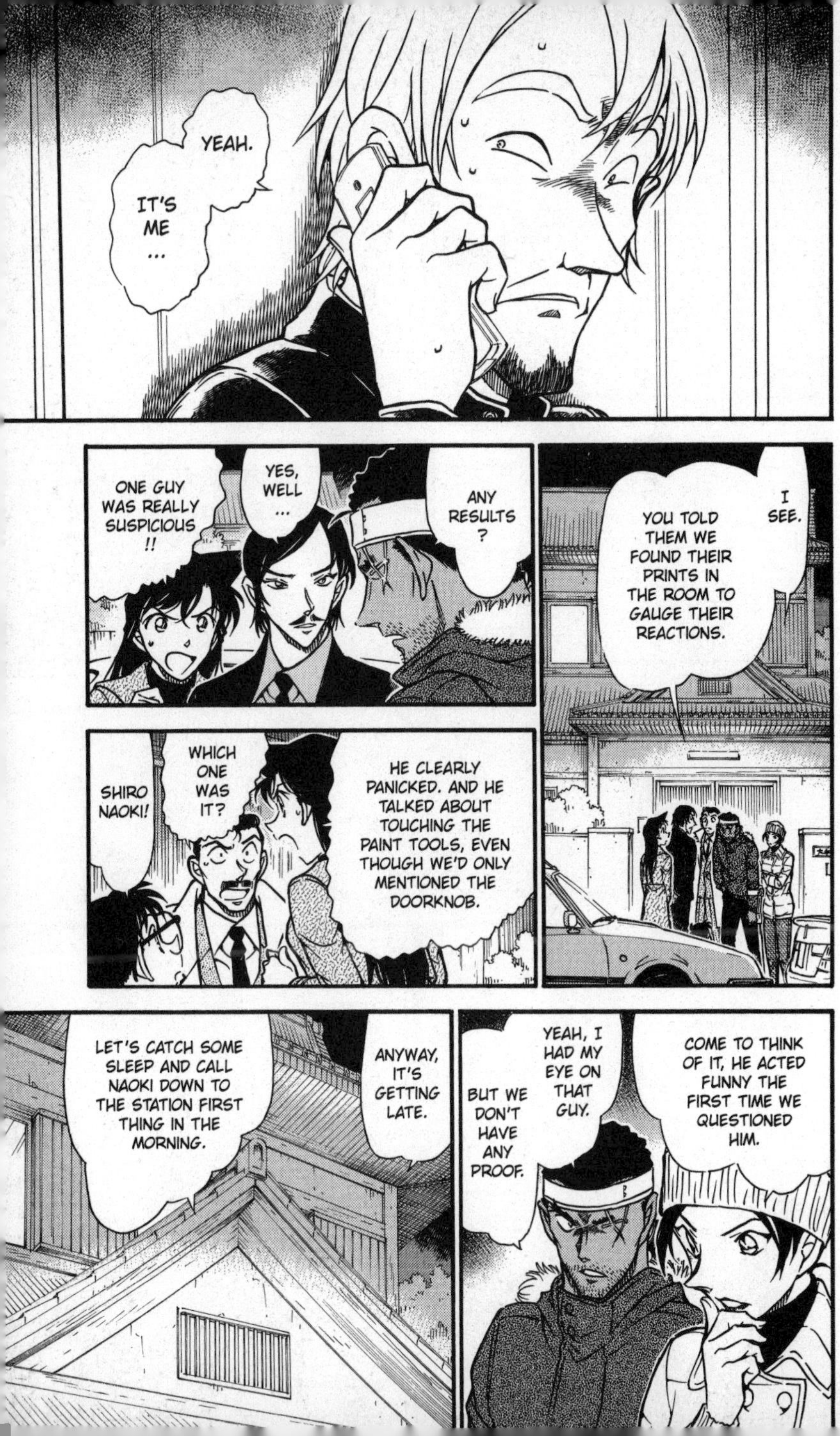
YEAH.
IT'S ME ...
I SEE.
YOU TOLD THEM WE FOUND THEIR PRINTS IN THE ROOM TO GAUGE THEIR REACTIONS.
ANY RESULTS?
YES, WELL ...
ONE GUY WAS REALLY SUSPICIOUS!!
HE CLEARLY PANICKED. AND HE TALKED ABOUT TOUCHING THE PAINT TOOLS, EVEN THOUGH WE'D ONLY MENTIONED THE DOORKNOB.
WHICH ONE WAS IT?
SHIRO NAOKI!
COME TO THINK OF IT, HE ACTED FUNNY THE FIRST TIME WE QUESTIONED HIM.
YEAH, I HAD MY EYE ON THAT GUY.
BUT WE DON'T HAVE ANY PROOF.
ANYWAY, IT'S GETTING LATE.
LET'S CATCH SOME SLEEP AND CALL NAOKI DOWN TO THE STATION FIRST THING IN THE MORNING.

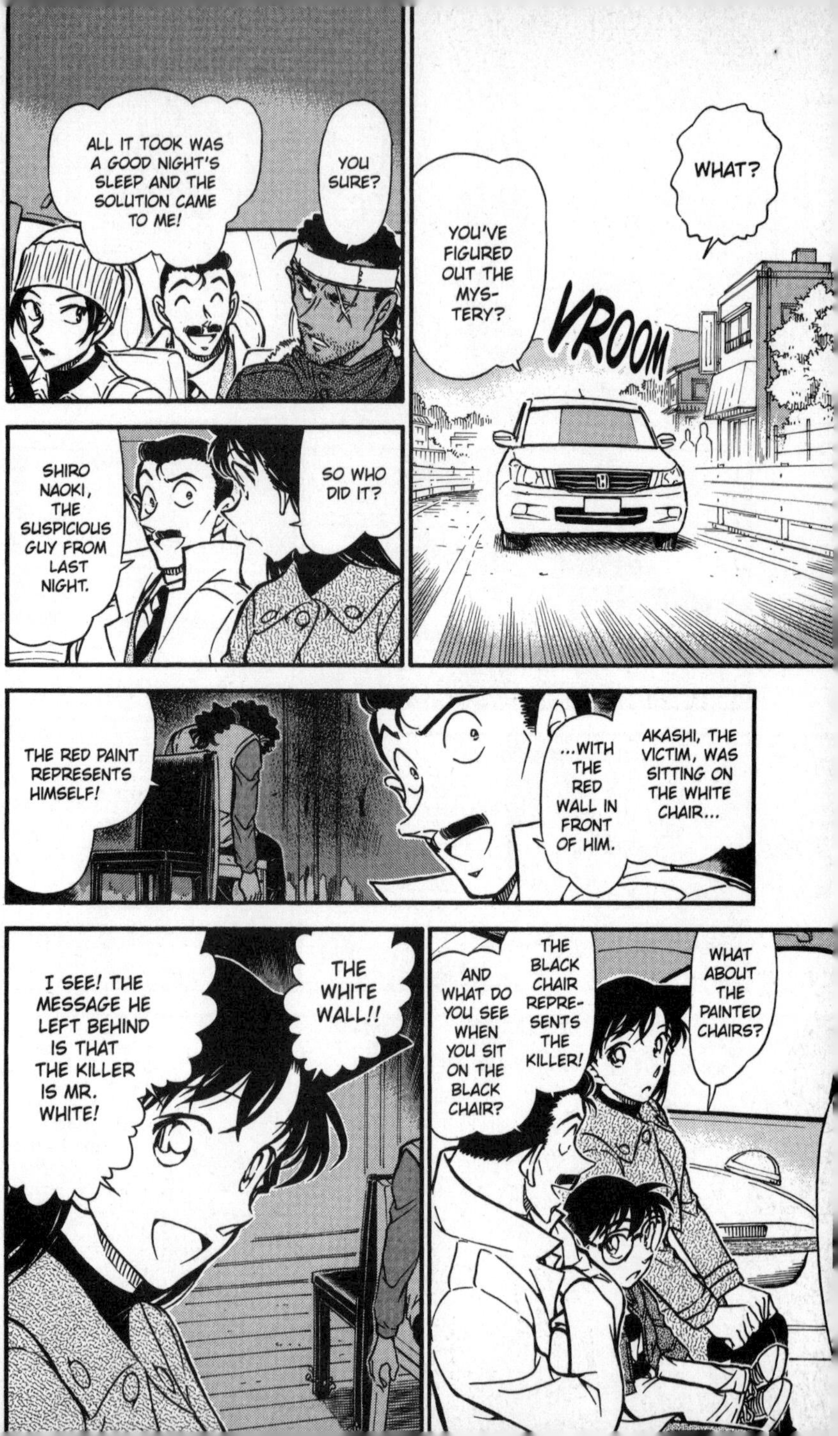
WHAT?
YOU'VE FIGURED OUT THE MYSTERY?
VROOM
YOU SURE?
ALL IT TOOK WAS A GOOD NIGHT'S SLEEP AND THE SOLUTION CAME TO ME!
SO WHO DID IT?
SHIRO NAOKI, THE SUSPICIOUS GUY FROM LAST NIGHT.
AKASHI, THE VICTIM, WAS SITTING ON THE WHITE CHAIR...
...WITH THE RED WALL IN FRONT OF HIM.
THE RED PAINT REPRESENTS HIMSELF!
WHAT ABOUT THE PAINTED CHAIRS?
THE BLACK CHAIR REPRESENTS THE KILLER!
AND WHAT DO YOU SEE WHEN YOU SIT ON THE BLACK CHAIR?
THE WHITE WALL!!
I SEE! THE MESSAGE HE LEFT BEHIND IS THAT THE KILLER IS MR. WHITE!

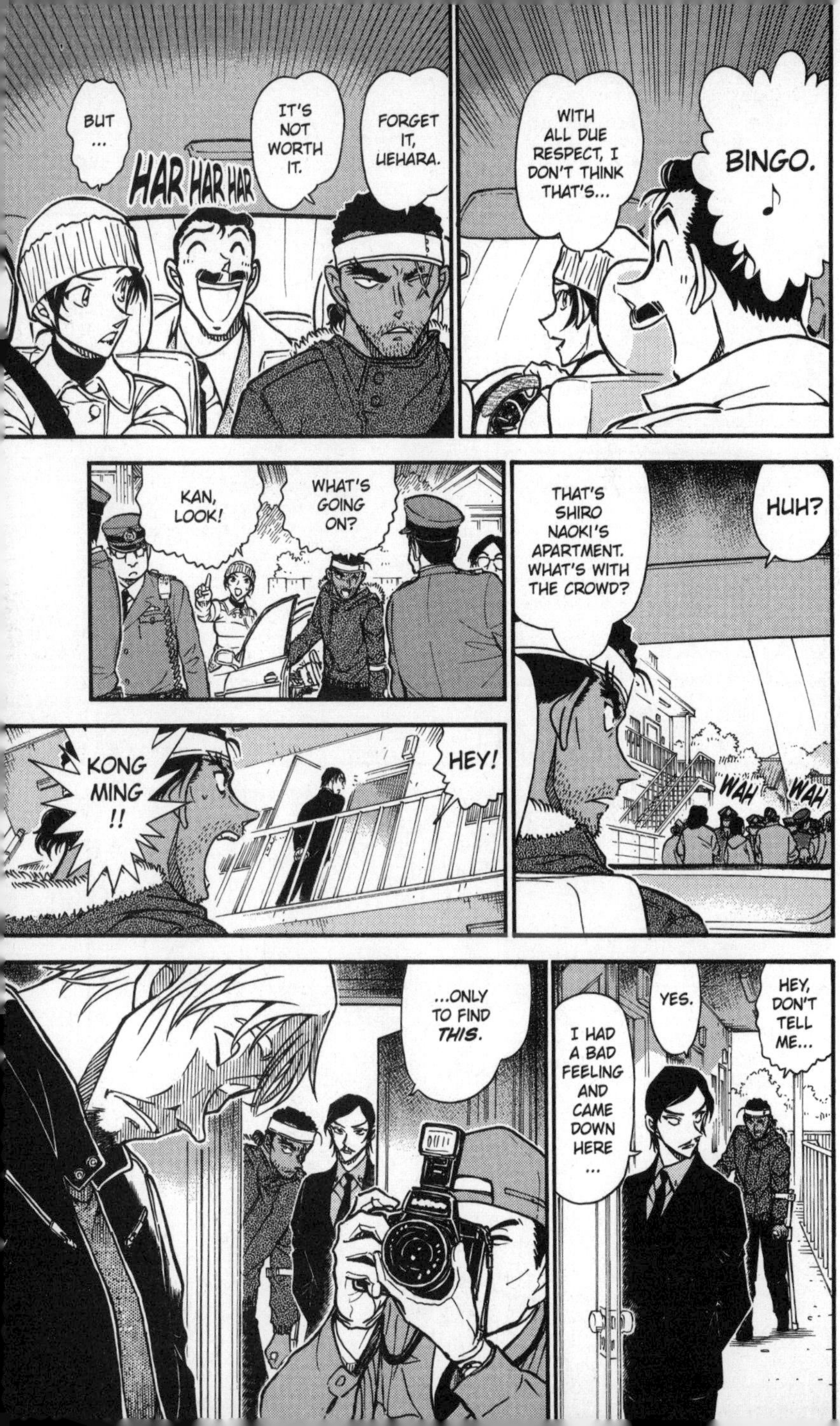
BINGO. ♪
WITH ALL DUE RESPECT, I DON'T THINK THAT'S...
FORGET IT, UEHARA.
IT'S NOT WORTH IT.
HAR HAR HAR
BUT ...
HUH?
THAT'S SHIRO NAOKI'S APARTMENT. WHAT'S WITH THE CROWD?
WAH WAH
WHAT'S GOING ON?
KAN, LOOK!
HEY!
KONG MING !!
HEY, DON'T TELL ME...
YES.
I HAD A BAD FEELING AND CAME DOWN HERE ...
...ONLY TO FIND THIS.

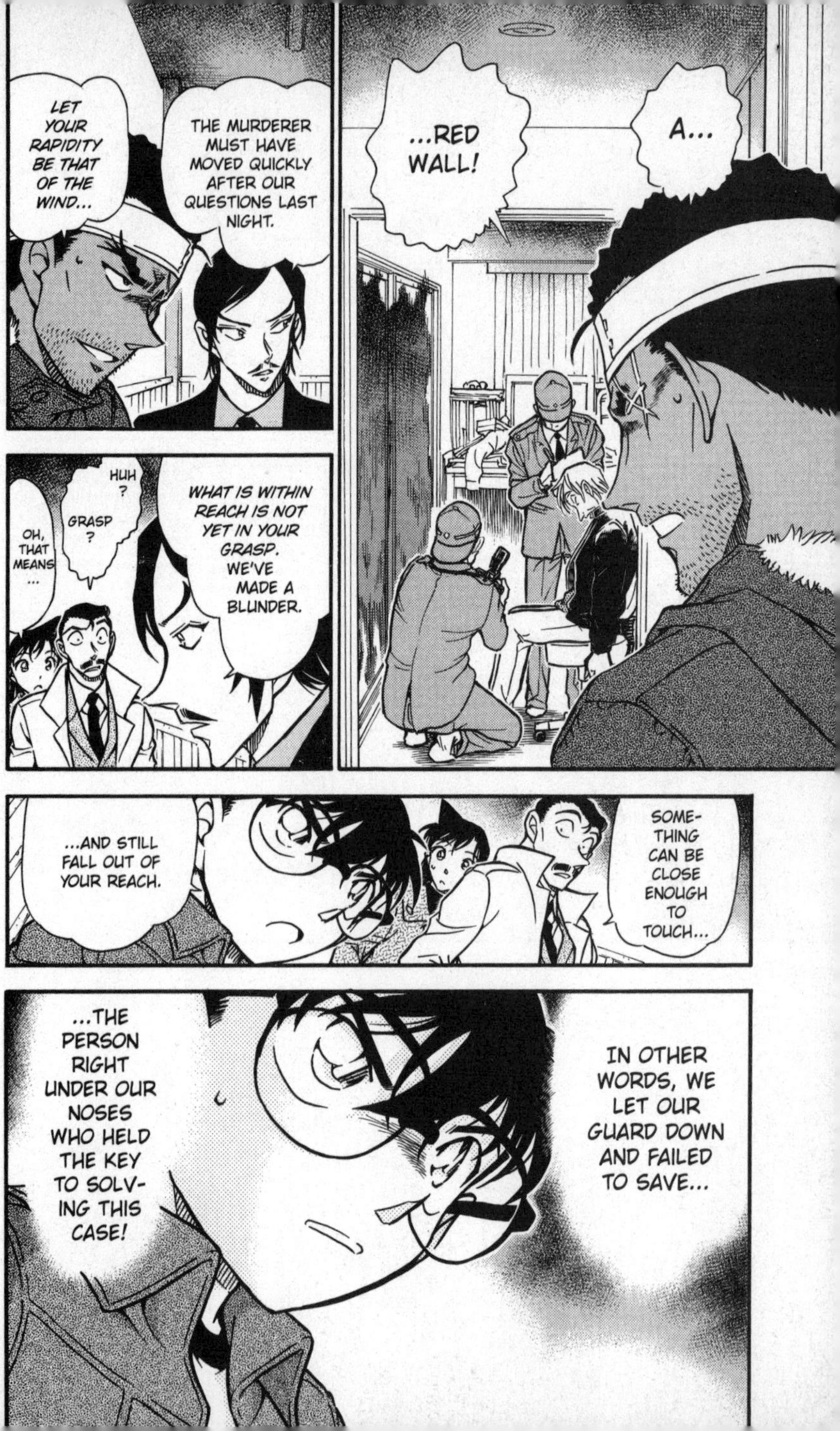
A...
...RED WALL!
THE MURDERER MUST HAVE MOVED QUICKLY AFTER OUR QUESTIONS LAST NIGHT.
LET YOUR RAPIDITY BE THAT OF THE WIND...
WHAT IS WITHIN REACH IS NOT YET IN YOUR GRASP. WE'VE MADE A BLUNDER.
HUH? GRASP?
OH, THAT MEANS...
SOMETHING CAN BE CLOSE ENOUGH TO TOUCH...
...AND STILL FALL OUT OF YOUR REACH.
IN OTHER WORDS, WE LET OUR GUARD DOWN AND FAILED TO SAVE...
...THE PERSON RIGHT UNDER OUR NOSES WHO HELD THE KEY TO SOLVING THIS CASE!

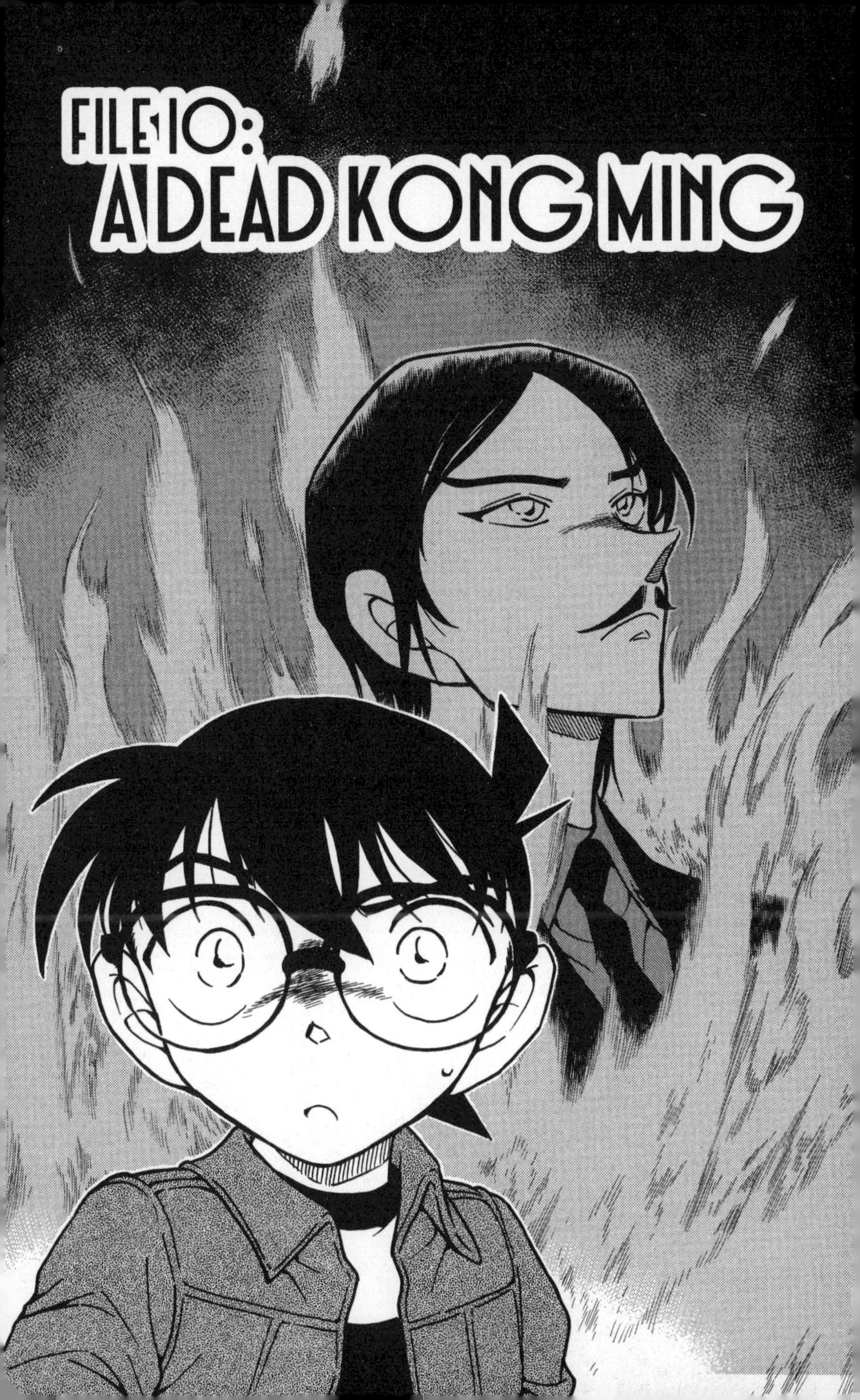
FILE 10:
A DEAD KONG MING

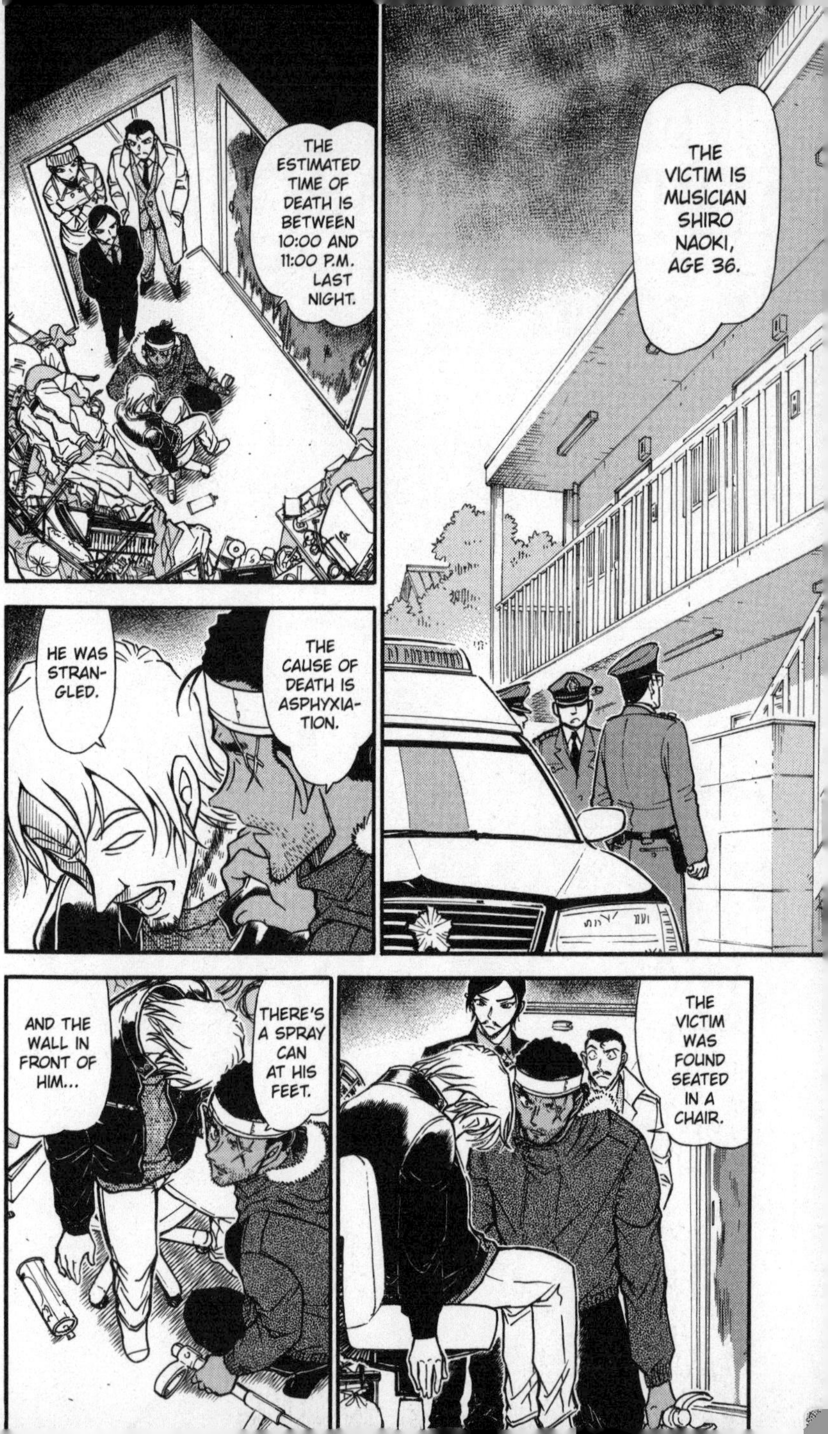
THE VICTIM IS MUSICIAN SHIRO NAOKI, AGE 36.
THE ESTIMATED TIME OF DEATH IS BETWEEN 10:00 AND 11:00 P.M. LAST NIGHT.
THE CAUSE OF DEATH IS ASPHYXIATION.
HE WAS STRANGLED.
THE VICTIM WAS FOUND SEATED IN A CHAIR.
THERE'S A SPRAY CAN AT HIS FEET.
AND THE WALL IN FRONT OF HIM...

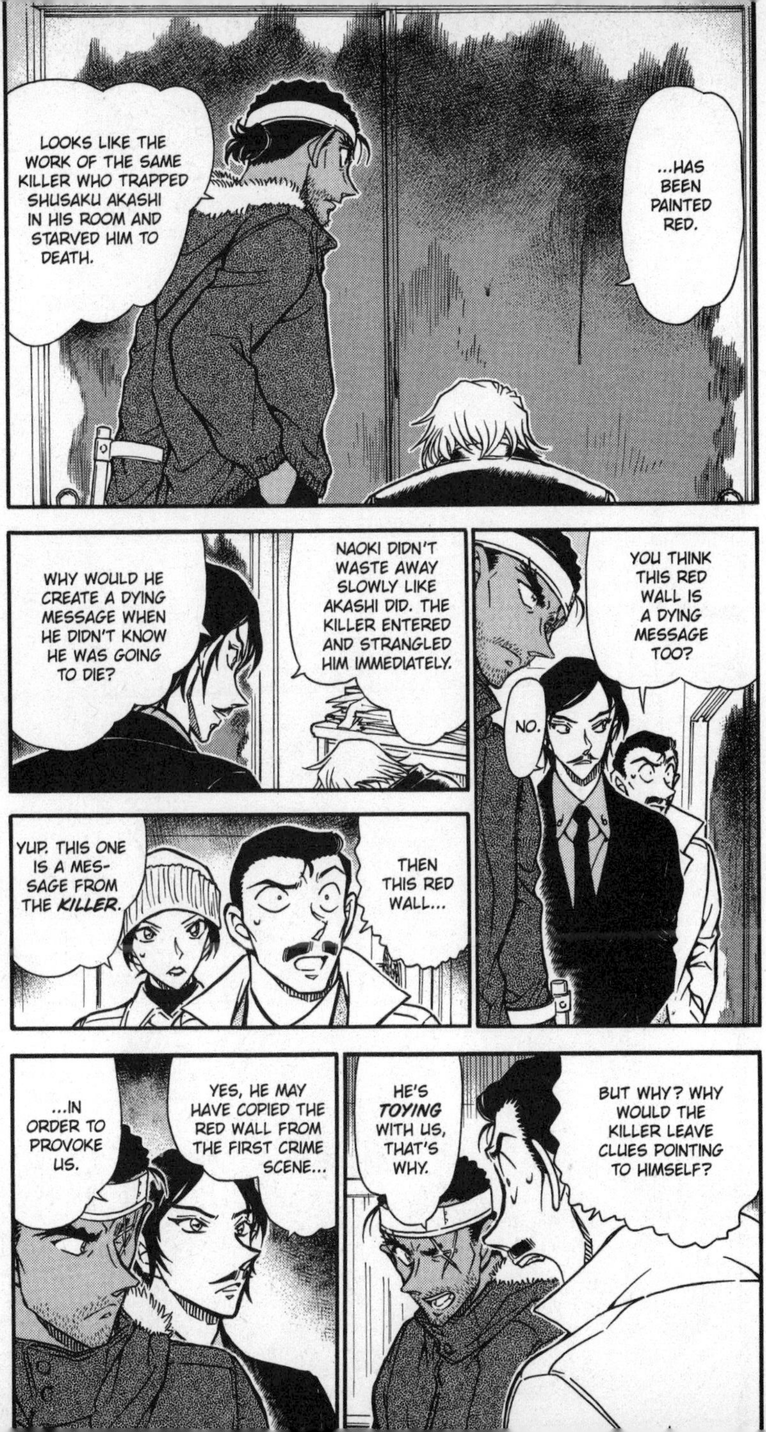
...HAS BEEN PAINTED RED.
LOOKS LIKE THE WORK OF THE SAME KILLER WHO TRAPPED SHUSAKU AKASHI IN HIS ROOM AND STARVED HIM TO DEATH.
YOU THINK THIS RED WALL IS A DYING MESSAGE TOO?
NO.
NAOKI DIDN'T WASTE AWAY SLOWLY LIKE AKASHI DID. THE KILLER ENTERED AND STRANGLED HIM IMMEDIATELY.
WHY WOULD HE CREATE A DYING MESSAGE WHEN HE DIDN'T KNOW HE WAS GOING TO DIE?
THEN THIS RED WALL...
YUP. THIS ONE IS A MES-SAGE FROM THE *KILLER*.
BUT WHY? WHY WOULD THE KILLER LEAVE CLUES POINTING TO HIMSELF?
HE'S *TOYING* WITH US, THAT'S WHY.
YES, HE MAY HAVE COPIED THE RED WALL FROM THE FIRST CRIME SCENE...
...IN ORDER TO PROVOKE US.

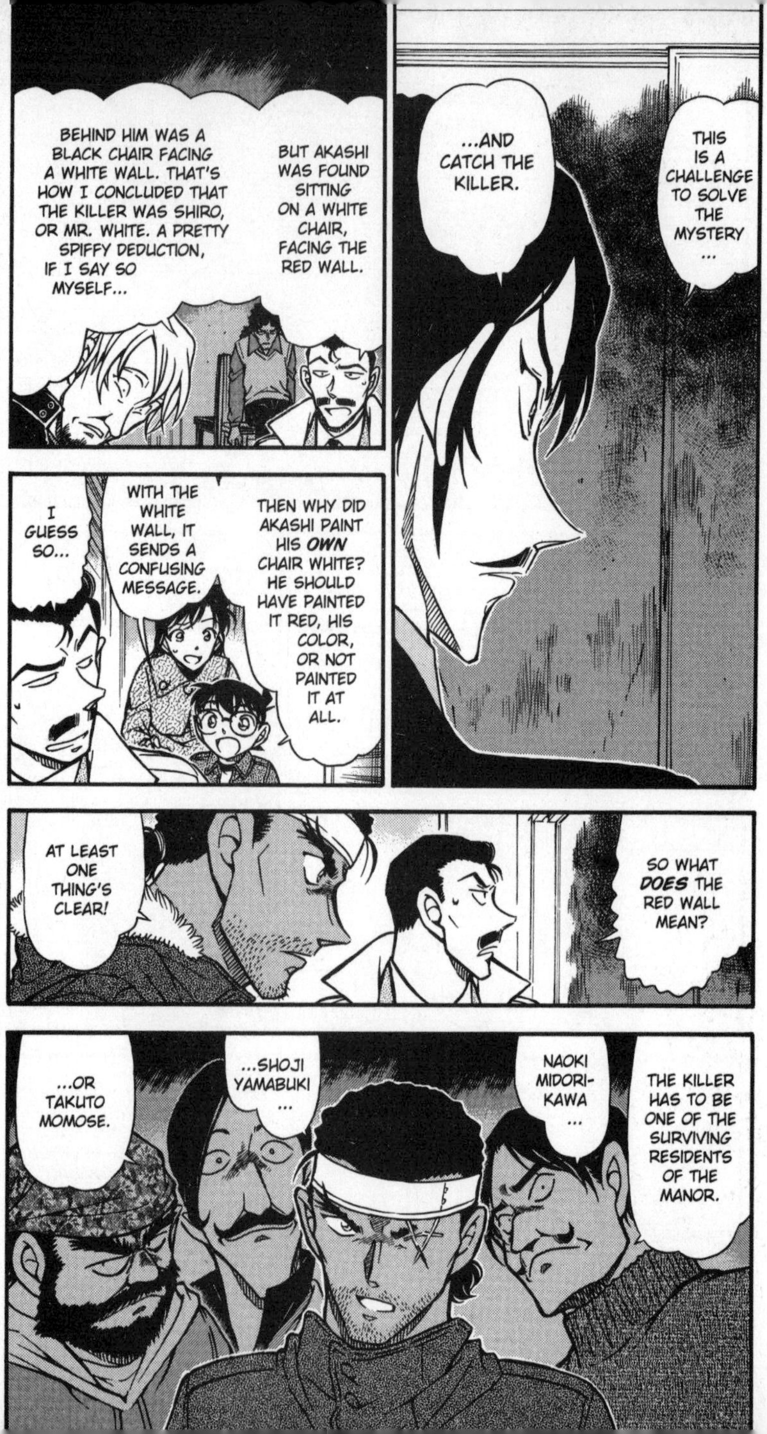
THIS IS A CHALLENGE TO SOLVE THE MYSTERY ...
...AND CATCH THE KILLER.
BUT AKASHI WAS FOUND SITTING ON A WHITE CHAIR, FACING THE RED WALL.
BEHIND HIM WAS A BLACK CHAIR FACING A WHITE WALL. THAT'S HOW I CONCLUDED THAT THE KILLER WAS SHIRO, OR MR. WHITE. A PRETTY SPIFFY DEDUCTION, IF I SAY SO MYSELF...
THEN WHY DID AKASHI PAINT HIS ***OWN*** CHAIR WHITE? HE SHOULD HAVE PAINTED IT RED, HIS COLOR, OR NOT PAINTED IT AT ALL.
WITH THE WHITE WALL, IT SENDS A CONFUSING MESSAGE.
I GUESS SO...
SO WHAT ***DOES*** THE RED WALL MEAN?
AT LEAST ONE THING'S CLEAR!
THE KILLER HAS TO BE ONE OF THE SURVIVING RESIDENTS OF THE MANOR.
NAOKI MIDORI-KAWA ...
...SHOJI YAMABUKI ...
...OR TAKUTO MOMOSE.

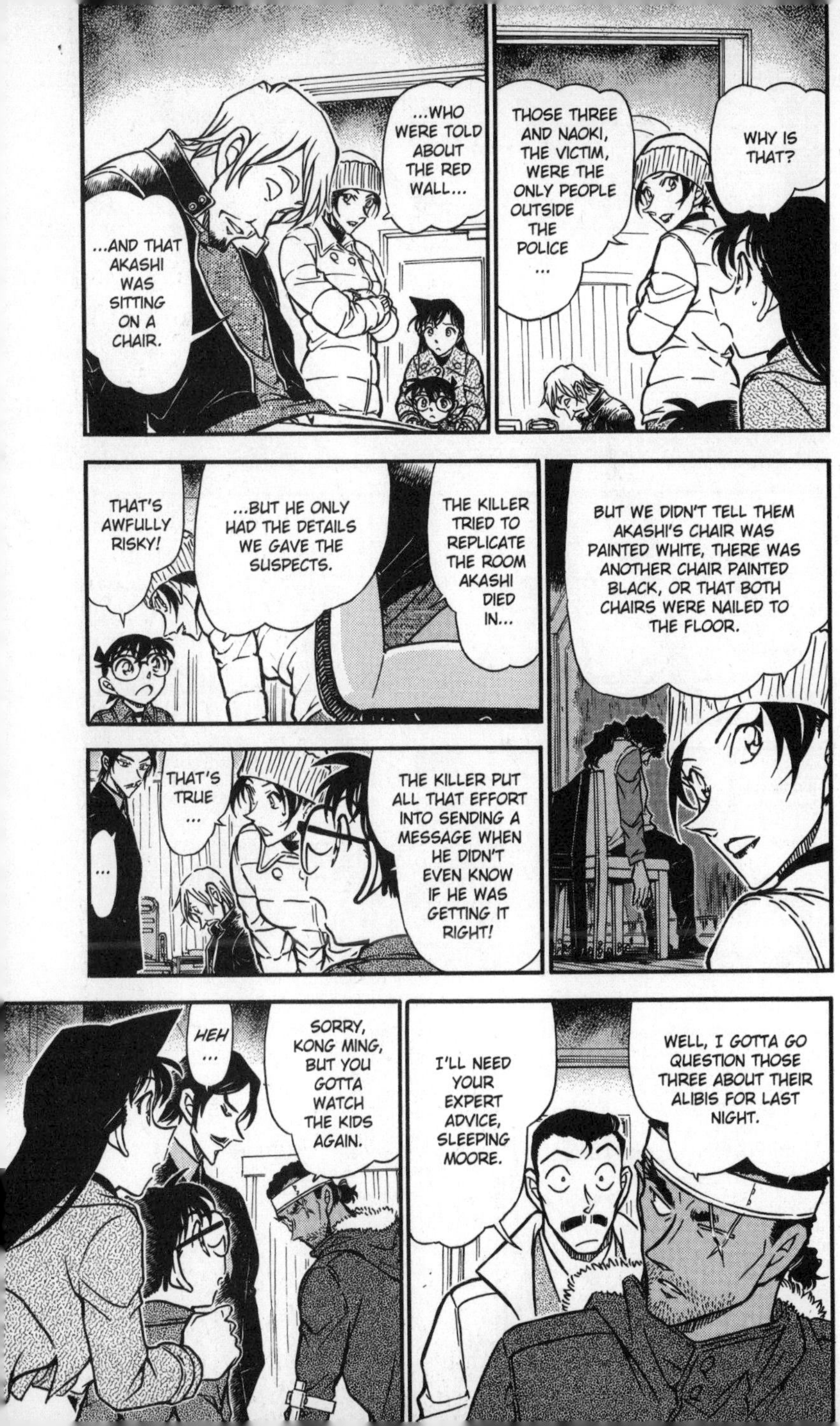
WHY IS THAT?
THOSE THREE AND NAOKI, THE VICTIM, WERE THE ONLY PEOPLE OUTSIDE THE POLICE ...
...WHO WERE TOLD ABOUT THE RED WALL...
...AND THAT AKASHI WAS SITTING ON A CHAIR.
BUT WE DIDN'T TELL THEM AKASHI'S CHAIR WAS PAINTED WHITE, THERE WAS ANOTHER CHAIR PAINTED BLACK, OR THAT BOTH CHAIRS WERE NAILED TO THE FLOOR.
THE KILLER TRIED TO REPLICATE THE ROOM AKASHI DIED IN...
...BUT HE ONLY HAD THE DETAILS WE GAVE THE SUSPECTS.
THAT'S AWFULLY RISKY!
THE KILLER PUT ALL THAT EFFORT INTO SENDING A MESSAGE WHEN HE DIDN'T EVEN KNOW IF HE WAS GETTING IT RIGHT!
THAT'S TRUE ...
...
WELL, I GOTTA GO QUESTION THOSE THREE ABOUT THEIR ALIBIS FOR LAST NIGHT.
I'LL NEED YOUR EXPERT ADVICE, SLEEPING MOORE.
SORRY, KONG MING, BUT YOU GOTTA WATCH THE KIDS AGAIN.
HEH ...

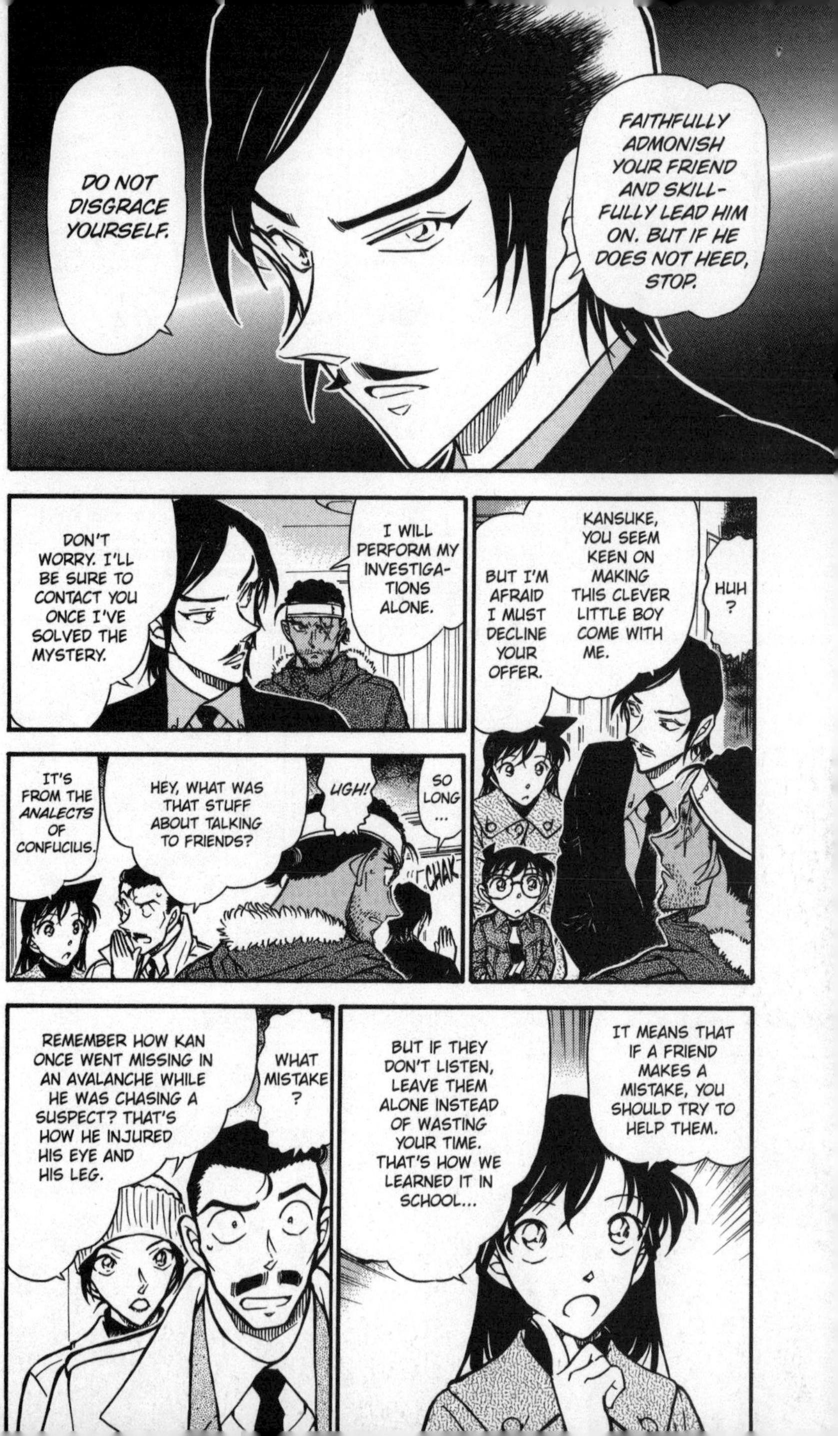
FAITHFULLY ADMONISH YOUR FRIEND AND SKILLFULLY LEAD HIM ON. BUT IF HE DOES NOT HEED, STOP.
DO NOT DISGRACE YOURSELF.
HUH?
KANSUKE, YOU SEEM KEEN ON MAKING THIS CLEVER LITTLE BOY COME WITH ME.
BUT I'M AFRAID I MUST DECLINE YOUR OFFER.
I WILL PERFORM MY INVESTIGATIONS ALONE.
DON'T WORRY. I'LL BE SURE TO CONTACT YOU ONCE I'VE SOLVED THE MYSTERY.
SO LONG...
UGH!
CHAK
HEY, WHAT WAS THAT STUFF ABOUT TALKING TO FRIENDS?
IT'S FROM THE *ANALECTS* OF CONFUCIUS.
IT MEANS THAT IF A FRIEND MAKES A MISTAKE, YOU SHOULD TRY TO HELP THEM.
BUT IF THEY DON'T LISTEN, LEAVE THEM ALONE INSTEAD OF WASTING YOUR TIME. THAT'S HOW WE LEARNED IT IN SCHOOL...
WHAT MISTAKE?
REMEMBER HOW KAN ONCE WENT MISSING IN AN AVALANCHE WHILE HE WAS CHASING A SUSPECT? THAT'S HOW HE INJURED HIS EYE AND HIS LEG.

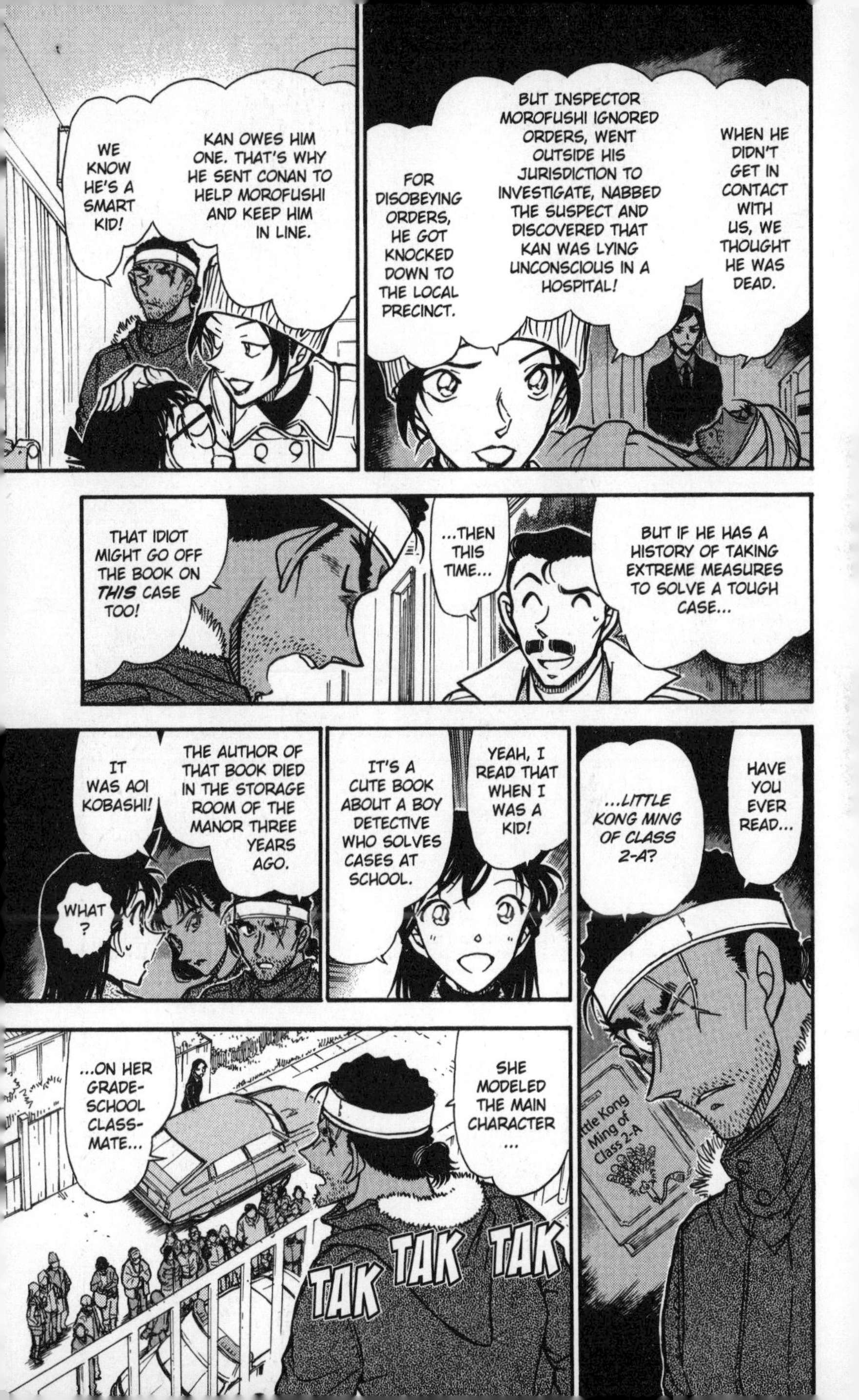
WHEN HE DIDN'T GET IN CONTACT WITH US, WE THOUGHT HE WAS DEAD.
BUT INSPECTOR MOROFUSHI IGNORED ORDERS, WENT OUTSIDE HIS JURISDICTION TO INVESTIGATE, NABBED THE SUSPECT AND DISCOVERED THAT KAN WAS LYING UNCONSCIOUS IN A HOSPITAL!
FOR DISOBEYING ORDERS, HE GOT KNOCKED DOWN TO THE LOCAL PRECINCT.
KAN OWES HIM ONE. THAT'S WHY HE SENT CONAN TO HELP MOROFUSHI AND KEEP HIM IN LINE.
WE KNOW HE'S A SMART KID!
BUT IF HE HAS A HISTORY OF TAKING EXTREME MEASURES TO SOLVE A TOUGH CASE...
...THEN THIS TIME...
THAT IDIOT MIGHT GO OFF THE BOOK ON *THIS* CASE TOO!
HAVE YOU EVER READ...
...LITTLE KONG MING OF CLASS 2-A?
ttle Kong Ming of Class 2-A
YEAH, I READ THAT WHEN I WAS A KID!
IT'S A CUTE BOOK ABOUT A BOY DETECTIVE WHO SOLVES CASES AT SCHOOL.
THE AUTHOR OF THAT BOOK DIED IN THE STORAGE ROOM OF THE MANOR THREE YEARS AGO.
IT WAS AOI KOBASHI!
WHAT?
SHE MODELED THE MAIN CHARACTER...
...ON HER GRADE-SCHOOL CLASSMATE...
TAK
TAK
TAK

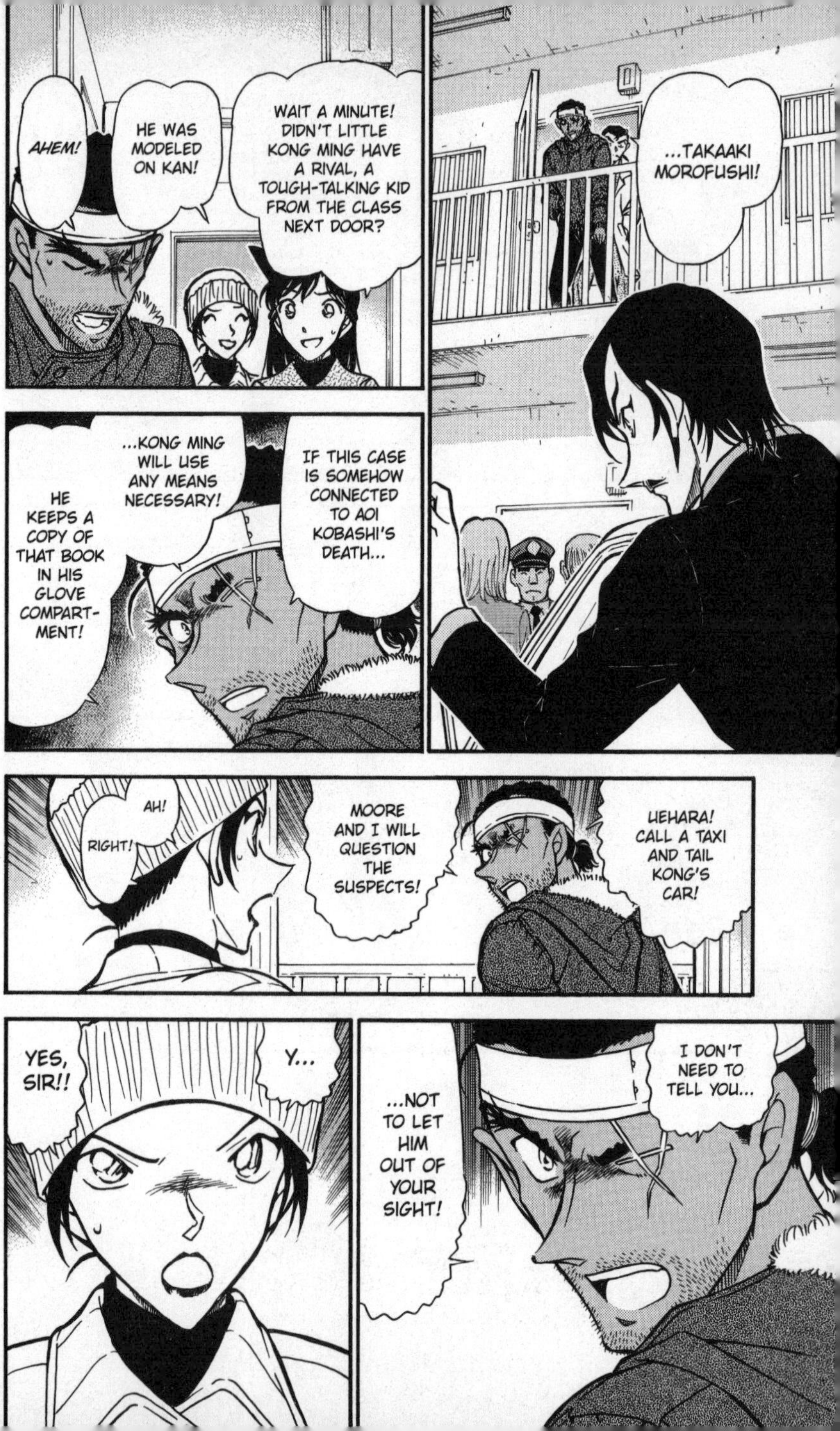
...TAKAAKI MOROFUSHI!
WAIT A MINUTE! DIDN'T LITTLE KONG MING HAVE A RIVAL, A TOUGH-TALKING KID FROM THE CLASS NEXT DOOR?
HE WAS MODELED ON KAN!
AHEM!
IF THIS CASE IS SOMEHOW CONNECTED TO AOI KOBASHI'S DEATH...
...KONG MING WILL USE ANY MEANS NECESSARY!
HE KEEPS A COPY OF THAT BOOK IN HIS GLOVE COMPART-MENT!
UEHARA! CALL A TAXI AND TAIL KONG'S CAR!
MOORE AND I WILL QUESTION THE SUSPECTS!
AH!
RIGHT!
I DON'T NEED TO TELL YOU...
...NOT TO LET HIM OUT OF YOUR SIGHT!
Y...
YES, SIR!!

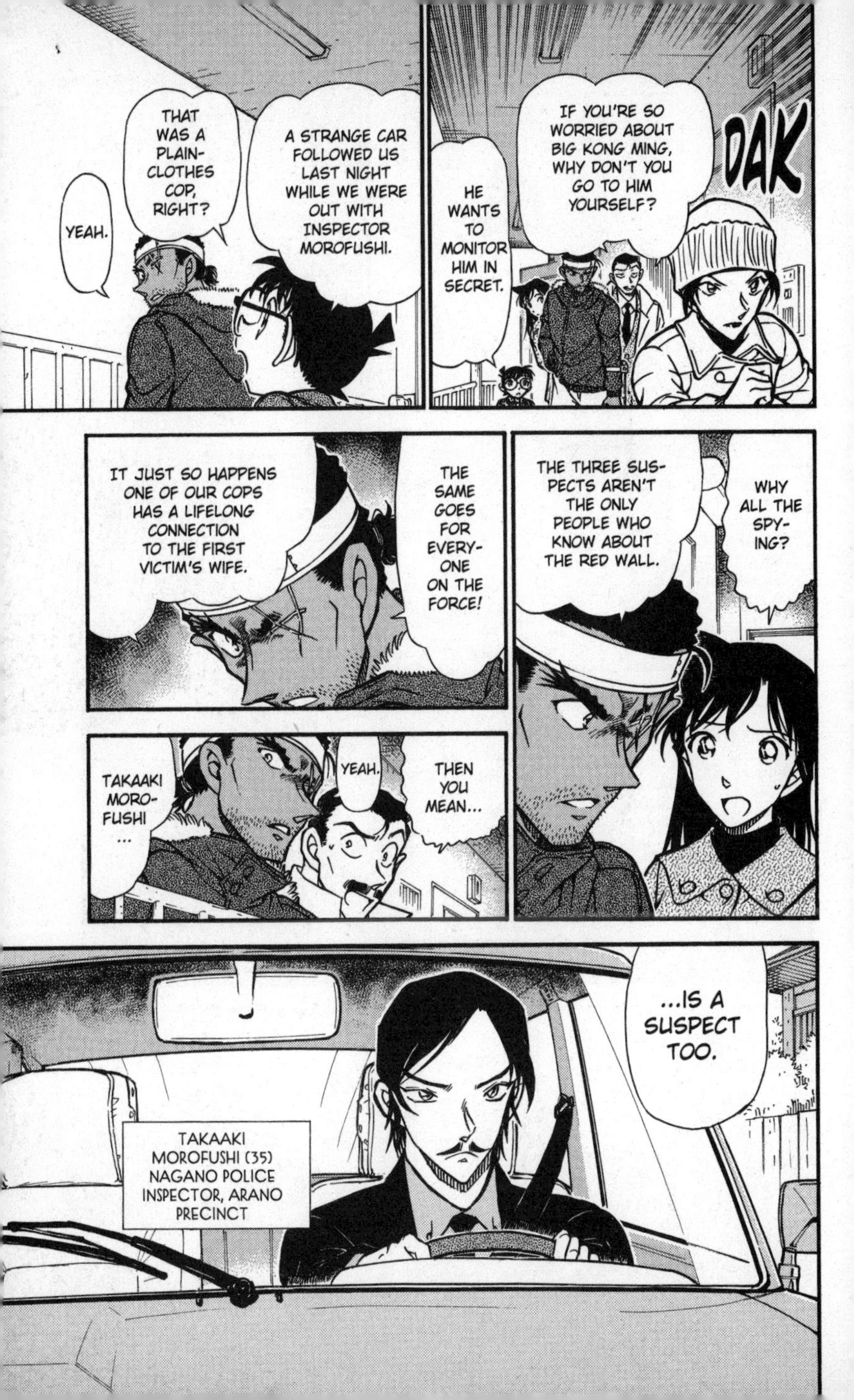
DAK
IF YOU'RE SO WORRIED ABOUT BIG KONG MING, WHY DON'T YOU GO TO HIM YOURSELF?
HE WANTS TO MONITOR HIM IN SECRET.
A STRANGE CAR FOLLOWED US LAST NIGHT WHILE WE WERE OUT WITH INSPECTOR MOROFUSHI.
THAT WAS A PLAIN-CLOTHES COP, RIGHT?
YEAH.
WHY ALL THE SPYING?
THE THREE SUSPECTS AREN'T THE ONLY PEOPLE WHO KNOW ABOUT THE RED WALL.
THE SAME GOES FOR EVERYONE ON THE FORCE!
IT JUST SO HAPPENS ONE OF OUR COPS HAS A LIFELONG CONNECTION TO THE FIRST VICTIM'S WIFE.
THEN YOU MEAN...
YEAH.
TAKAAKI MOROFUSHI ...
...IS A SUSPECT TOO.
TAKAAKI MOROFUSHI (35) NAGANO POLICE INSPECTOR, ARANO PRECINCT

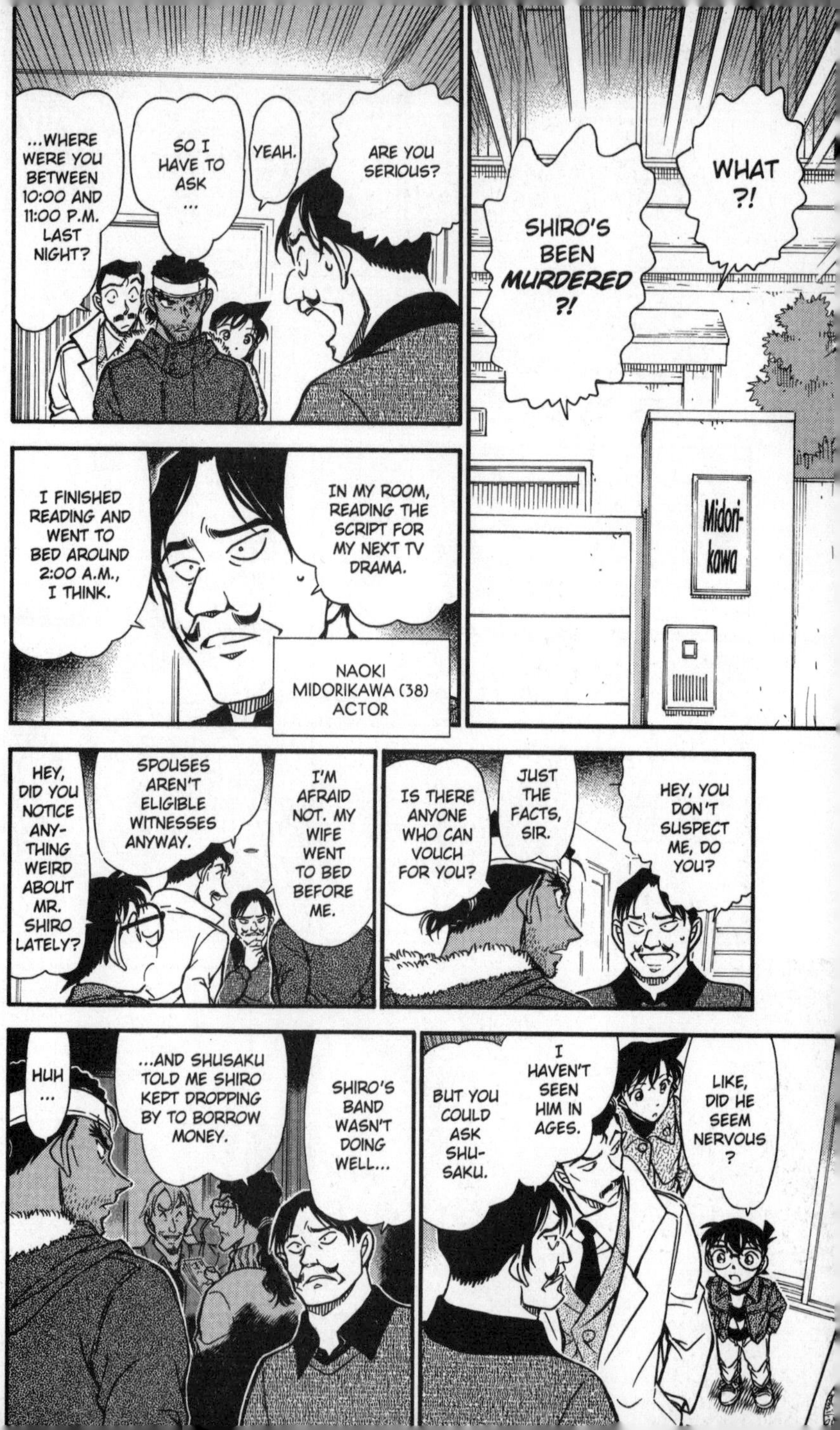
WHAT?!
SHIRO'S BEEN MURDERED?!
Midori-kawa
ARE YOU SERIOUS?
YEAH.
SO I HAVE TO ASK...
...WHERE WERE YOU BETWEEN 10:00 AND 11:00 P.M. LAST NIGHT?
IN MY ROOM, READING THE SCRIPT FOR MY NEXT TV DRAMA.
I FINISHED READING AND WENT TO BED AROUND 2:00 A.M., I THINK.
NAOKI MIDORIKAWA (38) ACTOR
HEY, YOU DON'T SUSPECT ME, DO YOU?
JUST THE FACTS, SIR.
IS THERE ANYONE WHO CAN VOUCH FOR YOU?
I'M AFRAID NOT. MY WIFE WENT TO BED BEFORE ME.
SPOUSES AREN'T ELIGIBLE WITNESSES ANYWAY.
HEY, DID YOU NOTICE ANYTHING WEIRD ABOUT MR. SHIRO LATELY?
LIKE, DID HE SEEM NERVOUS?
I HAVEN'T SEEN HIM IN AGES.
BUT YOU COULD ASK SHU-SAKU.
SHIRO'S BAND WASN'T DOING WELL...
...AND SHUSAKU TOLD ME SHIRO KEPT DROPPING BY TO BORROW MONEY.
HUH...

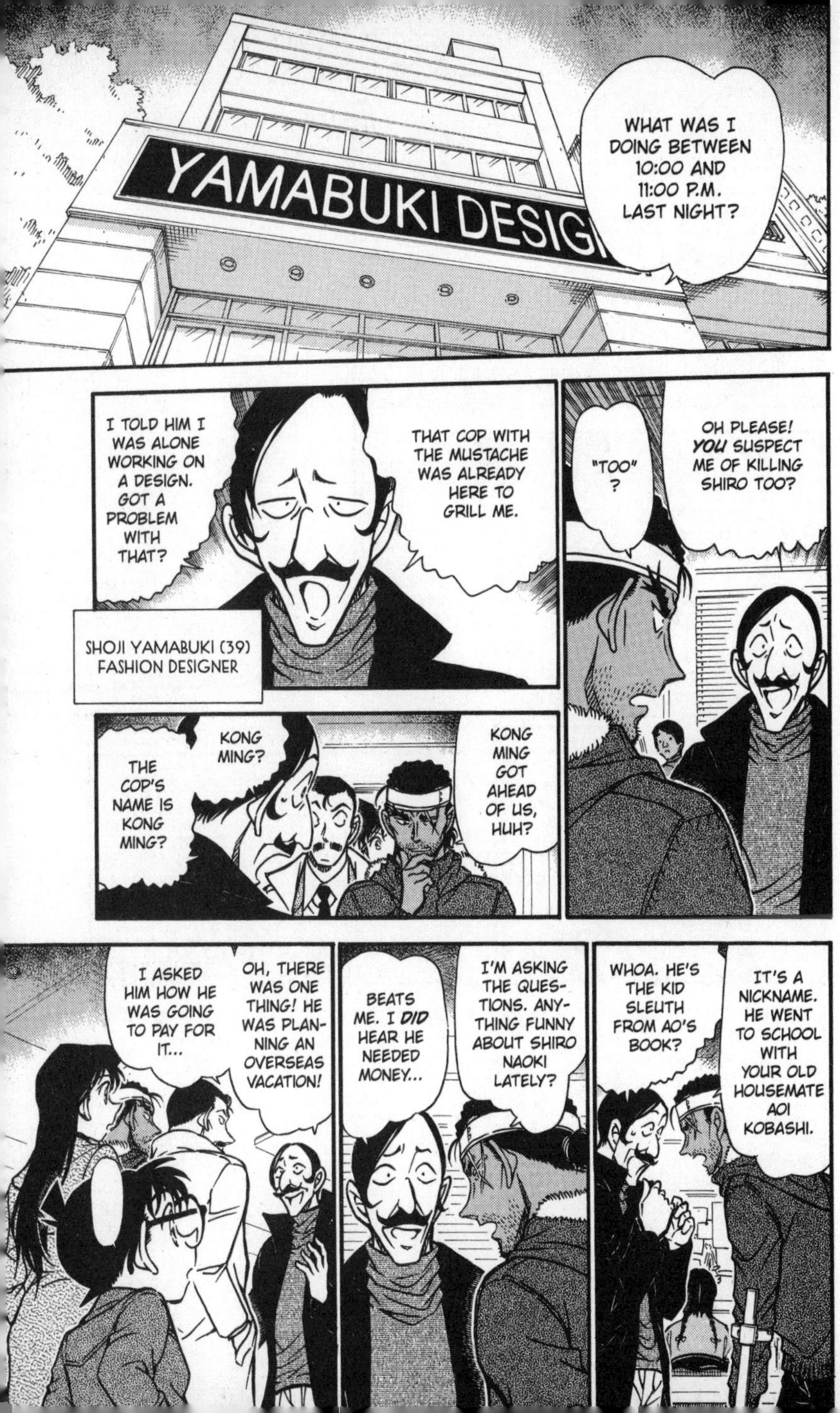
YAMABUKI DESIG
WHAT WAS I DOING BETWEEN 10:00 AND 11:00 P.M. LAST NIGHT?
OH PLEASE! YOU SUSPECT ME OF KILLING SHIRO TOO?
"TOO" ?
THAT COP WITH THE MUSTACHE WAS ALREADY HERE TO GRILL ME.
I TOLD HIM I WAS ALONE WORKING ON A DESIGN. GOT A PROBLEM WITH THAT?
SHOJI YAMABUKI (39) FASHION DESIGNER
KONG MING GOT AHEAD OF US, HUH?
KONG MING?
THE COP'S NAME IS KONG MING?
IT'S A NICKNAME. HE WENT TO SCHOOL WITH YOUR OLD HOUSEMATE AOI KOBASHI.
WHOA. HE'S THE KID SLEUTH FROM AO'S BOOK?
I'M ASKING THE QUES-TIONS. ANY-THING FUNNY ABOUT SHIRO NAOKI LATELY?
BEATS ME. I DID HEAR HE NEEDED MONEY...
OH, THERE WAS ONE THING! HE WAS PLAN-NING AN OVERSEAS VACATION!
I ASKED HIM HOW HE WAS GOING TO PAY FOR IT...

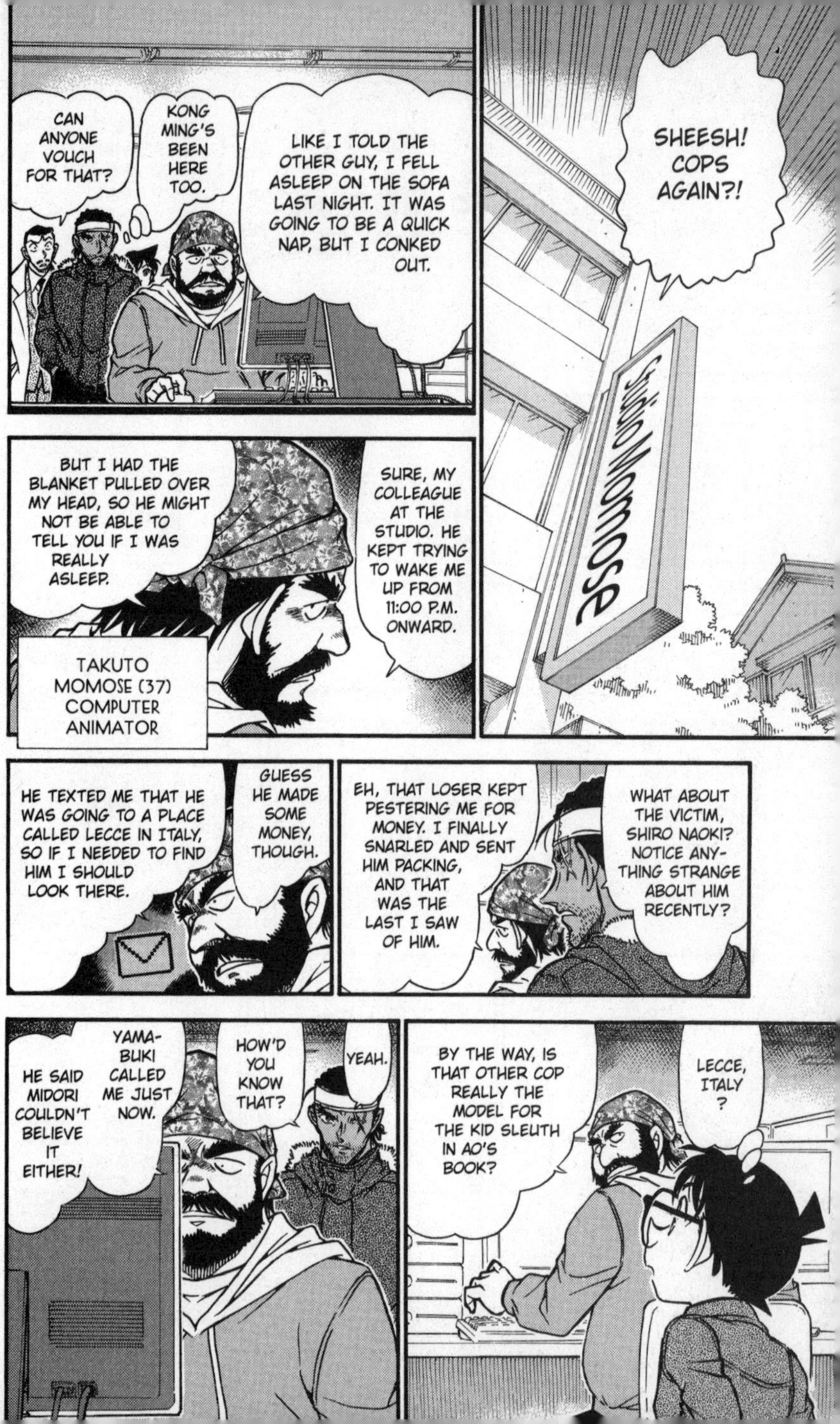
SHEESH! COPS AGAIN?!
Studio Momose
LIKE I TOLD THE OTHER GUY, I FELL ASLEEP ON THE SOFA LAST NIGHT. IT WAS GOING TO BE A QUICK NAP, BUT I CONKED OUT.
KONG MING'S BEEN HERE TOO.
CAN ANYONE VOUCH FOR THAT?
SURE, MY COLLEAGUE AT THE STUDIO. HE KEPT TRYING TO WAKE ME UP FROM 11:00 P.M. ONWARD.
BUT I HAD THE BLANKET PULLED OVER MY HEAD, SO HE MIGHT NOT BE ABLE TO TELL YOU IF I WAS REALLY ASLEEP.
TAKUTO MOMOSE (37) COMPUTER ANIMATOR
WHAT ABOUT THE VICTIM, SHIRO NAOKI? NOTICE ANY-THING STRANGE ABOUT HIM RECENTLY?
EH, THAT LOSER KEPT PESTERING ME FOR MONEY. I FINALLY SNARLED AND SENT HIM PACKING, AND THAT WAS THE LAST I SAW OF HIM.
GUESS HE MADE SOME MONEY, THOUGH.
HE TEXTED ME THAT HE WAS GOING TO A PLACE CALLED LECCE IN ITALY, SO IF I NEEDED TO FIND HIM I SHOULD LOOK THERE.
LECCE, ITALY?
BY THE WAY, IS THAT OTHER COP REALLY THE MODEL FOR THE KID SLEUTH IN AO'S BOOK?
YEAH.
HOW'D YOU KNOW THAT?
YAMA-BUKI CALLED ME JUST NOW.
HE SAID MIDORI COULDN'T BELIEVE IT EITHER!

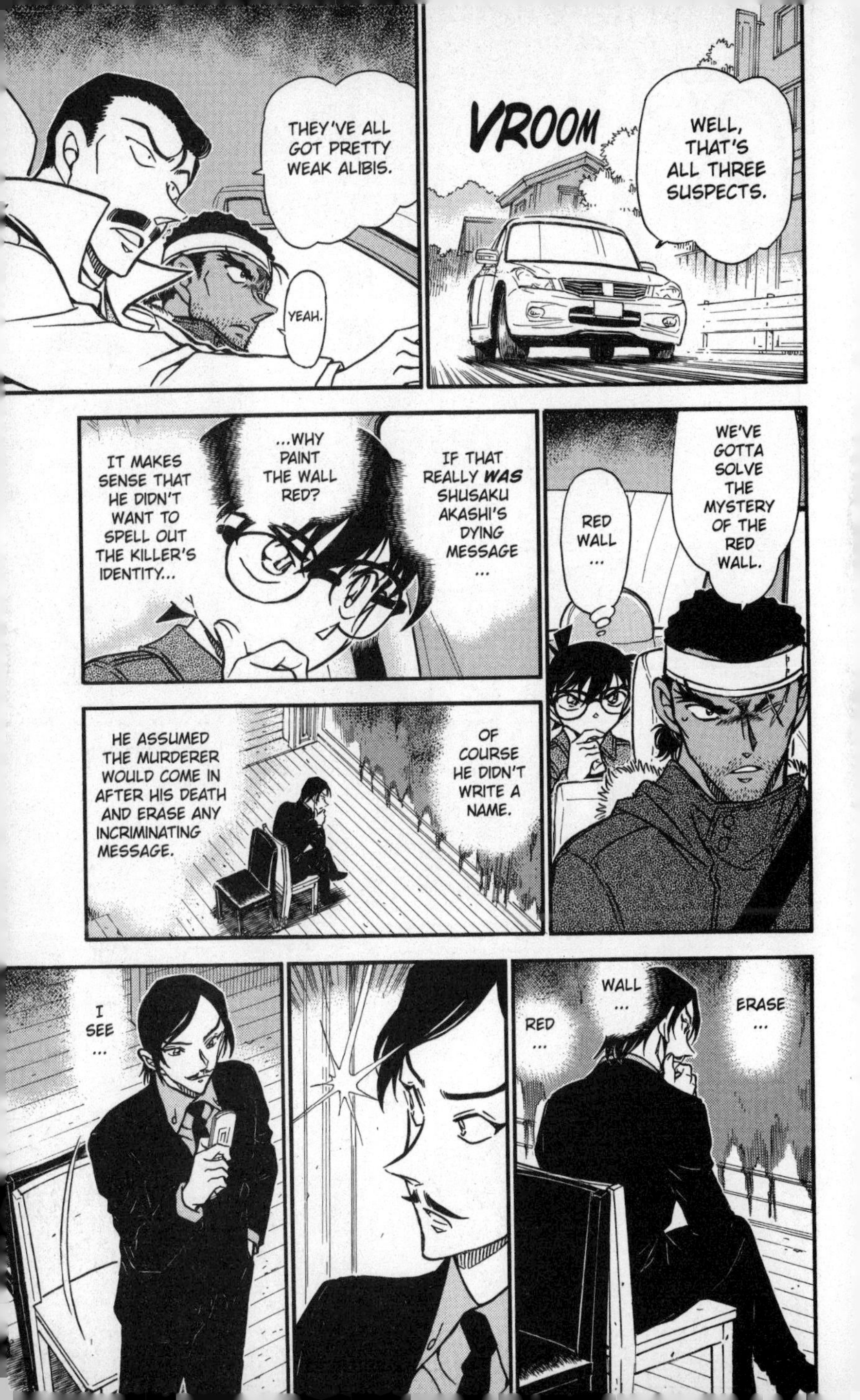
VROOM
WELL, THAT'S ALL THREE SUSPECTS.
THEY'VE ALL GOT PRETTY WEAK ALIBIS.
YEAH.
WE'VE GOTTA SOLVE THE MYSTERY OF THE RED WALL.
RED WALL...
IF THAT REALLY *WAS* SHUSAKU AKASHI'S DYING MESSAGE...
...WHY PAINT THE WALL RED?
IT MAKES SENSE THAT HE DIDN'T WANT TO SPELL OUT THE KILLER'S IDENTITY...
OF COURSE HE DIDN'T WRITE A NAME.
HE ASSUMED THE MURDERER WOULD COME IN AFTER HIS DEATH AND ERASE ANY INCRIMINATING MESSAGE.
ERASE...
WALL...
RED...
I SEE...

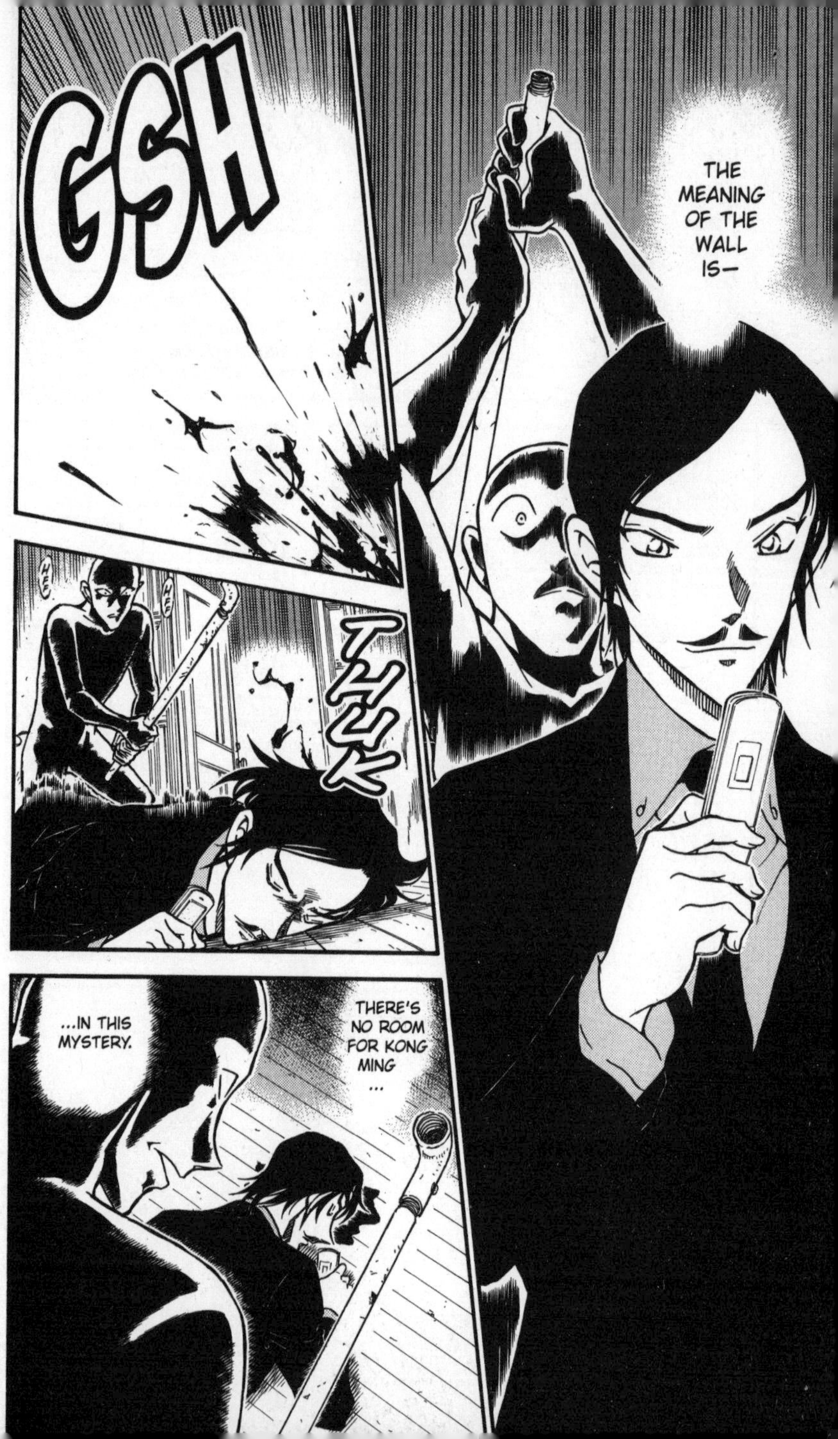
THE MEANING OF THE WALL IS—
GSH
THUK
THERE'S NO ROOM FOR KONG MING ...
...IN THIS MYSTERY.

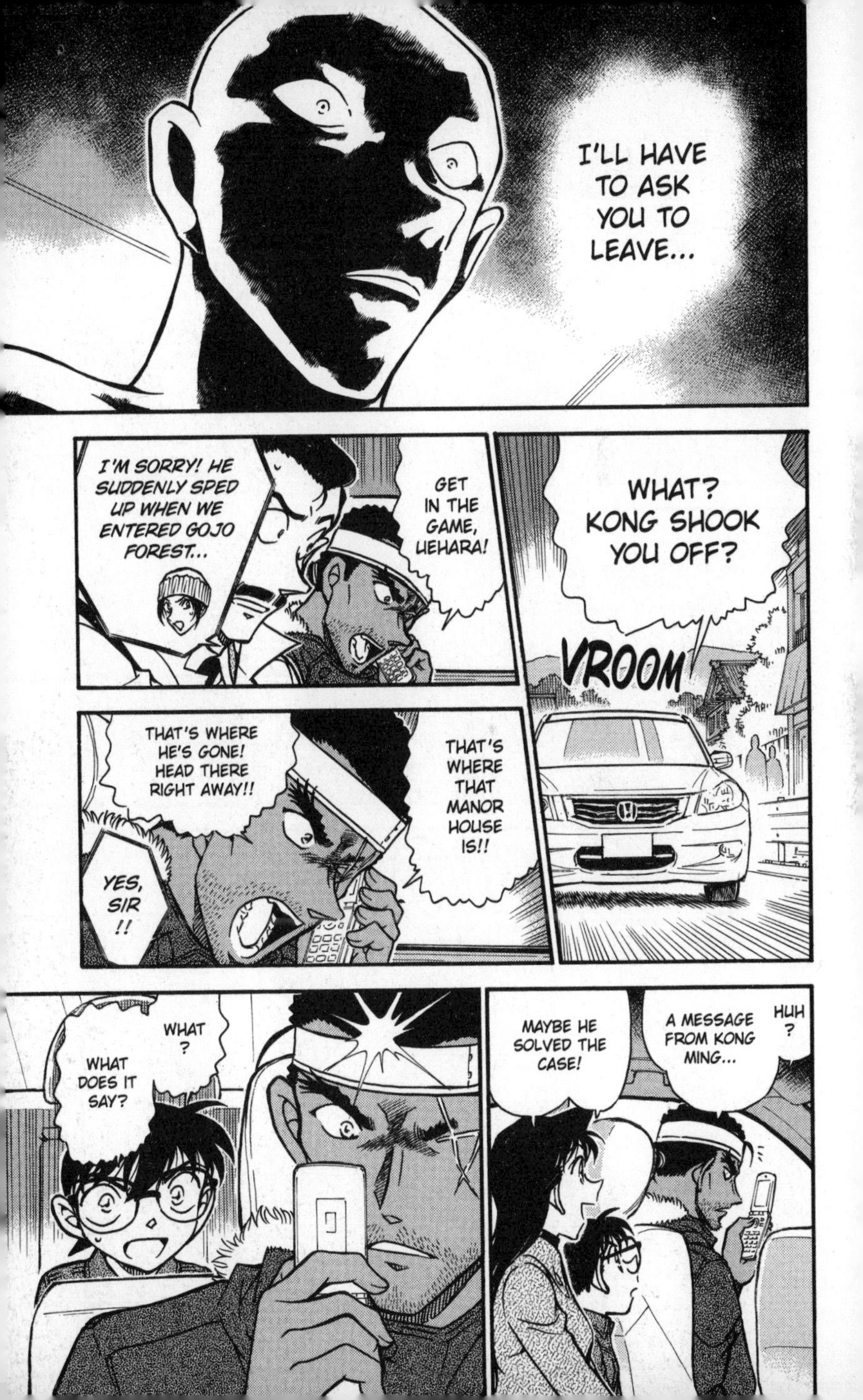
I'LL HAVE TO ASK YOU TO LEAVE...
WHAT? KONG SHOOK YOU OFF?
VROOM
GET IN THE GAME, UEHARA!
I'M SORRY! HE SUDDENLY SPED UP WHEN WE ENTERED GOJO FOREST...
THAT'S WHERE THAT MANOR HOUSE IS!!
THAT'S WHERE HE'S GONE! HEAD THERE RIGHT AWAY!!
YES, SIR!!
HUH?
A MESSAGE FROM KONG MING...
MAYBE HE SOLVED THE CASE!
WHAT?
WHAT DOES IT SAY?

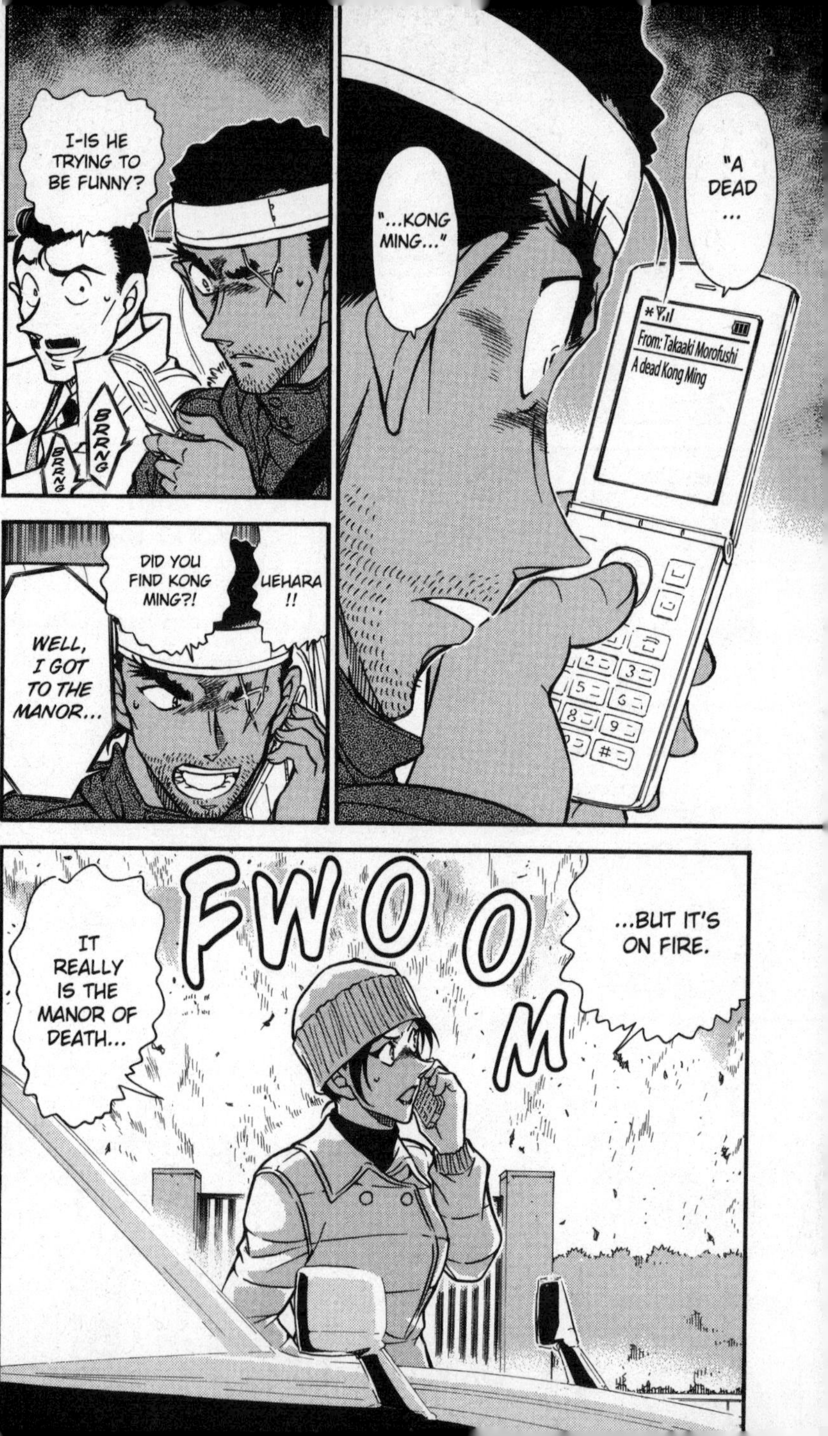
"A DEAD ...
"...KONG MING..."
From: Takaaki Morofushi
A dead Kong Ming
I-IS HE TRYING TO BE FUNNY?
BRRNG
BRRNG
UEHARA !!
DID YOU FIND KONG MING?!
WELL, I GOT TO THE MANOR...
...BUT IT'S ON FIRE.
FWOOM
IT REALLY IS THE MANOR OF DEATH...

FILE 11:
A LIVING ZHONGDA

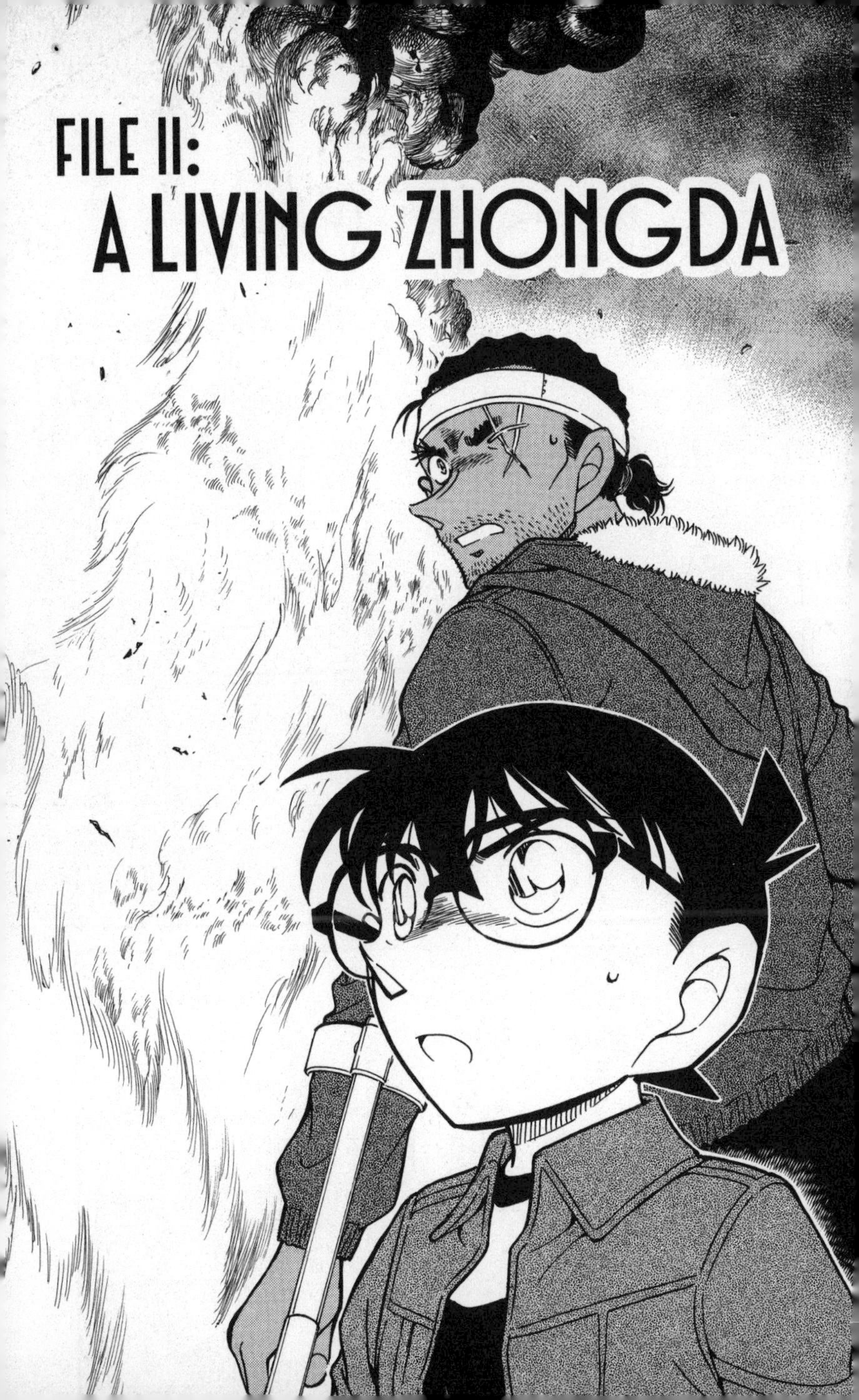

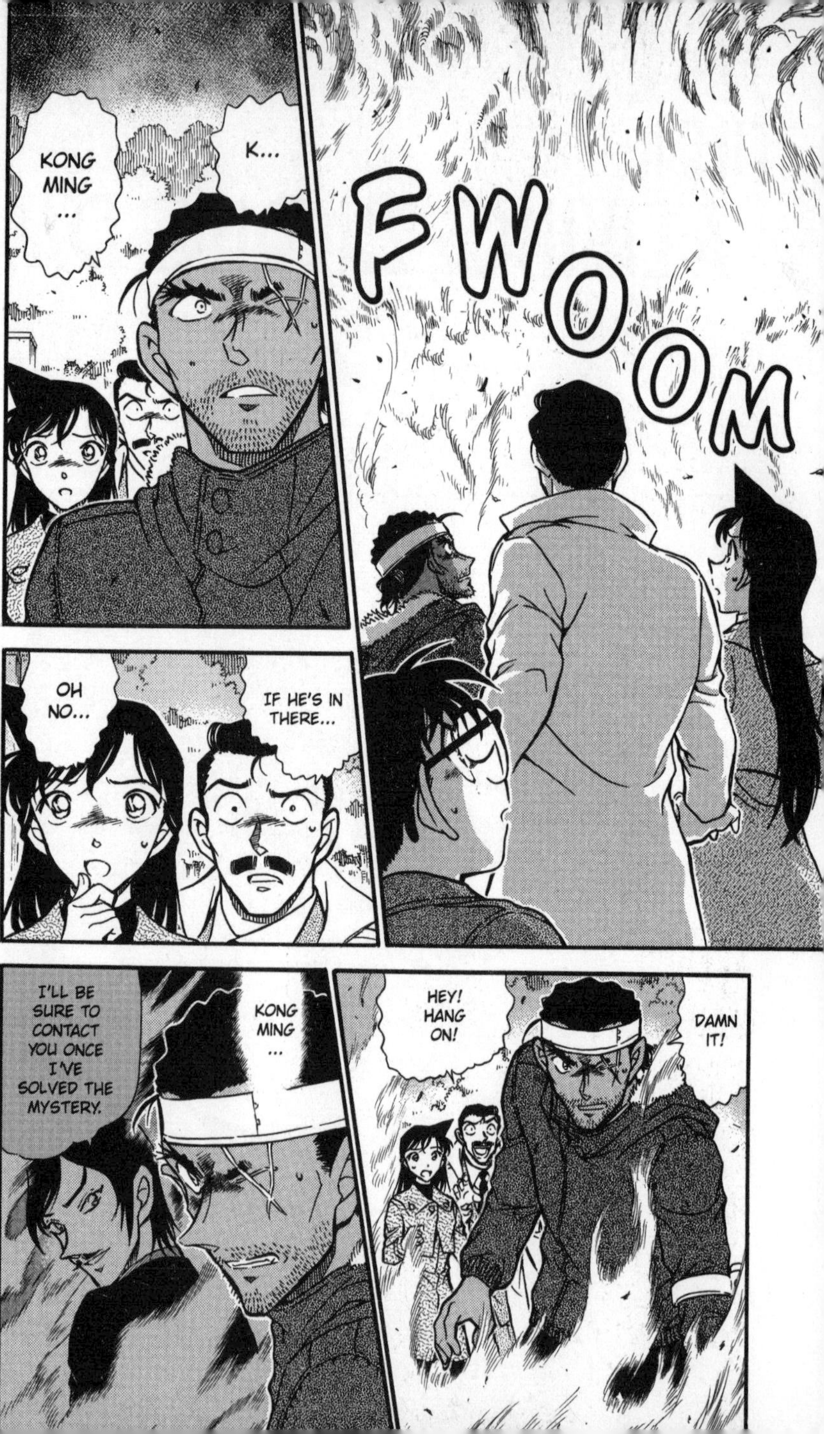
FWOOM
K...
KONG MING ...
IF HE'S IN THERE...
OH NO...
DAMN IT!
HEY! HANG ON!
KONG MING ...
I'LL BE SURE TO CONTACT YOU ONCE I'VE SOLVED THE MYSTERY.

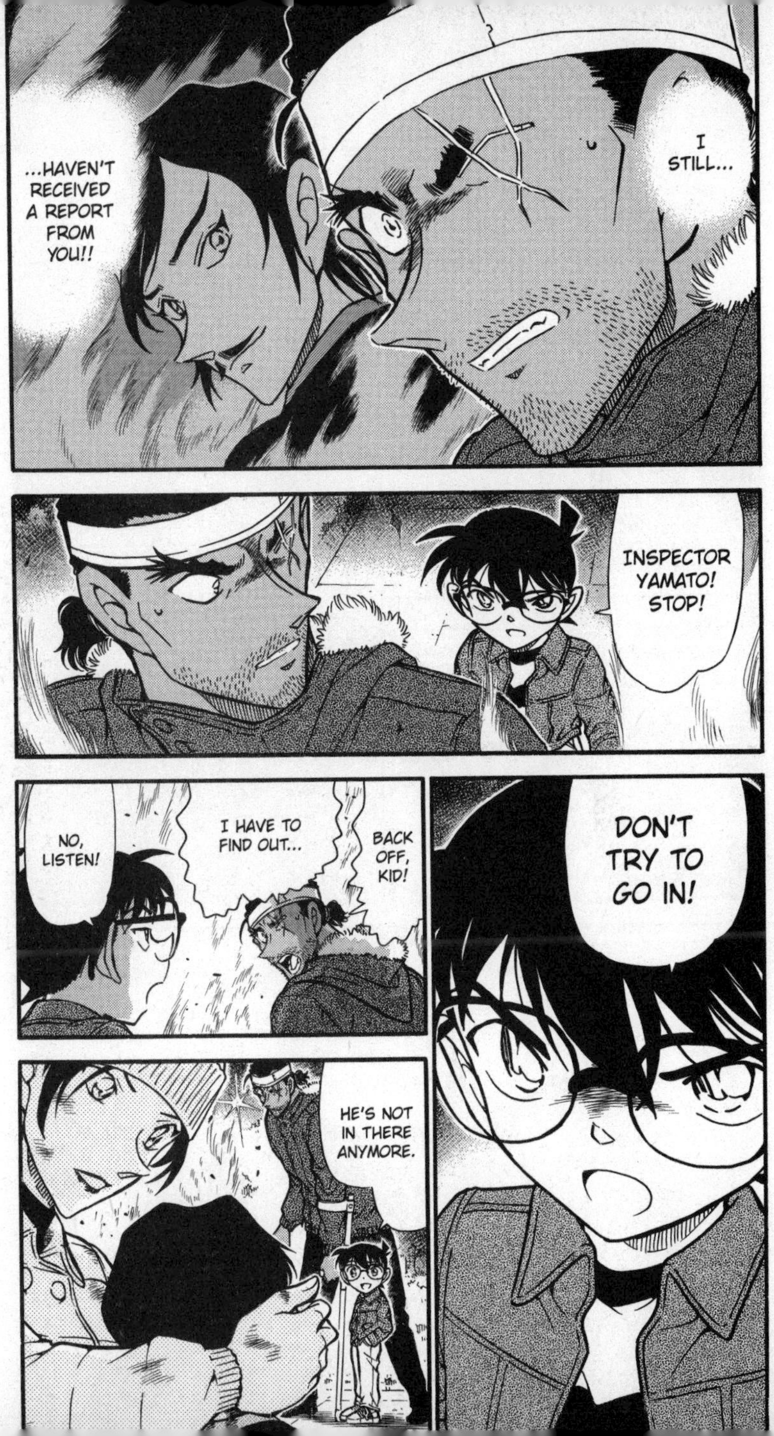
I STILL...
...HAVEN'T RECEIVED A REPORT FROM YOU!!
INSPECTOR YAMATO! STOP!
DON'T TRY TO GO IN!
BACK OFF, KID!
I HAVE TO FIND OUT...
NO, LISTEN!
HE'S NOT IN THERE ANYMORE.

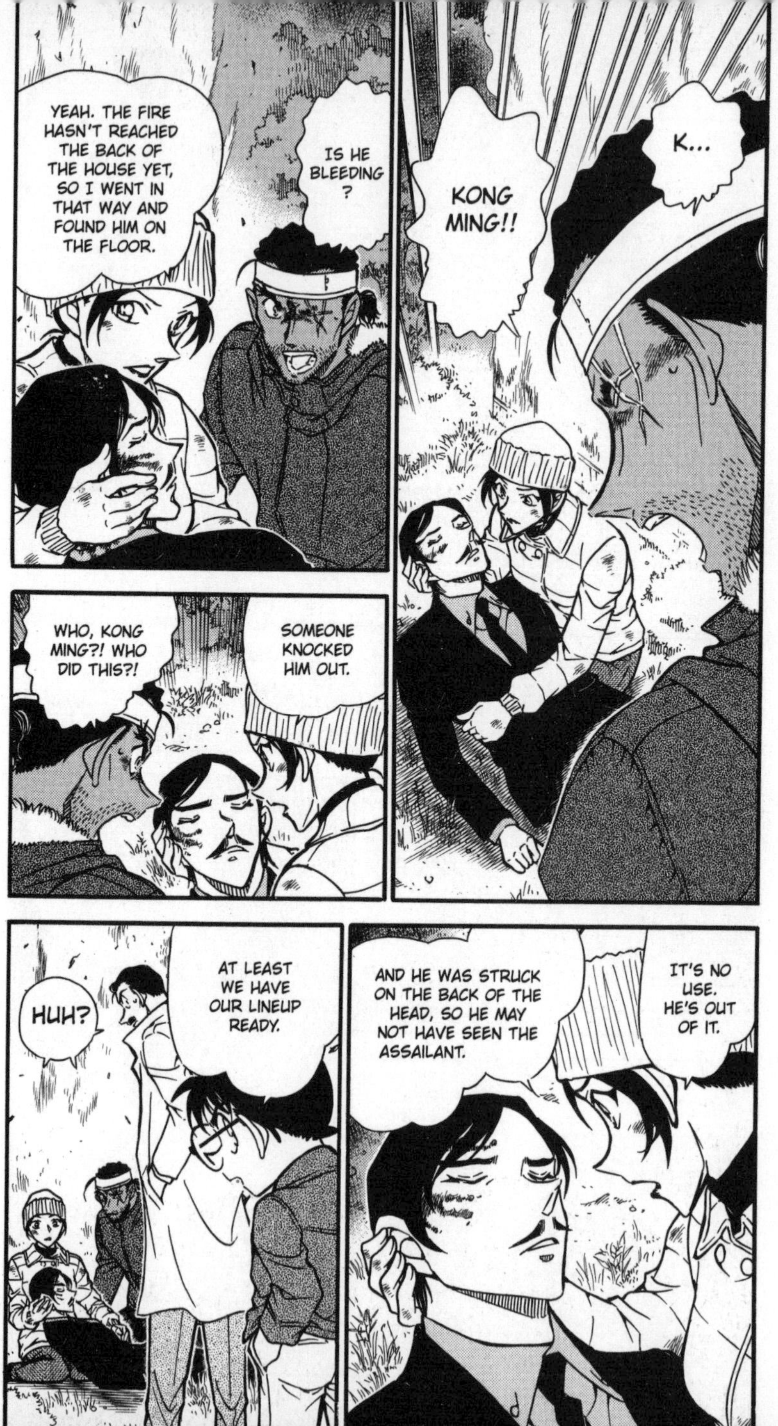
K...
KONG MING!!
IS HE BLEEDING?
YEAH. THE FIRE HASN'T REACHED THE BACK OF THE HOUSE YET, SO I WENT IN THAT WAY AND FOUND HIM ON THE FLOOR.
SOMEONE KNOCKED HIM OUT.
WHO, KONG MING?! WHO DID THIS?!
IT'S NO USE. HE'S OUT OF IT.
AND HE WAS STRUCK ON THE BACK OF THE HEAD, SO HE MAY NOT HAVE SEEN THE ASSAILANT.
AT LEAST WE HAVE OUR LINEUP READY.
HUH?

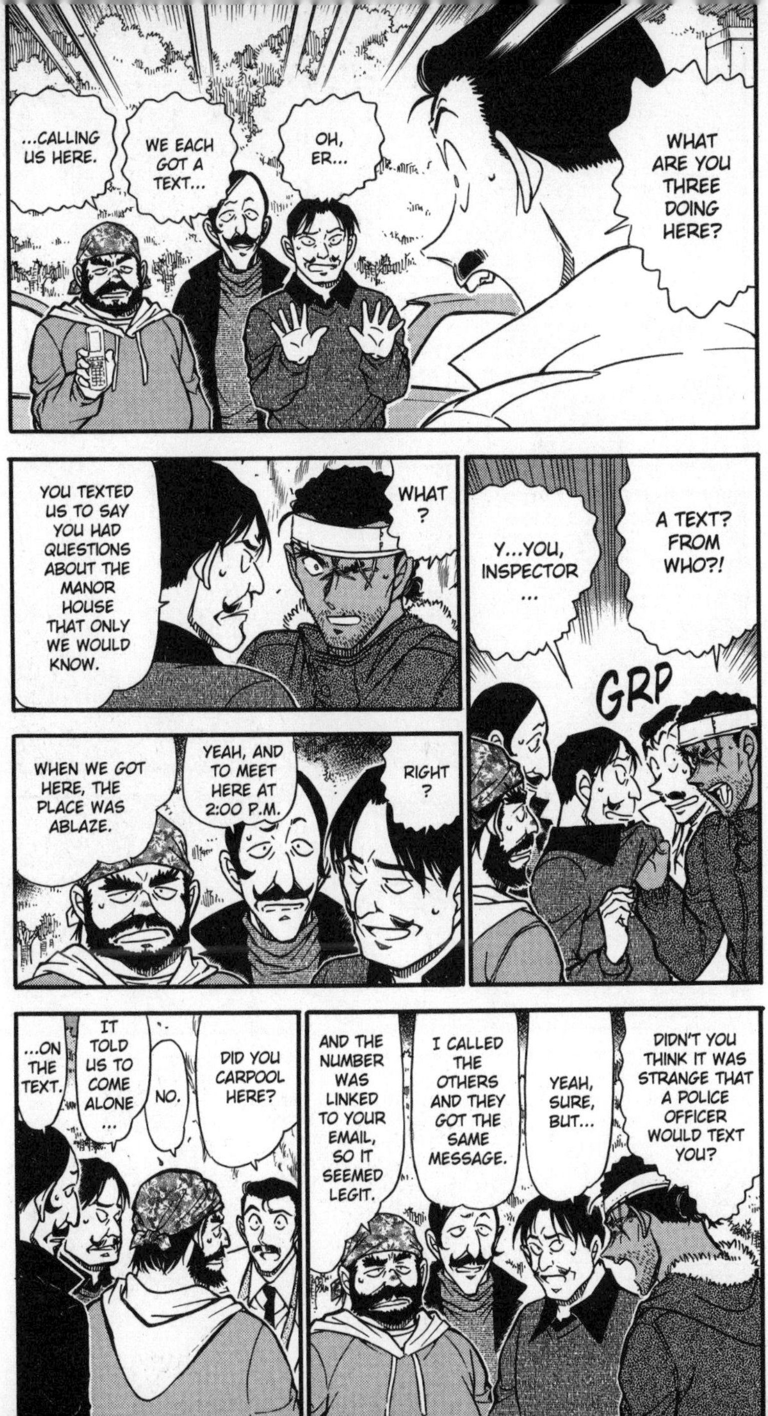
WHAT ARE YOU THREE DOING HERE?
OH, ER...
WE EACH GOT A TEXT...
...CALLING US HERE.
A TEXT? FROM WHO?!
Y...YOU, INSPECTOR...
GRP
WHAT?
YOU TEXTED US TO SAY YOU HAD QUESTIONS ABOUT THE MANOR HOUSE THAT ONLY WE WOULD KNOW.
RIGHT?
YEAH, AND TO MEET HERE AT 2:00 P.M.
WHEN WE GOT HERE, THE PLACE WAS ABLAZE.
DIDN'T YOU THINK IT WAS STRANGE THAT A POLICE OFFICER WOULD TEXT YOU?
YEAH, SURE, BUT...
I CALLED THE OTHERS AND THEY GOT THE SAME MESSAGE.
AND THE NUMBER WAS LINKED TO YOUR EMAIL, SO IT SEEMED LEGIT.
DID YOU CARPOOL HERE?
NO.
IT TOLD US TO COME ALONE...
...ON THE TEXT.

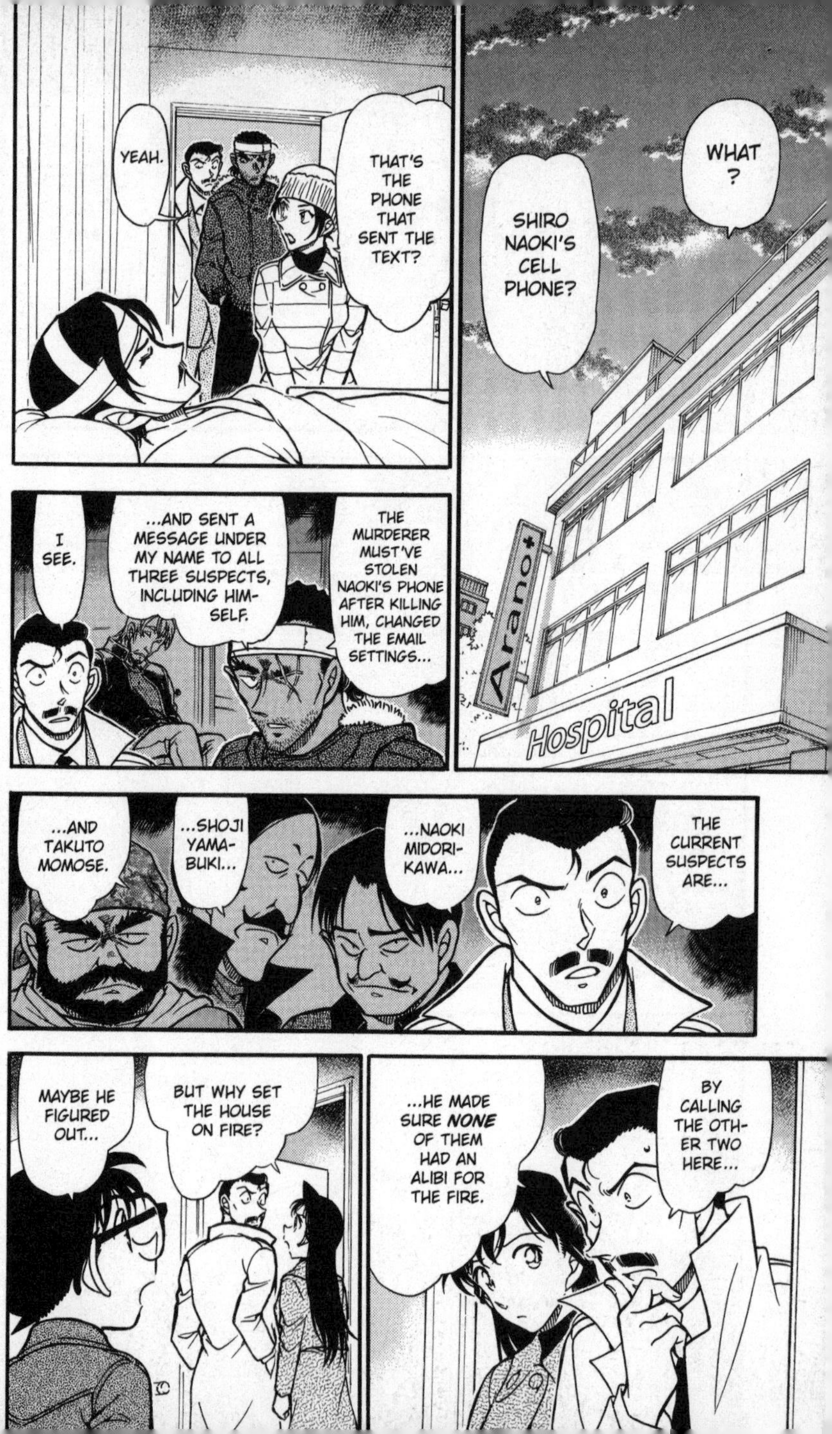
WHAT?
SHIRO NAOKI'S CELL PHONE?
Arano
Hospital
THAT'S THE PHONE THAT SENT THE TEXT?
YEAH.
THE MURDERER MUST'VE STOLEN NAOKI'S PHONE AFTER KILLING HIM, CHANGED THE EMAIL SETTINGS...
...AND SENT A MESSAGE UNDER MY NAME TO ALL THREE SUSPECTS, INCLUDING HIMSELF.
I SEE.
THE CURRENT SUSPECTS ARE...
...NAOKI MIDORIKAWA...
...SHOJI YAMABUKI...
...AND TAKUTO MOMOSE.
BY CALLING THE OTHER TWO HERE...
...HE MADE SURE ***NONE*** OF THEM HAD AN ALIBI FOR THE FIRE.
BUT WHY SET THE HOUSE ON FIRE?
MAYBE HE FIGURED OUT...

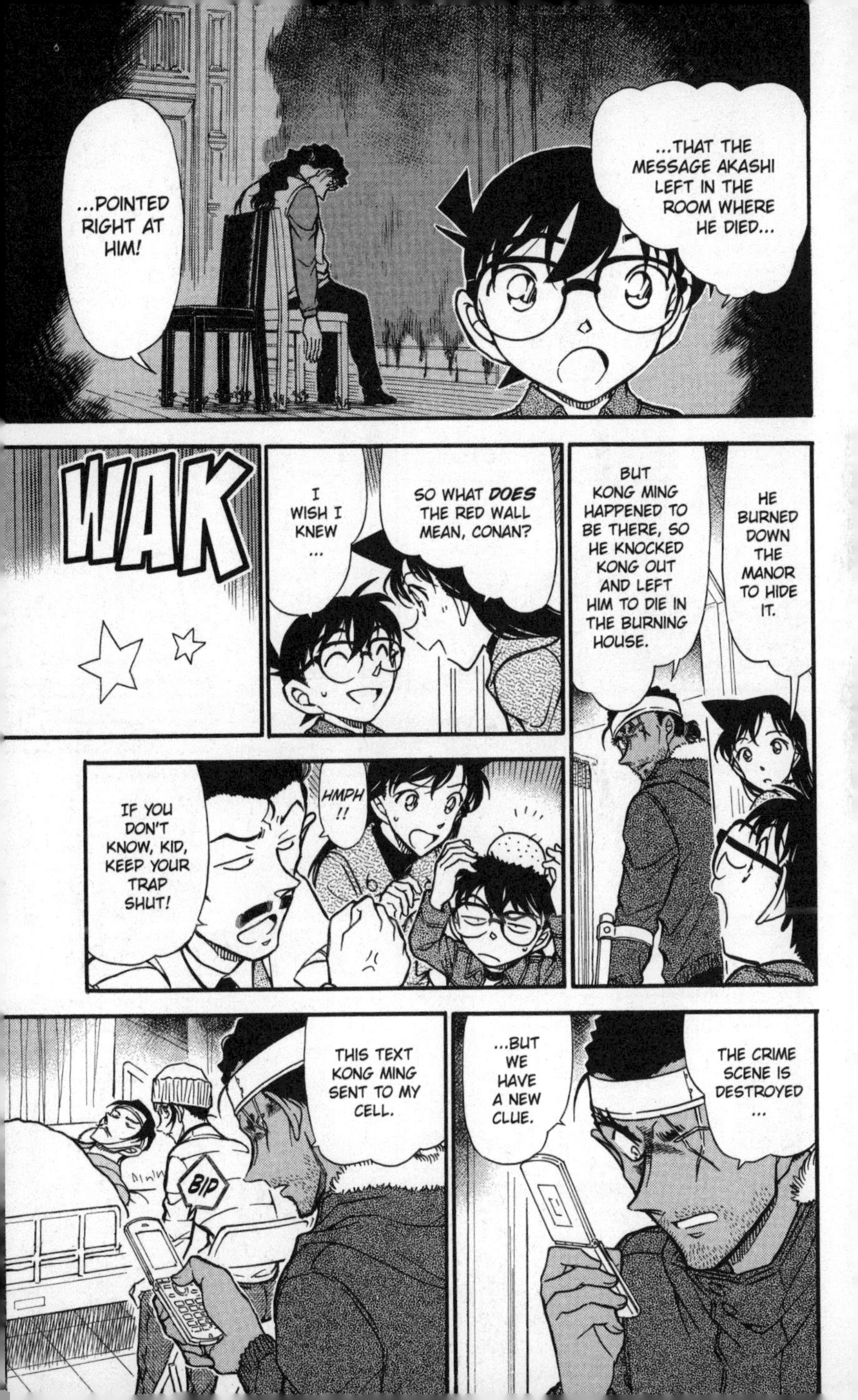
...THAT THE MESSAGE AKASHI LEFT IN THE ROOM WHERE HE DIED...
...POINTED RIGHT AT HIM!
HE BURNED DOWN THE MANOR TO HIDE IT.
BUT KONG MING HAPPENED TO BE THERE, SO HE KNOCKED KONG OUT AND LEFT HIM TO DIE IN THE BURNING HOUSE.
SO WHAT **DOES** THE RED WALL MEAN, CONAN?
I WISH I KNEW ...
WAK
HMPH !!
IF YOU DON'T KNOW, KID, KEEP YOUR TRAP SHUT!
THE CRIME SCENE IS DESTROYED ...
...BUT WE HAVE A NEW CLUE.
THIS TEXT KONG MING SENT TO MY CELL.
BIP

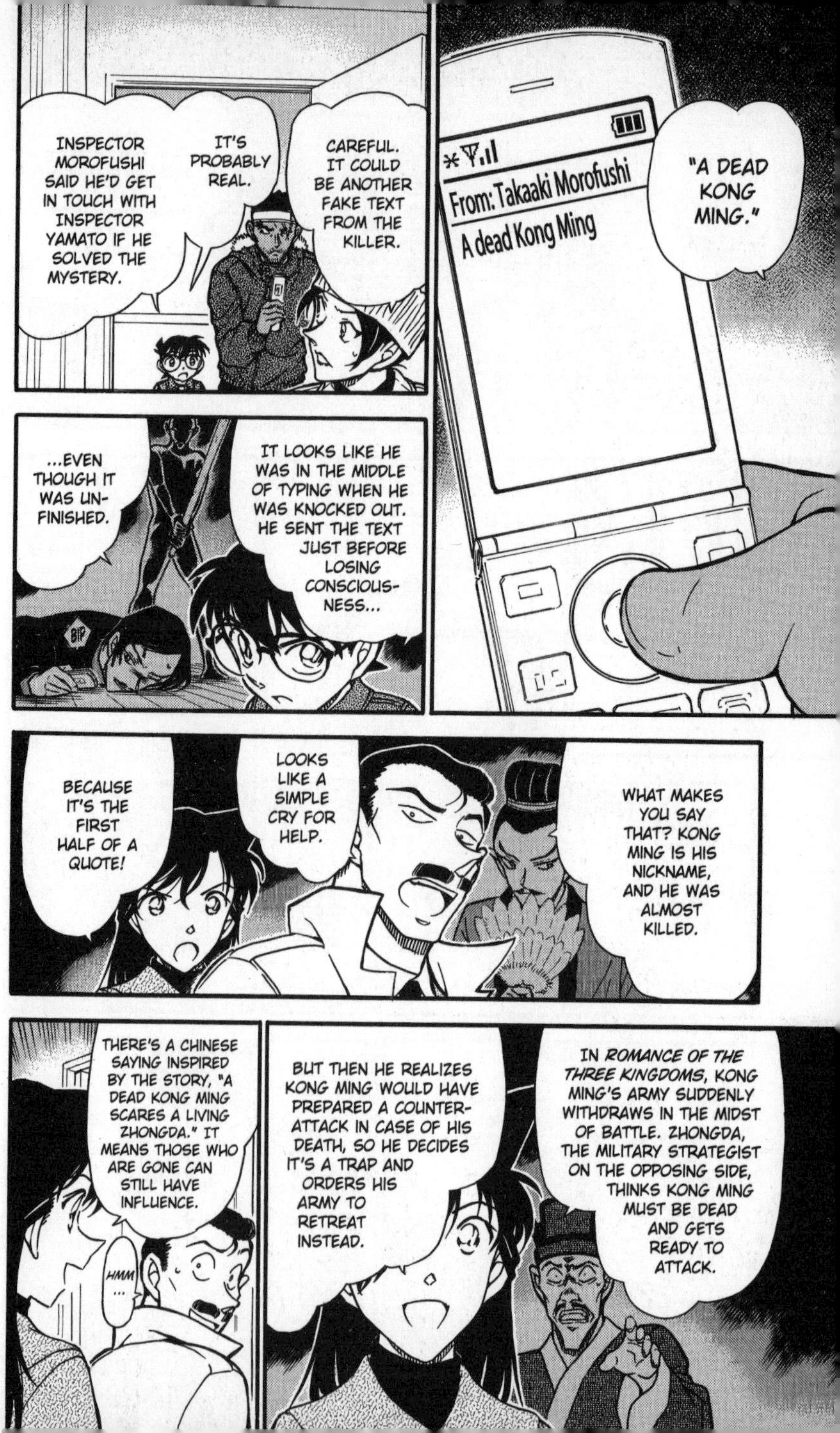
*
From: Takaaki Morofushi
A dead Kong Ming
"A DEAD KONG MING."
CAREFUL. IT COULD BE ANOTHER FAKE TEXT FROM THE KILLER.
IT'S PROBABLY REAL.
INSPECTOR MOROFUSHI SAID HE'D GET IN TOUCH WITH INSPECTOR YAMATO IF HE SOLVED THE MYSTERY.
IT LOOKS LIKE HE WAS IN THE MIDDLE OF TYPING WHEN HE WAS KNOCKED OUT. HE SENT THE TEXT JUST BEFORE LOSING CONSCIOUS-NESS...
...EVEN THOUGH IT WAS UN-FINISHED.
BIP
WHAT MAKES YOU SAY THAT? KONG MING IS HIS NICKNAME, AND HE WAS ALMOST KILLED.
LOOKS LIKE A SIMPLE CRY FOR HELP.
BECAUSE IT'S THE FIRST HALF OF A QUOTE!
IN *ROMANCE OF THE THREE KINGDOMS*, KONG MING'S ARMY SUDDENLY WITHDRAWS IN THE MIDST OF BATTLE. ZHONGDA, THE MILITARY STRATEGIST ON THE OPPOSING SIDE, THINKS KONG MING MUST BE DEAD AND GETS READY TO ATTACK.
BUT THEN HE REALIZES KONG MING WOULD HAVE PREPARED A COUNTER-ATTACK IN CASE OF HIS DEATH, SO HE DECIDES IT'S A TRAP AND ORDERS HIS ARMY TO RETREAT INSTEAD.
THERE'S A CHINESE SAYING INSPIRED BY THE STORY, "A DEAD KONG MING SCARES A LIVING ZHONGDA." IT MEANS THOSE WHO ARE GONE CAN STILL HAVE INFLUENCE.
HMM...

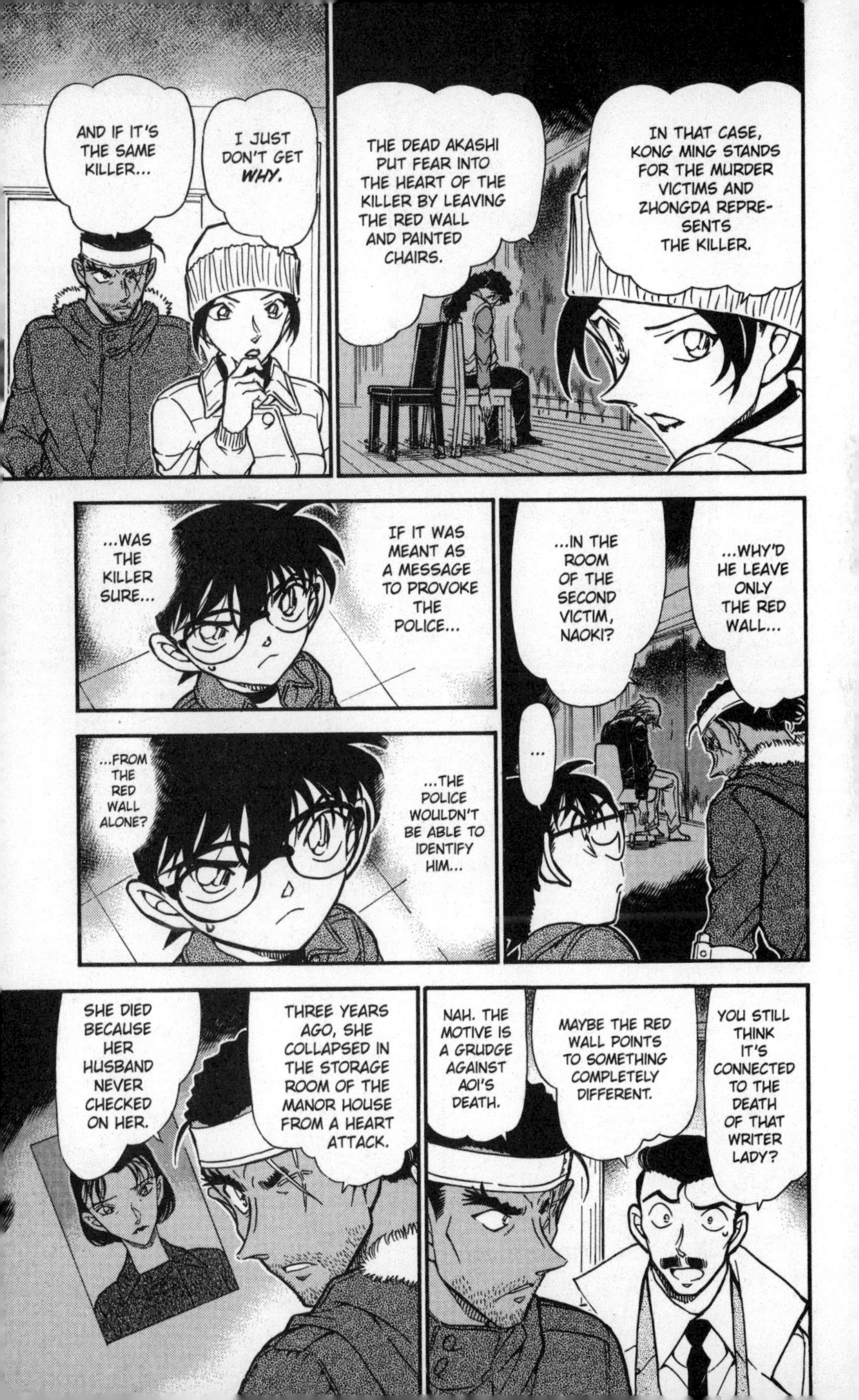
IN THAT CASE, KONG MING STANDS FOR THE MURDER VICTIMS AND ZHONGDA REPRESENTS THE KILLER.
THE DEAD AKASHI PUT FEAR INTO THE HEART OF THE KILLER BY LEAVING THE RED WALL AND PAINTED CHAIRS.
I JUST DON'T GET *WHY.*
AND IF IT'S THE SAME KILLER...
...WHY'D HE LEAVE ONLY THE RED WALL...
...IN THE ROOM OF THE SECOND VICTIM, NAOKI?
...
IF IT WAS MEANT AS A MESSAGE TO PROVOKE THE POLICE...
...WAS THE KILLER SURE...
...THE POLICE WOULDN'T BE ABLE TO IDENTIFY HIM...
...FROM THE RED WALL ALONE?
YOU STILL THINK IT'S CONNECTED TO THE DEATH OF THAT WRITER LADY?
MAYBE THE RED WALL POINTS TO SOMETHING COMPLETELY DIFFERENT.
NAH. THE MOTIVE IS A GRUDGE AGAINST AOI'S DEATH.
THREE YEARS AGO, SHE COLLAPSED IN THE STORAGE ROOM OF THE MANOR HOUSE FROM A HEART ATTACK.
SHE DIED BECAUSE HER HUSBAND NEVER CHECKED ON HER.

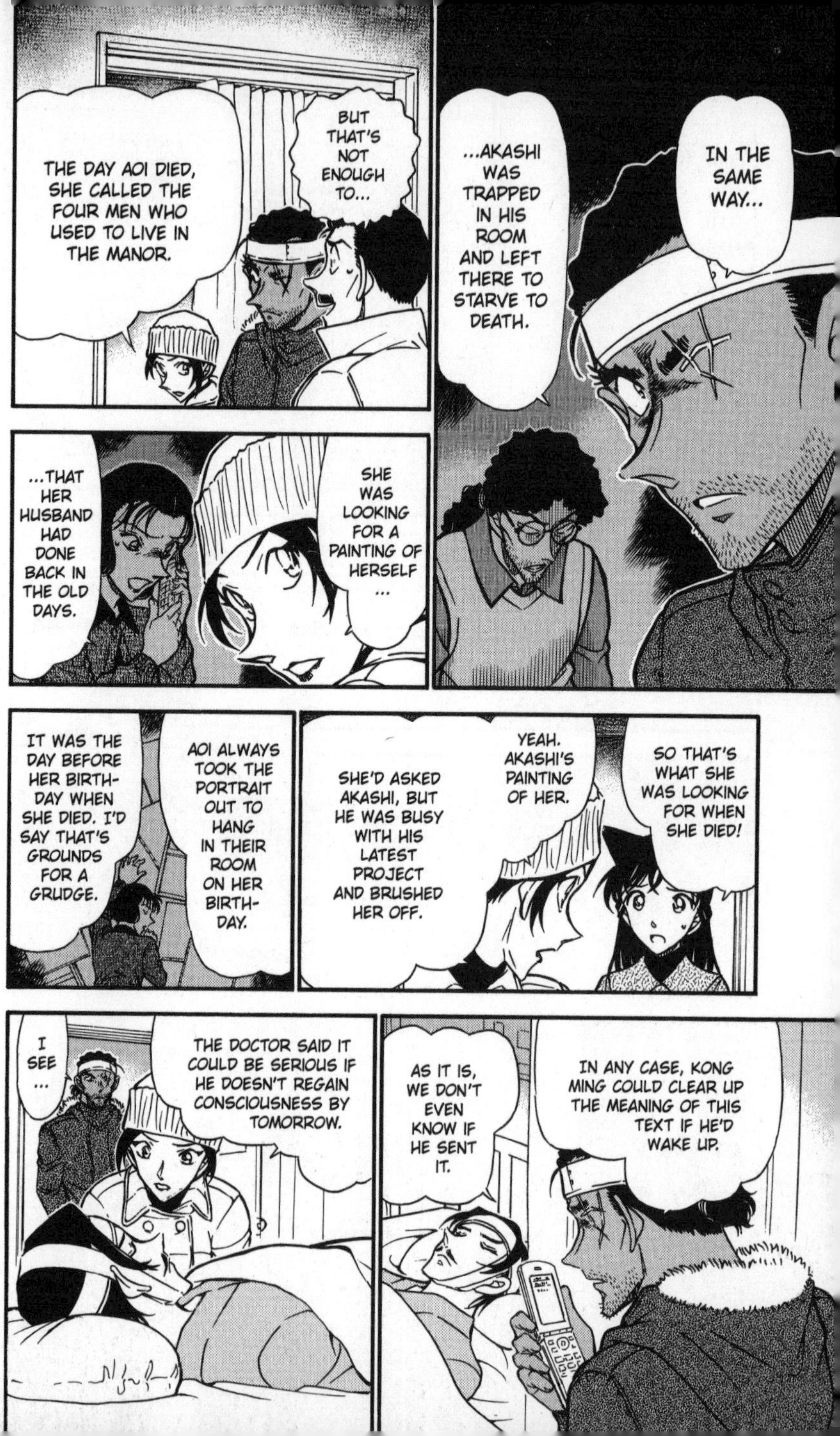
IN THE SAME WAY...
...AKASHI WAS TRAPPED IN HIS ROOM AND LEFT THERE TO STARVE TO DEATH.
BUT THAT'S NOT ENOUGH TO...
THE DAY AOI DIED, SHE CALLED THE FOUR MEN WHO USED TO LIVE IN THE MANOR.
SHE WAS LOOKING FOR A PAINTING OF HERSELF ...
...THAT HER HUSBAND HAD DONE BACK IN THE OLD DAYS.
SO THAT'S WHAT SHE WAS LOOKING FOR WHEN SHE DIED!
YEAH. AKASHI'S PAINTING OF HER.
SHE'D ASKED AKASHI, BUT HE WAS BUSY WITH HIS LATEST PROJECT AND BRUSHED HER OFF.
AOI ALWAYS TOOK THE PORTRAIT OUT TO HANG IN THEIR ROOM ON HER BIRTH-DAY.
IT WAS THE DAY BEFORE HER BIRTH-DAY WHEN SHE DIED. I'D SAY THAT'S GROUNDS FOR A GRUDGE.
IN ANY CASE, KONG MING COULD CLEAR UP THE MEANING OF THIS TEXT IF HE'D WAKE UP.
AS IT IS, WE DON'T EVEN KNOW IF HE SENT IT.
THE DOCTOR SAID IT COULD BE SERIOUS IF HE DOESN'T REGAIN CONSCIOUSNESS BY TOMORROW.
I SEE ...

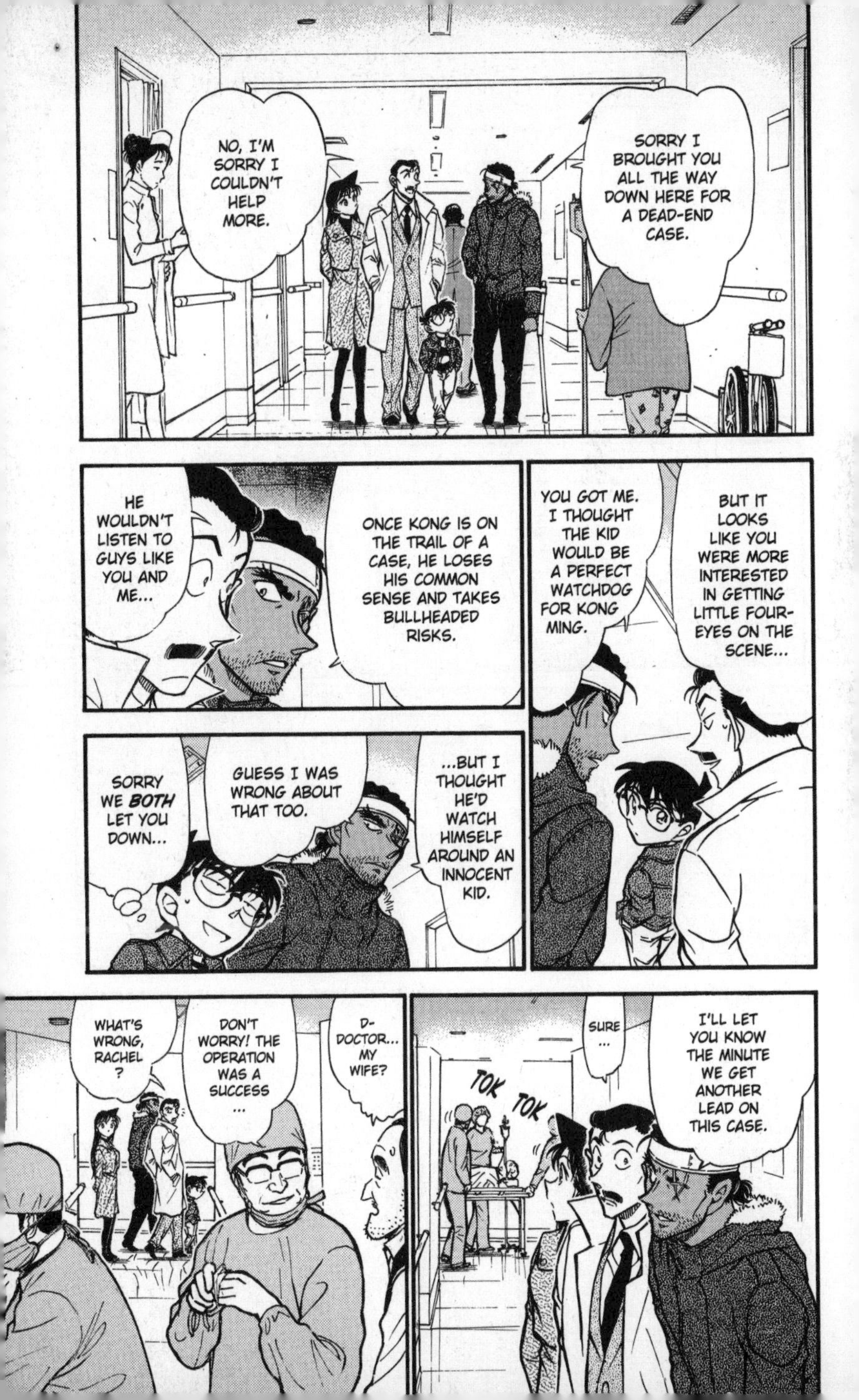
SORRY I BROUGHT YOU ALL THE WAY DOWN HERE FOR A DEAD-END CASE.
NO, I'M SORRY I COULDN'T HELP MORE.
BUT IT LOOKS LIKE YOU WERE MORE INTERESTED IN GETTING LITTLE FOUR-EYES ON THE SCENE...
YOU GOT ME. I THOUGHT THE KID WOULD BE A PERFECT WATCHDOG FOR KONG MING.
ONCE KONG IS ON THE TRAIL OF A CASE, HE LOSES HIS COMMON SENSE AND TAKES BULLHEADED RISKS.
HE WOULDN'T LISTEN TO GUYS LIKE YOU AND ME...
...BUT I THOUGHT HE'D WATCH HIMSELF AROUND AN INNOCENT KID.
GUESS I WAS WRONG ABOUT THAT TOO.
SORRY WE ***BOTH*** LET YOU DOWN...
I'LL LET YOU KNOW THE MINUTE WE GET ANOTHER LEAD ON THIS CASE.
SURE ...
TOK
TOK
D-DOCTOR... MY WIFE?
DON'T WORRY! THE OPERATION WAS A SUCCESS ...
WHAT'S WRONG, RACHEL ?

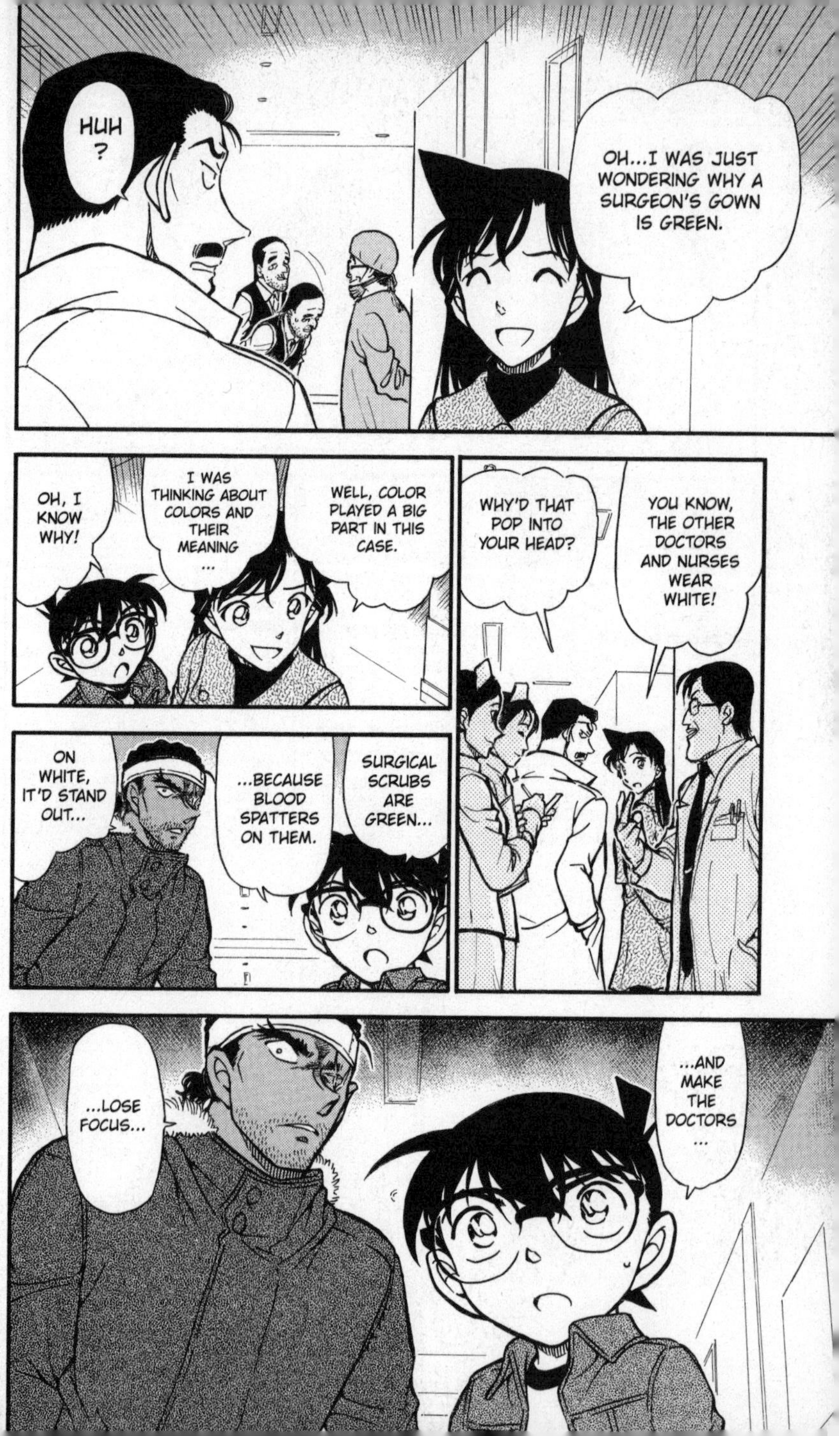
OH...I WAS JUST WONDERING WHY A SURGEON'S GOWN IS GREEN.
HUH?
YOU KNOW, THE OTHER DOCTORS AND NURSES WEAR WHITE!
WHY'D THAT POP INTO YOUR HEAD?
WELL, COLOR PLAYED A BIG PART IN THIS CASE.
I WAS THINKING ABOUT COLORS AND THEIR MEANING ...
OH, I KNOW WHY!
SURGICAL SCRUBS ARE GREEN...
...BECAUSE BLOOD SPATTERS ON THEM.
ON WHITE, IT'D STAND OUT...
...AND MAKE THE DOCTORS ...
...LOSE FOCUS...

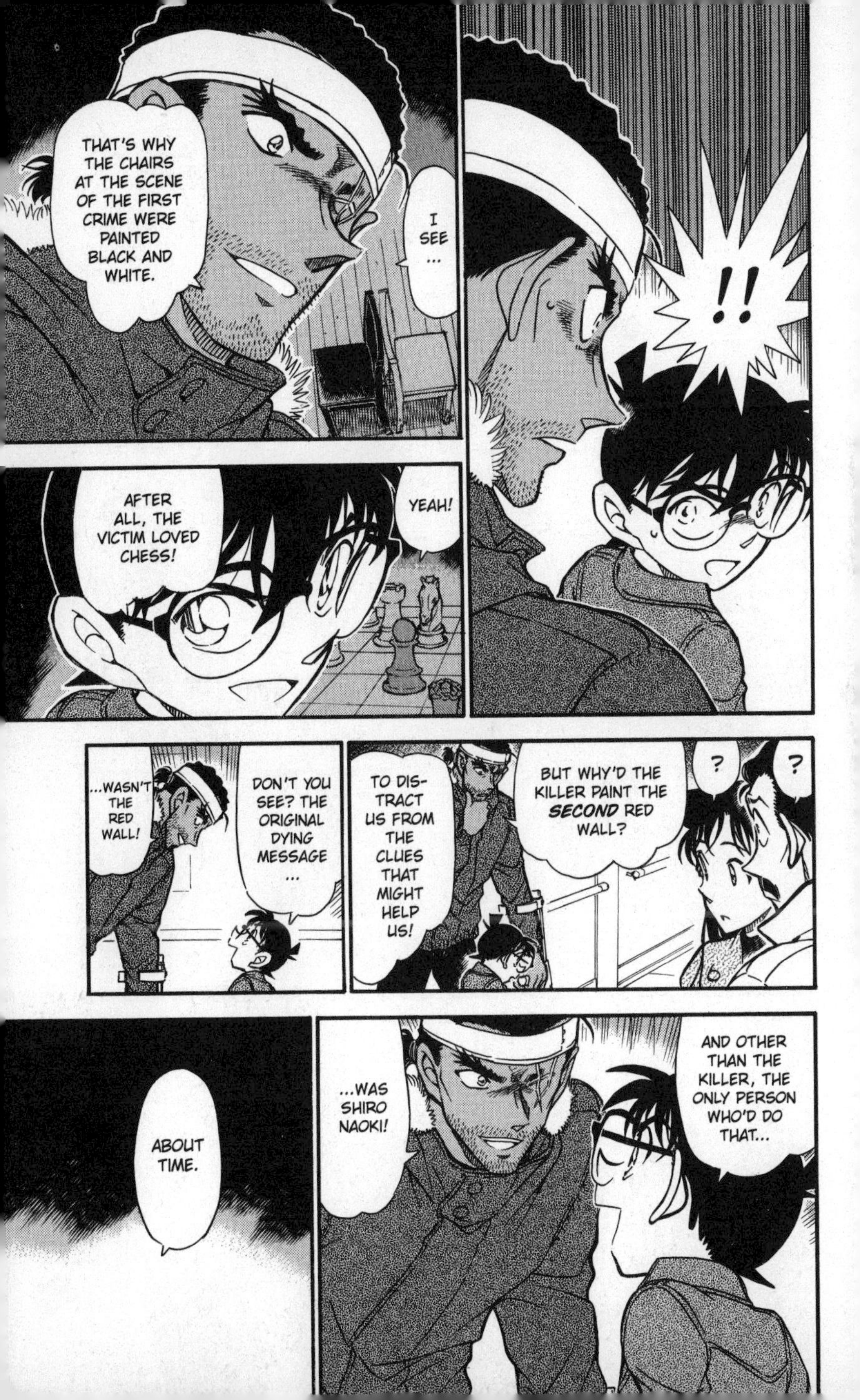
!!
I SEE...
THAT'S WHY THE CHAIRS AT THE SCENE OF THE FIRST CRIME WERE PAINTED BLACK AND WHITE.
YEAH!
AFTER ALL, THE VICTIM LOVED CHESS!
?
?
BUT WHY'D THE KILLER PAINT THE SECOND RED WALL?
TO DISTRACT US FROM THE CLUES THAT MIGHT HELP US!
DON'T YOU SEE? THE ORIGINAL DYING MESSAGE...
...WASN'T THE RED WALL!
AND OTHER THAN THE KILLER, THE ONLY PERSON WHO'D DO THAT...
...WAS SHIRO NAOKI!
ABOUT TIME.

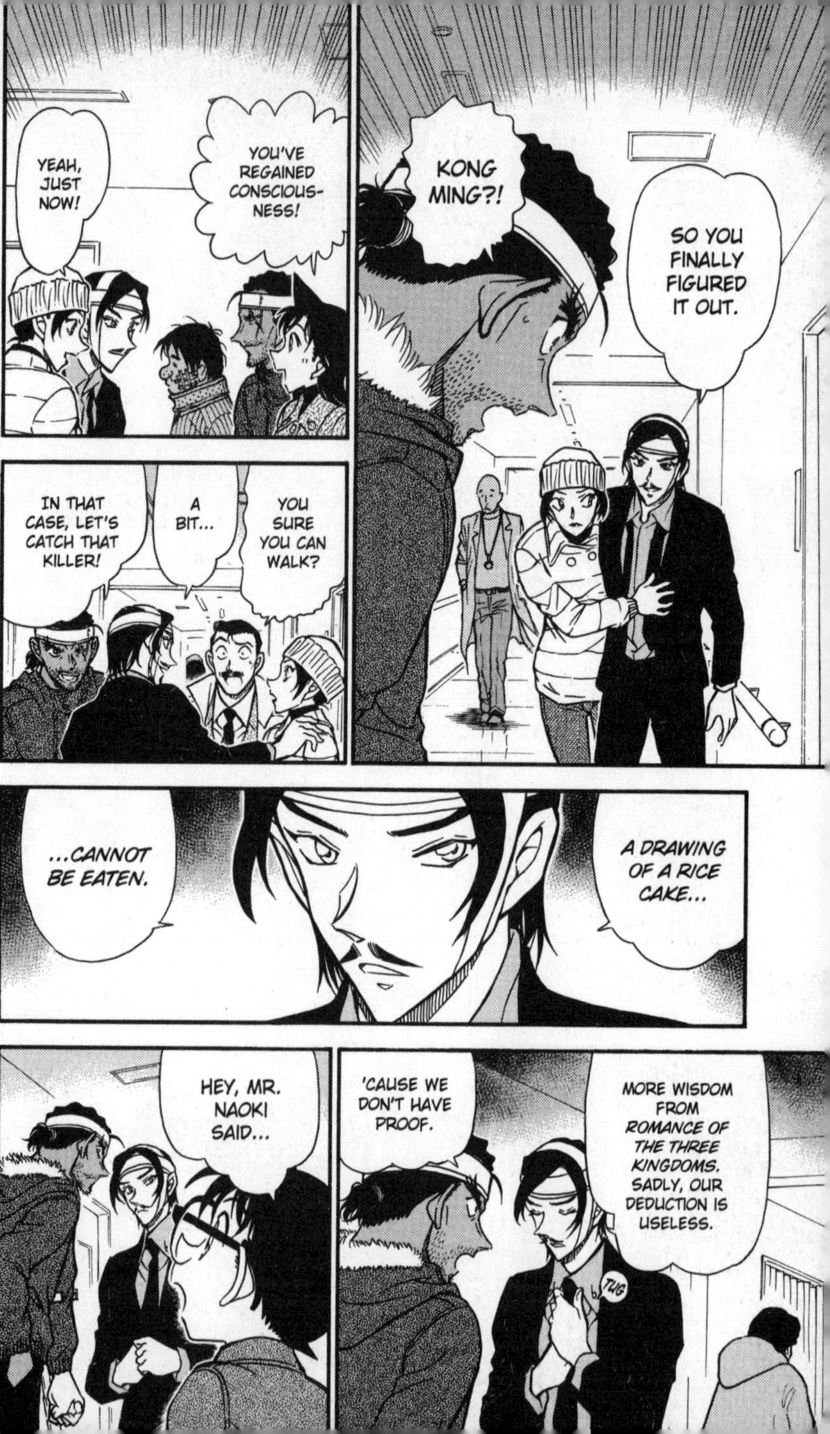
SO YOU FINALLY FIGURED IT OUT.
KONG MING?!
YOU'VE REGAINED CONSCIOUS-NESS!
YEAH, JUST NOW!
YOU SURE YOU CAN WALK?
A BIT...
IN THAT CASE, LET'S CATCH THAT KILLER!
A DRAWING OF A RICE CAKE...
...CANNOT BE EATEN.
MORE WISDOM FROM *ROMANCE OF THE THREE KINGDOMS*. SADLY, OUR DEDUCTION IS USELESS.
'CAUSE WE DON'T HAVE PROOF.
TUG
HEY, MR. NAOKI SAID...

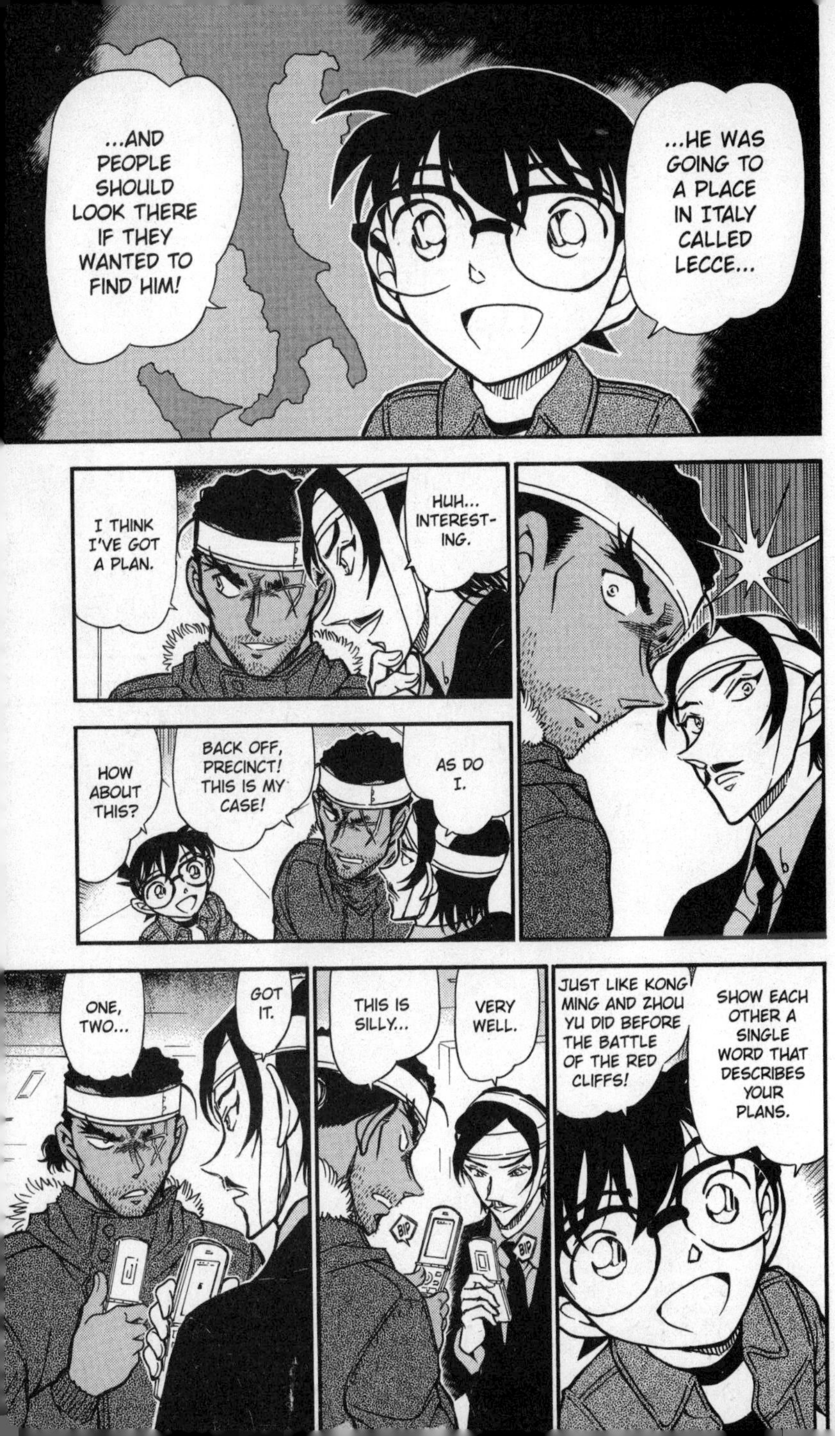
...HE WAS GOING TO A PLACE IN ITALY CALLED LECCE...
...AND PEOPLE SHOULD LOOK THERE IF THEY WANTED TO FIND HIM!
HUH... INTEREST-ING.
I THINK I'VE GOT A PLAN.
AS DO I.
BACK OFF, PRECINCT! THIS IS MY CASE!
HOW ABOUT THIS?
SHOW EACH OTHER A SINGLE WORD THAT DESCRIBES YOUR PLANS.
JUST LIKE KONG MING AND ZHOU YU DID BEFORE THE BATTLE OF THE RED CLIFFS!
VERY WELL.
THIS IS SILLY...
BIP
BIP
GOT IT.
ONE, TWO...

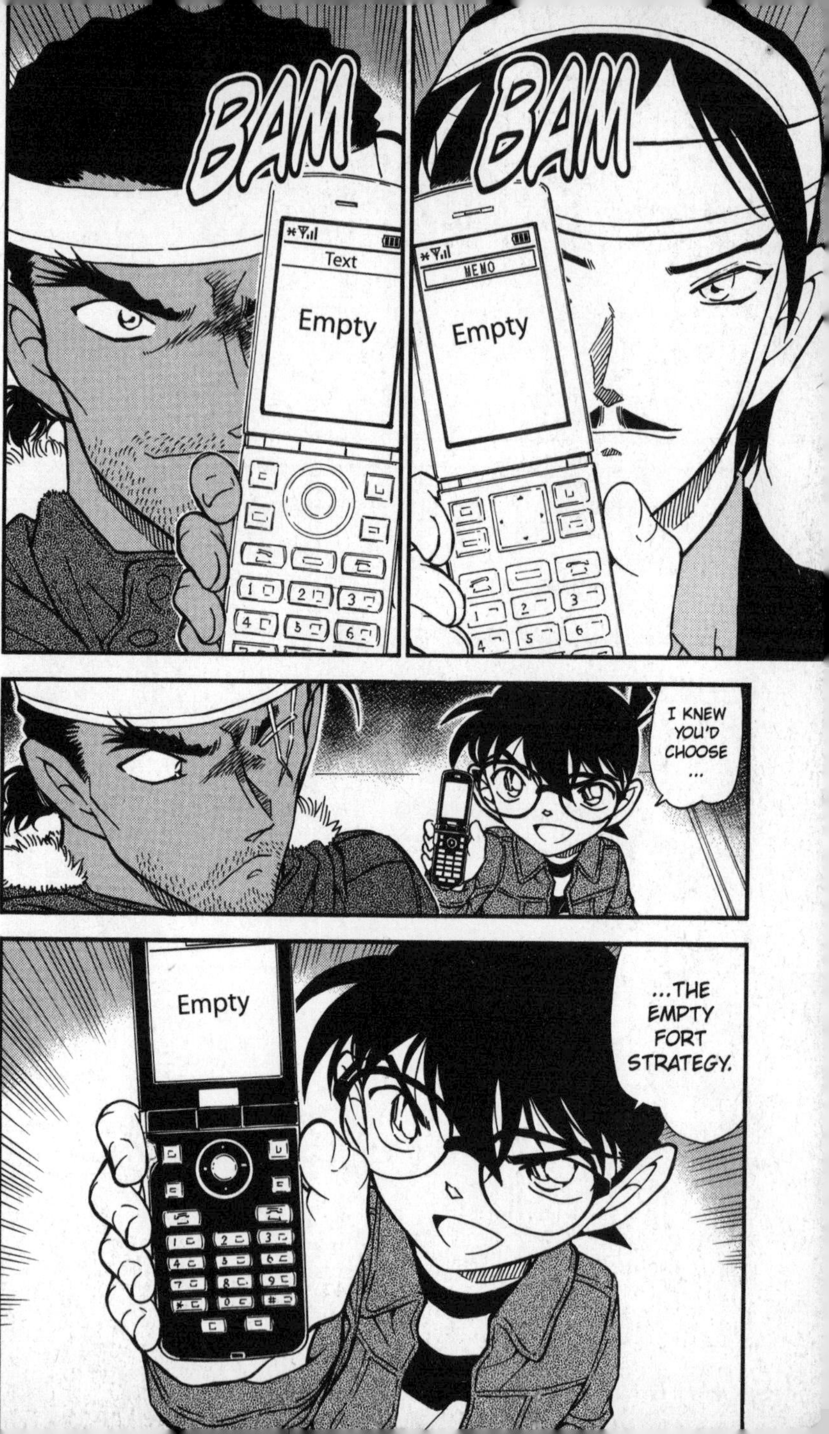
BAM
MEMO
Empty
BAM
Text
Empty
I KNEW YOU'D CHOOSE ...
...THE EMPTY FORT STRATEGY.
Empty

Hello, Aoyama here.

To be honest, I've never been a huge fan of Ichiro, the baseball player. He's an amazing player but he's a show-off and he jokes around all the time. I always got the impression that he was playing to the crowd...but wow! Top of the tenth inning at the second World Baseball Classic final, he kept hanging on and made the clutch hit that decided the game!! Ooh, he was like the great Shigeo Nagashima!

Congratulations, Samurai Japan! And Ichiro, from now on I won't mind if you show off or joke around. *Heh.*

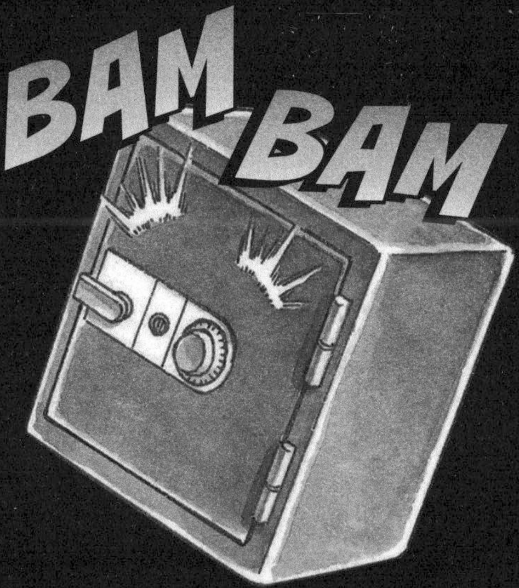
BAM
BAM

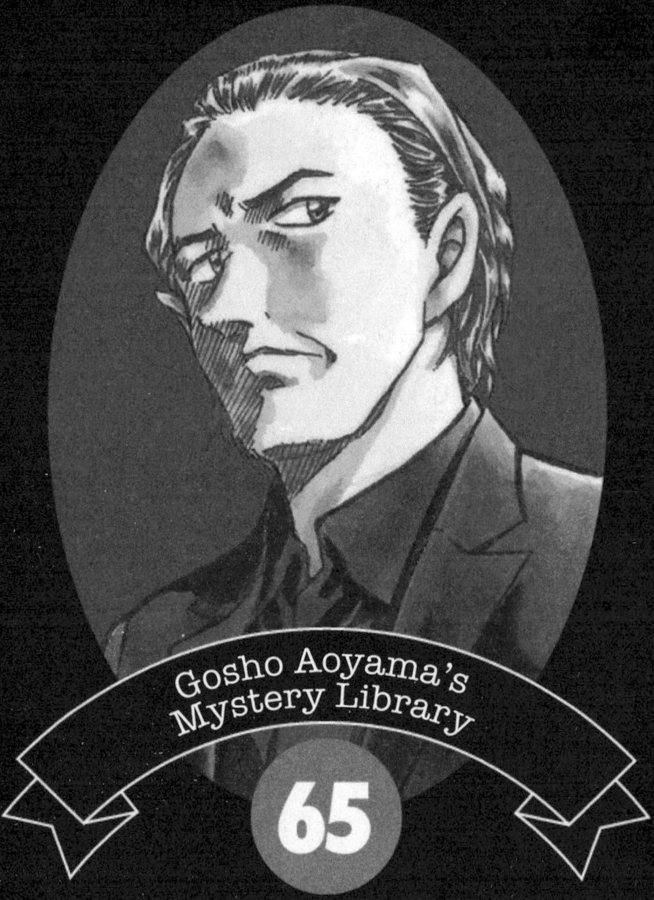
Gosho Aoyama's
Mystery Library
65

ROBERT LANGDON

Not all sleuths chase criminal cases. Allow me to introduce Professor Robert Langdon, who pursues the dark mysteries of history and religion! A professor of religious iconology and symbology at Harvard University, he's 45 and single. The cases he gets mixed up in are deeply connected to the dark secrets of Da Vinci's paintings, the secret society of the Illuminati and the history of Christianity. At times he finds himself framed as a criminal, but he continues to risk his life to solve these mysteries because of his undaunted curiosity as a scholar. His one and only weakness is claustrophobia. It's amusing that Langdon isn't afraid of anything else, yet he's terrified of ordinary elevators.

Author Dan Brown's parents were a mathematics teacher and a church musician, which explains a lot. My brothers are a doctor and scientist, so I was destined to become the creator of a detective manga! ...Or maybe not. *Heh.*

I recommend *The Da Vinci Code.*

Half Human, ALL ACTION!

Relive the feudal fairy tale with the new VIZBIG Editions featuring:

- Three volumes in one for $19.99 US / $22.00 CAN
- Larger trim size with premium paper
- Now unflipped! Pages read Right-to-Left as the creator intended

Change Your Perspective—Get BIG

大 VIZBIG EDITION

INUYASHA

Story and Art by Rumiko Takahashi

ISBN-13: 978-1-4215-3280-6

Available at your local bookstore and comic store.

www.viz.com

RATED T FOR OLDER TEEN ratings.viz.com

MANGA STARTS ON SUNDAY
SHONENSUNDAY.COM

SHONEN SUNDAY